FREEDOM OF THE PRESS IN ENGLAND 1476-1776

FREEDOM OF THE PRESS IN ENGLAND 1476-1776

THE RISE AND DECLINE OF GOVERNMENT CONTROL

By FREDRICK SEATON SIEBERT

UNIVERSITY OF ILLINOIS PRESS, URBANA, 1965

PREFACE

During the decade 1930-1940 I participated in the preparation of several briefs in court cases concerned with the problem of freedom of the press under the constitution of the United States. As a result of these researches and impelled by long-standing interest in American constitutional history, I outlined a program of study of the origins and development of the constitutional guaranties of freedom of speech and of the press in the American Bills of Rights.

Since most of our constitutional and political concepts of the late eighteenth century were inherited directly from English forbears, it seemed reasonable to begin with a study of the English origins and backgrounds of our American principles and institutions. It soon became evident that no thorough study of the development of freedom of the press in England from the introduction of printing to the time of the American separation had been undertaken by either British or American scholars. Available at that time was Wickwar's *Struggle for Freedom of the Press, 1819-1832* (1928), but neither Hanson's *Government and the Press, 1695-1763* (1936), nor Clyde's *The Struggle for Freedom of the Press from Caxton to Cromwell* (1938) had yet appeared. These latter two, together with Aspinall's *Politics and the Press, 1780-1850* (1949), are excellent accounts of chronological segments of the English backgrounds, but no study was available covering the entire period up to the drafting of the American Bills of Rights.

Further and equally serious handicaps were the lack of an adequate history of English printing and of a competent account of the developments in English journalism. The need for thorough studies of the history of both English printing and of English journalism remains. The best published work in the latter field is Mr. J. G. Muddiman's (J. B. Williams) *History of English Journalism to the Foundation of the Gazette* (1908). It was necessary, therefore, for a complete understanding of the American protections for freedom of the press to undertake an original study of the three hundred years preceding the American Revolution.

The purpose of the present volume is to trace the rise and decline of the government control of the press in England, to present the historical documents bearing on the problem of the relation of the government to the press, and to present a condensed interpretation of the observable trends over a three hundred-year period. This is a history not simply of an idea but of the application and practical working of an idea.

It was impossible to include in one volume, designed primarily as a background for later American developments, a complete account of the political and social trends which accompanied the rise and decline of the government control of the press. It should be emphasized, however, that the press was an integrated part of the entire social organism affecting and being affected by the society of which it was a part. For example, the decline of government controls in the eighteenth century parallels the growth of private enterprise capitalism and the increase in democratic processes in government. It is extremely difficult to assess the priority of one over the others either chronologically or in intensity. All three were inextricably interrelated.

Although logically the story of freedom of the press in England should have been carried on into the nineteenth century, this study was terminated in the last quarter of the eighteenth century for two reasons: first, the developments in England after 1776 had much less effect on American institutions, and secondly the period after 1780 has been adequately covered in the Wickwar and Aspinall volumes.

No attempt has been made in this volume to present a detailed account of the growth of the principles of the British constitution since this material is readily available in a number of standard histories. Nor has any attempt been made to trace the economic history of England for the same reason. Both the political and economic trends as well as religious movements were powerful forces shaping the government's policy concerning the press, and the impact of these forces is integrated as far as possible with the account of the contemporary press controls.

Other factors of significance in their effects on the history of freedom of the press have been passed over lightly, largely because they have not yet been adequately subjected to scholarly investigation. These fall in fields, like the history of English printing or the history of English journalism, where much preliminary work still needs to be done. Such factors as the size and distribution of printed editions, the extent of literacy, the cost of publications, and the economic status of newspaper proprietors have been mentioned where the information was readily available, but no original research of any significance was undertaken in the general fields of the history of printing or the history of English journalism.

The materials for this volume have been organized on two bases, chronological and by types of control. A glance at the table of contents will show that the three hundred years have been divided into five major parts according to standard English historical periods. Within each period, however, the chronological sequence is abandoned in the division into chapters. Each chapter discusses one or more of the important controls operating within the period. Within a chapter or a division of a chapter, developments are again presented in a chronological order. A defect of this type of organization is that each chapter within an historical period covers the same span of years although of course on a different subject. To keep the reader from becoming confused by asking him to follow four or five threads through a period, each thread is separated from the fabric and traced individually. The table of contents as well as cross references and the index should enable a reader to follow the history of a particular type of control from its earliest beginnings until its abandonment or until the last quarter of the eighteenth century. For instance, seditious libel, which did not become important as a control until the seventeenth century, is treated in

Chapter 5, pp. 116-26, for the period 1603-1640; in Chapter 13, pp. 269-75, 1660-1714; and in Chapter 18, pp. 380-92, 1714-1792. Under this method the reader must constantly keep in mind that other developments within the same period are taking place contemporaneously.

Acknowledgments

The research for this volume, including eight months of study in England, was made possible through a sabbatical leave of absence from the University of Illinois supplemented by a grant-in-aid from the American Newspaper Publishers' Association.

I am especially grateful to the officials and staffs of the various libraries and depositories here and in England who assisted me in my searches. My especial thanks to the officials and staffs of the British Museum, the Public Record Office, Dr. Williams Library, the Friends' Library, Lincoln's Inn Library (all in London), and for assistance over many years, to the staff of the Library of the University of Illinois.

The late Mr. Ralph Blumenfeld, editor of the *London Express,* contributed by giving me permission to examine the records of the Company of Stationers and Newspaper-makers at Stationers' Hall, London. Mr. R. T. Rivington, clerk of the Company, was especially helpful. I also appreciate the courtesies extended to me by Mr. Arch W. Shaw, Chicago, in permitting me to use his extensive collection of seventeenth- and eighteenth-century newspapers.

A host of correspondents both in the United States and England has helped me to check obstinate facts. I am indebted to Josephine Harper and George Wilkins for the detailed checking. Professor Harris Fletcher and the late Professor Theodore Pease, of the University of Illinois, read parts of the manuscript and made many suggestions for improvement. Professor Zechariah Chafee, Jr., of Harvard Law School, made extremely useful comments on the manuscript.

My thanks to the several generations of student typists from Vava Munson to Audrey Way. Two chapters have appeared in the *Journalism Quarterly,* Chapter 7, "Regulation of Corontos" in Vol.

XVI (1939), 151-60 and Chapter 15, "Control Through Taxation" in Vol. XXI (1944), 12-24.

My greatest indebtedness is to the historians, particularly the writers on constitutional history, who preceded me in this field. Instead of a formal bibliography, acknowledgment is made in footnotes which contain bibliographic details.

Fredrick S. Siebert
URBANA, ILLINOIS

CONTENTS

Part Five. Control of the Press in the Eighteenth Century, 1714-1776

FREEDOM OF THE PRESS IN ENGLAND 1476-1776

INTRODUCTION

Summary

The precipitous growth and gradual decline of the government control of the press in England from 1476 to 1776 can be traced along three main lines which cross and re-cross each other but which together present a discernible pattern of development.

The first line represents the number and variety of the controls operated by the central government. These varied in nature from the sixteenth-century royal proclamation having the force of law to the subsidization program of the Walpole administration in the second quarter of the eighteenth century. Whereas Elizabeth employed a variety of instruments in the operation of the control system, such as the Star Chamber, the ecclesiastical commissions, and the Stationers Company, William and Mary at the end of the seventeenth century were content to rely on the Regulation of Printing Act and the law of seditious libel.

The second line of development to be considered in any attempt to describe and evaluate the pattern of control is the effort made to enforce the regulations. This factor is as essential as the nature and variety of controls and more difficult to assess. Enforcement was more stringent during the reigns of Elizabeth and Charles II than at any other time, with the possible exception of short periods during the Protectorate. Enforcement was lax during the Commonwealth and again during the years 1685-1695.

More significant than the efforts at enforcement is the third line tracing the degree of compliance, either voluntarily or as a result of enforcement policies. Here again the pattern deviates from the graph of the first two lines of development. Compliance with government regulations was probably most general during the middle years of Elizabeth, the early years of Charles II, and the reign of George II. On the other hand, failure to comply with the controls reached high points during the late years of Charles I, the first years of the Commonwealth, and the reign of Anne.

Applying the three standards set out above to the five periods of English history covered in this volume, a blurred but nevertheless discernible pattern emerges. Printing did not become a social or political force until almost fifty years after its introduction into England in 1476. The rapid rise of the government control of printing took place during the reigns of Henry VIII and Elizabeth. Beginning with a few minor printing trade regulations, the control system was expanded by Henry with promulgation of the first list of prohibited books in 1529, the establishment of the first licensing system under secular control in 1530, and the granting of printing monopolies. This was followed by the establishment of the Stationers Company as part of the control system in 1557 under Mary. Elizabeth added the religious hierarchy as an instrument of control (Injunctions of 1559), but the climax of the regulation of the press under the Tudors was the Star Chamber Decree of 1586. These orders set the pattern of control for the next hundred years.

Enforcement was relatively uniform throughout the Tudor period and compliance by printers was general. Only in the later years of Elizabeth was there any serious attempt (by the Puritans) to evade the regulations. Elizabeth's reign is the high point of the entire three hundred-year period in the average pattern of the three factors, number and variety of controls, stringency of enforcement, and general compliance with regulations. From the opening of the seventeenth century, the pattern is that of a decline in government control. It took approximately eighty years to build up the system to its highest point; it took more than two hundred years to tear it down.

During the early Stuart period (1603-1640), although the number and variety of the controls increased slightly (the law of seditious libel and the Star Chamber Decree of 1637) and the efforts to enforce the regulations continued unabated, the degree of compliance was much less than during the sixteenth century. The Puritans, the disenfranchised printers, and a few political figures succeeded in circumventing the controls. So obnoxious did these controls on free discussion become that, when combined with the political and religious dissatisfactions under Charles I, their elimination was one of first reforms undertaken by the Long Parliament in 1641.

The period of the civil war, the Commonwealth, and the Protectorate (1640-1660) introduced drastic changes both in the government and in the press. Most of the social, religious, and political reforms undertaken during this period were ostensibly abandoned in 1660, but nevertheless they had permanent and serious effects on the social pattern of the late seventeenth century. All controls were abandoned or unenforced in the early years of the civil war. The Ordinances of Parliament, beginning with that of 26 August 1642, reinforced on 14 June 1643, and made more stringent on 20 September 1647, were attempts to revive the Elizabethan system but without success. Enforcement was lax and compliance at a low ebb. However, when the army took over and the Printing Act of 20 September 1649 was put into operation, enforcement efforts were increased and were relatively successful. Cromwell's order of August, 1655, reached a high point in the stringency of regulation and almost equaled Elizabeth in the degree of compliance enforced on printers and publishers.

This was the period which produced the first reasoned arguments for a free and uncontrolled press in the writings of the Puritan and nonconformist thinkers such as William Walwyn, Henry Robinson, John Milton, and John Lilburne. Unfortunately these writings had little or no effect on their times, but their arguments were to be revived and utilized in the contest with the government in the eighteenth century. The experiences of the period 1640-1660 demonstrated the folly of attempting to grant more freedom than the general temper and intellectual level of the times could absorb.

The later Stuart period (1660-1714) attempted to ignore the catastrophic experiences of the Interregnum, but nevertheless there was no returning to the standards of James I and Charles I. Under Charles II, responsibility for the controls was divided between the crown and Parliament, the latter participating through the Regulation of Printing Acts and the control of reports of its own proceedings. Controls were fewer and more definite than during the previous period with the result that enforcement was both active and effective under the office of the Surveyor of the Press.

The old alliance between the crown and the Stationers Company was abandoned late in Charles's reign, and its place was taken by the offices of two secretaries of state. Under William, the inability to operate a cumbersome licensing system under a two-party Parliamentary government resulted in the expiry of the Regulation of Printing Act in 1694. From this date until the first Stamp Act was passed in 1712 the only controls were the law of treason and of seditious libel and the regulation by Parliament of the reporting of its proceedings. This is the low point in the intricate pattern of controls, enforcement, and compliance. Queen Anne made repeated efforts to get Parliament to legislate against the flood of seditious pamphlets and newspapers, but she herself was impotent without the prerogative powers which Elizabeth enjoyed.

The government was not yet content to abandon all attempts to control the press, and the eighteenth century was scarcely well on its way before new methods were devised to supplant the old. Taxes on publications, including a stamp tax, a paper tax, and an advertising tax, replaced the licensing system. Subsidization of writers and newspapers replaced the controls formerly applied through the Stationers Company. Seditious libel and regulation of published reports of Parliamentary proceedings took on increased importance as methods of keeping the press in line.

Enforcement of the existing regulations in the eighteenth century was erratic. The tax system was effective in the first few years after 1712, but loopholes were discovered which were not closed until 1724. The Revenue Act of 1757 contained similar loopholes which were not eliminated until 1773. From that time on, particularly in the last decade of the century, definite efforts were made to enforce the taxes.

Parliament was more consistent in the enforcement of the rules against reporting its proceedings and in its insistence on its authority to punish libels on itself and on the government as breaches of Parliamentary privilege. The newspapers won the battle to report Parliamentary proceedings in the 1770's. The House of Commons gave up attempting to prohibit reports of its debates in 1771 and the House of Lords capitulated in 1775.

Enforcement of the laws against seditious libel was also erratic in the eighteenth century. After 1735 it was almost impossible to get a London jury to find a defendant guilty. A renewal of effort occurred during the early years of George III, but the contest with John Wilkes convinced the government that it was too difficult, if not impossible, to enforce the criminal libel laws. The battle for the right of juries to decide the criminal nature of the publication was won in Parliament in 1792 with the approval of Fox's Libel bill.

The last survivor of the Tudor system of control was the "general warrant" for the arrest of writers and printers and for the search of their premises. This method of procedure could trace its lineage back to the Regulation of Printing Acts of the Restoration period, from there back to the Star Chamber decrees of 1637 and 1586, and finally to the Charter of the Stationers Company of 1557. John Wilkes laid the plans for the overthrow of both the general warrants and the restrictions on Parliamentary reporting and, but for Chief Justice Mansfield, would have won the battle against seditious libel. Even the talented advocate, Lord Erskine, was unable to move the chief justice, who terminated his career firm in the belief that liberty of the press consisted in freedom from licensing but complete subjection to such laws of the land as were derived from common law or from legislative enactments.

The government control of the press did not disappear at the end of the eighteenth century. In fact, with the procedural rules renovated, seditious libel prosecutions were extremely effective in the early years of the nineteenth century. Subsidization was revived in the later years of George III, and taxes on publications increased to the place where they were almost confiscatory. Not until the 1860's was the press of England entirely free from objectionable controls by the government.

Theories of Control

Three theories of the function of the press in society, particularly in relation to organized government, are apparent from the study of three hundred years of English history. These three may be identified as the Tudor-Stuart theory, the Blackstone-Mansfield theory, and the Camden-Erskine-Jefferson theory.

The Tudor-Stuart theory of the function of the press which

justified its control was that the safety, stability, and welfare of the state depended on the efforts of the crown and therefore anything which interfered with or undermined those efforts was to be suppressed or at least controlled. Elizabeth was primarily interested in the safety and welfare of her people; so was James I and Charles II and most of the others. Even George III after 1782 abandoned his efforts to enhance the power of the crown and became sincerely interested in the welfare of his people. As long as the responsibility for protecting and advancing the public interest rested on the crown, it was a necessary corollary that the press should be regulated so as to ensure the success of the royal policies.

The English constitution underwent a profound change in 1689. Parliament, not the crown, became the predominant partner in the British system of government. Although the formal documents accompanying this change made no mention of the relation of the government to the press, the older theory of state control was necessarily revised to meet the new conditions. Parliament had been the predominant partner once before, in the days of the Commonwealth, and it had adopted the same principles of regulation of the press as its Tudor and Stuart predecessors. However, by the second quarter of the eighteenth century, as it became evident that the group in power in the government was subject to change under shifts in public opinion, a new theory of the place of the press in society became necessary.

The concept of "freedom of the press" is intimately related to the concept of "sovereignty." Both became accepted theories in the eighteenth century, and both appeared to be essential in any well-constituted system of society. They are alike in that although accepted by the eighteenth century neither was fully understood by its devotees. Neither had a place in John Locke's scheme of government. As theories, both were somewhat alien to the thinking of the British people in spite of the fact that their application and operation were taken for granted without philosophical misgivings.

Supporters of the theory of sovereignty in the king, Lords, and Commons assembled in Parliament under the British constitution were compelled to adopt a restricted definition of the concept of freedom of the press. Tory writers like Swift and Dr. Johnson were more articulate than the political leaders in expressing the theory that Parliament was the supreme sovereign power with no limitations on its authority. Sir William Blackstone and Chief Justice Mansfield accepted this theory of sovereignty and acted upon it. The meaning of the term, freedom of speech and of the press, as derived from this theory of sovereignty must necessarily be limited by those controls emanating from the sovereign power. Blackstone and Mansfield, as has been pointed out, concluded that although the press was free from previous restraints such as licensing, it was subject to penalties for the abuse of its freedom, the abuse to be determined by the common law and by Parliament.

Opposed to this traditional eighteenth-century view is the third theory, espoused by those who, like Thomas Erskine and Chancellor Camden in England and Thomas Jefferson and James Madison in the United States, looked upon the sovereignty of the king in Parliament as a limited power—limited by the rights of man as determined by natural law. Natural law in turn was identified with the law of God. Under this theory of sovereignty, freedom of the press became one of the natural rights of man as derived from the law of God and incapable of infringement by any man-made power. According to this position, a government could not restrict the right to speak and to print, even to save itself from destruction. This was the theory which was expressed at the end of the eighteenth century and which became a generally accepted principle of operation in America shortly after the opening of the nineteenth century and in England slightly later.

Causes of Changes

The evolution of freedom of the press from government control, beginning with the theory of the Tudor and Stuart monarchs, through the principles of Blackstone and Mansfield, to the interpretations of Erskine and Jefferson, can be attributed to three major trends: the political changes resulting from the Revolution settlement of 1689, the trade demands of the London printers and publishers and their desire to engage unhampered in the pursuit of wealth, and lastly, the philosophical principles of the freedom of the mind to explore and discuss all sorts of problems including political and social questions.

The first of these, which has been touched upon in explaining the relationship between freedom of the press and sovereignty, was the most important. The basic constitutional change occurred as the result of the overthrow of James II and the settlement of the crown on William and Mary. This in turn was a part of a more basic trend toward giving an ever-enlarging segment of the population a voice in the government. As this segment expanded through the late seventeenth and early eighteenth centuries, the older Tudor and Stuart theory that the people should not meddle in affairs of state became obsolete. As this meddling became more common, the need for information, discussion and criticism arose. As this need became more insistent, ancient regulations were abandoned and less stringent ones took their places. Licensing was abolished and the press was freed of one of its more obnoxious restraints. Regulatory taxation by Parliament took its place. The shift in political power within the British constitution was the basic reason for the withdrawal of many of the early controls.

A second reason for the change to new principles was the agitation on the part of the printers and publishers for more freedom to carry on the business of supplying information and comment free from government regulation. The abolition of printing monopolies and the breakup of the powers of the Stationers Company can be attributed to this cause. During the last half of the eighteenth century, the demand for political news became so insistent that the printers, urged on by a desire to tap this source of profit, allied themselves with other London tradesmen and with the leaders of the Whig party in their demands for more freedom. The Tudor-Stuart practice was to secure the printers as allies through a system of trade protection and printing monopolies. The printers of ephemeral materials such as newspapers and pamphlets needed no such protection. They were independent entrepreneurs seeking a livelihood from their trade, and their exclusion from profitable printing fields forced them into prohibited pastures. The printers of newspapers were a sufficiently large and cohesive group by the 1770's to provide the basis of support behind Wilkes in his campaign to remove the restrictions on newspapers. They made their demands effective by the discovery that they possessed an instrument (the newspaper) by which they could, if not directly influence votes, at least precipitate public demonstrations.

The third and least effective basis of the enlarged freedom acquired by the press at the end of the eighteenth century was the philosophical principle of freedom of the mind. Milton had formulated the theory in 1644 but had little effect on his own times. His principles were revived in the eighteenth century to lend support to the opposition to the restrictions. No other writer of prominence, not even John Locke, produced a statement of principles which could be used as a weapon against the government until John Stuart Mill published his "Essay on Liberty" in the nineteenth century. A few of the judges and several lawyers practicing before the courts enunciated some of the broad principles of freedom. Lord Camden, Lord Erskine, and John Glynn adverted to such principles in their arguments or opinions. Philosophical principles of freedom played a minor but nevertheless basic part in the transition from control by government to freedom.

Toward a Theory of Freedom of the Press

The present study of the rise and decline of government control of the press during three hundred years of English history points up a number of postulates which should be useful in the formulation of a comprehensive statement of the principles of freedom of the press.

One basic assumption appears to be common to all theories of liberty of the press, whether it is the theory of the Tudors, or of the eighteenth century as stated by Blackstone and Mansfield, or the theory of the late eighteenth- and early nineteenth-century libertarians. This assumption is that freedom of the press is not and never can be absolute. All agree that some forms of restraint are necessary and that the government has a legitimate function to define the limitations. They differ only as to the nature and number of these limitations.

Government must necessarily exert some control over the press as it must over all other types of institutions operating in society. All agree that it is the function of government to protect private reputations, to control to some unspecified degree the distribution of obscene matter, and to regulate to a still more vague degree publications which undermine the basic structure of organized society. Henry VIII, John Milton, John Locke, Walpole, George III, and even Lord Erskine agree that some government control of the press is necessary. The principal disagreements arise over the standards to be applied in devising and administering controls designed to protect the third objective mentioned above, the preservation of the basic structure of organized society. With this assumption in mind, the following propositions are advanced:

Proposition I. *The extent of government control of the press depends on the nature of the relationship of the government to those subject to the government.* This relationship, which in its nature provides for a greater or a lesser degree of accountability, has been identified under such general terms as Monarchy (absolute or enlightened), Democracy (more or less direct), and Totalitarianism (Communist or Fascist).

All types of government consider themselves responsible for the welfare of their peoples. The more direct the accountability of the governors to the masses, the greater the freedom of the press. As England progressed from a relatively absolute monarchy under Henry VIII to the more limited administration of Charles II, to the still more democratic government under George I, the area of freedom enjoyed by the press expanded. The contest to accomplish this expansion was long and arduous and not without retreats. As democratic forms superseded the ancient relationship between the government and its constituents, the press as a necessary corollary took on an extra-legal function, that of an informant and a watchdog of public affairs. The nature of this relationship between the central government and its subjects determines the degree of freedom from control under all types of government, monarchical, democratic, or totalitarian.

Proposition II. *The area of freedom contracts and the enforcement of restraints increases as the stresses on the stability of the government and of the structure of society increase.* This appears to be true for all types of governments. The more secure the existing government, the less restraint is imposed on the press. Henry VIII's insecurity due to the shift in religious allegiance prompted the enforcement of many of the controls during his reign. Elizabeth's insecurity during her early years caused by the flaw in her title to the crown was the primary cause of her interest in the products of the printing press. The stability of the government under Walpole in the eighteenth century was accompanied by few restrictions and lax enforcement. It is axiomatic that government does not exert itself in its own protection unless it is attacked or believes itself seriously threatened.

The three well-defined theories of the relation of the government to the press as described above are all based on these two propositions.

The first, the Tudor-Stuart theory of control, was derived directly from the first proposition, and its implementation and administration were based on the second.

The traditional, conservative, and Tory attitude toward democratic participation in government provides the foundation for the Blackstone-Mansfield theory of liberty of the press. Arbitrary monarchy was no longer tenable, but freedom was extended only to the abolition of licensing, leaving such restraints as the common law and the legislature provided.

The late eighteenth-century position, that of Lord Erskine and Lord Camden, also recognizes the two basic propositions. This theory, the dominant one in the nineteenth century in both England and America, insists on the right to discuss the government in a rational manner provided such discussion derives from a sincere belief in the necessity for a change. Jefferson went even further than Erskine and appears to approve of an absolute freedom to discuss political questions even if such discussion is intemperate and might result in the complete dissolution of the existing form of government. Such a position, however, has been modified in operation to coincide with the second proposition and with Erskine's stand, that the discussion must be addressed to reason and must urge change as an orderly rather than as a revolutionary process. The safety of the state is still a criterion for measuring the amount of freedom allotted to the press.

In addition to the three theories which grew out of the experiences of three hundred years, three additional positions on the relation of the government to the press have made their appearance in modern times. The first of these is the position on the question of the allowable area of freedom taken by the Supreme Court of the United States in a series of decisions since 1919. Justices Oliver W. Holmes and Louis D. Brandeis were largely responsible for the rule which interprets freedom of the press as prohibiting all types of restrictions on political discussion unless there is a clear and present danger that the government will be subverted or that other recognized evils which the government has a right to prohibit will ensue. This vague standard is the one in operation in the United States today. Like the others it is based on the principle that the people in a democracy have a right to speak and print on government affairs but that this right is limited by the immediate conditions under which such speaking and writing takes place. Congress and state legislatures can prohibit certain types of speaking and writing under certain conditions. The "certain" as used here is far from certain as that word is defined in standard dictionaries.

Two additional positions on the question of press freedom are implicit in the operation of the two basic principles in the modern world. The first of these grows out of the assumption that in his relation to his government, the citizen or subject has special duties and responsibilities. The principal duty is to participate in periodic decisions and selections in government affairs. As a participant, the citizen has an obligation to inform himself on the merits of current issues and on the qualifications of candidates for public office. Out of this grows the proposition that it is the duty of the press and of other media of mass communications to inform the citizen and to make available to him such materials as will enable him to arrive at sound and rational conclusions on public affairs. This is the theory of the Hutchins Commission on Freedom of the Press (1947) which would go so far as to intimate the use of government controls in the event that the press itself does not undertake to fulfill this obligation. This theory of social responsibility of the press is echoed in the Report of the Royal Commission on the Press (1949), but the British inquiry group unlike the American commission makes a firm statement that the social objectives stated above can be accomplished only through a private enterprise system of press ownership. The question of how the obligation to furnish the citizen with full, complete, and accurate information and interpretation can be met without government participation or enforcement is a problem for the twentieth century.

The third theory of press freedom in the modern world is that of the Communist government of Soviet Russia. Here again the two basic principles are at work. Because of the nature of the relation of the government to the people (much like that of Tudor times), the central administration takes the responsibility of providing for the welfare of the people as identified by the proletariat. As such it assumes more or less complete control of communications media. Nothing that tends to undermine the soviet system is allowed to appear. Bitter and widespread criticism of the operation of policies and of the administration of operating officials is permitted, but even mild questionings of the economic basis of the soviet system are severely punished.

A modern contribution of the soviet system of press control is the contention that emotional appeals·as presented in nonverbal artistic productions have definite and powerful political and economic implications. As such, the more abstract arts such as painting, music, and the dance are included under the theory of press control. In England and America these same nonverbal forms have been excluded from the freedom of the press on the ground that such arts have no political implications and should be regulated by an entirely different set of standards.

What applications or modifications of the principles of freedom of the press from government control will develop during the remainder of the twentieth century? Will the principles of Thomas Jefferson and John Stuart Mill be able to survive the ideological contest between democratic capitalism and totalitarian communism? Already we have seen instances of conflict. The second basic proposition mentioned above seems to have come into operation again in our own day. Whether with reason or not, the fear of communism is a powerful force both in England and in America. This fear places severe strains on the control system. As the stress from this fear and from other more tangible sources increases, the area of freedom of the press will contract. How much freedom we shall enjoy will depend on how widespread are the threats and the feeling of insecurity and instability.

The following chapters are presented in the nature of a documentation of these interpretations and postulates.

CALENDAR

EDWARD IV   1461-1483

    1468   Spurious date for first printing in England

    1476   First printing in England (Caxton)

EDWARD V   1483

RICHARD III   1483-1485

    1484   Act to encourage foreign printers

HENRY VII   1485-1509

    1504   First official printer (William Faques)

HENRY VIII   1509-1547

    1518   First book "cum privilegio regis"

    1520   Pope Leo's Bull against heretical writings

    1524   Warning to printers (heretical literature)

    1528   Decree regulating foreign printers

    1529   Henry VIII's first list of prohibited books (first index)

    1530   First licensing under royal authority

1534 Act of Supremacy—English church established
1534 Act to protect native printers
1537 First Bible printed in England
1538 First regular royal licensing system
1539 First patent for Bibles (Cromwell)
1542/43 Bible in English restricted

EDWARD VI 1547-1553

1547 Proclamation against seditious rumors
1551 Licensing system revived

MARY 1553-1558

1553 Proclamation against seditious rumors
1557 Stationers Company chartered
1558 Proclamation on heretical books

ELIZABETH 1558-1603

1559 Injunctions—Licensing system re-established
1566 Council order—Enforcement of licensing
1582 Wolfe contests patents
1586 Star Chamber decree on printing
1588/9 Marprelate tracts

JAMES I 1603-1625

1606 "De libellis Famosis" in Star Chamber
1621 First English newspaper (coronto)
1621 Proclamation against corontos

CHARLES I 1625-[1640]1649

1632 Suppression of corontos
1637 Prosecution of Puritans
1637 Second Star Chamber Decree on Printing
1638 Patent for monopoly of news

PURITAN REVOLUTION 1640-1649

1641 Star Chamber and Court of High Commission abolished

1641   First newsbook of Parliamentary News (November 29)

1642   Orders on Printing (August 26)

1643   Board of Licensers (June 14)

1644   Pamphlets on "freedom of the press" including *Areopagitica*

1647   Act for Regulating Printing (September 28)

1649   Warrant to Army to enforce printing ordinances (January)

1649   Trial and execution of Charles I

COMMONWEALTH   1649-1653

1649   Printing Act of September 20

1652   "Beacon Fired" controversy

1653   Printing Act of January 7

PROTECTORATE   1653-1659

1655   Cromwell's orders on the Press, August 28

CHARLES II   1660-1685

1660   Muddiman given monopoly of news

1660   Order of Lords against publication of proceedings

1661   Order of Commons against publication of proceedings

1662   Act to regulate printing (June 10)

1663   L'Estrange given monopoly of news

1665   Oxford (later London) Gazette

1679   Reorganization of Stationers Company

1680   Order of Commons to print "votes"

1680   Order of Charles II suppressing newsbooks

JAMES II   1685-1689

WILLIAM AND MARY   1689-1702

1694   Expiry of the Printing Act

1697   Order of Lords against publication of proceedings

ANNE   1702-1714

1702   First daily newspaper, *The Daily Courant*

1703 Order of Lords to print "votes"
1709/10 First Copyright Act
1712 First Stamp Act, 10 Anne c. 18

GEORGE I   1714-1727

1723 Commons restricts committee reports
1724 Second Stamp Act, II Geo. I, c. 8

GEORGE II   1727-1760

1738 Suppression of Parliamentary debates
1757 Pitt's Stamp Act, 30 Geo. II, c. 19

GEORGE III   1760-1820

1764 Prosecution of Wilkes (*North Briton*)
1765 General warrants held illegal
1765 Stamp tax on American publications
1766 Above repealed
1770 Prosecution of Junius letters
1771 Contest with Commons on reporting Debates
1773 Loopholes in Stamp Act closed
1775 Lords permit reports of Debates
1776 Increase in stamp taxes
1783 Dean of St. Asaph's case (seditious libel)
1789 New increase in stamp taxes
1792 Fox's Libel Act

PART 1

Control of the Press
UNDER THE TUDORS

1476-1603

CHAPTER 1

Printing and the Prerogative

The authority to control and regulate the printing press in England was claimed for two centuries by the crown as one of its prerogative rights. Beginning with Henry VIII, this authority was consistently and persistently exercised either by the king himself, by the Council, or by officers appointed by the king. Through royal proclamations, licenses, patents of monopoly, Orders in Council, and Star Chamber decrees, the press of England was effectively held in check throughout the Tudor period. The succeeding Stuart kings were less successful in operating the elaborate machinery which they inherited from their predecessors, and with the Revolution of 1688 the system of control through the royal prerogative finally collapsed.

The historical and constitutional origins of the right of the crown to regulate the printing press are somewhat obscure. It is characteristic that the Tudors worried not at all about the juristic bases of their powers; it was sufficient that they exercised them *de facto*. The Stuarts, however, were frequently disturbed in their claims and attempted to establish their authority *de jure*. The Tudors ruled arbitrarily without constitutional misgivings, while the Stuarts adopted the theory of the divine right of kings to substantiate their authority.

The right of the crown to regulate printing ultimately came to rest on these propositions: (1) that printing was first introduced into England at the behest of the king, who therefore held the original right to exercise the craft, (2) that the stability of government and the peace of the realm demanded strict control, and (3) that such regulation had in fact been exercised by the crown ever since the introduction of the first press in 1476. To the first, the answer is that the king probably did not introduce printing; to the second, the Tudor statesmen gave a categorical answer; to the third, the evidence shows that the crown did not regulate printing from the beginning but gradually, almost imperceptibly, assumed control over the press during the sixteenth century. These propositions will be examined in the following sections.

The Introduction of Printing

Two accounts of the introduction of printing into England have at different times been set forth. The early antiquarians (Stow and Ames) gave the credit to William Caxton (1424?-1491), who, according to them, on his own initiative set up the first press at Westminster in 1476.

In 1660, however, Richard Atkyns, a Stuart supporter, who had become involved with the Stationers Company over the right to print law books, published anonymously a broadside, later expanded into a pamphlet, designed to prove that printing was first introduced into England in 1468 at the instigation of Henry VI.[1] Atkyns' immediate purpose was to show that the right and title of printing rested with the crown and more particularly that his patent to print law books derived from the king was superior to the right of the Stationers.

The evidence stated in Atkyns' pamphlet was as follows: (1) A then recently discovered work in the library at Cambridge which was purported to have been printed at Oxford in 1468, (2) a manuscript at Lambeth palace, which was supposed to prove that another printer, Frederick Corsells or Corsellis, had at the king's suggestion set up a press at Oxford some eight years before Caxton, (3) Caxton's intimacy with persons of quality, (4) the statement by Stow in

---

[1] *The Original and Growth of Printing* (London, 1660 and 1664). The British Museum copy is bound up with *Orders, Rules and Ordinances of the Stationers Company* (London, 1682). See D.N.B. I, 700-702.

his *Annales* [2] that the press was set up within the precincts of Westminster Abbey under the direction of Abbot Islip, and (5) a woodcut in the first issue of Caxton's press at Westminster showing the presentation by a figure assumed to be Caxton's of a copy of the book to Edward IV.

Atkyns' pamphlet stated that "Thos. Bouchier, Archbishop of Canterbury, moved the king to use all possible means for procuring a printing-mold." The king, it said, confided the matter to a Mr. R. Turnour, who interested Caxton. Together they succeeded in bringing over Corsells from Haarlem, who set up a press at Oxford about eight years before Caxton. This claim was refuted in 1735 by Dr. Conyers Middleton, who showed that the book said to have been printed in 1468 (MCDLXVIII) by this press was misdated by ten years through the omission of a numeral X.[3] No other book was printed at Oxford until 1479. The error found its way into several dissertations on early printing, but all subsequent bibliographers have approved the contention of Dr. Middleton.

The Lambeth palace manuscript which was purported to prove the facts about Corsells has never been found despite diligent search by scholars.

It is undoubtedly true that Caxton, who set up his press in Westminster in 1476, was intimate with a number of important persons, some of whom were his patrons. In this he was like other men of letters of the times. He was in his own eyes first an author, translator, and patron of literature, and became a printer late in life largely as a means of advancing his avocation. The fact that his sponsors were numerous tends to preclude the contention that he set up his press at the order of the king.[4] No other evidence than his

[2] John Stow, *Annales, or, A Generall Chronicle of England* (London, 1580–).

[3] The title of the 1468 imprint (fourteen copies are known) as listed in Oxford bibliographies is *Exposicio Sancti Ieronimi in Simbolum Apostolorum* (Oxford, 1468? (1478)). Middleton published his *Dissertation Concerning the Origin of Printing* in London, 1735.

Falconer Madan, the modern bibliographer, reviews the evidence in *A Chart of Oxford Printing "1468"-1900* (Oxford, 1904), pp. 38-39, and in "Two Lost Causes," *The Library*, 3d Series, IX (1918), 90.

[4] William Blades, *The Biography and Typography of William Caxton* (2d ed.; New York, 1882), pp. 80-81. See H. B. Lathrop, "The First English Printers and Their Patrons," *Transactions of the Bibliographical Society*, 4th Series, III, 60-96.

intimacy with persons of quality has been discovered to suggest that Caxton's press at Westminster was sponsored by his patrons.

Other than Stow's statement that the press was set up at Westminster Abbey under the direction of Abbot Islip, there has been no evidence to indicate the exact location of the press in the city of Westminster, which was under the king's special jurisdiction, nor the reason for its being located there. Caxton was a member of the Mercers Company of the City of London, and it would have been natural for him to settle within the boundaries of that city upon his return from the continent. Since he had given up his business pursuits and was devoting his entire time to letters, it is probable that he set up his press in Westminster to be near his literary patrons and away from the distractions of the metropolis. The fact that Caxton died nine years before Islip was made abbot, together with evidence presented by Blades,[5] has effectively shown that Stow was not correct in stating that the press was situated within the walls of the abbey.

The woodcut used as an illustration in the *Dictes or Sayengis,* the first issue of Caxton's press at Westminster, portrays Edward IV on his throne with his young son standing by his side. Earl Rivers, tutor to the prince, is presenting the king a copy of his own translation. The other kneeling figure has been assumed to be Caxton, but this figure is actually an ecclesiastic as shown by his tonsure, and is apparently the scribe who engrossed and illuminated the copy.[6]

The conclusion to be drawn from this evidence is that Caxton introduced printing into England not at the mandate of the king but on his own initiative. The products of his press, although sometimes suggested or requested by his patrons, were probably his own selections. It may be assumed that he was subjected to neither censorship nor control by ecclesiastical or secular authority.

Caxton was soon followed by a number of foreign competitors, who set up their presses at London or Westminster. John Lettou, a native of Lithuania, settled in London in 1479; William de Machlinia, who came from Mechlin in Belgium, became his partner in

---

[5] *Ibid.,* pp. 72-75.

[6] *The Dictes or Sayengis of the Philosophers* (C.O.D.) Lambeth, 265. Translation from the French of Lehan de Teonville by Anthony Wydville, Earl Rivers, who completed the work in 1477. The ms. at Lambeth is stated by the transcriber to have been finished on December 14 in the 17th year of Ed. IV. The book as printed by Caxton differs slightly from the ms.

1482; Julyn Notary, a Frenchman, is found printing in 1496. Wynkyn de Worde, an Alsatian and one of Caxton's apprentices, took over his master's establishment on the latter's death in 1491. An unknown printer was at work at St. Albans before 1486, and there was a press at Oxford in 1478.[7]

To stimulate interest in letters, a proviso was added to the Act of 1484 to the effect that any foreign bookseller or printer might import books, bound or unbound, into England, and they or any foreign scrivener, illuminator, or bookbinder might live within the realm and carry on his business.[8] In 1500 there were only five printers in London; by 1523 there were at least thirty-three printers and booksellers actively engaged in the trade. In that year the influx of foreign craftsmen was undoubtedly responsible for the Act prohibiting an alien from taking an alien apprentice or keeping more than two alien journeymen.[9]

Tudor Statecraft

The Tudor policy of strict control over the press in the interest of the safety of the state was maintained throughout the sixteenth century. From Henry VIII to Elizabeth, the English sovereigns acted upon the principle that the peace of the realm demanded the suppression of all dissenting opinion and furthermore that the crown itself through its prerogative was the only instrument capable of carrying through such a program. That the Tudors, arbitrary rulers that they were, adhered to such a policy is not surprising, but that they encountered so little opposition is astonishing. Neither Parliament, the printers, nor public opinion such as it was, offered any appreciable resistance to the aggrandizement of the crown. The "liberties" of the British subject were for an entire century submerged. Dynasties were wiped out, the old nobility despoiled, the clergy made dependent on the crown; sects were persecuted and opinions punished as treason, all under rules contrary to the medieval common law and the liberties of the subject. The bases

---

[7] E. G. Duff, *Wynkyn de Worde and his Contemporaries* (London, 1925), contains the best account of these early printers. See also E. J. Worman, *Alien Members of the Book Trade* (London, 1906).

[8] 1 Ric. III, c. 9.

[9] 14 & 15 Henry VIII, c. 2 (1523) *An Acte Concerning the Taking of Apprentices by Straungers.*

of the policy of the crown as well as the reasons for the lack of opposition are found in the changed politico-economic situation, the New Learning, and the Reformation.

The opening of the sixteenth century found the people of England worn out from the dynastic struggles between the houses of York and Lancaster. The first Tudor, Henry VII, had brought them the blessings of peace, and they justly regarded his son, Henry VIII, as their best security against the anarchy from which his father had rescued them. The theoretical liberties of the middle ages were useless, they must have realized, in a state of perpetual civil war. Peace was what they wanted, and the opportunity to repair their fortunes. As much as the arbitrary extensions of the authority of the prerogative might have irked the sixteenth-century Englishman, he was content to put up with them in return for stability and continuity of government. As Professor A. F. Pollard has pointed out, during the entire Tudor period the citizen was willing to sacrifice his ancient liberties in return for domestic tranquility.[10] Henry VIII was not acting wholly against the will of his subjects when he sought to suppress dissenting opinion in the interest of the state.

Another political consideration conducive to Tudor policy was the growth of the spirit of nationalism. The feudal character of social institutions was fast disappearing, the internationalism of the Church of Rome was destroyed, and all over western Christendom new nations were emerging. The unsettled state of law and political institutions coincident with the change from feudalism to capitalism and nationalism gave the aggressive monarch an opportunity to extend his own authority. In the process of consolidation a strong rein on all public discussion was necessary if revolution and civil war were to be avoided. Both Henry VIII and Elizabeth succeeded in identifying themselves with the popular conception of peace and national unity to such an extent that opposition was reduced to a minimum.

The New Learning, while acceptable as providing arguments for the destruction of medieval institutions, was in fact irritating to the Tudors in its impartiality. With the fundamental principles of the new method of scientific inquiry, they had no quarrel; but they decried its lack of discrimination. Old institutions, religious, polit-

[10] A. F. Pollard, *Henry VIII* (Paris: Goupil, 1902), p. 34.

ical, and social, were properly analyzed under the glare of its searchlight, but it was exasperating to have the same light played on the substitutes invented by the crown. The interest in letters, in scientific inquiry, in political affairs increased with the spread of education and printed matter in the vernacular. The country strained to know more about what was going on behind the scenes, the workings of the courts, Parliament, the church, and the crown itself. During the sixteenth century there occurred many instances of the crown's being forced to crack the whip at printers who sought to satisfy this curiosity.

The early Reformation movement in England in the sixteenth century, instead of acting as a brake on the crown's progress toward absolutism, actually added its weight to the steam-roller methods employed under the prerogative. The religious dissensions of Henry VIII's reign were more political than theological. The crown was substituted for the Pope, but the idea of the direct relationship between the individual and his Creator, which was the mainspring of the German reformation and later of the Puritan revolt in England, remained taboo. Where political freedom disappeared, dissent was crushed and toleration unknown. Henry accomplished his unusual results by appealing to his subjects on religious grounds and using the results for political purposes. He attacked the Church of Rome on a theological basis; he built his own church on a political foundation. But he was not completely successful in substituting the authority of the crown for that of the church, for his methods returned to plague his successors. Henry, in common with other reformers, did not intend to introduce religious or political freedom, but the idea that any claimant to a position of authority in either political or religious matters should be subjected to a rational inquiry, once started on its way, was beyond his or anyone else's control. Religious freedom and political liberty both owed their inception to the primary freedom of inquiry and discussion. Whereas the political situation in the sixteenth century made it possible to control the press, to the Tudors the New Learning and the Reformation made it necessary.

The Tudor policy with respect to the press was carried out through instrumentalities based upon the authority of the prerogative or, in other words, upon powers inherent in the office of the king. The Orders in Council and the Star Chamber decrees owed whatever legal force they had to the crown. The right to exercise and delegate this authority was due solely to the Tudor sovereigns' usurpations, ably abetted by ingenious constitutional arguments. The Magna Carta, together with other feudal limitations on the power of the king, was discarded or at least held in abeyance during the sixteenth century. Distinctions were drawn between the "natural" and "politic" capacities of the king, between "separable" and "inseparable" prerogative powers, between the "absolute" and "ordinary" authority of the crown,[11] all directed toward, but incapable of, describing a situation in which the king used whatever powers he pleased whenever he saw fit.

The king's authority, therefore, to control and regulate the press was unlimited. From modest beginnings, such as the appointment of an official printer with special privileges, it had by the end of the century expanded into a complete and complex system of regulation. What Henry VIII began, his daughter Elizabeth completed. In no other country in Europe was the system so delicately balanced or so ingeniously operated. The result was the postponement until the next century of the serious problems arising from political and religious discussion.

The sixteenth century also witnessed a large increase in the powers — executive, legislative, and judicial — of the Council (or Privy Council) at the expense of both Parliament and the older courts, but to the distinct advantage of the crown. It was in and through this body that the monarchy performed its work. Through the authority of the king whom it was expected to advise and assist, the Council supervised the administration of the laws, regulated trade and wages, kept an eye on the courts, as well as controlled the press. As its independence of the crown decreased, its powers increased. It eagerly proceeded against what was called "lewd and naughty matters" — the sixteenth-century equivalent of modern political criticism.[12]

The Council assisted the king in preparing and enforcing his proclamations; it conducted investigations into seditious activities, or appointed commissions to conduct investigations; it handed indi-

[11] W. S. Holdsworth, *A History of English Law* (Boston: Little, Brown, 1924), IV, 190-217.

[12] Sir Harris Nicolas, *Proceedings and Ordinances of the Privy Council of England, 1540-1542* (London, 1837), VII, xxxviii.

viduals over to the Star Chamber for trial and sentence, and gave
orders compelling persons to do or abstain from doing almost any
kind of act. The proceedings were in secret, and although torture
was unknown to the common law of England, it was a recognized
prerogative of the king in Council. The Star Chamber, the judicial
offshoot of the Council, was the instrument most frequently employed in the control of the press in the later sixteenth century, but
the Privy Council itself frequently interfered.

Beginning in 1542 (the date of the first continuous record)
the acts of the Council report a long line of proceedings against
individuals for "seditious words," "unfitting worddes," "unsemely
words," or "evil opinions." The first conflict between the Council
and printers of which there is record occurred late in 1540 when a
number of ballads and broadsides appeared on the streets of
London for and against Cromwell, the late Privy Seal. Early in
January of the next year, Richard Grafton and Richard Bankes were
called before the Council charged with printing the invectives.[13]
Bankes denied the printing in spite of the fact that his mark appeared on some of the ballads, claiming that it had been forged
by the printer, Robert Redmon. (This fact continues to agitate
those bibliographers who had placed implicit reliance on printers'
marks.) Grafton confessed to printing part of the broadsides. When
he also admitted he had a copy of Melancthon's book written against
Henry's religious settlement, he was committed to prison by the
Council. How long he remained there is not known,[14] but he was
out of prison in time to be called and committed again by the
Council, 22 April 1543.[15]

The proclamation (or ordinance) was the legislative tool employed by the king and Council to give legality and force to the
rules and regulations for the press. The Tudors, who could control
Parliament, used the proclamation because of its dispatch; the
Stuarts, always at odds with Parliament, used it because of necessity. Based on the royal prerogative, the authority to issue procla-

---

[13] Eight ballads in the controversy are listed by Robert Lemon, *Catalogue
of a Collection of Printed Broadsides in the possession of the Society of Antiquaries* (London, 1866), pp. 2-5.

[14] *L. & P. Henry VIII, XVI*, Nos. 349, 366, 422, 424; Nicolas, *op. cit.*,
VII, xxxiv-xxxvi.

[15] *Acts of Privy Council.* n.s. I, 107.

mations having the force of law gave the king wide powers over fields left untouched by statute or common law. A further step was taken in 1538 when Henry VIII, apparently irked by frequent infringements of his proclamations, had Parliament pass an act giving them the status of enacted statutes.[16] The Act was repealed in 1547,[17] the first year of Edward VI's reign, but proclamations both before and after that date, as far as wording, promulgation, and enforcement were concerned, remained the same. That many of the Tudor proclamations were illegal, judged from seventeenth-century common-law standards, there can be no doubt, but they were made and enforced as law throughout the sixteenth century.

The Tudor sovereigns devised, amended, and repealed innumerable proclamations governing the press. From Henry VII's warning against "forged tydings and tales" in 1486 [18] to Elizabeth's announcement of 1601 submitting the question of patents to the common-law courts,[19] the royal proclamation was the chief implement employed in the control of printing. The method was quick, incisive, and effective, as we shall see.

The King Takes Control

As long as the "art and mistery" of printing remained merely an adjunct to letters, neither the king nor Parliament paid much attention to it, but as the trade in printed books increased and later extended into the field of religious and political controversy, the Tudor statesmen slowly but effectively concentrated the control of the new craft in the hands of the king and Council.

The encroachment of the royal prerogative was gradual. In spite of overlapping, four distinct steps leading to the establishment of a licensing system can be distinguished: (1) protection of the native printer against foreign competition; (2) the appointment of royal or official printers; (3) grants of privilege for purposes of control and trade protection; and (4) grants of patents of monopoly.

---

[16] 31 Henry VIII, c. 8; amended by 34 and 35 Henry VIII, c. 23. See E. R. Adair, "Statute of Proclamations," *English Historical Review*, XXXII (1917), 34-46.

[17] I Edw. VI, c. 12 sec. 4.

[18] Robert Steele, *Tudor and Stuart Proclamations, 1485-1714* (Oxford, 1910), Vol. I, No. 7.

[19] *Ibid.*, No. 922.

In 1528 Henry VIII proceeded to regulate the activities of foreigners through a decree by king and Council in the Star Chamber.[20] For the first time the royal prerogative was used to regulate the printing trade. The decree prohibited aliens from keeping more than two alien servants and from setting up any new shops, but it permitted foreign craftsmen to take subjects as apprentices. It was a modest beginning and scarcely hinted at the elaborate network of restrictions which was to emanate from the crown and Council during the course of the century. Evidently Henry was not at this date sufficiently sure of his powers as king for he felt it necessary to have the decree ratified by Parliament the following year.[21]

The final step in this series of enactments for the protection of native printers was the Act of 1534, which came into force on Christmas Day.[22] The preamble recites the reason for the statute:

Where As the provysyon of a statute made in the fyrst yere of the reigne of Kynge Richarde the thirde it was provyded in the same acte, that all strangers reparying into this Realme myght lawfully bryng into the seid Realme pryntyt and wrytyn bokes to sell at their libertie and pleasure; by force of which provysyon there hath commen into this Realme sithen the makyn of the same a marveylous nombre of pryntyd bokes and dayly doth; And the cause of the makyng of the same provysion semeth to be for that there were but fewe bokes and few prynters within This Realme at that tyme which cold well exercise and occupie the seid science and crafte of pryntyng; Never the lesse sithen the making of the seid provysion many of this Realme being the Kynges naturall subjects have geven theyme soo dylygently to lerne and exercyse the seid craft of pryntyng that at this day there be within this Realme a greatt nombre connyng and expert in the seid science or craft of pryntyng as abyll to exercyse the seid craft in all pynts as any Stranger in any other Realme or Countre; And furthermore where there be a great nombre of the Kynges subjects within this Realme which leve by the crafte and mystrie of byndyng of bokes and that there be a great multytude well expert in the same; yet all this not withstondyng there are dyvrse persones that bryng frome [behonde] the See great plentie of pryntyd bokes not only in the latyn tonge but also in our

[20] Henry VIII, February 25. The decree was purely an executive act by the king and Council as the distinction between the Privy Council (as an advisory body to the executive) and the Council in the Star Chamber (a judicial body) had not yet been completed. See p. 120.

[21] 21 Henry VIII, c. 16 (1529), *An Acte ratifying a decree made in the Sterre Chambre,* etc.

[22] 25 Henry VIII, c. 15, *An Acte for Prynters and bynders of bokes.*

maternall englishe tonge, somme bounde in bourds some in lether and
some in parchement and theym sell by retayle, whereby many of the
Kynges Subjects being bynders of bokes and havyng none other facultie
wherewith to gett theire lyvyng be destitute of worke and like to be
undone, except somme reformacion here in be hade. . . .

The act itself, after repealing the exemption in favor of foreign
printers in the Statute of 1 Richard III (1484), provided that no
book bound in foreign parts could be sold in England, no person
could buy from a foreigner in the retail trade any book brought
from beyond the sea, that steps could be taken against any printer
or bookseller who, taking advantage of the act, set unreasonable
prices for his books. Thus competition from alien printers almost
immediately ceased to the distinct advantage of the native craftsmen.

The appointment of an official printer was a further step leading to the concentration of the control of the press in the hands of
the king. The king's Stationer was a recognized position in the
royal household as early as the fifteenth century. His principal duty
was to supply written and printed books for the officials and the
members of the king's family. Henry VII, a patron of letters, first
gave official recognition to printing in the appointment of Peter
Actors as Stationer to the king, 5 December 1485. Actors, who was
not a printer, received a grant for life to "import, as often as he
likes, from parts beyond the sea, books printed and not printed into
the port of the city of London, and other ports and places within the
Kingdom of England, and to dispose of the same by sale or otherwise, without paying customes, etc. thereon and without rendering
any accoumpt thereof." [23]

The first official printer was William Faques, who held the
office from 1504 to 1508.[24] He was followed by Richard Pynson
(1508-1530) who received an annuity of 2 pounds and later 4
pounds and who styled himself "Prynter vnto the Kingis noble
Grace." Thomas Berthelet was appointed by Henry VIII in 1530,

[23] William Campbell, *Materials for a History of the Reign of Henry VII*
(London, 1873-77), I, 211.

[24] E. G. Duff, *A Century of English Book Trade, 1457-1557* (London,
1905), p. 45. Caxton was never an official printer. Arber's list (*Transcript*, V,
lix) headed by Caxton is erroneous. Although both de Machlinia and de Worde
printed royal proclamations (Steele, Nos. 3 and 35), neither was an official
printer.

and his is the earliest patent which has survived.[25] Berthelet used the legend "Regis impressor." Edward VI introduced an innovation when he deposed Berthelet and appointed Richard Grafton, who was given a patent for the sole printing of statutes and acts of Parliament.[26] Grafton was in turn succeeded by John Cawood in 1553 upon the accession of Queen Mary. Thus the custom of appointing a sort of book agent under Henry VII had expanded under the royal aegis into a monopolistic control of an important class of printed books.

Elizabeth, characteristically, made the office do as a reward for two adherents by appointing both Cawood and John Jugge as royal printers on 24 March 1560.[27] Cawood died in 1572 and Jugge continued as the sole owner of the office until his death in 1577. Christopher Barker, one of the most prominent printers of his day, purchased the office from Sir Thomas Wilkes, clerk of the Privy Council, who had acquired it as a reward for services.[28] In 1587 the imprint becomes "deputies of Christopher Barker" (George Bishop and Ralph Newberry), probably as an aftermath of the disgrace of Wilkes. Robert Barker, Christopher's son, obtained the reversion by patent in 1584,[29] but the imprint "deputies of C. Barker" continued until the death of Christopher in 1599 when the name of Robert appeared 14 January 1600.

Printing "privileges" made their appearance early in the history of the press. Under the medieval system of patent law the crown regarded itself as the sole patron of the destinies of new industries

---

[25] Rex Omnibus ad quos &. salutem. Sciatis quod nos de gracia nostra speciali, ac ex certa scientia, et mero motu nostris dedimus & concessimus, ac per praesentes damus et concedimus dilecto servienti nostro Thomae Barthelet impressori nostro quandam annuitatem, sive quendam annualem redditum quatuor librarum sterlingorum, habendum & annuatim percipiendum praedictam annuatim, sive annualem redditum quatuor librarum eidem Thomae Barthelet, a festo Pasche anno regni nostri vicesimo primo, durante vita sua de thesauro nostro ad receptum scaccarii nostri per manus thesaurarii & camerarii nostrorum ibidem pro tempore existendo ad festa sancti Michaelis archangeli: & Pasche per equales porciones, eo quod expressa mencio, etc. In cujus, etc., teste rege apud Westmonasterium, vicesimo secundo die Februarii: Per breve de privato sigillo, et de dat. etc. (Rot. Pat. 21 Hen. VIII, p. 2, m. 17).

[26] Rot. Pat. I Ed. VI, p. 7, m. 1 (22 April 1547).

[27] Rot. Pat. I Eliz. p. 7, m. 28.

[28] Rot. Pat. 19 Eliz. p. 8, m. 48.

[29] Rot. Pat. 31 Eliz. p. 9, m. 40.

which were introduced under its protection.[30] Although printing was not introduced under the royal patronage, the king could not refrain from extending his authority already used to allow special rights to the royal printer.

Special privileges were common on the continent at the opening of the sixteenth century. In 1467 a monopoly was granted for the manufacture and sale of paper in Berne and its jurisdictions;[31] and there is a record of a grant in 1469 to Johann von Speyer, who received an exclusive privilege of printing in Venice for a period of five years.[32] What a continental ruler could do, a Tudor could do.

The legal basis of the privilege in the Tudor period lay in showing that a particular patent was for the public interest or tended to develop industries through the protection of invention. As applied to printing, the first basis was so broad as to be readily susceptible of abuse; while the second was made applicable to the press by extending the meaning of "invention" to include any new publication. Without a doubt there were occasions when the grant of protection for a particular book hastened its publication, but never absent from the minds of Tudor sovereigns in allowing the royal protection was the realization that the privilege would either reward a compliant printer or seduce a recalcitrant one.[33]

The early sixteenth-century printers and booksellers were probably envious of the official sanction which soon attached to the works issued by the royal printer under the imprint "regis impres-

---

[30] E. W. Hulme, "History of the Patent System under the Prerogative and at Common Law," *Law Quarterly Review*, XII, 141-54; XVI, 44-56. Holdsworth, *op. cit.*, IV, 343ff. The legality of the medieval grants of patents of monopoly was based on *Year Book Ed. III*, Pasch. pl. 8 (ff. 17, 18) to the effect that the crown has power to grant many privileges for the sake of the public good, although *prima facie* they appear to be clearly against common right.

[31] W. H. Price, *The English Patents of Monopoly* (New York: Houghton Mifflin, 1906), p. 3, quoting Kholer, *Handbuch des deutschen Patenrechts*, p. 21.

[32] *Ibid.*, quoting Klostermann, *Das Patentgesetz fur das deutsche Reich*, pp. 15, 16. "Ut per annos quinque proxime futuros nemo omnino sit qui velit, possit, valeat, audeative exercere dictam arten imprimendorum librorum in hac inclyta civitate Venetiarum et districtu suo nisi ipse Mag. Johannes."

[33] That the Tudor patents of monopoly in printing were admittedly based on the ground that the restriction was necessary in the interests of the state, see argument of Dodderidge in Darcy *vs.* Allen, *Moore*, p. 673. Also Lands. Ms. 4.8 f. 194.

sor." It is more than likely that they themselves sought the king's approval for their printed works both as a protection against piracy (which was then common) and as an additional advertisement of authenticity. Whether the initiative came from the king, the author, or the printer is not known as no early original patent has been found, but by 1518 is found for the first time the legend "cum privilegio" on the colophon of a printed book. In one of the earliest books printed by John Rastell (Linacre's *Progymnasmata*), the colophon read: "Empryntyd in London on ye Sowth syde of Poulys by John Rastell with ye privylege of our most suverayn lord kyng Henry the VIII grauntyd to the compyler theof that no man in thys hys realme sell none but such as the same compyler makyth pryntyd for ye space of II yeare." [34] This author's privilege was probably obtained by Linacre, who had achieved preferment as a classical scholar and physician to the king.

The next instance is found in a sermon printed by Pynson, the royal printer, in 1518. The value of the publication to the printer was its timely appeal to the reading public. The privilege of exclusive printing of the pamphlet for two years is definitely given to the printer and not the author.[35] Rastell records an author's privilege for seven years in his edition of *Abbreviation of the Statutes*.[36] In Pynson's privilege for sole printing of William Horman's *Vulgaria* (1519) no term of years is mentioned. The sequence of grants was first an author's privilege for a term of years, then a printer's privilege for a term, and finally a printer's privilege for life.

By 1520 both Rastell and Pynson were issuing their books under a general privilege (i.e., a protection covering everything they printed) for which no original warrant can be found, although copies of the warrants are sometimes published in full in their books after 1538. Within a few years the entire craft was scrambling for printing "privileges" and the phrase "cum privilegio a rege" appeared in the colophons of almost all the printers. In addition

---

[34] A. W. Reed, "The Regulation of the Book Trade," *Transactions of the Bibliographical Society*, London, XV, 174, places the date before 1517.

[35] The colophon reads: "cum priuilegio a rege indulto ne quis hanc orationem intra biennium in regno Angliae imprimat aut alibi impressam et importatam in eodem regno Angliae vendat." Quoted by A. W. Pollard, "Regulation of the Book Trade," *The Library*, 3d Series, VII (1916), 20.

[36] Reed, *op. cit.*, p. 174.

to the aura of respectability which surrounded the phrase, it seems
to have been the only available protection against piracy.[37]

Henry VIII, who was just entering into his political and religious controversies brought on by the contemplated divorce, was
only too willing to extend the authority of the crown as a sort of
primitive copyright over the entire output of the press, realizing
that by grants of privilege he could the more readily exert pressure
on, and demand favors of, the printers. He was soon forced to face
the problem that he could not hand out grants of privilege indis-
criminately without incurring grave responsibilities. The religious
controversy had already broken out in print. Both orthodox and un-
orthodox were making an appeal to public opinion through printed
leaflets and books, and authors and printers did not scruple to use
the king's privilege as a mark of authenticity. Dr. Arthur W. Reed
recently discovered a Bill of Complaint addressed to Cromwell,
Lord Privy Seal, complaining that "though the king 'puts forthwith
Certyne bookes printed and openly sold with his ryght royal privy-
ledge sett unto the same to the intente (as we do take it) that no
man shoulde feare but rather be encoragede to occupye them'; yet
nevertheless they have been troubled by the said Vigorous [the
questman or prosecutor before the Ordinary] for reading, and making opportunities for reading, certain books so privileged." [38]

The king must have had such a situation as that above in
mind when he inserted in the proclamation of 1538, the most comprehensive set of regulations for printing up to that time, a section
designed to relieve the crown of responsibility. The Proclamation,
among other regulations for printers, required ". . . that no person
shall from hensforth . . . put these words *Cum priuilegio regali*,
without adding *ad imprimendum solum,* and that the whole copie,
or els at the least the effect of his licence and priuilege be there-
with printed, and playnely declared and expressed in the Englysche
tonge vnderneath them." [39] What was the meaning and effect of the
additional phrase *ad imprimendum solum?* It had never appeared

[37] John Scolar, who had set up a press at Oxford, printed a book in 1518
under a privilege for seven years granted by the Chancellor of the University.
II. R. Plomer, *Wynkyn de Worde* (London: Grafton & co., 1925), pp. 235-36.

[38] R. O. Misc. Bks., T. R., 120, p. 59, quoted in *Transactions of the Bibliographical Society,* London, XV, 177.

[39] Antiq. 2 (96). The licensing provisions of this proclamation are discussed in Chapter 2, p. 48.

on a book before 1538. The phrase is ambiguous to a modern reader; it can mean either "for sole or exclusive printing" or "for printing only," but an analysis of the reasons for its insertion in the proclamation by the king and the effect on contemporary printers as appears in a letter by Richard Grafton, the printer, clearly show that it was intended to mean "for printing only." The phrase "cum priuilegio" conferred the exclusive rights of printing, while Henry intended by the additional words to absolve himself of responsibility for the contents of books, many of which were issued under a general privilege without previous examination.[40]

Many books appearing after 1538 contained a full copy of the royal privileges. These were frequently general privileges extending to all the books printed by the grantee, and most of them were for a definite term of years. That the king continued to use the authority to grant privileges to keep printers in line is indicated by the grant to John Gough, who was on more than one occasion in trouble with the authorities. His privilege was made conditional upon his "Storyes or bokes being perused and overseen by two or three dyscrete learned persons." [41] No such condition appears on the grants issued to the more "respectable" printers. Grafton, who was at this time engaged in printing the Great Bible (a work undertaken with the cooperation of the Lord Privy Seal), objected to the addition of the qualifying phrase *ad imprimendum solum* on the ground that the Bible would not have the appearance of official sanction.[42] However, when the first edition appeared in 1538, it carried the full legend, *Cum priuilegio ad imprimendum solum,* as did all subsequent editions.[43]

---

[40] A. W. Pollard first gave the correct interpretation to this phrase in *The Records of the English Bible* (London: Oxford Univ. press, 1911), p. 241, restated on p. 6 of his *Shakespeare's Fight with the Pirates* (2d ed.; Cambridge, 1920). Reed, *op. cit.,* pp. 178-83 substantiates the interpretation. Miss Evelyn Albright has supported the other meaning in *Modern Language Notes,* XXXIV, 97-104. She is answered by Pollard in *The Library,* 3d Series, X (1919), 57-63. The Public Record Office has the original draft of the Proclamation (S. P. Hen. VIII, b. 139, f. 103). The B.M. has a fair copy with Henry's corrections in his own hand. (Cotton Ms. Cleo. E. V., 341.)

[41] See colophon of Gough's *Dore of Holy Scriptures,* 1540. Reed, *op. cit.,* p. 181, sets out a copy of a general warrant of privilege.

[42] Cotton Ms. Cleo. E. V., 323.

[43] Francis Fry, *A Description of the Great Bible* (1865). Place 2 presents facsimiles of the title pages.

Patents of monopoly were a natural development of the practice of granting warrants of privilege. Printers' privileges were grants for the protection from piracy of all works which a printer might issue. Patents of monopoly were primarily prohibitions directed against not only reprints but new works in the specially reserved field. Whereas under a grant or privilege to Bankes, Berthelet was prohibited from re-issuing books first printed by Bankes; under a patent of monopoly, such as that of law books to Tottell, another printer could issue no new works on the law. There had been, it is true, patents for the protection of single works issued in the latter half of the fifteenth century, but these were rather grants of privilege or copyright than patents of monopoly. John Norton had thus received by patent the royal protection for his *Specular;* and Richard Welsh was given the exclusive right to print the *History of Cornelius Tacitus.*

One of the earliest instances of the change from privilege to monopoly was the issuance of a patent for printing Bibles in English in 1539. Grafton, the printer, had written to Cromwell asking for an exclusive privilege.[44] On the same day that he received the letter, Cromwell hastened to the king and obtained a patent, not for the printer, but for himself. The warrant gave the Lord Privy Seal the exclusive right to print all Bibles in English for seven years.[45]

After Cromwell's fall, the king granted Anthony Marler, a merchant who had financed Grafton and Whitechurch, a monopoly over the printing of Bibles for four years.[46] In 1543, Grafton and Whitechurch received as compensation a patent giving them the exclusive right to print service books and primers for seven years.[47] A list of printing patents from 1559 to 1577 is found in the Burghley Papers:

R. Tottell held the exclusive printing during his life of "all manner of books concerning the common laws of the realm"; W. Seres had a license for life to print primers and prayer books; James Roberts and R. Watkins were given exclusive rights to print almanacks; John Jugge had Bibles and Testaments; John Day, the

---

[44] P.R.O. *L. & P. Hen. VIII*, XV, pt. 2, No. 517.

[45] Pat. Roll, 31 Hen. VIII, pt. 4, November 14, 1539.

[46] March, 1542. Thomas Rymer, *Foedera* (London: A. J. Churchill, 1712), XIV, 745.

[47] *L. & P. Hen. VIII*, XVIII, pt. 1, No. 68.

ABC's and catechisms; Thomas March, Latin grammars; Thomas Vautroller, Latin books; Byrde, music books and ruled paper; and Francis Flower, grammars.[48] Christopher Barker, the royal printer, submitted a report on monopolies December, 1582, which included the following: Barker, Old and New Testaments, statutes, proclamations, and Books of Common Prayer; Flower, grammars and school books; Day, psalms in meter and catechisms; Seres, school books and service books; Tottell, law books; Bynneman, dictionaries, chronicles, and histories; March, school books in Latin; Watkins, almanacks; Vautroller, Latin books.[49]

The change in policy from privileges to monopolies is attributed to Acontius,[50] an Italian jurist and engineer, who had settled in England. The new system had several distinct advantages. It strengthened the hand of the crown by making it possible to withdraw or threaten to withdraw a printing patent. Elizabeth shuffled the patents about among the printers, rewarding here and penalizing there. She also by an Order in Council made it a crime to print or import a book already assigned by letters patent.[51] Under the new policy the crown also retained the absolute right of jurisdiction in all cases arising out of their grants. The printer who disputed a grant before the Council or Court of Star Chamber undertook a task few would care to risk as these bodies were likely to regard any infringement as a want of respect for the queen's prerogative.

The most far-reaching effect of the indiscriminate grants of letters patent was the chaos resulting in the printing trade. Although the purpose of these grants was to bring order among the printers,[52] they had the opposite effect. Elizabeth, who was so astute in most things, failed to measure the results in this case. As larger areas of the printing field were awarded to loyal followers, the opportunities for the printer without a patent and the newly-released

[48] B.M. Lands. No. 48, f. 180, 181.

[49] B.M. Lands. No. 48, ff. 189-94.

[50] E. W. Hulme, "The History of the Patent System Under the Prerogative and at Common Law," *Law Quarterly Review*, XII (1896), 151.

[51] "Order against Seditious Books" (1566) John Strype, *Life and Acts of Matthew Parker* (London, 1711), III, Chap. 11.

[52] Barker's report, December, 1582 (B.M. Lands. No. 48, f. 194), gives the following as one of the reasons for the adoption of the policy of granting patents: "and if they should must of necessities, either wantt necessari lyving, or print bookes, pamphlettes, and other trifles, more dangerous then profitable."

apprentice to make an honest living decreased. Printers were forced from economic necessity to work on prohibited books in which there was always a large profit. Secret and surreptitious presses multiplied. A solution was not found until the crown was stripped of its prerogative rights in the seventeenth century.

CHAPTER 2

Tudor Licensing Systems

The Church (of Rome) and the Press

Having taken control of the press under its prerogative right to grant privileges and patents of monopoly in the printing trade, the crown proceeded almost immediately to the second step—control through a licensing system. This type of control, like that of the patents, developed through several stages, culminating in the complex licensing restrictions of Elizabeth.

The religious controversies of the sixteenth century, having found their way into print, afforded the immediate occasion for the additional restrictions devised by the Tudors. The two basic intellectual principles of the religious upheaval, the duty of free inquiry and the "priesthood of all believers," furnished the basic justification for the widespread discussion of religious questions.[1] To control religious discussion, the ecclesiastical authorities employed various means such as buying up and burning the supply of obnoxious literature, forbidding its circulation on pain of excommunication, licensing of the press, and the dissemination of counterpropaganda, all without success. In the end, the church was forced to call upon the crown for assistance.

---

[1] G. P. Gooch, *English Democratic Ideas in the Seventeenth Century* (2d ed.; New York: Cambridge Univ. press, 1927), pp. 7-8.

The most absorbing topic of public discussion in the early
sixteenth century was the relation of man to God. A new theory,
a new interpretation, was news of vital interest. The continental
printers, especially the Dutch, worked their journeymen overtime
to tap this rich source of profit, and the products of their presses
soon filtered across the Channel into the English market. Cardinal
Wolsey, Archbishop Wareham, and Tunstall, bishop of London,
immediately set into action the ecclesiastical machinery for the
control of the press.

As early as 1408 following the Wyclif heresies, the Provincial
Council of the English church had prohibited the translation of
the Bible into the vulgar tongue unless it was first submitted for
examination.[2] The order by inference permitted the circulation of
all manuscript translations made before the time of Wyclif (1382)
but if such translations ever existed, none has survived.[3] The
Council also ordered that censors were to be appointed by the
universities to approve all books sent to the Stationers to be copied.
In 1414 Parliament had confirmed the legal right of the ecclesiastical
officers to proceed in open court against the makers and writers of
heretical books.[4]

This machinery Cardinal Wolsey and his associates found
ready at hand when the first printed heretical books were imported
from the continent in 1520. Following the pronouncement against
the writings of Martin Luther issued by Pope Leo X, the English
clergy in May, 1521, staged the first demonstration against heretical
books at St. Paul's in London. Bishop Fisher preached the sermon
afterwards printed by de Worde, and Luther's books were put in
the fire. In July of the same year Henry VIII published his answer
to Luther,[5] which won for him the title "Defender of the Faith."

Within a few years it was evident that the efforts of the clergy
were meeting with little success. Since most of the printers and

[2] First adopted at Oxford in 1408 (Lyndewode's *Provinciale* (1525), f.
ccvi) and later at London (David Wilkins' *Concilia* (London, 1737), III, 317).

[3] Sir Thomas More asserts that such translations were available (*Dialogue*,
III, xvi) but William Tyndale (*An Answere vnto Sir Thomas Mores dialogue*,
f. cv) says he knew of no such "lawful translation."

[4] 2 Henry V, I, c. 7.

[5] Henry's book, *Assertio Septum Sacramentum*, contained some able argument and some vituperation which "Luther was at no loss to return with
interest."

booksellers of the kingdom resided within the diocese of London, Bishop Tunstall took it upon himself to call them in (12 October 1524), warning them of the penalties attached to the importation of pernicious books. His jurisdiction was based on the Provincial Constitution of 1408 and the confirmation by Parliament in 1414. No mention was made of books printed in England as apparently no danger was apprehended from that quarter,[6] but in the next year (19 October 1525) Wynkyn de Worde and John Gough, printers, were summoned before the ecclesiastical court for printing the *Image of Love*. They were warned and apparently allowed to depart.[7]

A second demonstration against heretical books was held at St. Paul's in February, 1526, and the clergy were spurred on to further efforts to stamp out the heresies. Within a month the ecclesiastical authorities called in Thomas Berthelet for printing three harmless works, one of them Fisher's sermon preached at the recent demonstration.[8] His offense was that he had not exhibited the books to the bishop before printing them. The censorship was on in earnest.

Unsuccessful attempts to suppress the circulation of Tyndale's translation of the New Testament with its Protestant bias demonstrated the failure of the ecclesiastical methods of control. With the approval of the king, Tunstall sent out to the archdeacons of his diocese an order calling in all copies of Tyndale's book.[9] He also summoned the booksellers and printers and in their presence delivered a second monition. According to the records of Foxford, vicar-general, the bishop warned them

under pain of suspicion of heresy that they neither themselves nor through others sell, hold, give or in any way part with any books containing Lutheran heresies or any other books conceived in Latin or

---

[6] A. W. Reed, "The Regulation of the Book Trade," *Transactions of the Bibliographical Society*, XV, 162-63, sets out the text of Tunstall's monition, taken from the first volume of the Consistorial records kept by Richard Foxford, vicar-general of the Bishop of London, and preserved in the Records Department at Somerset House, London.

[7] *Ibid.*, pp. 163-65.

[8] *Ibid.*, pp. 166-69.

[9] John Foxe, *Actes and Monuments* (1563), gives the text, pp. 449-50, and appends a catalogue of forbidden books which is obviously of a later date than October, 1526. G. H. Putnam, *The Censorship of the Church of Rome* . . . (New York: Knickerbocker, 1906), I, 87; II, 257, calls this the first Index.

English, and that they neither print nor cause to be printed any other works whatever (except only works before approved by the Church) unless first they exhibit the same to the Lord Legate, the Archbishop of Canterbury, or the Bishop of London. And further he warned them under the aforesaid pains, that if they import into England any books or works redacted in Latin or the vulgar tongue printed or that may be printed hereafter across the seas, or being imported if they buy such books, they shall not sell, hold, give or part with them in any way unless they first exhibit and show them really to the Bishops afore-said.[10]

Under this order, the most comprehensive yet announced, the Bishop of London and the Archbishop of Canterbury were consti-tuted the sole licensers of all books, religious and otherwise. Fox-ford records only one prosecution under this monition. Robert Wyer, printer, was cited before the vicar-general for printing *Symbolum Apostolicum* contrary to the warning, but no disposition of the case is found in the records.[11]

In 1527 occurred the first indication that Henry VIII was con-templating a divorce from Queen Catherine. While still publicly supporting the church, the king was privately encouraging the dis-tribution of heretical literature.[12] His strategy at this time was to obtain the Pope's permission for his divorce by rendering himself indispensable to the maintenance of the Catholic church in Eng-land. He planned to promote surreptitiously the circulation of Reformation books and then become a public hero by wiping out the resulting heresies. The clergy had already demonstrated its in-ability to control the press; with their blessings they turned the matter over to the king.

Early in 1529 Henry issued his first proclamation containing a list of prohibited books.[13] It provided that because of, among other things,

---

[10] Reed, *op. cit.*, p. 170.

[11] *Ibid.*, pp. 171-72.

[12] Letter by Bishop Nix. *Cotton Ms.* Cleo. E. V. 360; James Gairdner, *Letters and Papers Foreign and Domestic — Henry VIII, 1540-41* (London, 1882), p. 135.

[13] *Proclamation for resisting and withstanding of most damnable Heresies* . . . (London: R. Pynson, 1528-29). Only one folio in the possession of the Society of Antiquaries has survived. John Foxe, *Actes and Monuments* (1843 ed.), IV, 676, gives the text. Robert Steele (*Tudor and Stuart Proclamations* [Oxford, 1910], No. 114), dates it before 6 March 1528/29.

certain heretical and blasphemous books lately made, and privily sent into this realm by the disciples, fautors, and adherents of said Martin Luther, and other heretics, the king's subjects are likely to be corrupted, unless his highness (as Defender of the Faith) do put to his most gracious help and royal authority . . . wherefore his highness chargeth and straitly commandeth all and every his lords spiritual and temporal, judges, justices of peace, sheriff, mayors, bailiffs, constables, etc. . . . (to see that) no person or persons do from henceforth presume to bring into this realm, or do sell, receive, take, or detain any book or work, printed or written, which is made, or hereafter shall be made against the faith catholic, or against the holy decrees, laws, and ordinances of holy church, or in reproach, rebuke, or slander of the king, his honorable council, or his lords spiritual or temporal. . . .

The list, which preceded the first continental index by fifteen years,[14] was drawn up with the help of the clergy, but issued under the king's authority. The ecclesiastical officers were empowered to arrest anyone possessing one of the prohibited books and to assess fines which Henry carefully provided should go not to the church but into his own exchequer. All the royal law-enforcing officers were ordered to assist the clergy in apprehending culprits, the clergy, however, to pay the expenses of the secular officers while on such business. The sheriffs, mayors, justices, etc. were ordered to turn over all persons charged with violation of the proclamation to the ecclesiastical courts for trial and upon conviction were to receive back the prisoners for punishment. In 1530 Thomas Hitton was convicted of selling Tyndale's books and was executed by the state under the authority of the proclamation. Richard Bayfield and John Teukesbury were burned in 1531, and James Bainham suffered the same fate in 1532.[15] Occasional executions for circulation of Reformation literature took place until Henry's final breach with Rome in 1534; then begins the list of executions of the adherents of Rome headed by Sir Thomas More and Bishop Fisher.

In the meantime Henry had in June, 1530, issued another proc-

---

[14] The first continental index was not published until 1544. There is evidence that a list of prohibited reading matter was issued by the English clergy as early as 1521 (John Strype, *Annals*, I, 254; *L. & P. Henry VIII*, IV, pt. 2, No. 4260; Putnam, *op. cit.*, I, 86), but the list itself has not survived. Foxe's list of 1526 is spurious. See note, p. 43.

[15] James Gairdner, *The English Church in the 16th Century* (1912), pp. 128ff.

lamation containing an additional list of prohibited books including the English translation of the New Testament. The king's officers were charged with apprehending all persons found with such books in their possession and bringing them before the king's Council. While most of the prohibited books were printed on the continent and smuggled into England, the native printers were beginning to issue a few of the forbidden items. To deal with these Henry inserted a section in the proclamation of 1530,[16] establishing the first licensing system under secular authority. The ordinance provided that "no maner of person or persons take upon hym or them to printe any boke or bokes in englische tong, concernynge holy scripture, not before this tyme printed within this his realme, ontyll such tyme as the same boke or bokes be examyned and approued by the ordinary of the diocese, where the said bokes shalbe printed: And that the prynter thereof, upon euery of the sayde bokes so examyned, do sette the name of the examynour or examynours, with also his owne name upon the sayd bokes, as he wyll answere to the kinges highnes, at his uttermoste peryll." This early licensing system, the first based on the royal prerogative, extended only to books "concerynge holy scripture." Ecclesiastics continued to act as licensers.

The failure of the Church of Rome to stop the circulation of Reformation literature was due not to the inadequacy of the regulations but to the methods of enforcement. The very same regulations when adapted and modified by the Tudors served for over a century as effective controls. Aside from impediments secretly emanating from the crown, enforcement by the Church of Rome was rendered ineffective first through the general indolence of a large part of the ecclesiastical officers of the period and secondly through the leniency with which the regulations were administered. Censures, warning, and admonitions failed to impress the early printers and booksellers. The Church's ultimate punishment, excommunication, held little terror for the agents circulating Protestant books. With the advent of the king, who took control under the pretense of loyal devotion to the Church, the press found itself subjected to a more demanding master. Executions were substituted for excommunication, and fine and imprisonment for warning and censure.

[16] B.M. C. 18. e. 2 (113); Steele, *op. cit.*, No. 122.

Henry VIII's Licensing System

By 1535 the change in the hierarchy of the English church had been completed. The clergy had submitted to the king in 1532; the divorce had been denied by the Pope in 1533, and the Act of Supremacy was passed by Parliament in 1534. Whereas authority heretofore had been extended from heaven to earth, it was now concentrated on one point, a point on which the king was precariously perched. His control over the church, Parliament, and the press was complete, and he employed all three to strengthen and maintain his position. The part played by printed propaganda in effecting the revolutionary changes in the established religion is beyond the scope of this discussion, but let it be said that the king was fully aware of the aid he had received from the printed matter of the reformers. His policy henceforth was not only to eliminate undesirable reading matter but to stimulate the circulation of that which would strengthen his cause.

Henry's experience with the English translation of the Bible illustrates his methods. Before 1535 the king as "defender of the faith" had prohibited the circulation of Tyndale's translation, but he was one of the first to see its potential values. Nowhere in the translation was there support for the position of the Bishop of Rome as head of the church. When the break became inevitable, the king through Cromwell let it be known that there was no longer any objection to the translation. In 1537 the first Bible printed in England was published by James Nycolson. The translation, taken from Coverdale's edition of 1535 printed at Zurich, carried the legends "Newly ouersene and corrected" and "Set Foorth with the Kynges moost gracious licence." In that same year the London printers, Grafton and Whitechurch, commissioned an Antwerp printer to produce an edition of the Bible for them. They attempted to secure a license, but by this time the translations of Coverdale and Tyndale had been compared and complaints had reached the ears of the king that a large part of the New Testament was the same in both. The king, like the Pope, was not to be caught changing his mind. His face was saved by omitting Tyndale's name and substituting a pseudonym (Thomas Mathew).

Neither the king nor his bishops were satisfied with the new edition. Besides being obviously based on Tyndale's work, it con-

tained exceedingly dangerous matter in its annotations. It is true
it did not substantiate the claims of the Pope, but neither did it
support the king's position. In addition it was full of Protestant
theology. Henry was interested in bringing the English church
under his own control and not in reforming its theology. Cromwell
promptly secured his permission for a new translation to be edited
by Coverdale under the direction of the English clergy and printed
by Grafton and Whitechurch. Coverdale edited out most of the
Protestant theology, and the result was the "Great Bible" published
in 1538. But no amount of editing could eliminate what today would
be called the "democratic" and "socialistic" implications in the text.
This failure was one of the reasons Cromwell lost his head.

After exhausting all alternatives, the king finally put through
an Act of Parliament (34 & 35 Henry VIII, c. 1, 1542/3) prohibiting all English translations with annotations or preambles and
forbidding the reading of the Bible in church or by members of
the working classes, including artificers, apprentices, journeymen,
laborers, and women. Gentlewomen could read the Bible only in
the privacy of their boudoirs. The English Bible had been useful to
Henry in the separation from Rome; he was determined not to
allow it to disrupt the organization of his church, nor to disturb
his political position.

Having concluded the church settlement, Henry turned his
attention to the press. During the years immediately following the
changes in the ecclesiastical system, printing was permitted to
muddle along under the old regulations. Bible printing, however,
had brought these regulations, together with their violations, to the
attention of the king. A new system of control, with a more extensive scope and with better methods of enforcement, was necessary.

The Proclamation of 1538,[17] drawn up under the king's personal
supervision, was the first attempt to establish a regular censorship
and licensing over all kinds of printing. The purpose of the new
order was "for expellinge and auoydinge the occasion of errours
and seditiouse opinions." The new motif introduced by the king
was the "seditiouse opinions." Heretofore the church had confined
itself to stamping out heresy and theological error. Beginning with
Henry, the distinction between church and state, between heresy
and treason, between nonconformance and sedition becomes in-

---

[17] Antiq. 2 (97), Steele, *op. cit.*, No. 176.

creasingly obscure. An attack on Henry's church was an attack on Henry's government. Dissent in religion was no longer to receive the protection of the king, nor were critics of the government now safe in the garments of the church. The press which had proved so useful in the separation from Rome found it had only one master, the king.

The Proclamation of 1538, after disposing of such matters as books imported from abroad,[18] the indiscriminate use of the king's privilege,[19] and the printing of the Scriptures, set up a licensing system for *all* books printed in English. The earlier regulation of 1530 applied only to religious books. The ecclesiastic licensers were dismissed, and their places taken by the members of the Privy Council or "other such as his highness shall appoynte." Books of Scripture, however, could be licensed by a bishop whose name was to appear on the title page of the book. Henry had confidence in his councillors but not in the bishops appointed by the Council. The shift in the administration of the licensing regulations from the clergy to state officers was one of Henry's contributions to the regulation of the press. The method was subsequently adopted on the continent, even in Catholic countries.[20]

The penalties for infringement of the regulations were, "not only his Gracis most high displeasure and indignation, but also the loss and forfeiture to the king of all goods and chattels and fine and imprisonment at the will of the crown.[21] The king was careful to discard spiritual punishments for the more effective penalties of fine and imprisonment. A few years later he added another — the printers were required to post bonds to be forfeited upon their misbehavior. In 1543 the printers Beddle, Middleton, Maylour, Petye, Lant, and Keyle, all of whom had been imprisoned for printing "unlawful books," were released upon entering into a recognizance, the condition of which was that the printers "do make by writing a trew declaration what number off bookes and ballettes they have bowght wythin thiese iv yeres last past, and what they have sowlde

---

[18] See pp. 31-32.

[19] See pp. 36-37.

[20] In 1554 the Spanish Royal Council took over the licensing system. G. F. Barwick, "The Laws Regulating Printing and Publishing in Spain," *Transactions of the Bibliographical Society,* IV, 48.

[21] For the legal basis of the Proclamation, see pp. 29-30.

in grosse, and what merchantes they know to have browght in to
the Realme any Englisshe bokes of ill matter, and bring in the
saide writing before the Cownsell wythin v days after the date
hereoff, and paye all suche fynes as shall be sett upon theyre heddes
for suche offenses touching the printing off unlawfull bokes contrary to the proclamation they have prented and sold sythen the
tyme of the sayde proclamation, or ells etc." [22] A few days later
(25 April 1543) a group of twenty-five printers and booksellers
were called before the Council and were bound under bonds of
£100 each to obey the provisions of the Proclamation.[23]

The methods of enforcement of the regulations through the
Council proved successful. Few violations are recorded in the
minutes of the Council.[24] Besides the printers above mentioned,
Grafton and Whitechurch were imprisoned and fined; [25] Turke, a
bookseller, was committed to the Fleet, and a number of "leude
fellows" punished for reading or distributing dangerous books. In
1546 three persons were executed under the VI Articles of the
English church for "erronious opinions."

The Proclamation of 1538 continued as the principal regulation
of the press until the end of Henry's reign. Occasionally an instance
arose which called for special orders. In 1544 the king issued a
Proclamation [26] for "calling in and prohibiting certain books printed
of news of the success of the king's army in Scotland." Even at this
early date the printers found it extremely profitable to satisfy the
growing curiosity of the public in affairs of government. Henry
was moved to issue the prohibition both by the "unseemly" interest
of his subjects in matters of state and by the effect of the news on
scavengers who in those days followed in the wake of a successful
army. He also feared the effect of the news upon foreign states
with whom he was conducting negotiations. News, when properly
controlled, was even in Henry's day a useful pawn in the diplomatic game.

The king was also interested in seeing that his young subjects

[22] J. R. Dasent, *Acts of the Privy Council* (London, 1890-1907), I, 117.
[23] *Ibid.*, p. 120.
[24] However, the Register of 1543-1545 is missing, nor is there any record
of the books licensed by the Council.
[25] Dasent, *op. cit.*, I, 125.
[26] Antiq. 2 (132), Steele, *op. cit.*, No. 253.

were "properly" educated, particularly in matters of religion. In 1545 he personally inspected the primer then in use and ordered that no other than the approved primer be used by schoolmasters.[27]

Toward the end of his reign Henry was moved to issue further orders modifying the licensing system. The printers of the realm evidently found it difficult to conform to the orders of 1538, for it was proclaimed (1546)[28] that whenever a book was printed the first copy should be sent to the mayor and that no other copies were to be circulated for two days while an examination of the book was being made. The new method was an improvement over the previous order in that publication could no longer be indefinitely delayed by an indolent official. The licensers were forced to give a decision on a book within two days. As a further protection the printer was required to set out on each copy his own name, the name of the author, and the day of print. Unfortunately for future bibliographers, the order was in force for only a few months. With the death of the king and the accession of Edward VI (1547), new regulations for controlling the press were necessary.

Licensing Under Edward VI and Mary

No momentous changes in the licensing of the press were made by either Edward or his sister Mary in spite of the fact that the objectives of each differed from those of their father. Henry controlled the press in the interests of his own supremacy over the ecclesiastical system; the first years of Edward under the Duke of Somerset were honestly devoted to achieving a reformation in religion; Mary in her turn sought to re-establish the old order. All three monarchs used the licensing system with only such modifications as were necessary to accord with the changing objectives.

The early years of Edward VI's reign under the idealistic Protector Somerset provided sufficient proof to succeeding monarchs of the soundness of Henry VIII's methods of dealing with public opinion and the press. From 1547 to 1548 the press was for the first time free to print all kinds of Reformation literature. Instead of appealing to a calm and enlightened judgment the innumerable tracts which appeared at this time were directed to the emotions,

[27] Proclamation, Steele, *op. cit.*, No. 271.
[28] Proclamation Antiq. 2 (171), Steele, *op. cit.*, No. 295.

prejudices, and fiery dispositions of the sectarians. The result was religious dissension and confusion.

Mary also attempted to follow a policy of leniency in religious matters but was soon forced to change her tactics. Historians have deduced from the events of the early years of these two reigns that the Tudor policy of strict control over public discussion and the press was necessary if peace and order were to be maintained.[29] On the other hand while such a policy did in fact maintain peace and order in the sixteenth century, it merely postponed the inevitable conflict until the middle of the succeeding century.

Accompanying the religious din was the ominous rumble of political and social unrest—a rumble which grew in volume and became particularly threatening during the rudderless years of the reign of Henry's young son. The struggle to control the young king led to factions and parties. Each faction sought support. There was inevitable discussion of policies and powers among the upper classes, followed by an equally inevitable speculation on the outcome among the common people. Between the years 1547 and 1551 no less than nine proclamations were issued for the purpose of stamping out such presumptive speculations and rumors. An order of 24 May 1547 provided that taletellers should be punished as vagrants;[30] another in 1549 threatened to send such "lewd" (seditious) persons to the galleys to row as slaves;[31] later in the same year a proclamation,[32] after reciting evil qualities of "runagates who go from place to place stirring up ignorant folk to evil" and "spreading slanderous tales reflecting on the king and council," grants a bounty of 20 crowns reward and hearty thanks to all informers causing the arrest of such talebearers.

With the ascendancy of Northumberland and the fall of Somerset new orders were given; one on 10 October 1549 [33] against

---

[29] Professor A. F. Pollard maintains that "Freedom of worship was not permissible to those who could not agree to differ; and where differences were dangerous to peace the interests of order required uniformity." *History of England* (London, 1910), p. 23.

[30] Steele, *op. cit.*, No. 306.

[31] *Ibid.*, No. 350.

[32] *Ibid.*, No. 358.

[33] *Ibid.*, No. 374.

the bills, papers, and books defending the late Protector; others followed on 17 May 1550,[34] 28 April 1551,[35] and 20 May 1551.[36] All were directed toward suppressing news, rumors, or argument favorable to the opposing faction. The division into opposing groups, while not conducive to a strong or stable government, at least attracted the interest of the masses to the affairs of government. British democracy owes much to the "unstable" periods in its history.

To the religious and political questions of the short reign of Edward VI was added a third topic for public discussion — the coinage. Henry VIII, unfortunately, did not leave his son the same full coffers which he himself had received from his father, and the inroads of the members of the Council in their haste to gather while they could soon depleted what little funds remained. The easiest road was taken; the coinage was debased in 1551. Prices inevitably rose to compensate for the alloy. Rumors flew about that further debasement was planned; prices again rose on the basis of the rumors. Two proclamations[37] were issued to scotch the rumors under the penalty of pillory and loss of ears.

So busy were the councillors in maintaining their own positions that little attention was given to the licensing of printed matter. No revision of Henry's system was attempted until 1551. In the meantime the Register of the Council and the Patent Rolls indicate that at least some attempt was made to enforce a licensing system. In 1549 a Worcester printer was given a license to print religious books provided the copies were "perused and allowed by such as the king shall appoint." [38] A recognizance entered into by the bookseller John Mardeley dated 23 August 1549 provided that he would not print any "ballet or other work [until] siche worke shalbe licensed . . . . by my Lord Protector and the rest of the Kinges Majestes Counsaile, the same worke or workes to be first subscribed with the hand of William Cicill, esquier. . . ." [39] The recognizance

---

[34] *Ibid.*, No. 379.

[35] *Ibid.*, No. 395.

[36] *Ibid.*, No. 398.

[37] 18 July 1551 (*Ibid.*, No. 403); 16 December 1551 (*Ibid.*, No. 410).

[38] Pat. Rot. 2 Edw. VI, I, No. 269.

[39] Dasent, *op. cit.*, II, 311-12.

is followed by an order appointing as licensers Mr. Secretary Peter, Mr. Secretary Smith, and Mr. Cicill,[40] or one of them.

A revival of the licensing system was undertaken in 1551 following the flood of printed matter accompanying the fall of the Protector. A proclamation [41] provided that "no printer or other person do print nor sel, within this Realme or any other his maiesties dominions, any matter in th'englishe tong, nor they nor any other person, do sel, or otherwise dispose abrode any matter, printed in any foreign dominion in th'englished tong, onles the same be firste allowed by his maiestie, or his priuie counsayl in writing signed with his maiesties most gratious hand or the handes of six of his sayd priuie counsayl, vpon payne of Imprisonment, without balye or mayneprice, and further fine at his maiesties pleasor."

Two printing patents granted in the last year of Edward's reign indicate that additional licensers were drafted when necessary. The patent for law books to Richard Tathill (Tothill) provided that the books be licensed by "one of the justeces of the lawe or two serjantes or three apprentices of the lawe whereof th'one to be a reder in Courte." [42] The patent for primers to William Seres permitted licensing by either the Council, the lord chancellor, or any two of the king's four ordinary chaplains.[43]

Mary was proclaimed queen 19 July 1553. All her life she had been a devout Catholic, and as queen she made an heroic effort to lead the nation back to the old religion. After issuing a proclamation in the Tudor style against rumors and "brutes" touching on affairs of state and the queen's person,[44] she turned her attention to reconciling the divergent religious elements. Her first step was to restrain popular discussion and turbulence until such time as a religion "based on common consent" was established by law. The proclamation [45] declared that the "Queen will maintain her own religion, but at present will not force any subject to conform to it." All subjects were to live in accord eschewing abusive epithets such as "papist" and "heretic," an utterly reasonable but impractical order

---

[40] This is the first appearance of this celebrated name in the records of the Council.

[41] 28 April 1551, Steele, op. cit., No. 395.

[42] 12 April 1553, Rot. Pat. 7 Edw. VI, V, No. 47.

[43] 6 March 1553, Rot. Pat. 7 Edw. VI, V, Nos. 50-51.

[44] Steele, op. cit., No. 425 (28 July 1553).

[45] Ibid., No. 427.

for that age. No person was to be permitted to print or sell "false" books, ballads, rhymes, etc., unless they secured the queen's license in writing. With the exception of the ambiguous description of what books were to be licensed, this was the most humane and rational proclamation on the subject of religious discussion in the entire Tudor period.

Aimed as it was at moral suasion, the proclamation was incapable of enforcement. Scurrilous, rowdy, and defamatory pamphlets were spread about. A sensation was created by the appearance at this time of an English translation of Bishop Gardiner's treatise *De Vera Obedientia* written in 1535 to repudiate papal jurisdiction in England. The object of the republication was to discredit the recantation of both Gardiner and Bishop Bonner, who had written the preface. On the title page was a quotation "A double-minded man is inconstant in all his ways," followed by a violent introduction written by the translator who styled himself Michael Wood. The book although purporting to have been printed at Rouen was probably issued from a London press and has been ascribed to John Bale, a notoriously foulmouthed controversialist.[46] The publication of true and false recantations of Archbishop Cranmer particularly irritated the queen because of their tendency to stir up religious animosities.[47] On 14 March 1556 two London printers entered into a recognizance that they would print no further editions of the archbishop's recantation or other prohibited books.[48]

From the point of view of the government the policy of moral suasion and leniency was a failure. Freedom, instead of producing conversion, resulted in riots. Mary was no match for half a hundred pamphleteers whose tirades on the government and religion found eager readers. The early statutes against heresy and heretical books were revived.[49] A vehement proclamation was issued 6 June 1558 threatening execution under martial law of all persons possessing heretical or treasonable books. The zealots of the Protestant sects were the chief sufferers under the new orders. Few printers or booksellers were persecuted. The most important event of the reign for these latter was the establishment of the Stationers Com-

[46] Gairdner, *op. cit.*, pp. 326-28.
[47] *Ibid.*, pp. 370-77.
[48] Dasent, *op. cit.*, V, 247-48.
[49] Steele, *op. cit.*, No. 461 (13 June 1555).

pany, the trade organization of printers, under royal charter in 1557.[50]

The Elizabethan Licensing System

The long reign of Queen Elizabeth (1558-1603) witnessed changes and developments of great import in the history of the press. The number of master printers had increased from eight or ten in 1560 to more than thirty at the end of the century. With the increase in the number of printers came an increase in the number of books and pamphlets. However, the concentration of the "respectable" lists in the hands of "privileged" printers left the others to make a living as best they could. There was always available a number of these destitute printers who could be induced by the controversialists and pamphleteers to take risks. The government attempted to meet the situation principally through more stringent licensing regulations administered through the Council, the ecclesiastical officers, and the Stationers Company. The Elizabethan printer found himself enclosed in a triangle, one side of which was guarded by the queen, the Council, and the royal officials, the other by the church hierarchy and the ecclesiastical judges, and the third by the Stationers Company and its henchmen, with the officers of the city of London occasionally guarding the interstices.

The year after her accession Elizabeth paused long enough in framing the church settlement to devise a licensing system for the press. The royal injunctions of 1559 [51] (issued under the authority of the crown as head of the church) provided:

1. All new works must be submitted before publication for allowance by either the queen, six of the Council, an ecclesiastical judge (ordinary) above the rank of archdeacon within whose jurisdiction the book is to be printed, or finally by the Chancellor of one of the Universities and an ordinary of the place.

2. Pamphlets, plays, and ballads could be submitted to the three ecclesiastical commissioners of London for license to print. This class of printing had increased enormously, and practical considerations made it necessary to provide some way of delegating licensing authority to minor officials. The injunctions also imply that no printing of this type was to be done outside London.

---

[50] See Chapter 3.
[51] B.M. C. 37. 2. 53.

3. Reprints of works on religion and government were permitted if not expressly forbidden by the three ecclesiastical commissioners of London who were charged with inspecting these works and notifying the printer of their disallowance. The responsibility for inspection and notification was laid on the commissioners.

4. A further provision stated that the names of the licensers shall "be added in the end of euery such worke, for a testimonie of the alowance thereof." Only a few printed books of this period carried the licensing notice. Either the provision was not enforced or it was taken to mean that the names should appear on the manuscript only.[52] A proviso exempted the works of the standard classical authors from provisions of the Injunctions.

These Injunctions of 1559, which constituted the basis for all subsequent licensing in England, were issued by the crown under its authority as head of the church. The queen, as guardian of the religion of her people, assumed like her father that the authority to control the press was implicit in the powers of the sovereign.

The available evidence indicates that the licensing regulations were neither strictly obeyed nor wholly disregarded.[53] The failure to include the license notice in the printed work, as stated above, proves very little. Ordinarily the prosecution of printers for infringement of the orders would have taken place before the ecclesiastical commission, but the records have long since disappeared. Neither the minutes of the Privy Council nor the papers of the Star Chamber mention any prosecution of a printer for violation of the injunctions, although occasionally a translator or writer was committed to the Fleet for "putting a book to print without authority." [54]

Some record of the enforcement, however, is to be found in the papers of the Stationers Company. Both before and after its incorporation the printing craft organization maintained a desultory and unofficial licensing record. The list of works licensed,

---

[52] R. B. McKerrow, A *Dictionary of Printers* . . . (London, 1910), p. xii, found in his investigations that only an occasional book carried a printed license. John Day and Reyner Wolfe, however, frequently placed such notices on the title pages of their publications.

[53] Dr. McKerrow thinks the provisions were not generally ignored as sometimes has been stated. *Ibid.*

[54] Dasent, *op. cit.,* VII (1558-70), 108. The Public Record Office has a mass of Star Chamber papers of this period, but a cursory examination has failed to reveal any prosecution of a printer for violation of the Injunctions.

probably with the names of the licensers, was kept in a book which has since disappeared. However, the items were recopied into an account book for the purpose of keeping track of the fees. This book has survived and has been printed as Volume I (Register A) of Arber's *Transcript of the Stationers Register*. This account book contains the list of fees for licensing together with the fines for infringement or nonobservance. For instance in 1559, thirteen printers were fined for printing without license and one was imprisoned by the Company.[55] The entries of copies in the account book unfortunately do not state by whom the works were licensed, but it may be assumed that they were licensed either by the proper officials as set out in the Injunctions (and that the names of the licensers were duly listed in the original entry of copies) or by the officers of the Company. The clerk who made up the account book from the entry book listed only so much of the original entry as was necessary to account for the fees. Neither the Bishop of London nor the two Archbishops were frequent licensers but when these dignitaries did occasionally allow a work to be printed, the fact was recorded in the account book.[56] With the exception of a single book printed in Welsh licensed by a Dr. Yeale, no other ecclesiastical officer's name appears.

Elizabeth's first years were devoted to completing the change from the Church of Rome to the Church of England. The regulations for the control of the press were designed principally to suppress the Roman Catholic point of view, but no sooner were these regulations in force than the authorities found themselves attacked on the flank by Puritan pamphleteers. In June, 1566, a series of tracts criticizing the English church for failing to complete the reformation was circulated in England.[57] The government acted promptly with the Council Order of 29 June 1566.[58] The licensing

[55] Edward Arber, *A Transcript of the Registers of the Company of Stationers of London, 1554-1640* (1875), I, 100-101.

[56] The first license by the Bishop of London is a book listed under the date of March 8, 1561 (*Ibid.*, I, 155) while the first entry under the license of the archbishop is Stow's *Chronicles*, July, 1565 (Ibid., I, 272.)

[57] See *Parker Society Publications*, II, pp. xii-xiii; McKerrow, *op. cit.*, p. xii.

[58] Antiq. 57; reprinted in J. R. Tanner, *Tudor Constitutional Documents* (2d ed.; New York: Cambridge University press, 1930), pp. 245-47. The regulations have been frequently referred to as a Decree of the Star Chamber. The form of the Order and the fact that the separation between the Council

system of 1559 was left intact, but more stringent penalties for violations were provided. Any person who printed in violation of any statute, injunction, letter patent or ordinance was subjected to the following penalties: forfeit of all copies of books illegally printed, perpetual denial of the right to exercise the craft of printing, and three months imprisonment. Binders of illegal books were to be fined 20 shillings per copy. The most important provision of the order was that requiring each stationer, printer, bookseller, etc. to enter into a recognizance of "reasonable sums of money" that he would aid the wardens of the Stationers Company in enforcement and would observe all regulations. The Council Order gave the officers of the Company the right to inspect all incoming cargoes and also all shops and warehouses for illegally printed books.

Under the terms of the order, which was now based squarely on the prerogative powers of the crown, the ecclesiastical officers were retained as licensers. It is noteworthy that no mention is made of any delegation of licensing powers to the officers of the Stationers Company. In the wardens' account books the entries remain the same.[59]

Although the Stationers Company was made the principal agency of administration, it must be concluded that it made little effort to enforce the regulations[60] either through indifference or because of a secret sympathy with the principles of the Protestant sects, or more probably because of the bitter internal controversy on patents of monopoly which was at this time engaging its attention. Nor were the ecclesiastical licensers as efficient or as effective as the Council had expected. On 25 September 1577 they wrote the Bishop of London that they "do not a litle mervaile at the folly of the authors and the bouldnes of the printers presuming to put it [a pamphlet on the late devastating disease at Oxford] to the printe

and the Star Chamber was not complete at this date indicate that this reference is erroneous.

[59] The account book runs out in 1571 and after a gap of five years is resumed in Register B (Vol. II of Arber's *Transcript*). Dr. W. W. Greg presents an ingenious and convincing argument on the relationship of these various records in his *Records of the Court of the Stationers' Company* (London: Bibliographical Society, 1930), pp. viii-x.

[60] Since the early Court Book for the years before 1576 has disappeared, it is difficult to determine the degree of enforcement maintained by the company. *Ibid.*, p. ix.

without his Lordship's privity." The Council ordered the bishop to apprehend the printers and bring them before the board, and after chiding the bishop for his inefficiency ordered that thereafter the licensing should be done by the Council itself.[61]

The queen attempted to bolster the enforcement of the orders by a number of Proclamations, the first of which called in all books derogatory of the queen and the established religion.[62] Another was issued 1 July 1570 offering a reward to informers against persons dispersing seditious bills and books slandering the queen and the nobility.[63] The Council itself was at this date too busy to spend much time chastising printers, but on occasion it sought out a secret press [64] or gave further orders to the archbishop.

In spite of the regulations Puritan writers continued to find ways and means of dispersing their pamphlets.[65] Cartwright's *Second Admonition to Parliament* criticizing the book of common prayer, the administration of the Sacraments, and the order of the established church found a large body of readers. A proclamation confiscating the book was issued 11 June 1573.[66] Further orders against particular books were made on 28 September 1573,[67] 26 March 1576,[68] 27 September 1579,[69] 3 October 1580,[70] 30 June 1583.[71]

Since the combined efforts of government officials, ecclesiastical licensers, and Stationers Company searchers were insufficient to keep the writings of critics of the government and the established religion from finding their way into print, William Lambard, the eminent jurist, was commissioned in 1577 to draw up an act which would accomplish the desired results.[72] His suggestion, further revised in 1580, was to set up a licensing board of twelve, composed of three ecclesiastics, the recorder of the city of London,

---

[61] Dasent, *op. cit.*, X (1577-78), 25-26.

[62] Steele, *op. cit.*, No. 638 (March 1568/9).

[63] *Ibid.*, No. 656. And see also No. 659.

[64] For the Council Orders to search for the press of the Jesuit, Edmund Campion, see Dasent, *op. cit.*, XIII (1581-82), 148-49, 153, 185-86.

[65] The increase in printed matter on political and religious questions is discussed in Chapter 4, pp. 95-99.

[66] Steele, *op. cit.*, No. 687.

[67] *Ibid.*, No. 688.   [68] *Ibid.*, No. 702.

[69] *Ibid.*, No. 740.   [70] *Ibid.*, No. 752.

[71] *Ibid.*, No. 770.   [72] Arber, *op. cit.*, II, 751-53.

and eight others including four readers from the Inns of Court. Licenses were to be granted by three of the board of which only one could be an ecclesiastic.[73] All control was taken away from the Bishop of London.

The argument over the organization of an effective licensing system continued over several years. Archbishop Whitgift devised a scheme contained in sixteen articles which he presented to the queen for consideration. He suggested that the licensing be placed solely in the hands of the Archbishop of Canterbury and the Bishop of London. His suggestions were criticized by the Puritans in detail. The Puritans in turn suggested, not that the licensing system be abandoned, but that four divines and four lawyers were better qualified than the Archbishop and the Bishop of London, who were so busy that they often had to delegate the examination of books to "incapable inferiors." "Besides . . . ," the Puritans argued, "the Archbishop and the Bishop are known affectionate parties in some late differences touching the ordering of Church government and the reformation of manifold abuses in the Church of God." [74] The Stationers Company was also interested in the revision of the rules for the regulation of the press, particularly as these rules affected their patents of monopoly. The Company on 29 October 1584 agreed to reimburse the wardens for all sums spent in securing an act of Parliament.[75]

Elizabeth's answer to all this discussion was the Star Chamber Decree of 23 June 1586.[76] It was the most comprehensive regulation of the press of the entire Tudor period, continuing in effect until 1637. After reciting several provisions limiting the number of print-

[73] Lands. Ms. No. 48, f. 187.

[74] A. Peel, ed., *Seconde Parte of A Register* (1915), I, 175. Originals checked in Dr. Williams' library.

[75] Greg, *op. cit.*, p. 16. Greg (p. lxi) deduces from this entry that the initiative for the decree of 1586 came from the Stationers. Arber also expresses this view (*Transcript*, II, 13). The church was interested in suppressing dissent; the Stationers in maintaining their monopolies; and both in extending their authority over the printing trade; but the Council first conceived the plan for the new regulation in spite of the fact that Archbishop Whitgift's suggestions were followed and the Stationers' patents and authority confirmed.

[76] The Decree is misdated as 23 June 1584 in Calendar of State Papers, Domestic, Elizabeth, 1581-90, p. 184. Cora Scofield, *A Study of the Court of Star Chamber* (Thesis, University of Chicago, 1900), p. 32, and Tanner, *op. cit.*, p. 279, mistakenly assume this entry to refer to an earlier decree. The

ers, apprentices, and presses, and confirming the Stationers Company powers of search and seizure, the decree follows Whitgift's suggestions on the establishment of a licensing system. All books (with the exception of law books and books printed by the queen's printer) were required to be licensed by the Archbishop of Canterbury and the Bishop of London. Law books were to be licensed by the Justices.

The administration and enforcement of the regulations were entrusted jointly to the Stationers Company and the ecclesiastical officials. Archbishop Whitgift, unlike his predecessors Parker and Grindal, was a strict disciplinarian. He had successfully convinced the queen and the Council that licensing should be concentrated in his own hands, but the new system was in operation for only a few years when the fears of the Puritan critics were fulfilled. Both the Archbishop and the Bishop of London found that their duties as licensers for the press not only took up too much of their time but imposed on them grave responsibilities. If the queen and Council later objected to a licensed ballad, they as licensers must take the blame. The only alternative which would keep control in their hands yet relieve them of personal responsibility for a particular item was to delegate the licensing authority to subordinates. On 3 June 1588 the Stationers were notified of the appointment of deputies who were hereafter to license all printed works.[77] Authority was given by the Archbishop to Dr. Cosin, Dr. Stallard, Dr. Wood, Master Hartwell, Master Grauet, Master Crowley, Master Cotton, and Master Hutchenson, or any one of them to license books to be printed; or any two of the following—Master Judson, Master Trippe, Master Cole, and Master Dickens. All of the deputies with the possible exception of Judson were ecclesiastics.

Beginning in 1588 the licensing of printed matter as recorded in the Stationers' Register proceeded with more regularity. The provisions of the Decree of 1586 were obviously being enforced. Each book is listed (with a few minor exceptions) with the names

text of the decree is set out in Tanner, *op. cit.*, pp. 279-84, and Arber, *op. cit.*, II, 807-12. The provisions other than licensing are discussed in Chapter 3, pp. 69-70.

[77] Greg, *op. cit.*, pp. 28-29. Sir John Lambe, in his report on the licensing system misdates the letter June 30. Arber, *op. cit.*, III, 690.

of one or more of the deputies together with names of one or more wardens of the Stationers Company. The names of the latter were probably employed solely for copyright protection. Occasionally new names not mentioned in the Archbishop's original list appear, but these are evidently replacements or additions authorized by the primate. Some of the licensers' names occur more frequently than those of others; for instance, Hartwell, Whitgift's secretary and Stallard, rector of All Hallows, were the principal licensers from 1588 to 1591 while Hartwell continued to license most of the works from 1592 to 1603. On the occasion of a particularly doubtful book, it was not uncommon to have the license certified by the Archbishop, the Lord Chamberlain, and several other officials.[78]

An order of the Archbishop and the Bishop of London of 1 June 1599 indicates that by the end of the century the licensing system was not as effective as it had been a few years previously. Not only had writers succeeded in hoodwinking the licensers by disguising their real designs in the form of satires or epigrams, but there must have been some forging of signatures. The orders provided: (1) that no Satyrs or Epigrams be printed hereafter, (2) that no English histories be printed except those allowed by the Council, (3) that no plays be printed except as allowed by authority, (4) that all Dr. Harvey's books be taken wheresoever found, etc., (5) that all books similar to those above stated shall not be printed until the master or wardens of the Stationers Company have ascertained that the signature of the licenser is genuine.[79] Thus at the close of the Tudor period the inherent difficulties in the enforcement of a licensing system designed to protect existing institutions by suppressing popular political and religious discussion were already apparent.

---

[78] *Ibid.*, II, 564.

[79] *Ibid.*, III, 677.

CHAPTER 3

The Stationers Company

A large part of the administration and enforcement of the regulations governing the press in the late Tudor period was delegated by the crown to the printing craft organization. The printers and booksellers, being recipients of such royal favors as "privileges" and "patents of monopoly," were readily persuaded to take upon themselves not only the protection of their own advantages but the suppression of all printing which was in that day considered "dangerous" to the established authority. It is almost impossible to disentangle the efforts of the printers to maintain their "copy-rights" from their complacent cooperation in suppressing "unlawful" printing. The skillful use of the corporate organization of printers and publishers in the suppression and control of undesirable printing has long been considered a masterstroke of Elizabethan politics.

The Corporate Structure

A medieval society of writers of court hand and text letters existed in 1357,[1] and in 1404 these writers together with the limners (i.e., illuminators) and others employed in the binding and selling of books were formed into a guild governed by two wardens, one a limner and the other a text writer, whose duty was to provide

---

[1] Edward Arber, *A Transcript of the Registers of the Company of Stationers of London, 1554-1640* (1875), I, xxii.

for the "good rules and governance" of the members of the allied crafts. These producers and dealers in manuscript books received sometime during the fifteenth century the name "stacioners." [2]

By the opening of the sixteenth century the printers, who were beginning to supplant the earlier craft of manuscript writers, were admitted to membership. Pynson appointed royal printer in 1508, and Bedill (or Byddell), who worked with de Worde, were undoubtedly members of some form of printing craft organization. During this early period a number of printers continued as members of other city companies; Caxton was a Mercer and Richard Grafton a Grocer, while Whitechurch was a Haberdasher and John Day a Stringer. By the end of Henry VIII's reign most of the printers and booksellers had become members of the Stationers Guild.

The word "Stationer" came to be applied during the early sixteenth century to the publishers and dealers in books as distinct from the printers of books. The stationers bought their books in gross from the printers, bound them, and sold them in their shops.[3] These capitalists, being richer and more important, gave their name to the new organization.[4]

The charter for the incorporation of the Stationers Company was granted by Philip and Mary in 1557.[5] Whether the initiative came from the government or from the early craft organization has been a subject of much speculation, and the matter is further confused by the fact that it is not known whether the incorporation was sought by the printers and stationers for their own greater honor and the better regulation of the craft, or was foisted on the guild by the crown in order to exercise a more effective control.

[2] Christopher Barker, in his account of the company written in 1582, states, "In the tyme of King Henry the eighte, there were but fewe Printers, and those of good credit and compotent wealth, at which tyme and before, there was an other sort of men, that were writers, Lymners of bookes and dyverse things for the Churche and other vses, called Stacioners." *Ibid.*, I, xx.

[3] *Ibid.*

[4] For a history of the company before its incorporation, see J. G. Nichols, in *Proceedings of the London and Middlesex Archaeological Association*, Vol. II; Arber, *op. cit.*, I, xix-xxiv; II, 7-10, 19; IV, 24.

[5] The charter (3 & 4 P. & M., pt. 10 m 46) is set out in Arber, *op. cit.*, I, xxviii-xxxii. The original was destroyed in the fire of 1666, and the Company has exemplifications only which were obtained about 1684. The legality of the charter was called into question by quo warranto proceedings in 1663 and 1684-90. See Chapter 12, p. 252.

At least one attempt to secure incorporation was made by the Stationers as early as 1542 when an application for a charter was made to Henry VIII.[6] There were certain civic honors attached to a recognized city company which could not have failed to impress the craft members. On the other hand, the preamble to the charter clearly states that the purpose in granting the charter was to control "scandalous, malicious, schismatical, and heretical" printing. The available evidence seems to indicate that the printers and stationers themselves sought incorporation for the better regulation of craft practices, for the protection of copies, and for the incidental prestige. But the crown in granting the charter was actuated by altogether different motives. Mary offered the privileges of incorporation for cooperation in the control of undesirable printing—an offer accepted by the sixteenth-century printers and publishers.[7]

The charter, after reciting the reasons for granting the letters patent for the incorporation, proceeded to give the company wide powers for the control of the printing craft. Printing was limited to the members of the London Company or such others as secured a special license from the queen. No provision was made for printing outside London. The officers of the Company were given authority to search the premises of any printer for unlawful printing and to fine and imprison anyone resisting their efforts.[8] In 1559 Elizabeth confirmed the charter and the powers therein granted to the members,[9] and in 1560 the craft organization was created one of the liveried companies of the city of London.[10]

Since the bylaws and ordinances of this period have been lost,[11] the internal structure of the Elizabethan organization can be only partially reconstructed from fragmentary evidence. The classes of membership consisted of the apprentices, the brethren, the yeomanry or freemen, the master printers, and the livery. The apprentices were indentured to a master printer or stationer for a

[6] David Wilkins, *Concilia* (London, 1737), III, 862.
[7] Arber believes that stationers sought the charter (*Transcript*, I, xxvi), while A. W. Pollard (*Shakespeare's Fight With the Pirates* [2d. ed.; Cambridge, 1920], pp. 9-12) seems to think the organization was conceived by the crown.
[8] See pp. 82-83.
[9] Conf. Roll, I, Eliz., pt. 4, m. 5.
[10] Arber, *op. cit.*, I, 138.
[11] The earliest existing ordinances are dated 1678-82 and are reprinted in Arber, *op. cit.*, I, 3-26.

term of not less than seven years and upon arriving at the age of twenty-four were made free men of the Company. Under the rules adopted by the Company in 1558 an apprentice could not be employed in composition or press work as long as a competent journeyman was available.[12] The brethren were foreigners [13] (strangers) made free of the Company without serving an apprenticeship. Membership could also be obtained through patrimony (any son born subsequent to his father's freedom could claim freedom at the age of twenty-four) or by redemption or purchase.[14] Having achieved his freedom a printer could work for a master printer or publish books but he could not print by himself; this right was reserved to the master printers, the number of which was strictly limited by decrees emanating from the crown. Vacancies in the list of master printers were filled by the Court of Assistants with the approval of the Archbishop, or the position could be attained by marrying the widow of a master printer. As Arber says, "It must have been a lively time among eligible young printers when it was known that a Master Printer was dying. Whom would the widow take next? Every man must have calculated his chances with her. There are not wanting instances . . . of a widow having three husbands in succession." [15] The livery was composed of a selected group of master printers entitled to wear the "clothing" and to attend the Lord Mayor on ceremonial occasions. Between 1560 and 1596, sixty-three members were taken into the livery.[16]

The officers of the Company consisted of the master, the wardens, the Court of Assistants (Common Council), the renter wardens, the clerk, and the beadle. The master was the chief executive of the Company and was chosen annually by the livery or by the Court of Assistants. The two wardens, upper and lower, acted as his assistants. The Court of Assistants was the chief deliberative, judicial, and administrative body and was composed of the master,

---

[12] *Ibid.*, II, 43.

[13] The "brethren" was a sort of honorary membership accorded to foreign printers working in London. They were designated by the term "strangers," while the word "forreigners" was used to denote native printers other than Londoners. *Ibid.*, I, xl.

[14] George Buck paid thirty shillings for the freedom of the Company in 1560. *Ibid.*, I, 159.

[15] *Ibid.*, V, xxix.

[16] *Ibid.*, I, xliii.

the two wardens, the clerk, and eight or ten master printers. During the greater part of Elizabeth's reign meetings were held on the average of twice a week. Its duties were to choose the livery, to appoint (with ecclesiastical consent) the master printers, to hear complaints of all kinds, to choose officers, and to direct the affairs of the corporation. The renter wardens, of whom there were generally two, were the treasurers of the Company. They collected fines and dues and made an accounting to the Court of Assistants. The clerk's duty was to keep the records and the entries of copies. The beadle issued notices of meetings, kept records, looked after workmen, and acted generally as a referee in small disputes.[17]

The Right to Print

The principal regulatory provision of the charter of the Stationers Company prohibited all printing within the realm except by members of the Company or by those having special license from the queen.[18] The right to print could be exercised only with the permission of those already engaged in the craft (through control over admissions to membership) or by special dispensation from the crown. The established printers, who were thus able to maintain their own monopolies and at the same time assist the state in limiting the number of printers, desired even greater powers such as limiting *all* printing to members of the Company. The queen, however, though in fact permitting the Company to assume such powers, was reluctant to relinquish all official control to the craft organization.[19]

The internal ordinances of the Company, based upon powers conferred in the charter, made further restrictions on the right to print. The entire structure of membership was designed to safe-

---

[17] The best accounts of the membership and officers of the Company are found in C. R. Rivington, "The Records of the Worshipful Company of Stationers" reprinted in Arber, *op. cit.*, V, xxxvii-lxxv; W. W. Greg, *Records of the Court of the Stationers' Company* (London: Bibliographical Society, 1930), "Introduction"; and Arber, *op. cit.*, I, xxxix-xl. The Stationers Company, unlike the other existing companies of the City of London, has continued its craft connections to the present day. In 1928 it combined with the newspaper proprietors to form the Stationers and Newspaper-Makers Company, the largest of the several companies. (Information supplied by Mr. C. R. Rivington, clerk. See Arber, *op. cit.*, I, xvi.)

[18] Arber, *op. cit.*, I, xxviii-xxxii.

[19] S. P. Dom. Eliz., XV, No. 37 (1560).

guard and maintain the monopolistic position of the men who as officers controlled the company.[20] A freeman or yeoman could not engage in independent printing but must either work for a master printer or confine himself to publishing or bookselling. The privileges of the master printers, who alone had the right to print, were zealously guarded and no one was admitted to the rights of the position except upon the death of one holding such rights. Christopher Barker reported in 1583 that there were then in London twenty-three master printers (including two not members of the Company) operating a total of fifty-three presses. Both Barker and John Wolfe had five presses each, while Day and Denham each had four.[21] There is no reason to doubt that even before the Decree of 1586 the Company itself limited the right to print to master printers and carefully guarded admissions to this group.

The Injunctions of 1559 which set up the initial Elizabethan licensing system made no mention of the right to print, but the Council Order of 1566 [22] required all persons engaged in printing or bookselling to "enter into several recognizances of reasonable sums of money" as a guaranty that they would observe all rules and regulations for the control of printing.

The Star Chamber Decree of 1586 set up a detailed list of regulations governing the right to print: [23]

I. All printers (i.e., master printers) must register their presses with the Stationers Company.[24]
II. All printing prohibited outside the city of London except at Oxford and Cambridge.[25]
III. No new master printers to be appointed except with the concurrence of the High Commission for Causes Ecclesiastical.
IV. Licensing provisions.[26]
V. Penalty for binding unlawfully-printed books.

---

[20] See p. 67.

[21] Arber, *op. cit.*, I, 218. Note: Entries in Arber were checked with the original registers of the Stationers Company at Stationers' Hall. References are to Arber's reprint rather than to the original registers.

[22] Reprinted in J. R. Tanner, *Tudor Constitutional Documents* (2d ed.; New York: Cambridge University press, 1930), pp. 245-47.

[23] *Ibid.*, pp. 279-84.

[24] Arber reprints the registration list of 1586, *Transcript*, V, lii.

[25] The Company reported a list of eleven provincial printers in 1571. (Arber, *op. cit.*, V, lii.)

[26] See below, p. 71.

VI. & VII. The wardens of the Company given authority to search and
seize all unlawful printing and secret presses.

VIII. The number of apprentices limited to three, two, or one, according to the rank of the member of the Company.

IX. The printers at Oxford and Cambridge limited to one apprentice
each.

The most important single regulation in this Decree of 1586
was Item III which gave the High Commission [27] the right to name
the master printers. The procedure as laid down in the decree required the Archbishop of Canterbury and the Bishop of London
to determine how many master printers there should be and to
notify the master and wardens of the Stationers Company when
any new appointments were to be made. Candidates known for
their "skill, ability, and good behavior" were then nominated by
the Court of Assistants and presented to the Court of High Commission, six of whom together with either the bishop or the archbishop actually made the appointment.

A single appointment of a master printer for the period 1586-
1603 is recorded in the Court Records of the Company: [28]

vpon the letter of y[e] Archbishop of Canterburye the byshop of
London, Dc͞or Cosen and Dc͞or Walker Directed to this c͞upany & dated
.7. m' cij 1587. Thomas Orwin according to ye starch͞aber decree for
thelection of printers, was elected a printer, And p'sented the xviij[th]
day of May 1588, to the said archbishop, The lieutenant of the tower,
m[r] Recorder, The deane of Westm', m[r] doctor Aubrey, m[r] Dc͞or Cozen,
and m[r] Dc͞or Lewyn by m[r] Iudson, m[r] Coldock & m[r] Connewey wardens, m[r] watkins, M[r] Cooke, m[r] Denham, and m[r] howe. And there-
vppon the xx[th] day of maye. 1588. The said Orwyn was by the said
Archbishop, the ͘ Deane of wes[t]m' & m[r] Dc͞or Aubrey admitted to be
a printer according to the said Decree.

The refusal of the Court of Assistants to permit Mistress
Myddleton to print (March 4, 1587/8) until she had secured formal
admission as a master printer illustrates the cooperation given by
the Company in the enforcement of the Decree of 1586.[29] In March,

---

[27] The High Commission in Causes Ecclesiastical (Court of High Commission) was established in 1 Eliz. (1558). For the activities of this court in
controlling the press in the Stuart period see Chapter 6, pp. 138-41.

[28] Greg, *op. cit.*, p. 28. A separate list of those admitted as master printers
was kept by the Company but apparently has not survived.

[29] *Ibid.*, p. 26.

1597, the Company authorized the seizure of the printing materials of Simon Stafford for failure to be properly admitted as a master printer.[30]

The uprising of the journeymen printers in the early 1580's resulted in the adoption of a set of rules governing printing-trade practices for the purpose of creating employment. No forms of type were permitted to stand after an edition had been printed; the editions for several classes of works were limited; and the work done by apprentices was carefully circumscribed. The journeymen in return agreed to cease all further agitation against the exclusive printing rights of the master printers.[31]

The Company Licensing System

Soon after its incorporation the Stationers Company re-enacted an ordinance requiring all member printers to obtain a license from the officers of the Company before printing any work. The charter itself did not specifically require the establishment of a Company licensing system, but the ordinance was passed under the provision permitting the Company to "make and ordain and establish, for the good and sound rule and government of the free men of the art or mistery . . . , ordinances, provisions, and statutes' etc." [32] Although the early ordinances of the Company have been destroyed, the surviving records indicate the existence of a licensing provision. On 21 July 1555 (before the formal incorporation) Master Wallye was fined twenty shillings "for conselyng of the pryntynge of *a breafe Cronacle* contrary to our ordenances before he Ded presente the Copye to the wardyns." [33] Again on 17 December 1557, Robert Caley was fined four shillings "for pryntinge of a boke contrary to our ordenaunces that ye not havynge lycense frome the master and wardyns for the same." [34]

The sixteenth-century stationers were prompted to establish a trade licensing system by a variety of motives. In the first place, they were charged by the terms of the incorporation to bring "order" into the printing trade. Both Mary and Elizabeth expected

---

[30] *Ibid.*, pp. 59, 64, 68.

[31] Arber, *op. cit.*, II, 43-44.

[32] Charter in Arber, *op. cit.*, I, xxviii.

[33] *Ibid.*, I, 45.

[34] *Ibid.*, p. 70.

them to keep a tight rein on member printers in return for the grant of a royal charter. Secondly, the important stationers hoped to protect their patents and copyrights through the new registration system. If every printer were required to secure the permission of the officers of the Company before printing any work, piracy and infringement could be stopped. Lastly, the Company benefited by the fees charged for each permission, although neither the holders of special licenses under letters patent nor the masters and wardens were required to pay fees.

A section of the wardens' account book for the first year of the Company, 1557-1558, is headed "The entrynge of all suche Copyes as be lycensed to be prynted by the master and wardyns of the mystery of stacioners." [35] The fee was ordinarily four pence, although on occasion a fee of eight pence was charged. The rate was probably a penny for three leaves with eight pence the maximum. The standard entry was "for his license for pryntinge of" etc.

Neither the ecclesiastical licensing system set up under the Elizabethan Injunctions of 1559 [36] nor the added penalties of the Council Order of 1566 [37] seemed to have affected the Company's method of entering the fees for licenses. Occasionally there is notice of a license granted by the Bishop of London or the Archbishop of Canterbury, but from 1557 to 1586 the allowances were made principally by the Company officers. The common entry after 1578 was "lycenced vnto him vnder th [e h] andes of the wardens." [38] The beadle was the official charged with searching out unlicensed printing. An entry under the date of 15 June 1579 records the fine against Richard Jones for printing a ballad without license, "where of gyven to ye bedell for his paines vi d." [39]

The Star Chamber Decree of 1586 establishing a strict ecclesiastical censorship necessitated changes in the Company's ordinances.[40] Evidently before the issuance of the decree there had been some question as to the licensing requirement for ballads under the Stationers' ordinances, for on 1 August 1586 some hundred and

---

[35] *Ibid.*, p. 74.
[36] See above, p. 56.
[37] See above, p. 58.
[38] Arber, *op. cit.*, II, 338.
[39] *Ibid.*, p. 849.
[40] For the licensing provisions of the Decree, see above, p. 61.

eighty ballads already in print were hurriedly entered on the Company's books. The entries after 1586 contain the names of the deputy licensers appointed by the ecclesiastical authorities in addition to the names of the master or wardens of the Company. The ecclesiastics guarded against "dangerous" works, and the wardens against piracy. Occasionally a book was entered with the proviso that the publisher subsequently obtain a license; [41] and frequently the printer in the case of a questionable book was charged with getting the approval of either the ecclesiastical or secular authorities. In 1591 Richard Watkins occupied the office of official licenser for the Company.[42] His position must have been a special appointment for he was at this time neither master nor warden of the Company. After 1598 the under-warden of the Company (together with the ecclesiastical licensers) authorized the entrance of copies.

The Stationers Company enforced both its own licensing ordinances and those of the Council through its control of the members of the craft. A system of fines imposed by the Court of Assistants and collected by the renter wardens was in force throughout the second half of the sixteenth century.[43] Fines for failure to obtain a license ranged from twelve pence to twenty shillings. In 1558/9 thirteen printers were fined and one was imprisoned by the Company for failure to comply with the licensing ordinance.[44] Edward White was fined five shillings (12 May 1594) for printing a ballad contrary to the ordinance,[45] and on 28 June 1595 Andrew Wyse was fined forty shillings for twice reprinting a sermon without authority.[46] The ultimate penalty was the seizure of press and printing implements and the defacement of the type, and was imposed by the Court of Assistants only for more serious offenses such as violation of the Star Chamber decrees. Occasionally the penalty was imposed for violation of the Company's ordinances as in the case of Edward Aldee who was charged with printing a book "disorderlie w[th]out aucthoritie lycence [or] entraunce" and whose

---

[41] See entry *sub. nom.* Edw. Aldee, Reg. B, Arber, *op. cit.*, II, 514.

[42] *Ibid.*, p. 591.

[43] See Arber, *op. cit.*, I and II, *passim.* See above, p. 68.

[44] *Ibid.*, I, 100-101.

[45] Greg, *op. cit.*, p. 49.

[46] *Ibid.*, p. 51. The fine was later reduced to five shillings.

press and types were ordered to be made "vnserviceable for printing." [47] Since the objectionable book was a "popishe Confession,
Called a brief fourme of Confession," the harsh penalty was enacted
not only for the technical failure to register the copy but for the
dangerous nature of the publication.

Copyrights

The modern legal concept of copyright owes its inception to
the rights of patentees under royal grants and to the subsequently
developed rights of unprivileged printers in the copies lawfully
licensed and entered in the records of the Stationers Company. Its
threefold origin—the patents of monopoly, the licensing system,
and the copy records of the Stationers Company—is notably independent of either Parliamentary action or the common-law courts.

Rights of patentees [48]

The policy of granting patents of monopoly for certain classes
of books had been inaugurated by Henry VIII,[49] and by the last
quarter of the sixteenth century the number and extent of these
grants had so limited the already restricted fields of printing that
there was widespread discontent among the less favored printers.
The rights of patentees rested upon the authority of the crown
under its prerogative to control and regulate printing, and any
attack upon the legality of those rights or any infringement of
them necessarily resulted in a conflict between the alleged pirate
on one side and both the patentee and the crown on the other.
It was an unequal contest at best, but when it is considered that
the Council (later the Star Chamber) and not the law court was
the ultimate court of appeal in all questions involving the prerogative, it is nothing less than astonishing that the royal patents were
ever infringed or contested. But infringed and contested they were.
In 1577 Christopher Barker, the queen's printer, complained to

[47] *Ibid.*, p. 57 (1597).

[48] Since the original grants of letters patent were for either trade or political
purposes, the recipients were printers and booksellers rather than authors.
Creative rights in literary property were not definitely recognized until the
seventeenth century. The requirement of registration as a prerequisite to copyright protection persisted in both England and the United States until the
twentieth century.

[49] See above, pp. 38-40.

the Council that his patents were being violated.[50] John Wolfe, the leader of the insurgent printers, went so far as to question the right of the crown to grant the special privileges.[51] The dispute between the patentees and the unprivileged printers, which lasted from 1575 to 1586, ended in compromise. Wolfe, bought off by giving him a share in Day's patent, became a respectable and diligent law-enforcing officer of the Stationers Company. A number of the patents were surrendered for the benefit of the poor craftsmen, and the crown promised to abandon its policy of indiscriminate grants. On the other hand, both the legality of the existing patents and the power of the crown to issue new grants were sustained.[52]

Patentees at first made occasional appeals to the Council for protection from piracy, but after 1570 these appeals were made to the Star Chamber, the judicial off-shoot of the Council. Roger Ward was prosecuted before the Star Chamber 10 July 1582 for printing the *ABC* with John Day's trade mark thereon,[53] and Robert Bourne was called upon to defend himself before the same tribunal in 1586.[54] In 1601 the Privy Council ordered the Company to take steps to protect the privilege of Robert Barker, queen's printer, from infringement by Bonham Norton and John Norton, who were accused of printing Bibles at Dort. Barker pointed out to the Council that these printers having broken the law in one direction were extremely likely to break it in another by printing "lewde and seditious bookes and pamphlettes." [55]

It was inevitable that certain legal relationships should develop from the ownership of patents of monopoly for particular books or classes of books—relationships which had a profound

---

[50] J. R. Dasent, *Acts of the Privy Council* (London, 1890-1907), X (1577-78), 169-70.

[51] See H. R. Hoppe, "John Wolfe," *The Library*, 4th Series, XIV, 258-63. See also below, pp. 92-95.

[52] Arber reprints a number of important documents involved in the struggle over printing patents. Arber, *op. cit.*, I, 468; ii, 786-89, 804. The rights of patentees were confirmed by the Council Order of 1566 (above, p. 58) and the Star Chamber Decree of 1586 (above, p. 61).

[53] The preliminary papers are found in Star Chamber, Eliz. III, D, 16, reprinted in Arber, *op. cit.*, II, 753-69. The decrees of the court are missing.

[54] *Ibid.*, pp. 800-804. See also the preliminary papers in Richard Dan *vs.* T. Dunn, R. Robinson *et al.* (*Ibid.*, pp. 790-93) and in F. Flower *vs.* T. Dunn and R. Robinson (*Ibid.*, pp. 794-800).

[55] Dasent, *op. cit.*, XXXII (1601-4), 14-15.

influence on the early development of copyright law. These developments took place not in established courts of law but through the judicial machinery of the Stationers Company. The parties, being printers or booksellers, were almost always members of the craft organization, and were required under the Company ordinances to submit their trade disputes to the Court of Assistants.[56] When the parties were dissatisfied with the Company's ruling or did not wish to submit to it, an appeal could be taken to the Star Chamber. Before long the title to privileged copies was recognized in an assignee,[57] in a partnership, [58] or in a syndicate.[59] The Company sometimes acted as a trustee for a number of patents [60] and also took upon itself the duty of defending the privilege from outside attack.[61] The rights of a patentee in printed books became co-extensive with rights in other types of personal property and were limited only by the terms of the letters patent.

Questions of infringement were frequently presented to the Court of Assistants. In 1579 Thomas Dawson was called before the court charged with infringing Henry Denham's patent rights in prayer-books which had been assigned to him by William Seres.[62] The court decided that Dawson's book *A Handful of Honeysuckles* (1579) contained prayers in violation of the terms of the patent, and he was ordered to deliver the stock to Denham and to omit all prayers in future reprints.[63] The matter did not end then, for Denham, on the strength of the order, proceeded to reprint the entire

---

[56] See Ordinances of the Company, Arber, *op. cit.*, I, 14. The records of the Court of Assistants containing entries relating to patent rights have been reprinted by Greg.

[57] William Seres's privilege in books of private prayer was assigned to Henry Denham. Reg. A, Arber, *op. cit.*, I, 114.

[58] A partnership operated part of Day's privilege. Greg, *op. cit.*, p. 16. The privilege in Foxe's *Book of Martyrs* was exercised by a partnership. *Ibid.*, p. 51.

[59] Day's and Seres's privileges were amalgamated. *Ibid.*, pp. 70, 76. The Stationers Company received the patent for Psalters, Psalms, Primers, and Almanacks, etc. October 29, 1603. *Ibid.*, p. 94.

[60] *Ibid.*, pp. 39, 50, 76.

[61] *Ibid.*, p. 59.

[62] The valuable patent in the *Book of Common Prayer* belonged to the queen's printer. This patent was granted to Seres in order to (said Barker) "kepe back the infinite nomber of vnfrutefull prayer bookes, which vnskilfull persons do contynually offer to make." Arber, *op. cit.*, I, 116.

[63] Greg, *op. cit.*, pp. lxvi, 9.

work as his own for which action he was ordered to pay Dawson £6.[64] Penalties imposed by the Company for infringement of patent rights included both confiscation of copies and fines. Occasionally the punishment went further. A group of printers, including Robert Bourne, Henry Jefferson, and John Danter, were found guilty of infringing the patent for grammars (30 November 1586) and were by order of the Court of Assistants disabled from all printing other than as journeymen, and the press and materials with which the grammar had been illegally printed were seized and defaced.[65]

Rights in unprivileged printing

Like most Elizabethan concepts, the rights in unprivileged copies evolved slowly and without order or organization.[66] The royal patentees had rights in specially reserved fields. Why did not the ordinary printer have rights in books properly licensed and first published by him? The earliest evidence (1558/9) of recognition by the Stationers Company of a copyright in unprivileged printing is an entry of the assessment of a fine of 20 pence against Owen Rogers "for printing another man's copy." [67] The register of the Company listing the fees for permission to print took on a new significance as these entries became useful in establishing ownership of copies. This new use of the register resulted in a change of form. "Licensed vnto him" becomes by the end of the sixteenth century "Entered vnto him." [68] An entry in the name of John Wolfe in 1589 is more explicit—"that noe person shall prynte any parte or parcell thereof to his hindrance." [69] After 1591 the standard entry was "Entered for his copy" etc.[70]

Registration by showing prior publication became necessary to establish ownership of copies. Once this concept was accepted we find a rush to enter books and pamphlets, most of which were

---

[64] *Ibid.*, p. 18.

[65] *Ibid.*, pp. 20-21.

[66] For early history, see above, pp. 33ff.

[67] Arber, *op. cit.*, I, 101.

[68] *Ibid.*, II, 480. Arber dates the change about 1571-76; (I, p. xvii).

[69] *Ibid.*, p. 502.

[70] *Ibid.*, p. 601.

printed many years previously.[71] Even the royal patentees decided
that registration would afford them additional protection.[72] Books
were ordinarily entered in the name of a printer, but occasionally
a registration was made in the name of a publisher who was not a
printer.[73] Only members of the Company could register their
printed works, and provision was made for forfeiture of all copies
entered in the name of a Stationer who was not the real owner but
merely a cloak for outsiders who wished to avail themselves of the
Company's copyright protection.[74] Widows of printers as long as
they remained widows could register works in their own names.[75]
The University of Cambridge printer was permitted to enter his
work in the Company's register for copyright protection although
he was not a member of the corporation.[76] Entries in the names
of partners are not infrequent.[77]

Provisos, reservations, and conditions were occasionally attached to the official entry. The most common was the reservation
to the effect that if the item had been previously entered to another
the present entry was to be void.[78] The Company sought to protect
itself from conflicts over copies with powerful master printers by
such provisos as "yf this booke containe any thinge preiudiciall
or hurtfull to the booke of maister Askham that was printed by
Master Daie." [79] Entry was frequently made conditional upon the
printer's securing a license to print from the proper authorities.[80]
In 1588 *A Joyfull ballad of the Roiall entrance of Quene Elizabeth
into Her Cyty of London* was entered to John Wolfe several days

[71] Beginning 1 August 1586, 180 or more ballads were registered within
a week. *Ibid.*, pp. 450ff.

[72] *Ibid.*, pp. 419, 431.

[73] Entry to Andrew Mansell (1577), *Ibid.*, p. 308.

[74] Greg, *op. cit.*, p. 59.

[75] Arber, *op. cit.*, III, 82.

[76] *Ibid.*, p. 88 (1597).

[77] *Ibid.;* Greg, *op. cit.*, p. 90.

[78] John Charlewood was permitted to enter a list of books in 1582 with
this proviso: "That yf it be founde that anie other hath righte to printe anie
of theis Copies, That then this his lycence as touchinge euerie suche of those
Copies soe belonginge to anie other shallbe void and of none effecte." Reg. B,
Arber, *op. cit.*, II, 405.

[79] *Ibid.* (1581). See registration saving rights of patentees, *Ibid.*, p. 601
(1591).

[80] *Ibid.*, p. 480.

before the event took place and therefore before the item was printed.[81]

The bulk of the entries consist of new works first printed by the entrant, but occasionally there are registrations of other types of printing. Later editions were seldom registered.[82] John Danter succeeded in entering under his name in 1596 a book which had been printed by Day twenty years earlier but which Day had failed to register with the Company.[83] A curious rule for the ownership and registration of translations was evolved by the Court of Assistants in 1578. The translation of a privileged work belonged not to the owner of the privilege but to the printer of the translation and could be registered by him. However, the printer was required to list himself on the title page of the book not as the owner but as assignee of the holder of the privilege.[84] Translations from foreign tongues were listed under the name of the printer of the translation.[85]

As in the case of patents of monopoly,[86] various legal relationships followed the recognition of property in copies. A copyright could be sold,[87] exchanged,[88] assigned,[89] subdivided,[90] released by one partner to another [91] or settled in trust.[92]

---

[81] *Ibid.*, p. 506. This entry indicates how it was possible to control and even prohibit the publications of news through the copy-registration system of the Stationers Company.

[82] For two entries of second editions to Thomas East, see *Ibid.*, p. 449 (1586).

[83] *Ibid.*, III, 73.

[84] Greg, *op. cit.,* p. 7.

[85] Arber, *op. cit.*, II, 480, 514. However, in 1595/6 the Court of Assistants ordered that the copyright in foreign works should be open to any member who wished to share in the printing. Greg, *op. cit.*, p. 54. One of the earliest records of a recognition of a translator's (author) rights is an order of 1577 prohibiting all translations of *Titus Lucious* except the one made by Alexander Nevill. Reg. B, Arber, *op. cit.*, II, 312.

[86] See above, pp. 75-76.

[87] Arber, *op. cit.*, I, 259 (1564/5). A copyright for Calvin's *Chatechism* was sold for five shillings in 1565/6 *Ibid.*, II, 306.

[88] *Ibid.*, p. 359 (1579); I, 272.

[89] *Ibid.*, II, 309, 325, 351, 386. A widow of a printer if she married outside the Company was required to assign her copyrights but could reclaim them if she later married within the Company. *Ibid.*, III, 51.

[90] Publishing rights could be assigned reserving printing rights. *Ibid.*, pp. 70, 72 (1596). Greg, *op. cit.*, p. 37.

[91] Arber, *op. cit.*, II, 302 (1576).

[92] *Ibid.*, p. 316 (1577).

The duration of the copyright was ordinarily in perpetuity following the example set in the letters patent of the late sixteenth century. Occasionally an entry was made for life or for joint lives.[93] However, it was provided in 1577/78 that all rights in a book which was out of print and which the owner failed to reprint should lapse and become open for the benefit of the poor craftsmen of the Company.[94] The orders adopted by the Company in 1588 gave the owner six months within which to reissue a book which was out of print, after which it could be reprinted by any journeyman who was willing to take the original owner into partnership in the venture.[95]

Questions concerning the title to copies and infringement of rights were decided by the Court of Assistants. The records of this Court from 1576 to 1603 present numerous conflicts over copyrights, but unfortunately the facts are seldom fully set out. Dr. Greg has pointed out in his introduction to the Court records that "it was in fact a Court of conciliation rather than of law. At any rate we are able to observe a marked tendency, while giving an award in favor of one or other claimant, to allow some compensation to the unsuccessful rival, and many of the decisions are of the nature of a compromise." [96]

The ordinary punishment inflicted by the Court of Assistants for violation of copyrights was a fine. The account book of the Company lists the payment of these fines in the following fashion: "Received of Alexander lacye for his fyne for that he prented *ballettes* which was other mens copyes . . . xii^d." [97] The court frequently, in the case of disputed ownership, ordered an entry to one printer struck out and the name of the real owner inserted in the register of copies.[98] Claims were settled by a grant of books or

---

[93] *Ibid.*, III, 393.

[94] *Ibid.*, II, 43; Greg, *op. cit.*, p. 5.

[95] Arber, *op. cit.*, II, 43-44.

[96] *Ibid.*, p. lxxv.

[97] *Ibid.*, I, 274. The growing importance of the technical requirement of registration as a prerequisite to copy-ownership is evident in the following entry in 1597: "Yt is ordered that he shall pay ii^s vi^d for a fine for printinge a ballad to the wronge of Thomas Crede. And shall also pay to the seid Thomas Crede iii^s iiij^d for amendes for ye seid wrong. The fine is to be paid for that the ballad was not licensed and myllington performinge this order is to enjoy the copy ii^s vi^d paid. *Ibid.*, II, 826; Greg, *op. cit.*, p. 55.

[98] Arber, *op. cit.*, III, 60.

money to one party in a dispute [99] or by permitting the contesting printer to buy up the stock at a fixed rate; [100] by granting printing rights to one and publishing rights to the other; [101] or by ordering the rights to be shared equally.[102]

A practical method of dealing with the complex questions of copyright adopted by the Court of Assistants is illustrated by the controversy between Burbie and Dexter over *the English Schole-master*. The copy was entered on the Stationers' Register in 1596 to R. Jackson and R. Dexter as partners. Jackson transferred his interest to Burbie on 27 April 1602 and both printers (Burbie and Dexter) proceeded to put out separate editions. The decision of the court upon the controversy was:

Yt is found that m^r Burbie hathe broken thordoñances of the company in printinge the said book wthout Alowance [license] in this howse

Lykewise that M^r dexter hath broken the said ordoñances in print-inge the same booke wthout Lyke alowance

And yt is ordered that m^r dexter shall delyu' vnto Mr Burbye so many of his said bookes as will make m^r. Burbies said ympression equall with his

And all charges aswell to the Aucthor as otherwise to be equally borne betwene them parte and parte like

And that the said copie shalbe equally to them both parte and and parte lyke at all Impressions hereafter

And yt is further ordered that all Imp^{r}essions thereof hereafter they shall leave out of the same book the psalmes that are nowe printed wth yt

Also yt is ordered that m^r Burbie shall pay xx^s for A fine for break-ing thordañance as above appereth

And that m^r Dexter shall paie iij^s iiij^d for A fine for his breache thereof as is aboue exp'ssed.[103]

By the end of the sixteenth century property rights in un-privileged copies had achieved definite recognition in the trade practices of the members of the Stationers Company. Patent rights had furnished the model and the licensing register the evidence for ownership. Since no reference to copyrights has been found either in the common-law or the prerogative courts of the sixteenth

[99] Greg, *op. cit.*, pp. 2, 33-34, 40, 66, 79.

[100] *Ibid.*, pp. 7-8, 9, 12-13, 45-46.

[101] *Ibid.*, pp. 12-13.

[102] *Ibid.*, pp. 67, 88.

[103] *Ibid.*, p. 88.

century, it must be assumed that the rules for copy-ownership developed out of orders and decisions of the Court of Assistants. The further development of copyright protection in the seventeenth century is discussed in Chapter 6.

Search and Seizure

The problem of enforcing the detailed regulations for the control of the press which were devised by the crown, the Council, and the Stationers Company was solved by granting wide powers of search and seizure. Opposition from the printers, who would naturally have been most vehemently opposed to the methods of enforcement, was met by delegating the power of the search and seizure to the Stationers Company. Not only were the members of that organization which included all the London printers (with a few minor exceptions) silenced by drafting them as official "snoopers," but the policy seems to have been to appoint as searchers those printers who were notoriously addicted to violating the official regulations on the ground either that it takes a thief to catch a thief or that their reformation could be accomplished more easily by giving them a taste of responsibility and authority.

The charter of incorporation (1557) provided that "it shall be lawful for the Master and Keepers or Wardens . . . and their successors for the time being to make search whenever it shall please them in any place, shop, house, chamber, or building of any printer, binder or bookseller whatever within our kingdom of England or the dominions of the same of or for any books or things printed, or to be printed, and to seize, take, hold, burn, or turn to the proper use of the . . . community, all and several those books and things which are or shall be printed contrary to the form of any statute, act, or proclamation made or to be made." [104] Although the Company under the terms of the charter operated officially only within the city of London, no geographical limitations were placed on the right of search and seizure. In practice however, the Stationers confined their efforts principally to searching out any illegal printing within the city,[105] leaving the patrol of the provinces to the crown and to the local officers. The charter seems to limit the

---

[104] Charter provisions, Arber, *op. cit.*, I, xxxi.

[105] Hugh Singleton, however, while he was official searcher for the Company made trips into the country. *Ibid.*, p. 347.

power of search to the premises of printers and booksellers, but the practical question of determining beforehand whether or not the house about to be searched belonged to or was occupied by a printer never seems to have disturbed the Company. Anyone "disturbing, refusing, or hindering" a search could be imprisoned by the Company for three months and fined "a hundred shillings of lawful money . . . one half thereof to us (the crown) and the other half thereof to the Company." [106]

The Council Order of 1566 further clarified and expanded the powers of search and seizure enjoyed by the Company. After confirming the powers already granted in the charter, the Order gives the Wardens authority to inspect all incoming cargoes ("packs, dryfats [barrels], maunds [wicker baskets], and other things wherein books or paper shall be contained").[107] Under this order the Company appointed Hugh Singleton,[108] a notorious Puritan printer, and Thomas Purfoot as searchers for unlawful printing. The two inquisitors after receiving written authority and a grant of five pounds for the year ending July, 1567, proceeded to visit the London printing houses, catching six culprits, and then went to the provinces where they discovered that Thomas Marshe, John Wight, and Gerard Dewes were the principal dealers in prohibited Catholic books. Purfoot must have aroused the animosity of the printers for at their instigation he was called up before the Company and fined for selling primers to the haberdashers contrary to law. Singleton continued to act as Company searcher for several years.[109]

The clergy and other ecclesiastical officers under the direction of the Bishop of London kept a sharp lookout for illegal printing, and if their suspicions were aroused, they either directed the Company to make a search or conducted an investigation themselves. The bishop himself with two of his henchmen searched the premises of the eminent historian John Stow for heretical and papistical

---

[106] *Ibid.*, p. xxxl.

[107] Tanner, *op. cit.*, p. 246. The Order fails to give the Company authority to conduct searches on board ship.

[108] For an account of Singleton, see H. J. Byrom in *The Library*, 4th Series, XIV, 121-56.

[109] Arber, *op. cit.*, I, 346, 347, 348. In 1569 he was paid two shillings for "taken vp of bokes at the Water syde." *Ibid.*, p. 421. An account of the *Proceedings of the searchers* at York is set out by Robert Davies in *A Memoir of the York Press* (1868), pp. 30-33.

books and made an inventory of thirty-eight works found in his study.[110]

In 1576 the Stationers Company adopted an order that a search of all London printing houses be made once a week by two searchers. Twelve pairs of searchers were appointed to rotate in order. They were required to make a weekly report showing what work each printer was then engaged in, how many impressions he made, for whom they were printed, how many apprentices were kept, what journeymen were employed, and how many presses were in operation.[111] We can only echo Arber's lament, "What a tale these weekly Search-Reports would tell, if they were now extant." A new list was appointed 11 January 1585/6, but this time the searchers were divided into groups of three.[112] The Company agreed to pay for the dinner (13 pence each) on the day of the search. There must have been some active opposition to these weekly inquisitions for the Company agreed to stand the cost of prosecuting all those who molested the searching party.[113]

The Star Chamber Decree of 1586 confirmed the Company's authority to search out and seize unlawful printing. Item VI provided:

That it shall be lawful for the Wardens of the said Company for the time being or any two of the said Company thereto deputed by the said Wardens, to make search in all workhouses, shops, warehouses of printers, booksellers, bookbinders, or where they shall have reasonable cause of suspicion, and all books [etc.] . . . . contrary to . . . . these present Ordinances to stay and take to her Majesty's use, and the same to carry into Stationers' Hall in London; and the party or parties offending . . . . to arrest, bring, and present them before the said High Commissioners in Causes Ecclesiastical, or some three or more of them whereof the said Archbishop of Canterbury or Bishop of London for the time being to be one.[114]

Item II ordered the printers to set up their presses in places to which the Company's searchers had ready access.[115]

Further instructions were set out in Item VII of the Decree

[110] Lands. Ms. No. 11 (2-5), Arber, *op. cit.*, I, 393-94.

[111] *Ibid.*, II, 41.

[112] *Ibid.*, p. 42.

[113] *Ibid.*

[114] Tanner, *op. cit.*, pp. 282-83.

[115] *Ibid.*, p. 280.

authorizing the Company to seize and carry away all printing equipment employed in unlawful printing, and under orders from the Court of Assistants to proceed to the "defacing, burning, breaking, and destroying all of the said presses, letters, (*types*)" and other printing instruments. Finally the Company was ordered to return "the stuff of the same so defaced" to the owner to remind him of the results of his misbehavior.

The Court Book of the Company for 4 July 1590 reports the case of Roger Ward [116] before the Court of Assistants:

whereas vppon serche lately made by thappointm^t of ye w^{r}dens It was found that Roger warde had contrary to thorder of ye cũpany & decrees of ye starre chãber printed the Christian sacrifice beinge forbidden by my lords grace of Canterbury and burtons sermon, and a treatise of a Reformed churche and had a forme standing Redy to goo to ye presse of the iiijth Leafe of ye gramar in Viij^o And did also kepe & conceale a presse and other printing stuff in a Taylors house neere adioyninge to his own house and did hyde his letters in a henhouse neere St Sepulchres churche exp'ssely ag^t the decrees of the starchãber All the wch stuffe wth other his printing stuff were brought to the stac' hall according to the said decrees And yt is nowe therefore concluded thall [*sic*] all his presses and printinge instruments shalbe defaced & made vnserviceable for printing accordinge to the said Decrees.[117]

That the searchers were not always politely received is shown by the following entry of 7 August 1592:

whereas Abell Ieffes about the [*blank*] day of July last did Resist the serche which m^r Stirrop warden. Tho dawson and Tho [*Rente*] man renters were appointed to make & would haue made of his printinge house according to thordoñance & decrees, and for that he contemptuously proceded in printing a book wthout aucthority contrary to our m^r his coñaundem^t, and for y^t he refused to deliu' the barre of his presse neither would deliu' any of the Bookes to be brought to the hall accordinge to ye decrees, and also for y^t he vsed violence to our officer in the serche. — y^t is nowe therfore ordered by a full court holden this day. that for his offences he shalbe committed to ward according to the ordoñances and Decree in y^t behalf/[118]

All unlawful books seized by the searchers were taken to Stationers' Hall where they were inspected by the ecclesiastical officers. If they were merely infringements of patents or copyrights, they

---

[116] Ward had been tried in 1586. See Greg, *op. cit.*, p. 20 for an earlier offense.

[117] *Ibid.*, p. 34; also pp. 36-37.

[118] *Ibid.*, p. 42.

were turned over to the proper owner, but if they were books pro-
scribed by the authorities they were burnt.[119]

The Council could rely on but little assistance from the Stationers Company in the enforcement of the printing regulations
outside the city of London. This part of the work was carried on
principally by royal or local officers under directions from the
Council or by the local clergy under orders from the ecclesiastical
authorities. The Acts of the Privy Council for the latter part of
the sixteenth century contain frequent notices of orders, directions,
and reports to these provincial officers on the matter of enforcing
the printing regulations.[120]

The regulations were particularly difficult to enforce in seaports, open as they were to the importation of all the obnoxious
printing which was banned at home. Letters were dispatched by the
Council to the local officers in provincial seaports charging them
with enforcing the regulations.[121] The port of London was closely
watched, and special officers appointed by the crown were commissioned to cooperate with the Stationers Company and the city
officials to search all cargoes of incoming ships for illegal printing.[122] Although the officers of the Company assisted in these
searches and confiscated the books found in the ships, they seem
in each case to have operated under a warrant issued either by the
Council or by the High Commission. On 4 December 1594 the Company delivered to the Bishop of London "one barrel and ij firkins of
bookes of Alexander Humes doing of *Christes Descention into hell*
which by a warrant of his grace and other high Commissioners
dated 2 Decembris 1594 was seised in a ship of Andrew Blakes that
came forth of Scotland." [123]

The enforcement of the regulations for the control of the
press was remarkably successful during Elizabeth's reign, but by
the end of the century it was apparent that the system could not
long withstand the terrific strains put upon it. The basic authority

---

[119] Arber, *op. cit.*, II, 39, 40.

[120] Dasent, *op. cit.*, XXXI (1600-1601), 216; XXXII (1601-4), 85.

[121] For a letter to the Mayor, the clergy, and the customs officers of
Plymouth, see *Ibid.*, XXXII (1601-4), 412-13.

[122] *Ibid.*, XXII (1591-92), 486-87.

[123] Arber, *op. cit.*, II, 40. For a seizure of 768 copies imported from Scotland, see *Ibid.*, p. 38.

for the regulations (the prerogative powers of the crown) was soon to be attacked; the monopolistic position of the Stationers Company was particularly vulnerable; the exercise of secular powers by a clergy unsympathetic with national religious feeling was increasing the irritation; and above all, the low rumble of the demand of the people to see, to hear, and to know was gathering momentum. Elizabeth bequeathed a tottering system of control to her successors.

CHAPTER 4

Rumblings of Revolt

The regulations for the control of the press as they were applied during the Tudor period, taken all in all, were reasonably effective. There were infractions but few executions. However, as the sixteenth century progressed the number of violations increased. As the tension following the threat of the Spanish Armada eased, the focus of public interest shifted from foreign to domestic affairs. Matters which had been set aside under the threat of a foreign invasion were revived. The rights of the trading class of which the printers were naturally members, the grievances of the religious nonconformists both Protestant and Catholic, and the privileges of Parliament became before the end of the century volatile subjects of public discussion both in speech and in print.

Three groups were particularly outstanding in these preliminary forays against the Tudor restrictions — the insurgent printers, the religious nonconformists, and a few hardy members of Parliament. Among the printers William Carter, a Roman Catholic, was the only person put to death during the entire Tudor period. Printers of Puritan literature like Hugh Singleton, Robert Waldegrave, John Stroud, and John Hodgkins suffered less drastic punishments at the hands of the authorities. The printing patents of monopoly and the restrictions of the Stationers Company were attacked by such daring opponents as John Wolfe, Roger Ward, William Holmes, and John Charlewood.

The contests growing out of the publication of the *Admonition to Parliament* and the Martin Marprelate tracts illustrate the struggle for both religious freedom and liberty of the press. No statement of the intellectual principles of freedom is to be found in the writings of the early Puritan authors; in fact their attacks were directed not against the theory underlying the restrictions but against the application of these restrictions to themselves. They did not object to the doctrine that the press should be controlled, but they did object to the control of their own presses. Their avowed purpose was to substitute their regulations for those administered by the government — a purpose which was to be accomplished during the seventeenth century. The immediate contribution of the Puritans was assistance in destroying the existing system of control and thus establishing a precedent for attacks on their own subsequent regulations.

In the realm of political discussion, Parliament had first to establish its own rights in a contest which began with Peter Wentworth and culminated with the establishment of the Commonwealth. Here too the theory of freedom of speech was not recognized except as it applied to its own members. But the march toward freedom of the press, religious liberty, and democracy in government had begun. The printers, the nonconformists, and the representatives in Parliament fought the first battles.

Revolt Among the Printers

The careers of William Carter, Hugh Singleton, and John Wolfe illustrate the revolt among the printers. Carter, representing the Roman Catholic point of view, ventured into the field of political discussion. Hugh Singleton, the Puritan printer, dared to publish criticisms of the government of the established church; and John Wolfe conducted a running attack on monopolists and monopolies.

William Carter [1] was the son of John Carter, a draper in London, and at an early age was apprenticed to John Cawood, official printer under Mary and Elizabeth. He was suspected of having

---

[1] The authorities for the career of William Carter are found in the *Dictionary of National Biography*, IX, 207; *The Catholic Encyclopedia*, XV, 630; R. B. McKerrow, *Dictionary of Printers and Booksellers* (London: Bibliographical Society, 1910), p. 62; John Stow, *Annales* (London, 1600), p. 1176; Edward Arber, *Transcript* (1875), I, 196; II, 749.

had a hand in the printing and publishing of several Roman Catholic books, and on 30 December 1579 the Bishop of London reported: "I have found out a presse of pryntynge with one Carter, a verye lewd fellowe, who hath byne Dyvers tymes before in prison for the printinge of Lewde pamphlettes. But nowe in search of his House amongst other naughtye papysticall Bookes, wee have founde one wrytten in Ffrenche inty [t] led *the innosency of the Scotysshe Quene* a very Dangerous Book wherein he calleth her *the heire apparent of this Crown!*" [2] Carter was examined before the High Commission but refused to answer. Evidently the evidence was not sufficient to convict him of treason, and after a term in prison he was released.

In 1580 a new edition of Dr. Gregory Martin's *A treatise of Schism* appeared in London. The authorities contended that this book by allegorical allusion was designed to incite the women at court to assassinate Queen Elizabeth. With the assistance of the Stationers Company, the authorities traced the printing to Carter and seized copies of the book at his shop on Tower Hill. The printer was arrested, but torture failed to force a confession. On 10 January 1584, he was brought before the Old Bailey in London and there indicted, arraigned, and condemned for high treason. The next day he was taken from Newgate to Tyburn and then hanged, boweled, and quartered.[3]

Another of the printers to defy the Elizabethan regulations was Hugh Singleton. His antagonism to the established authority may be traced to his long and ineffective struggle with poverty as well as to his genuine attachment to the principles of the Puritan Reformation. Whether his poverty caused him to seek subsistence by printing prohibited works or whether his religious principles led him into dangerous as well as profitable fields is still a matter of dispute.[4] It is conjectured that Singleton learned his trade in one of the continental centers of reformed religion. During Mary's reign he was active as printer and dispenser of contraband books,

<hr/>

[2] Lands. Ms. No. 28, f. 177.

[3] Stow, *op. cit.*, pp. 1176-77. The Roman Catholic Church has bestowed on Carter the title *Venerable*.

[4] The sources for Singleton's career as a Puritan printer are set out in an article by H. J. Byrom, in *The Library*, 4th Series, XIV, 121-56, and by H. R. Plomer, *The Library*, 3d Series, I, 54-72.

and soon after Elizabeth's religious settlement his experience recommended him to the authorities as a person qualified to search out illegal printing.[5]

Elizabeth was at this period determined to maintain peace with her continental neighbors in order to give England an opportunity to build up her internal resources. She deftly used her eligibility in the matrimonial market as a means of keeping her enemies from uniting against her. When France was about to take over the control of the Netherlands from Spain, the queen adroitly forestalled annexation by offering herself in marriage to the younger brother of Henry III of France, the duc d'Anjou. This diplomatic wooing was pursued at intervals for more than ten years varying in intensity as England's interests veered toward Spain or France. The English public, at least the more Protestant part, could see nothing but evil resulting from a marriage between their queen and a Catholic prince. Elizabeth was probably never serious in her intention to wed Anjou and therefore was doubly vexed when either her councillors or others publicly condemned the projected marriage.

Late in August, 1579, there appeared on the streets of London a pamphlet entitled *The Discourie of a Gaping Gulf Whereinto England is like to be swallowed by another French marriage; if the Lord forbid not the banes, by letting her Maiestie see the sin and punishment thereof.* In phrases burning with indignation the author argued that the Reformation was about to be betrayed and cited instances from Biblical and secular history. Neither the author's nor the publisher's name appeared on the paper.

Elizabeth was furious. What right had anyone to discuss in public print any matter of state policy! She immediately issued a violent proclamation against the "lewde and seditious book." [6] An organized search for the authors and printers was begun, and in three days John Stubbe, the author, and Singleton, the printer, were apprehended. The queen wished to have them hanged, so they were first tried for felony but the jury refused to return a verdict. An indictment was then brought against them for conspiring to excite sedition under a statute passed in Mary's reign "for the protection of the queen's husband." At the close of a notorious trial the

---

[5] See above, p. 83.

[6] Robert Steele, *Tudor and Stuart Proclamations* (Oxford, 1910), No. 740.

prisoners were condemned to lose their right hands. On 3 November Stubbe underwent his punishment, and at its conclusion raised his remaining hand in a salute to his queen. For some undiscovered reason the sentence against the printer was never carried out; Singleton retained his hand but his printing business was ruined.[7]

The career of the insurgent printer, John Wolfe—his conflicts with the authorities and with the Stationers Company, his forays against the patents of monopoly of the privileged printers, his continuous chafing under the detailed Elizabethan regulations—was a forerunner of the more serious revolt of printers and publishers in the next century. Wolfe was apprenticed to John Day in 1562 for ten years, but after serving only seven years he went abroad studying printing in Italy and Germany.[8]

Upon his return to England (1579) the young printer was faced with the unpleasant fact that the more profitable fields of printing were pre-empted by the patents of the privileged printers.[9] Without a patent of monopoly a printer could scarcely make a living. Wolfe therefore petitioned the Privy Council for a patent of monopoly which was refused. Undaunted and rebellious he announced that "Just as Luther had reformed religion, so he Wolfe, would reform the government of the printing and bookselling trades." He proceeded to print "what pleased him best" of the books belonging to the men who had the most remunerative privileges.

Disdaining the small fry, the young reformer began by reprinting the properties of the most powerful printer of the day, Christopher Barker, queen's printer and owner of the right to print the Bible, the Book of Common Prayer, and the Royal Statutes and Proclamations. Barker became alarmed and for some undiscovered reason attempted to compromise with Wolfe rather than have him prosecuted in the law courts. The latter, however, while accepting Barker's commissions, turned his attacks upon other important printing privileges. On 19 June 1581 Francis Flower complained to the Council that Wolfe was infringing his patent in Latin grammars.

---

[7] William Camden, *Annales* (1625), Bk. III, p. 16.

[8] The authorities for the life of Wolfe are collected by H. R. Hoppe, "John Wolfe, Printer and Publisher," *The Library*, 4th Series, XIV, 241-88. See also entries under Wolfe in Arber's *Transcript*.

[9] See above, pp. 74ff.

The Council ordered the rebel to enter into bonds not to print more copies of the same.[10]

Sometime in 1582 Wolfe became the accepted leader of the unprivileged and discontented printers. Associated with him were Roger Ward, who was prosecuted for infringing the patent of John Day in the *ABC and Catechism;* William Holmes, and John Charlewood, printers; Henry Bamford, compositor; Frank Adams, maker of writing tables; William Lobley, bookbinder; Abraham Kidson, Thomas Butter, and William Wright, booksellers; and Robert Neak, lawyer. Robert Waldegrave and Thomas East were also members of the group.

Wolfe now took the lead by attacking the legality of the existing patents by questioning the authority under which they were issued. This raised the issue of the powers of the queen's prerogative and led him onto extremely dangerous ground. For his presumption he was committed to prison while two commissioners, Dr. John Hammond and John Norton, printer, were appointed to examine into the matter. Both commissioners were from the beginning prejudiced against the demands of the rebel group; but persecution merely increased Wolfe's aggressiveness. From prison he directed a campaign for the abolition of privileges and his presses continued to issue privileged works. His premises were raided by order of the Bishop of London and his presses and materials confiscated.

The Court of Aldermen of the city of London now took a hand in the matter and (in 1583) settled for a time Wolfe's organized raids on the monopolists. It was ordered that Wolfe should be transferred from the Fishmongers Company to the Stationers Company and that he should be given sufficient work to keep him busy. The success of his campaign is attested by the fact that in 1585 he owned five presses, more than any other printer except Barker. Waldegrave also capitulated for the first time and agreed to abide by the rules of the Stationers Company. Only Ward refused to be enticed into respectability.

Economic security and membership in the Stationers Company, however, failed to complete Wolfe's reformation. In 1583 he was nibbling into Day's patents. The latter secured a warrant for

[10] J. R. Dasent, *Acts of the Privy Council* (London, 1890-1907), XIII, 88.

the search of Wolfe's premises and confiscated his printing materials. Wolfe's fighting spirit was again aroused and he proceeded to prosecute Day in the Star Chamber for damages to his house and property.[11] After Day's death in 1584, his son Richard found it convenient to compromise with the infringing printers and assigned his interests to a group of which Wolfe was a member.

Himself an important patentee, Wolfe now rapidly climbed the ladder of respectability. He turned his energies against the unruly printers, and contrary to his earlier practice refused to compromise. In 1587 he was appointed beadle of the Company and given rooms in the Stationers' Hall. His principal duty was tracking down outlaw printers, and his experiences made him an exemplary bloodhound. He scented out Waldegrave, his former comrade, who was printing some of the Marprelate tracts. He pounced on the secret presses set up by Roger Ward in Southwark and Hammersmith. Abel Jeffes, John Charlewood, and John Danter were all hounded by the zealous beadle. In 1591 he was commissioned to prosecute the Cambridge printer, John Leggat, who was printing *Psalms in Metre*. In 1593 he was appointed printer to the City of London, and finally in 1598 he was admitted into the livery of the Stationers Company.

His temerity, however, led him into one more tussle with the authorities before the end of his career. In February, 1599, he published *The first part of the life and reign of King Henry IIII*, a play by John Hayward dealing with the deposition of King Richard II and the events leading up to it. In addition to a dedication to Essex, who was by this time out of favor with the queen, the book contained an epistle calling the attention of the reader to the obvious lessons learned from history. Denied the privilege of discussing current political affairs, the Elizabethan pamphleteers had frequently discussed personalities and state matters under feigned or historical guises. The authorities immediately suspected that the work was intended to draw an historical parallel between early and contemporary times.

The book, however, had been licensed by Samuel Harsnett, chaplain to the Bishop of London, who now sought to exculpate himself by shifting the blame to an associate. The edition was burnt by order of the Bishop of London, and Wolfe was forced to draw

---

[11] Star Chamber Proceedings, 26 Eliz. Bundle W 34, No. 23 (P.R.O.).

upon his skill in compromise to save his skin.[12] He died in 1602, a few months too early to participate in the conflict over patents which took place at the accession of James I.

Revolt Among the Puritans

The Elizabethan Puritans, pupils and heirs of those Edwardian reformers who were forced into exile during Mary's reign and who upon Elizabeth's succession returned to England filled with Genevan doctrines and evangelical zeal, were the first group to engage in an organized opposition to the established order. Failing to achieve further reformation in either the vestments or doctrines of worship as established by the Church of England through the Convocation (the ecclesiastical legislative body), they directed their appeals to Parliament. Elizabeth, however, in 1572 stopped the further consideration of bills for the reformation of the established church in Parliament. Her position was that church matters should be dealt with in Convocation, secular matters in Parliament.

Balked both in Convocation and Parliament, the Puritans discovered another avenue open to them—an appeal to the country through the medium of the press. The skill with which they conducted the campaign in spite of stringent regulations on printing and in spite of the opposition of both the crown and the ecclesiastical hierarchy demonstrated for the first time in English history the power of the press.

The first shot in the battle of pamphlets was the publication of *An Admonition to Parliament,* a small octavo tract of sixty pages without title page, author's name, or publisher's signature. The contents of the tract had previously been presented at the 1572 session of Parliament without results; they were now presented to the people of England. Whether publication took place before or after the proroguing of Parliament on 30 June 1572 is still a matter of dispute.[13] The sponsors of the pamphlet were the Puritan group in London, with two of their number, John Field and Thomas

---

[12] G. B. Harrison, "Books and Readers, 1599-1603," *The Library,* 4th Series, XIV, 10-13; M. Dowling, "Sir John Hayward's Troubles over his *Life of Henry IV,*" *The Library,* 4th Series, XI, 212-24.

[13] See A. F. S. Pearson, *Thomas Cartwright and Elizabethan Puritanism, 1553-1603* (New York: Cambridge University press, 1925), pp. 58-61; W. H. Frere and C. E. Douglas, *Puritan Manifestoes* (London, 1907), p. 88.

Wilcocks, acting as their scribes. The authors, in characteristic Elizabethan prose, attempted to point out the errors existing in the established system of ecclesiastical government and argued for a return to the church organization of apostolic times as set out in the Bible. They attacked the bishops and the remnants of Romanism remaining in the Church of England.

The authorities immediately went into action, and in June, 1572, Field and Wilcocks were apprehended. An organized search, however, failed to discover who or where the printer was. Thomas Cooper, Bishop of Lincoln, was appointed to preach against the pamphlet at St. Paul's cross on Sunday, June 27. In September, the two Puritan authors, having languished in prison all summer, received a visit from the Archbishop's chaplain. To him they admitted writing the pamphlet but insisted they had committed no crime since they "wrote it in Parliament time, which should be a time of speaking and writing freely." [14] For the first time the ancient right of Englishmen to petition Parliament was translated as an argument for a free press. On 2 October 1572, Field and Wilcocks were sentenced to a year's imprisonment.

Outside the prison the friends of the Puritan authors had not been inactive. The *Admonition* was issued in several editions and in enlarged form. Archbishop Parker wrote (25 August 1572) as follows: "For all the devices that we can make to the contrary, yet some good fellows still labour to print out the vain 'Admonition to the parliament.' Since the first printing it hath been twice printed, and now with additions, whereof I send your honour one of them. We wrote letters to the mayor and some aldermen of London to lay in wait for the charects, [sic] printer and corrector, but I fear they deceive us." [15] The secret press was skillfully guarded. The printer Day and the Bookbinder Toy were commissioned by the Stationers Company to discover the press, but they failed in their efforts.

A *Second Admonition* [16] attributed to the Puritan reformer, Thomas Cartwright,[17] appeared on the streets of London late in

---

[14] A. Peel, ed., *Seconde Parte of A Register* (1915), I, 87-90.

[15] John Bruce and T. T. Perowne, *Correspondence (Letters by and to Parker)* (Cambridge, 1853), CCCIII, 397.

[16] Reprinted by Frere & Douglas, *op. cit.*, pp. 79ff.

[17] Pearson, *op. cit.*, p. 74, disclaims Cartwright's authorship.

1572. It was soon followed by an official refutation prepared by John Whitgift and printed and published by Henry Bynneman and Humphrey Toy (February, 1673). It was entitled *An Answere to a certain libel intituled An Admonition to the Parliament.* The Puritans were elated. The controversy was at last being forced into the channels they desired. Both sides were compelled to appeal to a nascent public opinion for support. Let the better argument win. The press was accomplishing what Convocation and Parliament failed to do.

The hopes of the bishops, that Whitgift's *Answere* would silence the discontented Puritans, were blasted when on 30 April 1573 Cartwright's *Replye to an Answer* was issued from the secret Puritan press. A second edition appeared on June 11 with an address to the reader signed with the initials "J. S.," i.e., John Stroud, the much sought-after Puritan printer. "Some perhaps will marvel," says the printer, "at the newe impression of thys boke . . . notwythstanding our most gracious Princes late published proclamation, procured rather by the Bishops then willingly sought for by her maiestie. . . . But cease to muse, good christian reader, whosoever thou art, and learne to know that no lawes, were they never so hard and severe, can put out the force of Gods spirite in hys children. . . . For the profite therefore of the godly and their instruction have we hazarded ourselves, and as it were cast ourselves into such daungers and troubles as shalbe layed upon us if we come into the hands of the persecuting Bishops. . . ." [18] In this preface Stroud, the Puritan, translates his religious zeal into defense of the rights of Stroud, the printer.

On the same day as Stroud's pamphlet appeared, Elizabeth issued a proclamation calling in all copies of the *Admonition* and all books written in its defense.[19] The pursuivants of the Ecclesiastical Commission and the Stationers Company increased their activities. Twenty days after the publication of the order, although there were hundreds of copies of the Puritan tracts circulating in and about London, not a single copy was brought in. In August, 1573, the searchers for the Stationers Company discovered a secret press in Hampstead. Two assistants, Lacy and Asplyn, were arrested, and the printing materials were confiscated and turned over to Bynne-

---

[18] Peel, *op. cit.,* I, 112n; Pearson, *op. cit.,* p. 87.

[19] Steele, *op. cit.,* No. 688.

man, Whitgift's printer.[20] Stroud himself was captured soon afterward and was examined 25 November 1573 at the Guildhall in
London by the Ecclesiastical Commission. A record of the proceedings made by Stroud has been preserved.[21] He was released
after agreeing to submit to the printing regulations. He continued,
however, to trouble the authorities until his death by the plague
16 October 1582. With the destruction of the Puritan presses and
printing materials, the government was once more in control of
the situation.

The most notorious defiance of the Elizabethan printing regulations is popularly known as the Martin Marprelate tracts, anonymous pamphlets sponsored by the Puritan group.[22] These tracts,
which were published in the years 1588 and 1589, undertook to
answer the arguments for the episcopal form of church government
which had been set out in a ponderous volume by Dr. John Bridges
entitled *A Defence of the Government Established in the Church of
England for Ecclesiastical Matters.* By satire, by ridicule, by humor-
ous quips, as well as by theological argument, the pamphlets sought
to demolish the ponderous and labored work of the defender of the
established church. Both the style and format of these diminutive
publications were designed to appeal to the public at large rather
than to the theologians and church dignitaries. The first of the
tracts, familiarly called *The Epistle,* was secretly printed at the
home of Mrs. Crane a few miles above Kingston by Robert Waldegrave,[23] a Puritan printer, who had already attracted the attention
of the authorities by printing anti-episcopal tracts from the pen of
John Udall. On 13 May 1588, the searchers for the Stationers Company in obedience to directions from the Star Chamber had seized
and defaced the printing materials found on Waldegrave's premises.
With new type and a press furnished by the Puritans, the printer
produced *The Epistle* on 15 October 1588.

---

[20] Frere and Douglas, *op. cit.,* pp. 155, xxix; Pearson, *op. cit.,* pp. 109, 110.

[21] Peel, *op. cit.,* I, 114.

[22] The history of the Marprelate tracts is amply set out in William Pierce,
An Historical Introduction to the Marprelate Tracts (London, 1908); Edward
Arber, *An Introductory Sketch to the Martin Marprelate Controversy* (London,
1879); J. D. Wilson, "Martin Marprelate and Shakespeare's Fluellen," *The
Library,* 3d Series, III (1912), 113. The tracts themselves have been reprinted
by William Pierce, *The Marprelate Tracts* (London, 1911).

[23] See above, p. 93.

Immediately the search was on again. The Kingston press, being much too near the center of the activities of the official searchers, was laboriously transported to the north of England and lodged at Fawsley House, Northamptonshire, the residence of Sir Richard Knightly, a Puritan sympathizer. The printer, however, was detained in London on suspicion, but since no evidence could be produced against him he was released. He immediately made his way to Northamptonshire and there issued the second of the Marprelate tracts, *The Epitome* (27 November 1588). An itinerant cobbler, Humphrey Newman, alias Brownbread, trudged back and forth between the Midlands and London, distributing the parcels of books. In the meantime, the secret press had been traced to the house of Mrs. Crane near Kingston. To avoid all chance of disclosure the press was again moved from Fawsley, this time to Coventry. Here the third tract referred to as *Mineralls* was printed by Waldegrave on 20 March 1589. A fourth and more elaborate work, *Hay any Worke for the Cooper,* was issued from the same place a few days later. Although no evidence had as yet been discovered connecting Waldegrave with the printing, he was carefully watched; finally unable to shake off his pursuers, he crossed over to France where he continued to print Puritan attacks on the Church of England.

The sponsors of the tracts again moved the press which Waldegrave had left behind, this time to Wolston Priory, the residence of Roger Wigston. John Hodgkins, who had learned to print on the continent, was persuaded to take on the task. With two young assistants, Valentyne Simms and Arthur Thomlyn, he was installed in the Priory as "embroiderer" and on 29 July 1589 issued *Theses Martinianae*, written by John Penry. The following week they finished another tract, *The Just Censure and Reproofe* by Job Throkmorton. The searchers were again hot on the trail of the secret press. Again the press was dismantled and the type packed in boxes, and under cover of the night the printers and their materials set out in a cart for Lancashire. At Warrington a curious crowd which had gathered to watch the unloading was surprised to see a number of small pieces of metal which fell from one of the boxes Hodgkins explained that it was "shott," but one of the bystanders must have picked up a piece of the metal and showed it to a person sufficiently well informed to explain that it was a piece of printing type. Officers of the law arrived immediately, and the printers and their equipment were seized.

After a preliminary hearing before the Earl of Derby, the three printers were taken to London to appear before the High Commission in Causes Ecclesiastical. Hodgkins was one of the most stubborn witnesses yet to appear before the bishops. He was turned over to the secular authorities for torture,[24] but his meager confession proved insufficient to convict him. He denied that the books printed by him were seditious or slanderous and demanded that he be confronted by two witnesses produced within one month. After almost a year in Marshalsea the prisoner was taken back to the Tower where he was again racked. His two assistants suffered the same fate, but evidently the authorities failed to obtain satisfactory confessions.

Of Hodgkins' fate there is no further knowledge. The authorities may have been satisfied with having stopped the productions of the Marprelate press and thereupon released the prisoners. The government was again victorious, but not before the Puritans had made a deep impression upon the public consciousness through the Marprelate publications. Both sides were convinced of the power of the press, a conviction which led the authorities to increase their surveillance and the nonconformists to a fixed determination to surmount the restrictions.

Rumblings in Parliament

While religious diversification following the Reformation provided the subject matter for the initial steps in the development of a theory of freedom of discussion, the earliest legal recognition of such liberties was first demanded in Parliament. The Elizabethan Parliaments standardized the formula presented by the Speaker at the opening of each session requesting the three great privileges, freedom from arrest, freedom of access to the sovereign, and freedom of speech.[25] The medieval Parliamentary practice was to claim freedom of speech for the Speaker alone, but by Elizabeth's time this claim had been extended to the entire membership of the House. However, the Parliamentary supplication of freedom of

---

[24] Pierce, op. cit., p. 197.

[25] G. W. Prothero, Select Statutes . . . of the Reigns of Elizabeth and James I (4th ed.; Oxford, 1913), p. lxxxvii.

discussion was during the Tudor period a privilege in name only. Elizabeth, as sovereign, could not afford to recognize such a privilege as complete freedom of speech in Parliament. The struggle for these liberties lasted in at least one phase until the Long Parliament and in another until the Wilkes affair in the eighteenth century. In the sixteenth and seventeenth centuries the contest for freedom of speech in Parliament involved the right to initiate discussion upon any subject. This privilege was recognized in 1649.[26] Not until the eighteenth century, was the concept extended to include the right to criticize both the crown and the government.[27]

Queen Elizabeth regarded the introduction and discussion of bills on certain subjects such as religion, the succession, and her marriage as presumptuous infringements of her prerogatives. The ensuing conflict between the queen and individual members of Parliament furnished the first reasoned statement of a theory of freedom of speech. The issue was skillfully evaded by the queen when in 1566 after pre-emptorily prohibiting the discussion of the succession, she revoked her commandment upon agreement by the House to drop the matter. In 1571 she replied to the Speaker's petition by referring to her "experience of late of some disorder" and warned the Commons "to meddle with no matters of State but such as should be propounded unto them." [28]

The high-handed action of the queen in resisting Parliamentary intrusion into the sphere of religion led Peter Wentworth to deliver his famous address on "liberty of speech" *thus* preceding Milton in his reasoning by some sixty-five years.[29] Wentworth argued for freedom of discussion in Parliament on the ground that "how can Truth appear and conquer until falsehood and all subtilties that should shadow and darken it be found out?" and further that "an evil can do less harm when it is known." He also attacked the particular methods of suppression used by the crown—indirectly by rumors of the queen's displeasure, and directly by messages from

[26] J. R. Tanner, *Tudor Constitutional Documents* (2d ed.; New York: Cambridge University press, 1930), p. 555. See below.

[27] See below, Chapter 18.

[28] Sir Simonds D'Ewes, *Journals of all the Parliaments during the Reign of Queen Elizabeth* (1682), pp. 141-42.

[29] Strickland's case, *Ibid.*, pp. 166, 167, 168, 175-76.

the throne. Wentworth was, of course, committed to the Tower but upon submission was pardoned by the queen.[30]

In 1587 Wentworth returned to the fray by introducing a series of questions on the privileges of members,[31] but these were not even considered by the House and the author was returned to prison.[32]

Although freedom of speech in Parliament made little progress during the sixteenth century, the germ of the idea had been implanted. Elizabeth had recognized, in theory at least, the claim of privilege presented by the Speakers, but she had reserved the right to draw a distinction between liberty and license. The first reasoned statements for liberty of expression had been made in Parliament, but the essential conflict was postponed until the next century.[33]

The sixteenth century also witnessed the beginnings of the assault on the privacy of debate in the House of Commons. The Parliamentary rule that the proceedings of the House should be held in secret was, during the Tudor period, largely a protection for members against royal displeasure and therefore conducive to freedom of discussion within the House itself. The aggressive policy of the crown in controlling and directing Parliamentary legislation especially on religious matters led to the earliest attempts to break through the privacy of debate and to publicize the proceedings.

The Tudor Parliaments closely guarded the precincts within which meetings were held and proceeded with dispatch against anyone not a member who attempted to attend the sessions.[34] Similarly they proceeded against members or others who divulged or discussed Parliamentary proceedings.

In 1580 Arthur Hall, a member from Grantham, published a pamphlet reflecting upon Sir Robert Bell Knight, late speaker, and criticizing the proceedings in regard to an affair between the author, Hall, and his servant which had come before the House of Com-

---

[30] *Ibid.*, pp. 236-44, 259, 260.

[31] *Ibid.*, p. 411.

[32] Wentworth was imprisoned again in 1592 for presenting a bill on the succession (*Ibid.*, pp. 470, 497) and there is reason to believe that he died in prison in 1596 (*Dictionary of National Biography*, LX, 263.)

[33] See below, pp. 112-16.

[34] D'Ewes, *op. cit.*, pp. 156, 248, 334.

mons.[35] At the next session of Parliament (1580) Hall was called
before the bar of the House and sentenced to imprisonment for
five months, to pay a fine of 500 marks, and to lose his membership
in the House during the current session of Parliament.

Again in 1589 the discussion of Parliamentary matters among
outsiders prompted the Speaker to admonish the members of the
House "that Speeches used in this House by the Members of the
same be not any of them made or used as Table-talk, or in any wise
delivered in notes of writing to any person or persons whatsoever
not being Members of this House." [36]

As the sixteenth century drew to a close, the elaborate structure erected by the Tudors for the control of the press was being
subjected to stresses which it could not long withstand.

Elizabeth and her ministers had labored long and arduously
to keep both printed and spoken discussion within restricted channels. Such bulwarks as royal proclamations, Star Chamber decrees,
the Stationers Company, and patents of monopoly had been erected
against the flood of printed matter. In addition, public expression
was circumscribed by Orders in Council, by Convocation, by the
High Commission, by Parliament, and by exhortations from the
queen.

Isolated groups had already begun to challenge the system of
government controls, the printers for economic reasons, the Puritans for religious reasons, and at least one member of Parliament
for political reasons. Printers like Wolfe chafed under the rules of
the Stationers Company. They rebelled against the printing privileges and the patents of monopoly. The religious nonconformists,
denied the privilege of appealing to public opinion, darted about
inserting wedges with which they eventually wrecked the entire
structure. And in Parliament the faint stirrings of rebellion were

[35] The pamphlet is entitled, "A letter sent by F. A. touching the Proceedings in a private Quarell and Unkindnesse, between Arthur Hall and Melchi-
sidech Mallerie, Gentleman, to his very friend L. B., being in Italy with an
admonition by the Father of F. A. to him . . ." (London, 1579). Printed by
Henry Bynneman. The tract is reprinted in *Miscellanea Antique Anglicana*
(London, 1816), I, 5, and a copy of the trial of Hall by Parliament, included
in the appendix to H. G. Wright's "The Life and Works of Arthur Hall of
Grantham," *Publications of the University of Manchester*, English Series No.
IX (1919).

[36] D'Ewes, *op. cit.*, p. 432.

discernible. Peter Wentworth had dared to discuss forbidden subjects and, in his own defense, had made the first reasoned appeal for liberty of speech to be heard in the halls of Westminster.

PART 2

Control of the Press

UNDER THE EARLY STUARTS

1603-1640

CHAPTER 5

Restrictions on Political

Discussion

The Crown Under James I and Charles I

When James I became king of England in 1603, he inherited a vaguely defined monarchical system of government together with numerous constitutional problems which the Tudors had left unsolved. The political questions, which Elizabeth had successfully avoided and which were revived upon the accession of a new sovereign, were the position of the crown and the powers of the prerogative, the religious settlement involving particularly the church government, and finally the powers and privileges of Parliament. But the central point of all political questions was the crown. What position did it hold both in theory and in practice in the constitutional system of government? What were its inherent rights? What was its position in the ecclesiastical government? What controls and restrictions could it impose upon Parliament? With a trusted and beloved sovereign in her grave, the people of England looked with suspicion upon the arrival of the son of Mary Stuart. Could he be trusted with the powers of the prerogative, with maintaining the established religion, with harmonizing the already rebellious elements in Parliament? Perhaps now was the time to place some definite limitations upon the powers of the crown.

For the first time in almost a century the fundamental problems of government were discussed on all sides. Henry VIII was too strong a monarch to permit such discussion and Elizabeth had avoided it by a combination of circumstances, such as prosperity at home, threatened invasion from abroad, and her own astute statesmanship. James I, foreign-born philosopher king, found himself the center of a widespread and articulate political discontent.

The new king was just as insistent on maintaining the existing powers of the crown as the popular movement was intent on curtailing them. His son, Charles I, who came to the throne in 1625, was equally determined to retain his heritage. Both kings were handicapped by a philosophical disposition and an immense conceit which led them to open argument. In publicly presenting a defense for their sovereign powers, they unconsciously invited retaliation and rejoinder. James I was especially articulate and thoroughly enjoyed political and religious disputation. Adept at picking flaws in an opponent's argument, he was incapable of building a positive case which would withstand the same type of attack. In his early years he solicited the support of public opinion,[1] but in his later years he sought to abolish it. His son, who followed his later policy with vehemence, paid for his mistakes with his head.

The principal controversial question at the opening of the seventeenth century, then, was the constitutional position of the king. The Tudors had accepted their powers without argument or consultation with either Lords or Commons.[2] James, however, must set up a constitutional theory to justify his own position and to serve as a major premise in subsequent disputations. The fundamental principle of the early Stuart state was the unity of spiritual and temporal authority under one divinely anointed head. The king was the embodiment of all political power, and from him lesser satellites received such powers as they were permitted to exercise. Neither the law, nor the Constitution, nor the Church, nor Parlia-

---

[1] See detailed account of political discussions engendered by James's own writings, particularly his *Apologie for the Oath of Allegiance* (1607), in C. II. McIlwain's edition of *The Political Works of James I* (1918).

[2] See below, pp. 25ff. W. S. Holdsworth, *A History of English Law* (Boston: Little, Brown, 1924), IV, 202-14; VI, 20-31.

ment was superior to the king. All were subject to him; and since the king held his position directly under God, it became the religious duty of the subject to obey his sovereign.[3]

Under this theory of government, the prerogative powers of the crown as they had been defined under the Tudor constitution became confused since now all authority flowed directly from the God-head. The Tudors maintained prerogative rights as inherent in the office of king, inferentially recognizing certain constitutional powers in Parliament and the law. The Stuarts insisted upon divine rights, inferentially denying the existence of any powers correlative with their own.[4] Unity, not balance, was the keynote of their state. Dissention and dissatisfaction, paradoxically, were nourished by their persistent attempts to establish a unified control. Dissatisfaction bred public discussion, and public discussion in turn inflamed dissatisfaction. Mutual reverberations gave birth to a hostile public opinion before which the prerogative powers of the crown were helpless.

The religious aspect of the political questions of the first half of the seventeenth century permeated all controversial discussion. Henry VIII had obliterated the division between church and state, between religion and politics, and since his time all political thinking was directed toward a religiously-minded public and all religious speculation inevitably involved the constitution of the state. James I was anointed by God as head of both secular and ecclesiastical government. Any attack upon the established government of the church was sedition; any questioning of the ecclesiastical powers of the crown was heresy.

The theory and doctrines of the established Church of England as codified in Elizabethan times were accepted wholeheartedly by James I,[5] who recalled with a shudder his trying experiences with the Presbyterian kirk of Scotland.[6] Here in England was a happy medium, neither Romanism nor Calvinism. Above all, the

[3] J. N. Figgis, *The Divine Right of Kings* (2d ed.; Cambridge, 1922), *passim*. James I, *Basilikon Doron* (1598), *The True Law of Free Monarchies* (1598), both reprinted in McIlwain, *op. cit.*

[4] "James I's Speech in the Star Chamber," (1616), McIlwain, *op. cit.*, pp. 326-45.

[5] "Speech at Whitehall," (1609), McIlwain, *op. cit.*, pp. 306-25.

[6] S. R. Gardiner, *History of England* (London: Longmans, 1896), I, 47, 55-65.

English church coincided with the Stuart theory of unity. From God through the king all blessings flowed, both secular and ecclesiastical. Elizabeth had supported the church settlement because she had no other choice; her legitimacy and therefore her inheritance depended upon it. James, however, supported the established church because it provided a simplified and unified solution for the religious problem; it squared with his conception of the ideal church-state.

Haunted by an inherited fear of Romanism and Romanists, the English people could not dispel a deep-seated suspicion that the Stuarts were more Roman Catholic than Protestant. Every move of the crown was carefully inspected for traces of Romanism. The entertainment of ambassadors from Catholic countries, the negotiation for the marriage of the Stuart heir to a Catholic princess, the failure to prosecute English Recusants, the insistence upon high church ritual, the preferment of anti-Puritan churchmen, and above all the open persecution of Puritan nonconformists served merely to confirm the people in their suspicions.

At the opening of the seventeenth century both James and his subjects were loyal supporters of the established doctrines of the Church of England.[7] Unfortunately their mutual distrust drove them into opposite camps. As larger numbers became convinced of the Romanistic designs of the Stuarts, they deserted for the Puritan ranks; and as James and Charles saw their subjects destroying the unified political edifice, they found themselves much to their surprise forced into a conflict with their own subjects for the maintenance of the national religion. From the Stuart point of view, both Puritans and Catholics were political renegades. The theology of the Puritans tended to destroy the unity of ecclesiastical government by introducing division and democracy.[8] The Catholics were intent on the separation of church and state, or at least upon the separation of secular and ecclesiastical authority, and these latter, too, were introducing theories of vile republicanism.[9]

---

[7] Millenary Petition of 1603, G. W. Prothero, *Select Statutes and Other Constitutional Documents* . . . (Cambridge, 1894), p. 413.

[8] G. P. Gooch, *English Democratic Ideas in the Seventeenth Century* (New York: Cambridge University press, 1927), pp. 42-48.

[9] Prothero, *op. cit.*, p. xlviii. "Under monarchical government it was natural that the first assertions of anti-monarchical opinions should proceed from those

By the time Charles I ascended the throne (1625) the national distrust of the king's professed religion found a voice in Parliament. In 1625, in 1628, and in 1629 the ecclesiastical policy of the crown was subjected to a searching analysis. Both the matter (ecclesiastical government was supposedly under the prerogative) and the manner (Convocation, not Parliament, was the ecclesiastical legislative body) were calculated to irritate the haughty ruler. Dissolving Parliament, he sought with the aid of his zealous minister, William Laud, to settle religious questions in his own way. Laud, who succeeded as Archbishop of Canterbury in 1633, held political and religious views which coincided exactly with those of his king.[10] He was intellectual and liberal in religious matters, but he was a strict disciplinarian determined above all costs to translate his principles into practice. "The liberty which he claimed for men's minds, he denied to their actions." [11] He was determined to uphold the unity of the state and the uniformity of religion at all costs. He stretched the political and ecclesiastical machinery to the utmost in the prosecution of political offenders for their religious nonconformity. In the Star Chamber and before the Ecclesiastical High Commission he was adamant both as prosecutor and judge. He succeeded in arousing public resentment against both institutions, until finally the whole carefully constructed edifice including the royal prerogative tumbled about his head.

Since uniformity was the Stuart ideal and diversity was the intellectual climate, persecution was inevitable. No single faction or single person stood for complete toleration. Religion was conceded to be a state matter because you were right and the others were wrong. Being right gave you a moral and therefore a political basis for exorcising the wrong. Schism existed but was not recog-

---

upon whom the weight of persecution fell heaviest, or from such as saw the least hope of converting their rulers to their own religious views." McIlwain, *op. cit.*, p. xvii. See also *Bellarmine, De Romano Pontifice.* Lib. V, cop. i-viii (McIlwain, *op. cit.*, p. xlvii). Robert Parson, *Conference about the next succession to the Crown of England* (1594) contains the most succinct statement of the Jesuit antimonarchial doctrine.

[10] Charles was so pleased with Laud's views as expressed in the trial of Burton, Bastwick, and Prynne that he ordered the speech to be published. Gardiner, *op. cit.*, VIII, 230.

[11] *Ibid.*, III, 244.

nized.[12] Only because no party or faction could subdue, extermi-
nate, or banish the others was toleration finally achieved.[13]

The first half of the seventeenth century was an age of suspicion and mistrust, of wild rumors and fanatical tales. Neither the
king nor the people could understand each other, or for that matter
made any attempt at understanding. With the principal avenues of
communication in the hands of the crown, the arguments and information conveyed along these routes were to many persons tainted
at the source. Out of the mouths of rebellious preachers flowed the
only opposition argument or information which a large part of the
population received. Sober theological discourses, uninspiring
royal proclamations, censored political writing, and dull reviews of
foreign news could hardly vie with the fulminations of aggrieved
and self-righteous orators. Repressive controls were inadequate
and positive substitutes were ineffective. Like religious schism and
like political opposition, the circulation of falsehood and error
eventually was permitted because there was no way to stop it.
Freedom was a practical concession, not an intellectual ideal.

Parliament and Freedom of Speech

The Parliaments of the early Stuart period made startling
assertions of authority over the discussion of political affairs. In
the first place James found it impossible to confine, as his predecessor had done, the consideration of religious matters to Convocation
and himself. Having fused civil and religious authority in his own
person, he could not maintain the distinction before Parliament,
and it was on the political implications of religious questions that
the legislative body made its excursions into the realm of freedom
of speech. These excursions are for the present purpose divided
into two groups, (1) the attempts by Parliament to control and
suppress discussion by outsiders or nonmembers and (2) attempts
to maintain and extend the Parliamentary privilege of freedom of
speech by members in the face of royal and ecclesiastical opposition.

Parliament was no more willing than the crown to see its rights
and privileges infringed by reflections on its principles. The cases
of Dr. Cowell (1610), Floyd (1621), Montague (1625), and Man-

---

[12] McIlwain, *op. cit.*, pp. xvii, xxx.

[13] J. N. Figgis, *Studies of Political Thought From Gerson to Grotius* (1st
ed.; Cambridge, 1907), *passim*.

waring (1628) indicate that the legislative body was as jealous
of its privileges and opinions as a James or a Laud. The first case,
that of Dr. Cowell, professor of civil law at Cambridge University,
arose over the publication of *The Interpreter* (1607), a dictionary
of legal and political terms. Parliament as well as the common-
lawyers were offended by the definition therein of such constitutional terms as King, Parliament, Prerogative and Subsidy.[14] The
king was able to quiet the consternation created by the book by
publicly denouncing the author and calling in all copies.[15]

The case of Floyd, an aged Catholic barrister, raised problems
of grave constitutional import, and the whole affair demonstrates
the emotional tension and intellectual climate of the time. Public
interest was at this time (1621) centered on the affairs of the
Protestants in Germany where James's daughter Elizabeth and her
husband were fighting for the crown of Bohemia. Floyd was arrested and imprisoned by order of the Council for rejoicing at the
news of the battle of Prague in which the Protestant forces were
routed. Themselves prohibited from discussing the religious affairs
on the continent, the Commons pounced upon poor Floyd and
arraigned him before the bar of the House. Witnesses attested the
truth of the stories which Floyd continued to deny. Then followed
a scene the like of which has seldom been exhibited in an English
Parliament. Each member vied with the others in inventing atro-
cious punishments. It was finally ordered that the old man should
be pilloried three times, to ride from station to station on a bare-
backed horse with his face to the tail and a paper on his hat explaining the nature of his offense, and finally to pay a fine of £1,000.
The next day the Commons were amazed to find that the king had
interfered, questioning their authority to punish a nonmember for
his religious opinions. The king's position was unanswerable. Coke,
the eminent lawyer, could do no better than to argue that the words
against Elizabeth were spoken against her father, the king, and
the king is ever intended to be a resident of the House, and therefore the House had jurisdiction. The House of Lords then proceeded

[14] See *Parliamentary Debates*, 1610 (Camden Society), Vol. 81, pp. 22-25;
Holdsworth, *op. cit.*, V, 20-22, 432; several of the objectionable definitions are
given in Prothero, *op. cit.*, pp. 409-11.

[15] Proclamation 25 March 1610, Robert Steele, *Tudor and Stuart Proclamations* (Oxford, 1910), No. 1092.

to take up the matter, and to show that they had no kindly feelings for the Papists raised the fine to £5,000 and ordered the culprit to be whipped from London Bridge to Westminster Hall and then imprisoned for life. The jurisdiction of the Lords was left unquestioned, but James through the intercession of the Prince of Wales remitted the whipping.[16]

The persistent interference by the House of Commons in matters pertaining to religious doctrines is illustrated by the cases of the two divines, Richard Montague and Roger Manwaring. The former, canon of Windsor and later Bishop of Chichester, was an adherent of high church principles, and in 1625 published in support of his position a pamphlet entitled *Appello Caesarem*. The Commons immediately took offense at this attack upon the Protestant theories of church government and proceeded to appoint a committee headed by Mr. Pym to investigate the matter. Articles were drawn up against Montague, but the threat of the plague and the approaching impeachment of the Duke of Buckingham engrossed the attention of the House, and the matter was dropped.[17]

Dr. Roger Manwaring, later made bishop of St. David's, was another divine whose support of the king's position annoyed the Commons. Manwaring insisted in two sermons, which were later published, that the authority of Parliament was not necessary for the raising of aids and subsidies. The author was cited by the Commons who framed a declaration which was presented to the Lords. Neither house seemed troubled over the question of jurisdiction, but proceeded to pass judgment. Manwaring was ordered to be imprisoned at the pleasure of the House, and to pay a fine of £1,000 to the king, and he was suspended for three years from exercising the ministry and disabled forever from holding any ecclesiastical or secular office. His books were ordered to be burnt and the king was asked to issue a proclamation inhibiting the further circulation of his printed works.[18] Charles I conformed to the latter desire by issuing a proclamation 24 June 1628,[19] but he canceled whatever effect this might have had upon Protestant opinion by immediately

[16] The best statement of Floyd's case together with the authorities is found in Gardiner, *op. cit.*, IV, 119-24.

[17] 2 State Trials, p. 1258.

[18] 3 State Trials, p. 335.

[19] Steele, *op. cit.*, No. 1551.

presenting the disenfranchised Manwaring with the rectory of Stamford Rivers in Essex.

At the same time as it was attempting to suppress the public presentation of the Stuart point of view, Parliament was insisting upon its own privilege of free and unrestricted discussion of such questions as foreign policy and church government. Elizabeth had regarded such matters as properly within her prerogatives, and James was of the same mind. On 3 December 1621 the king warned the Houses of Parliament to keep off his preserves.[20] Parliament, however, was not to be put off as in the days of the Tudors and sent back a petition protesting the attempt "to abridge us of the ancient Liberty of Parliament for freedom of Speech, Jurisdiction and Just Censure of the House.[21] The king answered by asserting that whatever rights the House enjoyed were "derived from the grace and permission of our Ancestors and Us." [22]

The famous Protestation of the House of Commons was then drafted and entered on the Journal as of 18 December 1621 with unanimous consent. The instrument declared that "the arduous and urgent affairs concerning the King, State and defence of the realm, and of the Church of England, and the maintenance and making of laws, and the redress of mischiefs and grievances which daily happen within this realm, are proper subjects and matter of counsel and debate in Parliament; and that in the handling and proceeding of those businesses every member of the House of Parliament hath, and of right ought to have, freedom of speech to propound, treat, reason, and bring to conclusion the same. . . ." [23] James, at a full meeting of the Council, ordered the offending matter ripped out of the Journal,[24] but no physical act could alter the determination of the Commons to protect the kingdom from the moral and territorial extensions of Papist authority, even though such action might infringe on "matters of state." The king also appealed to public opinion by stating his position in a royal proclamation 6 January 1622.[25]

[20] John Rushworth, *Historical Collections* (London, 1701), I, 43-44.

[21] *Ibid.*, pp. 44-46.

[22] *Ibid.*, pp. 46-52.

[23] *Ibid.*, p. 53.

[24] J. R. Tanner, *Constitutional Documents of James I* (2d ed.; New York: Cambridge University press, 1930), p. 275.

[25] Steele, *op. cit.*, No. 1323.

The Parliaments of the early part of the reign of Charles I refused to relinquish the position which they had taken on the privilege of freedom of speech although in the confusion and tension which accompanied each of the sessions no single controversy between king and Commons presented the issue squarely. The proceedings in the King's Bench against Eliot, Holles and Valentine in 1629,[26] on a charge of assaulting the Speaker and making seditious speeches in Parliament illustrate how the issues were confused. The courts claimed jurisdiction over all crimes; assaulting the Speaker was a crime; speaking seditiously was a crime; therefore the members could be punished in a court of law. It was not until 1688 that the House of Lords finally untangled the issues by declaring the speaking of seditious words in Parliament not a crime.[27] Parliament in the early Stuart period was too opinionated, too obsessed with its own righteousness, too convinced of the soundness of its own positions to make a stable contribution to the doctrine of freedom of speech. It was right; the king and church were wrong. The sole contribution of the period 1603-1641 on this subject was the insistence of the right of Parliament to extend the limited sphere set for it by Tudor precedents. Of opinions contrary to its own, it was as intolerant as any Tudor or Stuart monarch.

Judicial Suppression of Political Discussion

The courts as well as Parliament were in the early seventeenth century employed as instruments for the suppression of political discussion. The legal precedents established during this period (1603-1640) form the basis for the notorious judicial persecutions of the Restoration. Controversial writers and daring speakers bore the brunt of the attacks during this early period, but the same rules of law were applied in a later age against printers and journalists. The development of the legal basis for the suppression of controversial discussion is a distinct contribution of the Stuart period. The causes of this phenomenal growth which finally came to bloom during the reign of Charles II [28] are to be found in the Stuart philosophy of government, in the inchoate state of the legal system inherited from the Tudors, and finally in the political neces-

---

[26] 3 State Trials, p. 293.

[27] *Ibid.*, p. 332.

[28] See above, pp. 121ff.

sities of an age which was witnessing the emergence of a nascent public opinion. The judicial system at the opening of the seventeenth century was ripe for reorganization. The jurisdiction of the ecclesiastical courts was being gradually circumscribed, and the supremacy of the common law was being asserted by such a genius as Edward Coke.

Where Parliament failed to legislate, the common law courts by developing the theory of judicial interpretation of medieval law attempted to fit the ancient legal system to what were conceived to be contemporary needs or even at times to make it conform to the expressed desires of persons in authority. Judicial hairsplitting, appeals to precedents (frequently of doubtful authenticity), and insistence on correct procedural forms were characteristic of the age.

The law of seditious libel is a characteristic example of the legal development which was taking place. It was in the first place an attempt to check at its source the growing power of public opinion. The old medieval and Tudor law of treason was no longer adequate. Rules of law which were developed to combat armed rebellion against the state were too cumbersome to be used to suppress the fleabites of political or religious pamphleteers. Humanity, although not particularly tolerant, was beginning to object to capital punishment for such trivial offenses. A new offense, or at least a new interpretation of an old offense, was necessary if irritating discussions of public affairs were to be stopped. To this end the Jacobean judges found at hand several medieval statutes, a body of medieval law, and a powerful judicial organism, the Star Chamber.

The legal doctrine of seditious libel as it was applied in the seventeenth century has never been satisfactorily described. Its terminology has been so various, its sources so obscure, its application so inconsistent that legal historians have contented themselves with the mere outlines of its development.[29] In spite of the investigations of a few competent scholars, the following problems remain obscure: the origins of common law jurisdiction; the origin of the

---

[29] See Frank Carr, "The English law of defamation . . .," *Law Quarterly Preview,* XVIII (1902), pp. 255, 388; Van Vechten Veeder, "The History of the Law of Defamation," *Select Essays in Anglo-American Legal History* (Boston: Little, Brown, 1909), III, 446. These studies touch on the law of seditious libel as a part of the broader subject, the law of defamation.

distinction between criminal and civil libel; the historical development of the defense of "truth"; the origins of the distinctions between slander and libel; the contribution of Statutes such as *Scandalum Magnatum*; and finally the procedural and substantive rules developed in such sixteenth- and seventeenth-century judicial bodies as the Council, the Star Chamber, the Ecclesiastical, and the local courts.

The medieval statutes, popularly referred to as *Scandalum Magnatum*, had been enacted for the purpose of suppressing rumors affecting the king and the nobility (or in other words the government). Their immediate purpose was not to give damages to defamed persons but to stop contentious discussions and aspersions which tended to disturb the peace of the realm. "From henceforth none be so hardy to tell or publish any false News or Tales, whereby discord or occasion of discord or slander may grow between the King and his People or the Great Men of the Realm." [30] To accomplish this purpose the statute provided for the imprisonment of the teller [publisher] until such time as he was willing to reveal the original inventor. The inventor [author] was punishable *without* the statute; the reporter or disseminator was punishable *under* the statute, "and he that doth so, shall be taken and kept in Prison until he hath brought him into the Court which was the first Author of the Tale." [31] Between the lines of the statute it can be seen that the medieval authorities had run into difficulties in suppressing rumors. A person apprehended for disbursing such stories could successfully defend himself by pleading that he was merely repeating what he had heard. He had invented nothing. Under the statute of 1275, he could now be forced to reveal the source of his information or go to prison.

A century later evasion of the penalties prescribed by the original statute through the interpretation of "great men of the realm" resulted in the enactment of an amendment defining the quality of peers about whom it was illegal to circulate rumors. "Prelates, Dukes, Earls, Barons, and other Nobles, and Great men of the Realm and also the Chancellor, Treasurer, Clerk of the Privy Seal,

---

[30] 3 Edw. I, (West.) c. 34 (1275); 2 Rich. II, Stat. 1, c. 5 (1378); 12 Rich. II, c. 11 (1388); 1 & 2 Phil. & Mary, c. iii (1554); 1 Eliz. c. vi (1558). 4. 3 Edw. I, c. 34.

[31] *Ibid.*

Steward of the King's house, Justices of the one Bench or of the other, and other Great Officers of the Realm" were included in the list of persons of whom it was a crime to tell tales.[32] A few years later the provisions of the statute were made still more definite by confirming the jurisdiction of the offense in the king's Council and by providing for further punishment of those offenders who continued to refuse to reveal the source of the tales.[33]

Two characteristics are apparent from the text of these statutes: (1) the matter objected to was *false* ("false news or tales") which would lead to the conclusion that the falsity of the matter would have to be both alleged and proved by the prosecutor,[34] (2) to disseminate such false matter, aside from inventing it, was a crime, but the invention was the greater offense. These two elements of the law of *Scandalum Magnatum* were obstacles to complete and successful prosecutions. Judicial interpretation, however, soon made short work of them. That truth was a defense to an action under the statutes is attested by all the early seventeenth-century authorities.[35] In 1606, however, the Star Chamber in the famous case, *de Libellis Famosis* [36] threw overboard this restriction on the operation of the medieval statutes and set out boldly into the open sea of criminal libel. Why should "Great Men of the Realm" be forced to establish the truth of the tale when the local and common-law courts were permitting prosecutions for libels on lesser men without the impediments of the medieval statutes?

The case *de Libellis Famosis* set down four propositions: (1) Libel against an ordinary person is a criminal offense, (2) libel is still a libel although the person defamed is dead, (3) the prosecution can be either at common law or before the Star Chamber, (4) truth is immaterial. A fifth was soon derived by implication. To publish libelous or seditious material was just as criminal as to invent it. This result was obtained by insisting that the "manner" of

[32] 2 Rich. II, Stat. 1, c. 5 (1378).

[33] 12 Rich. II, c. 11 (1388).

[34] See Veeder, *op. cit.*, quoting Hudson, p. 467.

[35] William Hudson, *Treatise on the Court of Star Chamber* (1633), p. 104; Crompton, *The Jurisdiction of Divers Cours Courtes de la Reigne* (1594), p. 19; Earl of Northampton's Case, 12; Edward Coke, *Fourth Institute* (1613), p. 132.

[36] 5 Coke Reports, 25a, 3 Jac. 1.

publication (by writing or printing) was the principal basis for prosecution.

Thus was the stage set for the use of this body of law by the Court of Star Chamber in the well-known prosecutions for seditious libel during the reign of Charles I.

At the opening of the seventeenth century the Court of Star Chamber had become a separate court with distinct rules of procedure. The historical development of the court is obscure, and the rules of law laid down by its judges will probably never be clearly understood since all the decrees and orders of the court have disappeared.[37] Throughout the medieval period the king's Council exercised judicial functions which were later delegated to a special committee of the Council. This committee sitting in the "starred chamber" at Westminster became by 1570 a separate court with a definite jurisdiction inherited from the Council. The court consisted in varying numbers of the members of the Privy Council, (the Chancellor, the Treasurer, the Lord Privy Seal, a bishop, and a temporal lord) and two of the king's judges.

The procedure followed by the court was of two kinds, ordinary and summary.[38] An ordinary proceeding was both civil and criminal in nature. It was begun by filing a bill of complaint by the aggrieved party signed by counsel. A writ of subpoena was issued under the Privy Seal requiring the appearance of the defendant. At a private hearing he was required to answer upon oath to articles prepared against him. If he refused to answer, he was imprisoned and thence held to have confessed. If he agreed to answer, he replied to a set of interrogatories prepared by plaintiff's counsel. Witnesses were produced and examined in private. Next, an open hearing was held at which the depositions of witnesses, complaint and answers were read to the judges. Both sides were represented by counsel. Upon these pleadings the court gave its decision.

The summary procedure of the Court of Star Chamber was based upon the ancient practice of the Council called *Ore Tenus*. This method of procedure was designed not for the protection of the innocent but for the conviction of the guilty. Acting on private

---

[37] Gladys Bradford, *Proceedings in the Court of Star Chamber* (Somerset Record Society, Vol. 27, 1911), p. 14.

[38] Tanner, *op. cit.*, p. 140.

information or on mere suspicion, the court would send a pursuivant to arrest the defendant. He was examined in private but not under oath, and if he refused to answer he was imprisoned. If he made damaging admissions, he was liable to be condemned at once (ex ora suo). The common-law rule that a person could not be forced to make incriminating admissions was not a part of the summary procedure of the Star Chamber.

The court, however, was limited in the punishments which it could inflict. It could not punish with death. Fine, imprisonment and corporal punishment (pillory, whipping, branding, mutilation) were the available remedies. These were not new punishments invented by the Stuarts but were relics of Tudor times. The subsequent unpopularity of the court was due, not to the invention of new or drastic remedies, but to the application of these remedies to political offenders with whom a large part of the public sympathized.

The jurisdiction of the court at the opening of the seventeenth century was especially concerned with breaches of the peace, breaches of proclamations, regulation of trade, and seditious libels. Whatever may be thought of the Star Chamber in the later years, during the Tudor period it performed functions which no other tribunal could discharge. It put down anarchy among the nobles, and it supplemented the defects of the already crystallized common law. It acted during the period of its ascendancy as a court of criminal equity serving the same function in relation to the Court of King's Bench that Chancery fulfilled in civil matters not cognizable before the Court of Common Pleas. Its advantages lay in its deft procedure (designed for the prosecution of the guilty), in its freedom from the restraint of common-law precedents, and above all in the exalted positions occupied by those who sat as judges.

It was perhaps fortuitous circumstances which placed such a powerful weapon and one which might have developed into an efficient arm of the law, in the hands of the arrogant and undisciplined monarch, Charles I, who proceeded to employ it for political purposes. The prosecutions against Leighton (1630) and against Bastwick, Burton, and Prynne (1637) illustrate both the law of seditious libel and the causes which led to the overthrow of the Court of the Star Chamber in 1641.

Dr. Alexander Leighton, a Scotsman, was informed against in the Court of Star Chamber [39] 4 June 1630 for writing and publishing a pamphlet entitled, *An Appeal to Parliament, or a Plea against Prelacy,* in which the clergy of the English church were declared to be "anti-Christian and satanical." The author went on to say that "the church hath her laws from the scripture, and no king may make laws in the house of God, for if they might, then the scripture might be imperfect." Leighton defended his publication by saying his intention was to call the attention of Parliament to existing grievances to the end that redress might be had "for the honour of the King, the quiet of the people, and the peace of the church."

The judges were all agreed that the book was "seditious and scandalous." The two Lord Chief Justices (of the King's Bench and Common Pleas) who sat on the court declared that if the defendant had come before them he would have been convicted of treason. Not being permitted to inflict capital punishment under the rules of procedure, the court proceeded to make the sentence as oppressive as possible. Dr. Leighton was sentenced to be degraded from the ministry, to be pilloried at Westminster and there whipped, one of his ears cut off, his nose slit, and his face branded; the whole performance to be repeated, after the prisoner recovered, at Cheapside on a market day; and finally he was to be imprisoned at his majesty's pleasure. The prisoner, however, escaped from the Fleet before the sentence could be carried out. He was apprehended and on 16 November 1630 the first part of the corporal punishment was carried out, and a week later the second part took place at Cheapside. The populace for whose benefit the punishment was staged was impressed, not with the heinousness of the offense but with the enormity of the sentence.

The proceedings against Dr. John Bastwick, Henry Burton, and William Prynne were begun by an information exhibited in the Star Chamber in 1637 by the Attorney-General charging the three men with seditious libel.[40] Bastwick (1593-1654) had participated in disputations as early as 1623 attacking the Pope's supremacy and favoring Presbyterianism. For these early errors which he

---

[39] 3 State Trials, p. 383; Rushworth, *op. cit.,* II, 55.
[40] 3 State Trials, p. 711; Rushworth, *op. cit.,* II, 380.

published in book form [41] Bastwick had been imprisoned in the Gatehouse.[42] While in prison the unrepentant physician published another book against the High Commission in which he reasserted his position on political and religious matters.[43] In 1637, abandoning Latin, he produced in English his *Letanie of Dr. John Bastwick* in which he kept no quarter with the bishops. The information in the Star Chamber was based on these last two works.

Henry Burton (1578-1648) had entered the ministry in 1618 when he was forty years old. He was extremely suspicious of the Popish tendencies of the second Stuart monarch. His sermons and letters brought him to the attention of the High Commission and he was in 1626 banished from the court. As a preacher he inveighed against episcopal practices and incumbents. For publishing *The Baiting of the Pope's Bull* (1627) he was summoned before the Privy Council, but was allowed to depart with a warning. Undaunted the preacher continued with his vituperation of the bishops in *Babel no Bethel* (1629). In two sermons which he published under the title *For God and the King* (1636) he attacked the tables turned into altars, the crucifixes set up, and the bowing toward the east with a fierce relentlessness which was certain to tell upon the popular mind. Refusing to appear before a special High Commission, the author was imprisoned and cited to appear before the Star Chamber.

William Prynne (1600-1669), the youngest of the three defendants who were prosecuted for their religious and political opinions, had a more immediate effect on the religious, social, and political life of his time than did the other two men. His attitude was one of hostility to all existing practices which did not coincide with his Puritanical ideals. He was irritated into action by what he considered the Stuart defection from the Protestant cause. He espoused the central idea of Calvinism in his first book published in 1627.[44] In succeeding works he attacked both Presbyterianism and Romanism and then went on to castigate the social foibles of

---

[41] Bastwick's early publications include *Elenchus Religionis Papisticae* (1624) and *Flagellum Pontificis* (1624).

[42] *Dictionary of National Biography*, I, 1309.

[43] *Apologeticus ad Praesules Anglicanos* (1636).

[44] *The Perpetuity of a Regenerate Man's Estate.*

the times. For condemning such "immoralities" as dancing, hunting, play-acting, and public festivals in his *Histrio-Mastix* (1632), he was haled before the Star Chamber (1633) and was sentenced to be pilloried, to lose both ears, to be disbarred from his profession, and to be fined £10,000.[45] Like his co-defendants Prynne was not to be silenced. In prison he continued his writings including an attack on prelates in an appendix to Bastwick's works and in an anonymous work assailing Dr. Wren, Bishop of Norwich. For these publications he was again cited to appear before his enemies on the Court of Star Chamber, along with Bastwick and Burton.

The judges of the court had only to read the offending publications to be convinced of the guilt of the defendants. Procedural obstructions, which were few in the Star Chamber, were easily wiped away but not without resistance from the offending authors. Instead of confessing, the defendants prepared answers which no counsel of that day was willing to sign. They argued for permission to sign their own answers, which was denied, and then proceeded to file a cross-bill charging the Archbishop of Canterbury and other prelates with "usurping upon his majesty's prerogatives." Burton's answer, which was eventually signed by an attorney, was admitted but only after the contents were stricken out as being scandalous and libelous of the court and bishops, leaving only the beginning and the end. The case against the three men was then judged *pro confesso* [46] and they were called to the bar to be sentenced. Prynne, still adamant, moved that the cross-bill be considered, but his motion was denied. He then objected to the presence on the bench of those prelates who felt themselves personally attacked in his writings. This motion was also denied. No full or official report of the decision of the judges has been preserved, but it is evident from the speech of Archbishop Laud reported by Rushworth [47] that the judges recognized a distinction at least in the gravity of the offense between spoken and printed seditious libel. The detail into which the archbishop went in pointing out the errors, inaccuracies, and misconstructions in the *News from Ipswich* (1636)

---

[45] 3 State Trials, p. 562. It was assumed by the members of the court that the attack on play-acting was directed particularly against the queen. *Ibid.*

[46] See discussion of Star Chamber procedure above, pp. 120ff.

[47] *Historical Collections*, II, 380.

supports the conclusion that truth was, in some instances at least, still a defense to an action for words in the Star Chamber.[48]

The sentence of the court was then pronounced. The defendants each were to be fined £5,000, to be degraded from their several professions, to be pilloried and to lose their ears, and to be perpetually imprisoned in different parts of the realm without access to writing materials. The execution of the sentence was the occasion for a public holiday. The authorities themselves encouraged public interest in the spectacle hoping thereby to impress the people with the seriousness of the crime and the consequent punishment. The trial itself had been a public proceeding. The episcopal clergy and secular authorities were convinced of the righteousness of their own position and were at this time unafraid of the reactions of public opinion. They were certain that their reasoned arguments would prevail over the emotional outbursts of the defendants. The acclamation which the three men received when they stepped onto the platform for their mutilation and spoke at length to the assembled crowd showed plainly that the authorities were mistaken. Instead of quieting the mob, the public punishment served only to arouse its sympathy for the three martyrs and its antagonism toward the bishops.

The publicity attending the trial and punishment of the three propagandists did, however, bring toleration and freedom of the press one step nearer. The government was not yet ready to concede defeat; it continued to attempt to bring about unity and uniformity both by repressive measures and by direct appeals to public sentiment. These methods had failed in the present instance, and an accumulation of such failures was in the end bound to impress the statesmen and ecclesiastics. Freedom to express an opinion was accepted only after all possible methods of suppression and control proved useless. As a last resort, liberty to discuss was granted not because the principle was intellectually sound but because there was no alternative. This lesson was implicit in the cases of Bastwick, Burton, and Prynne, but neither side was able at this time to grasp it.

The new learning, the Reformation, and the Counter-Reformation were having their effect. The civilized world was broken into schisms, sects, and nations, all searching for Truth and as yet unwilling to recognize the illusive character of that intellectual con-

[48] 3 State Trials, 725ff.

cept. But public discussion and inquiry, once started, would eventually convince dissenters of the impossibility of achieving unity
without force. The unity of the medieval world was still an ideal;
but the heterogeneity of the modern world was in the offing. In
the meantime the early Stuart kings continued on their way, extending their repressive measures as their efforts to convince by argument and exhortation failed.

CHAPTER 6

Printing Trade Regulation, 1603-1640

During the reigns of the first two Stuart kings, the system for regulating the press was subjected to strains and stresses which it could scarcely withstand and which ultimately under the combined pressure of religious, political, and trade interests resulted in its collapse. In 1640 Parliament was forced to create its own system of control out of the remnants of the Elizabethan and Stuart methods. Until then, however, the regulation of the press proceeded from four quarters: the crown with its Patents of Monopoly, the Stationers Company with its trade regulations, the church principally through the High Commission, and the licensing system.

The Crown and Patents of Monopoly

The Tudor monarchs, as we have pointed out,[1] consolidated their authority over the press by exercising their power to appoint an official printer with special privileges, by extending these privileges to other members of the trade, and by the creation of patents of monopoly. The appointment of a book agent to the king under Henry VII had been the first step, followed by grants of exclusive

[1] See above, pp. 30-40.

127

rights to the royal printer, and culminating in the lateral extension
of similar rights over large areas of the printing field to "respectable
stationers." The sixteenth-century privileges in books granted to
both printers and booksellers and the subsequent patents of monopoly not only served to establish control of printing in the hands
of the crown but furnished the only available protection against
piracy. The same seed produced both the Star Chamber decrees
and copyright.

The early Stuart kings proceeded to build upon the foundations
laid out by Elizabeth. To the Tudor policy of awarding patents
of monopoly in commercial fields, James I and Charles I continued
to make extensions and changes. Elizabeth had granted trade patents of monopoly for three purposes — for control in the interests
of the state, for the protection of rights of inventors, and finally
as in inexpensive and opportune method of paying off deserving
supporters without dipping into the royal treasury. The Stuarts,
while ostensibly following Elizabeth's policy, grasped at the prerogative powers as a means of raising money which a disgruntled
Parliament refused to supply. As a result the agitation against commercial monopolies which disturbed the last years of Elizabeth's reign grew in volume during the early seventeenth century.
The growth of the commercial classes and their contest with the
crown through the instrumentalities of Parliament and the common
law and the establishment of the principles of commercial freedom
(laissez-faire) could not fail to have an effect upon the printing
trade and upon the printing patents.

The Stuart grants of patents in the printing field in the early
seventeenth century fall into four classes: grants to the royal printer,
grants of reserved fields, grants to the Stationers Company, and
finally grants for individual works.

The office of king's printer was during the entire seventeenth
century the subject of numerous family and legal squabbles. Robert
Barker, who had obtained a patent for the reversion of the office
on the death of his father Christopher Barker,[2] took up his duties
early in 1600. He was reappointed by King James in 1603 and secured the reversion for his two sons, Christopher II and Robert II.
Trade and financial arrangements with John Bill and later with

[2] See above, p. 33.

Bonham Norton ultimately led to a series of lawsuits over the emolu-
ments of the office.[3] The Barker family continued to print for the
Stuart kings until the removal of the royal government to Oxford
during the civil war. Under his patent the official printer secured
exclusive rights to print all statute books, acts of Parliament, proclamations, Bibles, and New Testaments. In addition, Robert Barker
secured a patent from James for the printing of books in Latin,
Greek, and Hebrew.[4]

The second class of patents, those embracing more or less extensive sections of the printing trade, was rapidly extended under
both James I and Charles I. The more valuable grants were those
for printing and publishing grammars (variously held by John
Norton and John Willie),[5] law books (held by Wright and Norton
with reversion to John Moore), songs (Edward Alday), hymns and
songs of the church (George Wither). Charles I carried the system
further than any of his predecessors by granting exclusive rights to
print ballads, briefs, and other things printed on one side of the
paper to Thomas Symcock.[6] Even the printing of the early newspapers (corontos) was soon gathered within the fold of patent
rights.[7]

Political and commercial circumstances led to the creation
of a third class of printing patents, those granted to the Stationers
Company. This step was a logical result of the Stuart policy of controlling the various trades through their "corporate bodies."[8] The
agitation against monopolies, carried on largely by the less fortu-
nate tradesmen, was silenced at least for a time by withdrawing
grants to private individuals and turning them over to the trade
organizations ostensibly for the benefit of the poorer members of

---

[3] H. R. Plomer, "The King's Printing House under the Stuarts," *The
Library*, n.s., II, 365, traces the sequence of the royal imprints and the legal
difficulties of the patentee. See also Robert Steele, *Tudor and Stuart Proclamations* (Oxford, 1910), I, xxxv.

[4] List of patents granted by James I in Edward Arber, *Transcript . . .*
(1875), V, lvii.

[5] *Ibid.* The exact sequence of the early Stuart patents of monopoly for
the printing trade remains to be worked out.

[6] Symcock's patent is discussed below.

[7] See below, Chapter 7, pp. 156ff.

[8] W. H. Price, *The English Patents of Monopoly* (New York: Houghton
Mifflin, 1906), pp. 36-37.

the trade. However, as these trade bodies became more restricted and wealthy, fewer of the poorer tradesmen were benefited. By gradual accretion, the Stationers Company secured title to a number of valuable patents. These patents, or "stocks" as they came to be called, were leased out to prominent and wealthy members and were directly under the control of the officers of the Company. They included the English stock, the Bible stock, the Irish stock, the Latin stock, and the ballad stock.[9] The English stock alone in 1620 consisted of the following: law books (58 items), school books (32 items), ABC's and primers (5 items), psalmes and psalters in all volumes, almanacks, kalendars, prayer books (13 items) and eight general works.[10] The Bible stock was probably the most profitable, as it is recorded that eight auditors were necessary to take care of the accounts and the partners in the stock on occasion loaned money to the Company at 6 per cent. With such valuable properties concentrated in the hands of a few prominent printers and stationers, it is small wonder that the independent printer was forced to take to piracy, surreptitious and seditious printing, and finally to rebellion. On the other hand, it is also apparent why the principal printers of the day were not in the vanguard of the social and political revolution which was soon to take place.

The fourth class includes the grants of exclusive property rights in individual works. Arber lists twenty-nine such grants during the first forty years of the seventeenth century.[11] These exclusive rights, based upon sound public policy, were granted not only to printers but to authors and translators as well. Caleb Morley was given a patent "for the sole printing, selling and transporting of a book invented by him for the helpe of memory and grounding of Schollars in several languages." George Sandes secured the sole right of printing and selling his translation of fifteen books of Ovid's *Metamorphoses*. Two important contributions toward the development of a copyright law are apparent in this last group of patents, ownership of a copy outside the Stationers Company and ownership for a limited duration.

While the extension of the patents in printing during the early Stuart period was intimately connected with the general Stuart

[9] Arber, *op. cit.*, V, xlvii.
[10] *Ibid.*, III, 668-71.
[11] *Ibid.*, V, lvii-lviii.

policy toward industry and trade, the agitation against the prerogative grants and the attacks on their legality had little effect on
the printing monopolies. In fact, while the exclusive grants in other
fields of trade were being contracted, those in printing were
expanded. One of the last official acts of Queen Elizabeth was to
recall certain particularly obnoxious patents such as those for salt
and starch and to open the question of the legality of existing patents for hearings and decision by the courts of common law.[12]
Her successor, James, a few days after his arrival in London also
called in a large number of the existing monopolies, but soon afterward they began to increase again. Beginning in 1614 the House
of Commons listed the monopolies among their grievances, and
after presentation of a bill against them in 1621, the king was
moved to recall the more oppressive grants. In 1623/24 Parliament
enacted the Statute of Monopolies,[13] which placed the control of
monopolies under the courts of common law. Printing patents, however, were excepted from the purview of the statute.[14] No printing
patent was included in the general revocations of the first two
Stuart kings, and the legality of these grants was not successfully
questioned until the end of the century.[15]

Opposition to the monopolies, however, was not lacking among
the unprivileged printers. The journeymen, in particular, revived
their protests of Elizabethan days. How was an honest man to
make a living when all the profitable fields were in the hands of
a few entrenched printers? In 1614 the journeymen printers presented a petition to Parliament in which they set out their grievances. They complained that they were deprived of the right to set
up their own presses by the Decree of 1586, that the master printers
had acquired and held by patents and privileges all the valuable

---

[12] Proclamations, British Museum G6463-388. The patents of monopoly,
because they originated under the prerogative powers of the crown, were
subject only to the Council and Star Chamber courts and not to the courts
of common law.

[13] 21 Jac. I, c. 3.

[14] *Ibid.*, X. Provided also, "and be it enacted that this act or any declaration, privision, disablement, penalty, forfeiture, or other thing before mentioned shall not extend to any letters patents or grants of privilege heretofore
made or hereafter to be made of, for or concerning printing." A further exception (ix) included grants to chartered companies.

[15] See above, Chapter 12, pp. 244-49.

printing properties, and that as a result the journeymen were without means of making a living. They also complained of the restrictive trade arrangements made between printers and booksellers and against the high-handed methods employed by the wealthy printers in breaking into journeymen's homes in search of illegal printing. The petition ended by questioning the legality of the printing decrees which, it was claimed, "are contrary to the laws of God and Nations." [16]

George Wither, the poet and pamphleteer, carried on a running attack against the privileged stationers in the public prints until he was silenced, as John Wolfe had been in the preceding century, by grants of special privileges. Wither was twice imprisoned in Marshalsea for political allusions in his satires, and when the booksellers refused to print or retail his books, he turned his fire on them.[17] In 1623 the pamphleteer was granted a patent for hymns and songs of the church [18] and for a time he was quiet, but when the stationers refused either to include his hymns in their collections or to sell the song books which he had privately printed he again attacked them. In 1625 he published a scathing denunciation of both the printing patents and the organized printers. According to Wither "the Bookseller hath not onely made the Printer, the Binder and the Claspmaker a slave to him, but hath brought Authors, yea the whole Commonwealth and all the liberall Sciences into bondage." [19] Wither's grievances were that the Stationers resisted his patent, let him invest money in print, and then boycotted his books, appealed to the king against him, spread rumors that his grant was a monopoly to the oppression of the people, and clam-

---

[16] British Museum, *Harleian Manuscripts*, No. 5910, Item 136.

[17] See *Dictionary of National Biography*, XXI, 730-39. Also "Scintilla, or a Light Broken into dark Warehouses with observations upon the Monopolists of Seven severall *Patents*, and two *Charters/* Practiced and performed, By a Mistery of Some *Printers*, Sleeping *Stationers*, and Combining *Book-sellers/* Anatomised and layd open in a Breviat, in which is only a touch of their *forestalling* and *ingrossing* of books in *Pattents* and Raysing them to excessive prises," (London, 1641). This pamphlet addressed to Parliament presents a very unflattering picture of the contemporary printer and bookseller.

[18] Calendar of State Papers, Domestic, James I, 1623-25, p. 143.

[19] "Schollars Purgatory, Discouered in the Stationers Commonwealth, and Described in a Discourse Apologeticall, as vvell for the publike advantage of the Church, the State, and whole Commonwealth of England as for the remedy of priuate iniuries" (London, 1625). Copy in the Huntington Library.

ored against him at Parliament. In the reign of Charles I (1633/4) Wither made his peace with both crown and Stationers.

The system of control of the printing trade through special grants from the crown eventually brought about its own downfall. This collapse was accelerated by the case of Thomas Symcock, who was in 1618 granted exclusive rights to print all *Briefs* printed on one or both sides of a single sheet. This grant served to unite the opposition from both the master printers and the journeymen. Such an extensive grant was bound to disrupt the livelihood of a large number of the poorer printers. Dr. R. B. McKerrow character-izes this grant as "one of the most daring and merciless attempts to secure a monopoly of which the annals of the Stationers Company furnish an instance." [20] The Stationers Company joined with the journeymen in presenting a petition to the king at Greenwich in May, 1629, requesting the recall of the patent. The matter was referred to a commission consisting of the Earl of Holland, Viscount Dorchester, and the Bishop of London. A hearing was held at Whitehall, and the Commission reported to the king that it was "cleerely of the opinion that the Patent was surreptitiously procured from your Mat[ie] (upon untrue suggestions) and that the same pattent is verie dishonorable to your Mat[ie] and exceeding hurtful to the commonwealth." The commission further recommended that the patent be withdrawn but that Symcock be compensated for the printing materials which he purchased for the purpose of carry-ing out the terms of the patent. In July, 1629, the king referred the report of the commission to the Lord Keeper. By this route the mat-ter came before the Court of Chancery. For the first time a law court was allowed to consider the legality of a printing patent. The decision of the court, annulling the patent, was, however, some-what weakened as a legal precedent since the jurisdiction was ac-quired only upon the express wish of the king. The crown and not the law was still the final authority in the printing trade, but a beginning had been made in the eventual overthrow of the powers of the royal prerogative.[21]

[20] R. B. McKerrow, *Dictionary of Printers and Booksellers, 1557-1640* (London, 1910), p. 261.

[21] The papers in the Symcock case are preserved in State Papers, 4 Charles I, s66/13.

The Stationers Company

Throughout the early years of the seventeenth century, the corporate trade organization of printers and publishers continued to increase its control over both the members and the practices of the craft.[22] The motives which prompted the Company to cooperate with governmental and ecclesiastical officials in the enforcement of printing regulations are obvious. The entire structure of the organization was based on a royal grant. The principal officers were frequently the recipients of valuable patents of monopoly, continuation of which depended on obedience to the royal will. Orders to suppress from the Council were obeyed with alacrity.[23] The master printers, whose monopolistic position was closely guarded by the Ecclesiastical Commission, were eager to assist their benefactors.

Toward the end of the reign of Charles I the authority of the Company reached its highest point. By the Decree of 1637 all printing was placed in its hands.[24] Printing outside the Company was forbidden. The identification of the interests of the crown with those of the Stationers was complete.

The internal regulation of the printing trade begun in the sixteenth century continued unabated during the early Stuart period. The crown determined the number of printing houses and the number of presses; the Ecclesiastical Commission passed on the qualifications of the master printers; [25] but the Company itself controlled the number of apprentices and consequently the number of journeymen. Between 1603 and 1637, an average of thirty printers a year was admitted as freemen. After 1637 the Company was forced to follow the regulations of the Star Chamber decree limiting the number of apprentices, but the admission of freemen remained in the hands of the Company. The master printers found it profitable to employ young and unskilled labor, as a result of which the journeymen found themselves without employment and,

[22] The origin of the Company and its operation as a regulatory force in the sixteenth century are discussed below in Chapter 3.

[23] See order of the Lord Treasurer to the Company of Stationers requesting the suppression of all printed matter concerning the French king's death. Cal. St. P. Dom., James I, 1603-10, p. 609.

[24] A gratuity of £20 was given the king's attorney for safeguarding the interests of the Company in drafting the Decree of 1637. Ct. Bk. C, f. 150.

[25] See below, pp. 136ff.

forbidden to set up presses of their own, frequently resorted to secret printing as a means of gaining a livelihood. To remedy this situation each master printer was ordered to take on one unemployed journeyman.[26]

The rules for impressions and editions adopted in Elizabethan times received only desultory enforcement. The Company was chiefly engaged in protecting the rights of its prominent members. The Court of Assistants was busy administering the properties of the Company as represented in the various "stocks" and in adjusting the rights of partners in large undertakings. There seems to have been no regulation of the prices charged for printing; and Arber laments the poor quality of workmanship.[27]

Copyrights in both privileged and unprivileged printing were assiduously protected. The registers of the Stationers Company had become the record book of ownership in copies,[28] and even ballads and news-sheets were entered. In the case of the latter, entry frequently took place in advance of printing, for the sole purpose of establishing exclusive rights.[29]

The principal function of the Company in the regulation of printing was to detect and prosecute secret and seditious printers. Throughout the early seventeenth century, the Company enjoyed wide powers of search and seizure. The legal bases of these powers were the charter granted by Mary and confirmed by Elizabeth, the royal proclamations of both Elizabeth and James, and the Star Chamber decrees of 1586 and 1637.[30] Most of the excursions against illegal printers were carried on by deputies of the Company without warrants, but on occasion the Council would issue a special warrant.[31] Just how energetic the searchers were, we have no way of knowing, but we may be sure that any printer infringing the rights held by the officers of the Company was promptly detected. Not so successful were the attempts to stamp out seditious or Puritanical literature.

[26] Decree of 1637 (20). Decree reprinted in Arber, *op. cit.*, IV, 529-36.

[27] *Ibid.*, p. 26.

[28] The sixteenth-century origins of copyrights are discussed below in Chapter 3, pp. 71ff.

[29] Arber, *op. cit.*, III, 293, 303.

[30] See below, Chapter 3. For proclamation of James reaffirming the powers see Steele, *op. cit.*, No. 1362 (1623); No. 1383 (1624).

[31] Cal. St. P. Dom. James I, 1623-25, p. 141.

Having detected and apprehended the unfortunate printer the Stationers would proceed to the prosecution. If the culprit was a member of the Company, he was tried before the Court of Assistants. The common sentence was the destruction or confiscation of printing materials.[32] A typical entry in the records of the court is the following: "This day [9 April 1632] a presse being erected in Shoredich by John Ham [m] on contrary to the decree in Star-Chamber was defaced and made unserviceable the ninth day of this month following in ye presence of the wardens & divers of the assistant. Likewise one presse taken in the Minorie supposed to be William Harris being unlawfully erected, was also defaced & made unserviceable in the presence as aforesaid."[33]

If the person engaged in illegal printing was not a member of the Company, the case was turned over to the Ecclesiastical Commission. None of the orders or decrees of this court has survived, but a scattering of preliminary pleadings is found among the State Papers. The penalty imposed by the commission was total disbarment from printing, fine and confiscation.[34]

The Company was able to render a creditable account of its stewardship during the reigns of the first two Stuarts. Few secret presses existed in London. The products of the recognized presses were relatively pure in content if poor in quality. Piracy was practiced but was always under fire. No well-equipped or responsible printer defied the regulations, except, perhaps, Nicholas Bourne, the news-publisher. The principal points of leakage were the border and the ports. Over the first the Company had little control; and over the latter they exercised whatever authority they possessed with indifference except in the case of importation of works which infringed the patents of monopoly.

Ecclesiastical Control of Printing

The failure of the Church of Rome to control the importation of Reformation literature in the early years of the reign of Henry VIII was due largely to the inefficacy of "censure" and "excommunication" as punishments.[35] Elizabeth, after the Marian inter-

---

[32] Ct. Bk. C, ff. 69, 79.

[33] Ct. Bk. C, f. 119b.

[34] The powers of the High Commission are discussed below, pp. 138ff.

[35] See above, Chapter 2, pp. 41-47.

lude, had revived the judicial powers of ecclesiastical officers, adding the authority to fine and imprison [36] in addition to excommunicate. Armed with such weapons, churchmen were well equipped and frequently were eager to maintain the established doctrines of both church and state. Their authority progressed easily from the suppression of heretics and heretical writings to the control of what was called under the Tudor theory of church-and-state "seditious opinions," and culminated in the reign of the first two Stuarts in the complete regulation of *all* printing.

The administrative and judicial functions involved in controlling the press were spread over the ecclesiastical hierarchy. At the head was the Archbishop of Canterbury, who aside from the power to appoint lesser officials, frequently intervened directly in the affairs of the printing trade. The crown limited the number of printing establishments, but the archbishop retained the power to name the master printers to vacancies. In 1615 there were nineteen printing houses exclusive of the king's printers; [37] in 1634 the number of master printers had increased to twenty-three; [38] and in 1636 there were again nineteen printing establishments operated by twenty-one master printers.[39] The petition of John Dawson to the archbishop for the place as master printer vacated by the death of his uncle, Thomas Dawson, is preserved in the State Papers.[40]

This power to appoint the master printers was an especially powerful weapon in the hands of the archbishop. Since the enjoyment of their occupation depended upon his will, the master printers were alert to carry out his wishes. These wishes took three forms, orders to suppress, orders to print, and requests for special services. The archbishop occasionally ordered a licensed work withdrawn from circulation and canceled from the Stationers' registers.[41] He also initiated the printing of works upholding the arch-episcopal

[36] 1 Eliz. c. 1. Edward Coke, the common-lawyer, contended that neither this statute nor the commissions issued under it were a sufficient warrant for the penalties of fine and imprisonment but the fact remains that for almost 100 years such penalties were imposed. *Fourth Institute* (1644), Chapter 4.

[37] Arber, *op. cit.*, III, 699.

[38] *Ibid.*, p. 701.

[39] *Ibid.*, p. 704.

[40] Dom. James I, 1621, Vol. 119, Art. 29, f. 39.

[41] Prynne's *Histrio-Mastix* was thus withdrawn. Arber, *op. cit.*, IV, 241.

government under a "speciall commandment," [42] and he was not
above extracting contributions for the repair of St. Paul's cathed-
ral in return for favors granted.[43] The archbishop's ire was aroused
by the mistakes made by the printer in the 1631 edition of the
Bible. In 20 *Exodus* a line read: "Thou shalt commit adultery";
and in 20 *Deut.* "the Lord hath shewed us his glory and his great
asse." The primate exploded, "I knew the tyme when great care
was had about printeing, the Bibles especiallie, good compositors
and the best correctors were gotten being grave and learned men,
the paper and letter rare and faire every way of the best; but now
the paper is nought, the composers boyes, and the correctors un-
learned: There is a farmer [assignee] and he makes the benefitt,
and careth for nothing about it. They heertofore spent their whole
time in printeing, but these look to gaine, gaine, gaine. . . ." [44]

The lesser clergy from the bishops down took an active interest in protecting the purity of the reading matter. The Bishop
of London in particular, besides serving on the Ecclesiastical Commissions, superintended the search for unlawful printing in vessels
docking at the port of London. The episcopal chaplains and the
doctors of civil law bore the burden of the detailed work involved
in regulating the press. They acted as licensers, detectives, searchers, and prosecutors. At Archbishop Laud's request, Sir John Lambe
assumed direction of these lesser officials, and under propulsion
from above he whipped these servants of church and state into
the most efficient regulatory organization of the early Stuart period.
He was a worthy predecessor of both Hunscott and Sir Roger
L'Estrange.

The principal instrumentality of the church in the control of
printing was the Court [or Courts] of High Commission which
evolved from the re-establishment of Protestant ecclesiastical jurisdiction under Henry VIII and Elizabeth.[45] By 1570 the High Commission had developed into a regular court entertaining cases in-

---

[42] *Ibid.*, III, 306.

[43] Cal. St. P. Dom., Charles I, 1629-31, p. 379.

[44] Cases in Courts of Star Chamber and High Commission, Camden Society,
p. 304. London, 1884.

[45] See R. G. Usher, *The Rise and Fall of the High Commission* (Oxford,
1913).

volving matters of matrimony, church attendance, church practices, nonconformity and libel.[46] The distinctive feature of its procedure was the oath of "ex officio" whereby the prisoner was required to answer questions which the court put to him. If he refused to answer, he was imprisoned for contempt, and if he took the oath, he could be convicted on his own confession. Facts thus elicited were used as the basis for "articles" against him. The accused was then required to plead to the articles without the advantage of knowing their contents, and the whole proceeding was conducted in secret for the reason, as advanced by the clergy, that it was "too demoralizing to society to see such an exhibition of crime." [47]

It was only natural that the ecclesiastical courts should progress by easy stages from jurisdiction over the religious opinions of the clergy and laity to complete control over the products of the printing press. By 1611 this progress was completed. In the commission of that year issued by James I as head of the English church, authority over the press was given to the ecclesiastical judges:

VI. And also we . . . do give full . . . authority unto you or any three or more of you, . . . to enquire and search for . . . all heretical, schismatical and seditious books, libels, and writings, *and all other books, pamphlets and portraitures offensive to the state or set forth without sufficient and lawful authority in that behalf,* and all makers, devisers, printers and wilful dispersers of any such . . . books [etc] and their procurers, a counsellors and abettors; and the same books [etc] and their printing-presses themselves likewise to seize *and so to order and dispose of them . . . as they may not after serve or be employed for any such unlawful use, restoring nevertheless the materials in such case as they may not afterwards be so abused or otherwise the value of them to the owners thereof: and also all persons which shall offend against any decree heretofore made by the high court of Star-Chamber . . . or hereafter to be made touching the reformation of divers disorders in the printing and uttering of books.*[48]

Printers were brought before the Commission for the publication of Puritan or Catholic literature, for aspersions cast upon the clergy, for seditious words against the state, for violations of the

---

[46] The jurisdiction of the ecclesiastical courts over libel is discussed below.

[47] For the procedure before the High Commission, see W. H. Hale, *A Series of Precedents and Proceedings . . . from Ecclesiastical Courts* (1847), p. lx.

[48] Pat. Roll, 9 Jac. I, Part 18. Italicized portions were added in the Commission of 1613. *Ibid.,* II, Jac. I, Part 15.

licensing system, and for general "disorders" in printing. It is impossible to present the complete history of any single case before the High Commission during the early Stuart period as the decrees and orders have all disappeared. Occasional examinations and articles are, however, preserved among the State papers for the period,[49] and from this source the following examples are drawn.

No printer of the early Stuart period troubled the authorities more than Michael Sparke. He succeeded in becoming involved either as printer or publisher with almost every piece of "seditious" printing of the time. In 1629 articles were drawn up by the High Commission charging Sparke, along with Nathaniel Butter, William Jones, and Augustine Matthews (all printers) with publishing four works [50] without license.[51] In his answer [52] to the charges, Sparke, who was already in prison, shocked the court by questioning the binding authority of the Star Chamber decree for regulating printing as "directly intrenching on the hereditary liberty of the subject's persons and goods and being contrary to Magna Charta, the Petition of Right, and other statutes." Sparke, the lowly printer, raised his voice against the combined authority of the crown, the Church, and the corporate printers. In his answer he laid firm foundation for the freedom of the press theories propounded by his more famous compatriot, John Milton, a decade later. In spite of his plea the printer was kept in prison, but for how long we do not know.

Two years later Sparke was again cited before the High Commission,[53] this time as a bookseller for dispersing a number of "obnoxious" works printed by William Turner at Oxford. It is stated in the articles that "Sparke although within ten years past eleven times committed to prison and admonished and although he promised to submit to his governors as other moderate men do, has yet been more refractory and offensive than ever; that he also seized and detained . . . a messenger of the chamber charged to

---

[49] See Cal. St. P. Dom. Charles I, 1628-29, pp. 364, 513-14, 539; 1629-31, pp. 159, 202, 203-4; 1635-36, p. 468.

[50] The books were *Babel no Bethel*, by Henry Burton; *The Antithesis of the Church of England*, by William Prynne; *The Reconciler*, and *Musquil Unmasked*, by Thomas Spencer.

[51] Cal. St. P. Dom. Charles I, 1628-29, p. 525.

[52] *Ibid.*, p. 538.

[53] Cal. St. P. Dom. Charles I, 1631-33, p. 3.

seize [the books] and attach Sparke." The prisoner again attempted
to justify his actions by questioning the legality of the proceedings and by insisting on the rights of an Englishman to be free
from search without a legal warrant. Again he was kept in prison.
Later in the same year he was again cited for assisting in publishing a scandalous book entitled *Rome's Ruin*.[54] No record of this
prosecution seems to have been preserved. The next year Sparke
was the center of extended proceedings both before the High Commission and the Council over the publication of Prynne's *Histrio-
Mastix*[55] No man of his time waged such persistent warfare against
the regulation of the press.

The Licensing System Under the Early Stuarts

The licensing of printed matter in the early seventeenth century
followed the outlines laid down in the Star Chamber Decree of
1586.[56] The successful operation of the Elizabethan system was
based on a delicate balance of crown, ecclesiastical, and trade organization authority. Founded on the king's prerogative powers,
administered by the archbishop and his subordinates, and operated
with the assistance of the Stationers Company, the licensing system
continued as the basic printing regulation during the early Stuart
period. That this method of controlling the press was not as successful under James and Charles as it had been under Elizabeth was
due not to innovations introduced by the Stuarts but to a failure to
adjust the system to those changes which were taking place in the
social, economic, and religious life of the people. Under Elizabeth,
the crown, in spite of its arbitrary character, had represented the
political ideals of the nation; the clergy was in conformity with
general religious opinion; and the Stationers Company was a cohesive organization of master printers, journeymen, and apprentices.
Under the Stuarts, the crown failed either to represent or to direct
general political opinion; the clergy was insulated against the prevailing religious climate; and the Stationers Company had become
an autocratic oligarchy principally engaged in pursuing the pecuniary advantage of its officers. It is not surprising therefore to find

[54] *Ibid.*, p. 231.

[55] See Preface to Cal. St. P. Dom. Charles I, 1631-33, p. xx; 1633-34, pp.
135-36.

[56] See above, pp. 61ff.

the licensing system more stringently administered and at the same time less effective as the century wore on. In 1610 James by royal proclamation [57] orated against the "itching in the tongues and pennes of most men, as nothing is unsearched to the bottome . . . . from the very highest mysteries in the Godhead, and the most inscrutable Councels in the Trinitie, to the very lowest pit of Hell. . . ." He promised the appointment of a number of commissioners to investigate "what shall be put to the Presse, either concerning our Authoritie Royall, or concerning our government or the Lawes of our Kingdome." [58] Again in 1623 [59] following the political and religious disturbances accompanying the opening of the Thirty Years War the king ordered the observance of the regulations set out in the Star Chamber Decree of 1586. But the printers of "seditious" books were not deterred. Another proclamation restating the licensing provisions followed in 1624.[60]

The Star Chamber Decree of 1637,[61] the most complete and detailed regulation of the early seventeenth century, was designed to stop the abuses and evasions which had crept into the operation of the licensing system. All books and pamphlets, including "title, epistle, proem, preamble, introduction, table and dedication" must be licensed. Specific licensers for particular classes of books were appointed.[62]

Evasions and alleged misunderstandings were checkmated by requiring two manuscript copies of every work submitted for licensing, by insisting on the appearance of the name of the author, printer, and licenser on the printed work, and by requiring a new license for all reprints. All printers were required to make a deposit of "£300 as surety not to print anything not licensed." These regulations had been in operation only a few years when the Long Parliament took over the control of printing in 1640.[63]

[57] B.M. 506. h 12 (71). Steele, *op. cit.*, No. 1092.

[58] No commissioners seem to have been appointed at this time. Three ecclesiastical commissioners were named to oversee the press in 1634. Arber, *op. cit.*, III, 15.

[59] Steele, *op. cit.*, No. 1362.

[60] *Ibid.*, No. 1383.

[61] Reprinted in Arber, *op. cit.*, IV, 529-36.

[62] These are discussed below.

[63] See below, Chapter 9.

The administration of the licensing system continued under the joint supervision of the ecclesiastical authorities and the Stationers Company with occasional interference by a state official. The Stationers employed and supported the licensing provisions as guaranties of their property rights in registered works. The clerical licensers carried the brunt of the detailed work involved in reading and certifying acceptable manuscripts. For those printed works issued under a royal patent, no license was necessary. The patent itself was sufficient allowance, and the fear of losing his monopoly usually kept the privileged printer from venturing on forbidden ground.

The operation of the system as it applied to unprivileged printing during this period can be followed in the registers of the Stationers Company. Before anything could be printed, it must have been approved both by an agent of the Stationers Company (usually a warden) and by an official or approved licenser.[64] Ordinarily, medical books were licensed by a recognized medical authority; plays by the Master of Revels; Heraldic books by the Earl Marshall; law books (when registered) by a judicial officer; works on politics or history by one of the secretaries of state; and finally religious and all other works by ecclesiastical officers. In this last group the practice was to refer controversial works to licensers of higher rank. Ordinary works were regularly licensed by chaplains, episcopal secretaries, or doctors of divinity appointed to the task. Questionable writings were frequently handled by members of the Ecclesiastical High Commission, and more suspicious works were on occasion referred to the Archbishop of Canterbury or the Bishop of London. Archbishop Laud relieved himself of responsibility by turning the matter over to three special commissioners, Sir John Lambe, dean of the Arches, Sir Nathaniel Brent, and Doctor Duck.[65]

The vagaries and inconsistencies of the licensing system are most apparent in its operation. As the gap between the politico-religious opinions of the licensers and of the nation widened, evasions became more numerous. These in turn were followed by a more stringent application of the regulations. One of the principal

[64] For a time, 1603-37, ballads were entered with the approval of the warden alone, but after 1637 an official license was required for them also.

[65] Arber, *op. cit.*, III, 15. See entries in Registers for period 1603-40.

methods of avoiding the licensing requirement was to issue the forbidden matter not as a book but as a single sheet. No effort seems
to have been made until 1632 to require licenses for such ephemeral and insignificant publications. News-sheets, ballads, and
almanacks were thus published without licensing.[66]

Another popular method was to obtain a license for the book
proper and then to insert the questionable matter in a dedication
or introduction. This evasion was remedied in the Decree of 1637
by prohibiting the insertion of introductory matter which was not
licensed along with the main body of the book. There is evidence
that certain publishers were not above forging a license to get the
permission of the Stationers Company to print. The Company's
regulation of 1631 and the Decree of 1637 sought to avoid forgeries
by requiring the printer to print the licenser's name and imprimatur
in the printed copy.[67] The requirement that two written copies be
submitted to the official licenser was designed to offset the possibility of changes introduced by the printer after official allowance.
The licensed copy was returned to the printer; the duplicate was
kept by the licenser for future comparison. Another method used
by publishers was to insert objectionable matter in a reprint of an
already licensed work. The Decree of 1637 prohibited all reprints
without new licenses. A common method of avoiding liability was
to shift the responsibility for obtaining the license from the author,
to the printer, to the publisher. The author would insist it was the
printer's duty; the printer would excuse himself on the ground that
he had been informed by the author that the work had been properly licensed; while the publisher would plead ignorance of what
had been done either by the author or the printer.[68]

As the number of works submitted for licensing increased, the
burden imposed by the regulations on the official licensers became
almost insupportable. Detailed revision of the manuscript was frequently undertaken. For instance the official licenser of *The general*

[66] Ballads continued to be published without license until the Decree of
1637. The Stationers Company ordered all almanacks to be licensed in 1634.
(Court Book C, f. 129) The licensing of newsbooks is discussed below in
Chapter 7.

[67] Ct. Book C, f. 117. Item 4, Star Chamber Decree, 1637.

[68] See answer of Henry Burton, author, before the Ecclesiastical Commission in which he insisted that it was the printer's duty to obtain the license.
St. P. Dom. Charles I, 1628-29, p. 364.

history of Spayne in thirty books insisted on a revision of every page of the manuscript and on an allowance by him of all such revisons.[69]

The examiner continually ran the risk of making a mistake or of overlooking an obnoxious passage. Boccaccio's *De Cameron* was licensed under the hand of Master Auernor and later recalled by the Archbishop of Canterbury.[70] An official licenser also passed upon Prynne's *Histrio-Mastix*, much to the confusion of the crown and the episcopal primate.[71]

The licenses for news-sheets were occasionally withdrawn,[72] and Nathaniel Butter, when questioned before the Ecclesiastical Commission for publishing a work for which a license had been refused, introduced the opinions of two bishops to show that the licenser had made a mistake.[73]

The official licensers frequently found themselves in hot water in their attempts to censure the controversial writings on ecclesiastical matters. For instance, the Bishop of London was embarrassed before the Court of Star Chamber in the trial of Dr. Manwaring [74] when it was pointed out in defense of the doctor that his book had been licensed by the bishop himself.[75] To extricate himself the bishop was obliged to call upon Laud, then Bishop of Bath and Wells, who admitted he had at the express command of the king written the Bishop of London asking him to license Manwaring's work.[76]

---

[69] Arber, *op. cit.*, III, 395. See also revisions required by the Master of the Revels. *Ibid.*, IV, 270 (26 January 1631/32).

[70] *Ibid.*, III, 677 (22 March 1619/20).

[71] *Ibid.*, IV, 241 (16 October 1630). William Buckner, chaplain and official licenser, who passed upon Prynne's book was proceeded against in the Star Chamber along with the author and the printer. Evidence introduced in that proceeding showed that Prynne had submitted the work to two previous licensers (Dr. Goade and Dr. Harris) who refused to sanction the work. 3 State Trials, p. 568. Buckner testified in his defense that he had passed upon only 64 pages and that the author and printer had proceeded to put on the entire work on the basis of the preliminary license. He was fined £ 50 for his negligence in failing to follow up the licensing and printing.

[72] Arber, *op. cit.*, IV, 222 (13 November 1629).

[73] Cal. St. P. Dom. Charles I, 1628-29, p. 539. A charge that official licenses were inconsistent is listed in *Ibid.*, p. 472.

[74] See above, Chapter 5, p. 114.

[75] 3 State Trials, p. 353.

[76] *Ibid.*, p. 356.

For his refusal to license Dr. Sibthorp's sermon, *Apostolical Obedience,* in which the authority of the king to impose taxes without the consent of Parliament was asserted, Archbishop Abbot was sequestered from his office, and a commission was granted to a group of bishops to act in his place. The book was then licensed by the Bishop of London.[77] Thus, bishop was frequently set against bishop, with neither party willing to license publication presenting the opposing point of view.

The judicial interpretations of the licensing regulations for the early Stuart period are found in the records of the Court of High Commission and in the minutes of the Court of Assistants of the Stationers Company. Ordinary infractions by printers and publishers were adjudicated before the Company's court; more serious cases were called before the Commission.[78]

W. Aldee, printer, was called before the Court of Assistants, 8 October 1621 and charged with imprinting books "without license or entrance (in the registers)." The judgment of the court was that "he shall not be warned [notified] to attend any more as a liverie man, untill he shall submitt himself to this table [court]." [79]

The court records support the conclusion that very few respectable printers were charged with violation of the licensing provisions. There was too much to lose and very little to gain. The publishers did not object to the theory of licensing but merely to its application in particular cases and by particular individuals.

[77] 2 State Trials, p. 1450; John Rushworth, *Historical Collections* (London, 1701), I, 422.

[78] Very few of the records of the Ecclesiastical Commission have survived. See below, pp. 138ff.

[79] Ct. Bk. C, f. 70.

Regulation of Corontos

Origin and Growth of Corontos

The first quarter of the seventeenth century witnessed a phenomenal growth in the English people's interest in public affairs both domestic and foreign. The rise of England as a maritime power and the establishment of colonial possessions extended her horizons. The accumulation of wealth by trade instead of from the land had created a powerful commercial class which insisted in its own interest upon sharing the burdens of government with the king and the landed aristocracy. The House of Commons and the Courts of Common Law provided the battleground for the contest of this group for political power. Religion, too, as we have seen, was a matter of primary importance to a large part of the population. The nonconformists especially insisted upon publicly discussing questions which the Tudors had presumed to settle a hundred years before. The taverns as well as the churches resounded with the moral fervor of religious argument.

In periods of conflict, news is of transcendent importance. Here were political, social, and religious interests engaged in a terrific struggle which eventually broke out into a rebellion. The participants were hungry for information. What moves had been made by Parliament? What successes had been achieved by the Puritans? What concessions had been made by the king? What new restric-

tions on trade were contemplated? The established means of communication were unable to satisfy the demand. News ballads had
existed from the sixteenth century, but poetry, no matter how bad,
was too restricted a medium for the presentation of such a burning
question as the rights of members of Parliament. Prose pamphlets
were better, as the Marprelate writers proved, but what the public
wanted now was information as well as argument. Besides, the
pamphlets were issued without regularity and with long sterile
intervals. There were, of course, the newsletter writers, or intelli-
gencers as they were called, like John Chamberlain, John Pory,
William Locke, and the two Reverends, Larkin and Mead. They were
the first English reporters and correspondents. To the persons for-
tunate enough to be able to pay for and secure their services, they
rendered a satisfactory account of the events of the day. But the
circulation of these newsletters was limited. A more disinterested,
regular, and widespread medium was demanded. The time was
ripe for the appearance of the first English news-sheet or coronto.

In 1620 the attention of the people of England was attracted to
the events taking place in Germany. The popular Princess Elizabeth
of England had in 1613 married Frederick, Elector of the Palatinate,
a Protestant prince much in favor with the nonconformists. His
decision to accept the Crown of Bohemia in the face of the opposition of the Holy Roman Emperor had precipitated the Thirty Years
War. What was happening in Germany? What would King James
do to assist his daughter and her German husband? The English
people looked out from their insular position with eager eyes at
darkening clouds over Europe. What was happening?

The enterprising Dutch printers were quick to capitalize on
their opportunities. They were situated midway between the source
of information and the market for it. Soon, news-sheets in English
printed in Amsterdam found their way into the British market.
Nathaniel Butter, a bookseller of not too eminent a standing, provided one of the London outlets. The first of these Dutch corontos
must have been imported late in 1620.[1] The only known surviving
Dutch corontos in English are dated 2 December 1620—18 Septem-

---

[1] Chamberlain to Carlton (February 16, 1622) "for since two yeares that
the forge or mint was set up at Amsterdam we have never left coyning, so
apish are we in imitation of what is worse." R. F. Williams, *Court and Times
of James I* (London: Henry Colburn, 1849), 2 vols.

ber 1621.[2] The success of these publications must have been immediate for we find the Intelligencer, Joseph Mead, writing (30 June 1621) that he was unable to get a copy.[3]

The less prosperous among the English printers were alarmed. The Dutch were taking the bread from their mouths. Why should not they themselves print the English corontos and gather in the pennies? Why should the Amsterdam printers be allowed to sell their wares under the very noses of the London workmen? Thomas Archer was probably the printer and Nathaniel Butter the publisher of the first English-printed newsbook which appeared on the streets of London sometime during the summer of 1621. These early corontos were probably pirated Dutch copies, reprinted in London.[4]

The business of selling news-sheets must have proved profitable with the entire population anxious for news of the German affairs. In the meantime James was pursuing what to him was a diplomatic course. He refused to be stampeded into sending armed forces to assist his son-in-law in acquiring a crown. The English king was too much the philosopher not to be disturbed over the consequences of supporting a claim based solely on the will of the people in the face of the "legal and rightful" owner of the title. The divine right of kings was too much a part of his thinking to be cast lightly aside even in the interests of his own flesh and blood. The king

---

[2] The collection was acquired by the British Museum in 1913. A bibliographical description of these items is found in the *Times Handlist* under the year 1620-21. Photostatic reprints of eighteen of the Dutch corontos in English were published by P. Jon Stockum, Jr., at the Hague (1914) on the occasion of the International Exhibition of Graphic Art, Leipzig, 1914. The most complete bibliographic description of the corontos is to be found in a "Short-Title Catalogue of English Corontos and Newsbooks, 1620-1642," by Folke Dahl, *The Library*, 4th Series, XIX (1938), 44-98.

[3] Mead to Stuteville, *Court and Times of James I*, II, 263. The best discussion of the early corontos is found in (J. B. Williams) J. G. Muddiman, *A History of English Journalism to the Founding of the Gazette* (London: Longmans, Green, 1908), Chapter II. The exact sequence of these early publications as well as the relations between Butter, Bourne, and Archer remains to be discovered.

[4] Six copies of the English corontos of 1621 are known to have survived. They are listed in M. A. Shaaber, *Some Forerunners of the Newspaper in England, 1476-1622* (Philadelphia: Univ. of Penn. press, 1929). Chamberlain to Carlton (August 4, 1621) refers to the fact that both Dutch and domestic corontos were in circulation. *Court and Times of James I*, II, 272. See also Folke Dahl's short title list, above Note 2.

delayed, vacillated, and played for time. He hoped to avert the war through diplomatic negotiations with the emperor.

But the people of England were of another mind. Even a king should not desert his only daughter. The Protestants and non-conformists insisted on intervention on the side of Frederick. Even the commercial classes favored a war which would bring back prosperity. The Dutch and then the English corontos tended to feed this appetite for participation in the Thirty Years War.[5]

Once James had made up his mind to suppress the corontos he found several implements at hand. Through the English ambassador to the Netherlands James persuaded the States General of Holland to forbid the printing and exportation of corontos to England. The Dutch printers were warned by proclamation not to "send the same [books and pamphlets in various languages] to other countries and realms and particularly not to send some twelve scandalous writings and pamphlets concerning other kings and potentates, friends, and allies, touching their political or ecclesiastical governments, and especially also none against the king of Great Britain and his principal ministers, spiritual and temporal.[6]

James next proceeded against the domestic product by reissuing, on 21 July 1621, a proclamation[7] which had first appeared the previous December, at which time it had been directed against the "great liberty of discourse concerning matters of State." The same order was revived to suppress the corontos. "No man," said James, was "to think himself free from punishment because there are so many offenders." Such threats seem to have had little effect for we find the newsletter writer, Chamberlain, commenting on the proclamation "which the common people know not how to understand, nor how far matters of state may stretch or extend, for they continue to take no notice of it, but print every week, at least, corrantos, with all manner of news, and as strange stuff as any we have from Amsterdam."[8]

---

[5] The Amsterdam Gazette of this period supported the Catholic party in Germany, but very little news from this source was used by Dutch printers of English corontos. These latter for the most part supported the Protestant Frederick.

[6] Groot Placet Boeck (1658), I, 409 and 441, quoted in Times Handlist, p. 9.

[7] B.M. 506. h. 12 (88).

[8] Chamberlain to Carlton, August 4, 1621. Court and Times of James I, II, 272.

The entire subject of news publication must have been discussed before the king's Council, for the Stationers Company soon received a request from the secretary of state, Calvert, to imprison the printer, Thomas Archer. The immediate charge was the publication of a news-sheet on the war in the Palatinate without license. In vain did the news publisher plead that it was not the practice to submit news ballads or news-sheets for licensing and registration. He was ordered to be kept in prison and "the barres of his presses . . . taken downe." [9]

There now enters upon the scene the second printer of corontos, the eminent and respectable Nicholas Bourne, a master printer and a capable business man. Soon after Archer's imprisonment he, together with Nathaniel Butter, must have appeared before the Council requesting permission to print newsbooks, provided always that the subject matter be properly licensed and acceptable to the Council board. No record of this petition is preserved, nor is any mention of it made in the Council registers. Some arrangement must have been made granting Bourne and his associates the right to print corontos and for the appointment of Francis Cottington, clerk of the Council, to read and authorize the publication of each issue.[10]

Thus within a short space of time all the devices of the crown for the control of printing were employed in regulating the first newspapers—royal proclamations, prosecution by the Council, the licensing system, the machinery of the Stationers Company, and finally the power of the crown to grant privileges of monopoly.

Bourne and Butter, Publishers of News

The first corontos "published with authority" appeared sometime late in 1621. No early copies have survived, nor do the registers of the Stationers Company reveal any entries prior to 18 May 1622. In spite of this evidence it would seem that Nicholas Bourne and his associates began to issue translations of foreign newsbooks

---

[9] Court Book C, f. 69b. 13 August 1621.

[10] Mead to Stuteville (22 September 1621) writes "My corrantor, Archer, was laid by the heels, for making, or adding to his corrantos, as they say. But now there is another that hath got license to print them, and sell them, honestly translated out of the Dutch." *Court and Times of James I*, II, 276, 277.

soon after the receipt of their grant (September, 1621).[11] Not all the corontos subsequently issued by Bourne were entered in the Stationers' Register, so that there is no reason to suppose he entered his first productions. Since his grant came from the crown, he was not required under Company rules to enter his publications except as additional protection against piracy. The earliest surviving coronto is dated 23 May 1622, entered in the Stationers' Register May 22, and its contents dated May 21. Thomas Archer, now out of prison, probably did the printing; Nathaniel Butter was evidently the editor and circulation manager, while Bourne himself was the publisher.[12]

From 1621 to 1632 Bourne and Butter enjoyed their monopolistic position in the field of news publication, but their reign was not without its trials. One of the devices employed by both Elizabethan and Jacobean printers for their pecuniary advantage was the "blocking entry" whereby the printer who first entered a current news subject under his name on the Stationers' Register thereby stated a claim and established his prior rights to any and all publications describing the event. Examples of this tactic are to be found in the registers of the Stationers Company under the dates of the most important events such as the death of Queen Elizabeth (1603),[13] the death of Prince Henry (1612),[14] and the marriage of Princess Elizabeth (1613).[15] Nathaniel Newberry, an enterprising publisher, had the foresight to enter for his copy "The Edict of the King of France." [16] Bourne and Butter in one of their corontos presumed to print the contents of the decree of the French king for which they were ordered to appear before the Court of Assistants of the Stationers Company where they were fined and ordered to pay damages to Newberry.[17] It seems probable that the news publishers decided

---

[11] Court Book C, f. 69b. 13 August 1621.

[12] The Burney collection of early newspapers in the British Museum contains a number of corontos for 1622.

[13] Edward Arber, *Transcript* . . . (1875), III, 230.

[14] *Ibid.*, p. 501.

[15] *Ibid.*, p. 515. See also G. B. Harrison, in The Library, 4th Series, XIV (1933), 6.

[16] Copy in the Burney collection dated 4 November 1622.

[17] Court Book C, f. 75b (February 3, 1622/3). Thomas Archer *(Mercurius Britannicus)* published occasional newsbooks, but whether on his own account

that in order to avoid further troubles of this nature they would enter the corontos on the register of the Stationers Company.

The licensing of newsbooks was undertaken by Sir Francis Cottington, clerk of the Council, for the period of 1621-1624. Before this Sir George Calvert, principal secretary to his majesty, licensed the occasional pamphlet of news content.[18] Francis, Lord Cottington (1578-1652), was a distinguished English diplomat. His experiences as an agent in Spain (1609-1611) and travels on the continent made him acquainted with European politics and therefore competent to censor corontos which purported to discuss continental affairs. In October, 1622, Sir Francis was made secretary to the Prince of Wales, but this appointment did not interfere with his duties as licenser. The first newsbook licensed by Cottington as registered in the books of the Stationers Company is "a relation of News from Poland," 23 October 1621.[19] The first "Currant of generall newes" by Bourne and Archer, 18 May 1622, which is listed in the registers is stated to have been licensed by the clerk of the Council.[20] All subsequent issues of the privileged corontos are licensed by the same hand until September, 1624, when the name of Dr. Worall appears.[21] Cottington seems to have filled the position of licenser of news in a satisfactory manner at least from the point of view of the king. He permitted the publishers, Bourne and Butter, to print only foreign news, probably in conformance with the agreement made between the printers and the Council. He successfully suppressed all controversial discussion of the war in the Palatinate, and on the few occasions when he permitted the publication of domestic news (11 November 1623), he escaped censure.[22] Dr. Worall, already an experienced censor, took over the duties in September, 1624. He was followed in this office by Master Wackerlyne in 1627.[23] Occasional unlicensed newsbooks, however, continued to

---

or in conjunction with Butter and Bourne is not known. See items in Burney collection for 1625.

[18] See Arber, *op. cit.*, IV, 52 (5 April 1621), for license by Calvert for the publication of an oration by the Polonian ambassador.

[19] *Ibid.*, p. 60.

[20] *Ibid.*, p. 68.

[21] *Ibid.*, p. 128.

[22] *Ibid.*, p. 107.

[23] *Ibid.*, pp. 122, 182.

appear. William Phillips, a hack writer, was in 1623 committed to
the Gate House by the secretary of state for translating a small
French pamphlet for Newberry, the stationer.[24] The wardens of
the Stationers Company, under color of a warrant from Secretary
Calvert, nailed up the printing house and broke down the presses
of William Stansby for printing a tract, *A demonstration of the Unlawful Succession of the New Emperor,* for Nathaniel Butter, the
bookseller.[25]

The domestic printing of newsbooks was well under control,
but the importation of foreign corontos continued to trouble the
authorities. Late in 1621 the mayor of Dover seized a consignment
of these books found in the possession of a Frenchman who had
just landed.[26] Pursuivants were sent out into the streets of London
to buy all the copies of two issues of the *Mercurius Gallo-Belgicus*
printed in Germany which it was contended "contained foul and
untrue matter concerning our sovereign's speech to the lords about
his purpose in sending the prince into Spain, as also of approving
the Romish religion." [27]

To curtail the circulation of continental newsbooks James
issued a royal proclamation (25 September 1623),[28] calling attention to the existing decrees [29] "the true intent and meaning of which
. . . hath been cautelously abused and eluded by Printing in parts
beyond the Sea, and elsewhere, as well as sundry seditious, schismaticall, and scandalous Bookes and Pamphlets . . . and by importing the same unto this our Realme." The king ordered the
existing laws against importing foreign printing put into speedy
execution and charged the wardens of the Stationers Company as
well as the "justices of the peace, Mayors, Sheriffes, Bayliffes, Constables, and Head-Boroughes, and all Customers, Comptrollers,
Searchers, Wayters, and all other Our officers, Ministers, and Subjects whatsoeur, as they tender our fauour, and will auoyd Our

---

[24] Calendar of State Papers, Domestic, James I, 1623-25, p. 141.

[25] *Ibid.*

[26] Cal. St. P. Dom. James I, 1619-23, p. 324.

[27] Letter to Joseph Mead, 24 October 1623, *Court and Times of James I,*
II, 421.

[28] B.M. 506 h. 12 (109). Robert Steele, *Tudor and Stuart Proclamations*
(Oxford, 1910), No. 1362.

[29] Star Chamber Decree of 1586. See above, pp. 61ff.

indignation and displeasure, from time to time, to their uttermost powers, to see this Our Royal pleasure duely executed. . . ."

All was not smooth sailing for the authorized publishers of corontos, Bourne and Butter. The latter, particularly, was frequently in difficulties as the result of his efforts to supplement his income outside his arrangement with his partner Bourne. On 22 October 1624 he was haled before the Court of Assistants of the Stationers Company and fined for "printing a corontos contrary to order."[30] Irritated by what he considered an unwarranted interference with his private business, the printer must have used strong language before the court, for on December 24 he was again fined, this time for "unfitting speeches." [31] His activities as a bookseller finally brought him before the Court of High Commission where he was accused of associating with the notorious printer, Michael Sparke, in the publication of controversial pamphlets without license, including *Babel no Bethel* by Henry Burton and *The Antithesis of the Church of England* by William Prynne.[32] In his defense the astute publisher introduced the opinions of two bishops to the effect that the matter complained of was not objectionable.[33] The judgment of the court in the case has not been preserved.

The "responsible" publisher of corontos, Nicholas Bourne, also found himself summoned before the Ecclesiastical Commission in 1630 for selling controversial pamphlets. He admitted selling thirty copies but stoutly disclaimed all knowledge of the authors, printers, or purchasers.[34] Several others, including Sparke and James Bowler who were similarly accused, followed the journalistic precedent set by Bourne and refused to disclose either the author or the purchasers of the leaflets.

The ax finally fell on both Bourne and Butter. Whether their activities as publishers of controversial pamphlets on domestic affairs or their failure to follow the suggestions of the official licenser in their weekly corontos on foreign affairs was the cause of their downfall is not known. On 17 October 1632 the king's Council consisting of the Lord Keeper, the Lord Privy Seal, the Earl Mar-

[30] Court Book C, f. 83b.

[31] *Ibid.*, f. 84b.

[32] Cal. St. P. Dom. James I, 1628-29, p. 525.

[33] *Ibid.*, p. 539.

[34] Cal. St. P. Dom. James I, 1629-31, p. 202.

shall, the Earl of Kelley, Lord Wimbledon, the Lord Bishop of London, Lord Cottington, and Mr. Serjeant Windebank issued the following order:

> Upon consideration (had at the Board) of the great abuses in the printing and publishing of the ordinary Gazetts and Pamphletts of Newes from forraing parts: And upon signification of His Maieties express pleasure and comand, to the Board for the present suppressing the same. It was thought fitt and hereby ordered that all printing and publishing of the same be accordingly suppressed and inhibited and that as well Nathaniell Butter and Nicholas Bourne Booksellers under whose name the said Gazetts have been usually published, as all other Booksellers Printers and Stationers, presume not from henceforth to print publish or sell any of the said Pamphlets as they will answere the contrary at their peril. And Mr. Secretary Windebank is likewise prayed to send for the said Butter and Bourne and to lay a strict command upon them on that behalfe.[35]

The reason for the suppression as given by Butter was that the news from the continent was so unfavorable that "the lords would not have it known." [36] The last entry of a coronto by Bourne and Butter before the order of suppression was received is dated 27 July 1632,[37] but the last surviving coronto is dated 12 October 1632.[38] By exercising his prerogative powers, Charles I was thus able to suppress all newsbooks.

Patents for Foreign News, 1632-1640

The years immediately preceding the civil war were troublous times for Charles and his supporters. The more stringent the regulations against printing and public discussion, the more the purveyors of news were forced underground. The church and its minions were of little help in searching out offenders since the main body of the clergy had completely alienated itself from the populace. Even the Stationers Company by virtue of its commercial interests tended to sympathize with the London merchants and tradesmen who were making a stand in Parliament against the

[35] P.R.O., St. P. Dom. Charles I, 1632, pp. 224/33. Erroneously called Star Chamber Decree in *Times Handlist*, p. 19.

[36] Pory to Luce, November 1, 1632. R. F. Williams, *Court and Times of Charles I* (London, 1848), II, 188.

[37] Arber, *op. cit.*, IV, 282.

[38] Folke Dahl, *op. cit.*, p. 79, No. 267.

encroachments of the crown. The period was one of unrest, confusion, and dissatisfaction. Interest in foreign affairs gave way to a
more immediate interest in domestic happenings. The German religious wars could hardly vie in importance with the possibilities of
new and increased taxation at home.

No sooner had Charles and his Council prohibited the publication of corontos than the enterprising printers discovered a loophole
in the orders. No mention had been made of ballads. The streets
of London were immediately flooded with news ballads touching by
indirection or by metaphor the current events of the day.[39] In spite
of Charles the people were demanding news, and the printers were
willing to furnish it as long as they could supply it and at the same
time save their necks.

Encouraged by the failure of the crown and Council to suppress the publication of news, Butter and Bourne on 30 September
1633 petitioned the king for a revival of their former privilege of
publishing translations of foreign corontos. In the meantime they
translated several Antwerp corontos to show the Council "how they
lie upon us and our friends, and we in the meantime must be
muzzled and our mouths stopped." [40]

The petitioners humbly requested upon their promise "of being
carefull in time to come that nothing dishonorable to Princes in
amitie with your Matie shall pass the presse" that they be permitted to resume publication of their newsbooks.[41] The king referred
the petition to his secretary of state with the notation that "if they
find that the printing and publishing of the Gazettes and Weekly
Newes may be permitted again without inconvenience, that then
their Hon[es] may settle it in some fitting course, and give order
therein as is humbly desired."[42]

The two printers soon discovered that it was more difficult to
deal with the secretary than with Charles himself. How much were
the petitioners willing to pay for the approval of their petition for
the exclusive printing of foreign news? Surely such a monopoly
was worth something. To determine the market price the secretary
asked for bids. John Locke, the intelligencer who found his market

[39] See amazing entry of ballads in 1632, Arber, *op. cit.*, IV, 297.
[40] Pory to Luce, November 1, 1632. *Court and Times of Charles I*, II, 188.
[41] P.R.O., St. P. Dom., Charles I, 1633, pp. 246/92.
[42] *Ibid.*

pre-empted by the publishers of corontos, was one of the bidders. There is an undated paper preserved in the Public Record Office in the handwriting of Locke pointing out the advantages accruing to the crown from the supervised publication of news.[43]

Walter Wardner and George Moore, two entrepreneurs, made another offer with the evident idea of farming out the patent. They carefully suggested that "whereas Gentlemen of England desirous of news doe ordinarily furnish themselves with the Gazettes, such as strangers and careless persons doe provide them, whereby not onlie diverse untruths, but rumors also prejudiciall to the designs of your Ma[ties]s happy gouvernement are dispersed through the kingdom" it would be in the king's interest "to command that noe such Gazettes bee hereafter sent abroad [published] before they bee viewed and reformed by some person of understanding that shalbe thought fittest by youre Ma[tie] for that purpose." Furthermore by granting the petitioners the exclusive right to print corontos for twenty-one years the king would have at hand an outlet for "such reports as upon occasion may tend to the good of your Ma[ties] service." [44] Suppression and propaganda were the baits held out by the two gentlemen to the king; something more tangible was in all probability offered to the secretary of state.[45]

---

[43] Cal. St. P. Dom. James I, 1619-23, p. 330. Where the document is mistakenly attributed to Sir Thomas Wilson. Locke, in his petition, gave the following as reasons for granting his request:

(i) To settle a way that when there shall be any revolt or backsliding in matter of religion or obedience (which commonly grows among the vulgar) to draw them in by the same lines that drew them out, by spreading amongst them such reports as may best make for that matter to which we would have them drawn.

(ii) To establish a speedy and ready way whereby to disperse into the veins of the whole body of a State such matter as may best temper it, and be most agreeable to the disposition of the Head and the principal members upon all occasions that shall be offered.

(iii) To devise means to raise the spirits of the people and to quicken their conceits and understanding by giving them tastes of matters clear from the common mire of worldliness. It makes such apt to be drawn from the cold sodish humour of sloth (and) extends the sense by degrees to the conceit of the right rules of reason, whereby they are wrought easily to obey those which by these rules shall command them.

[44] Summary given in Cal. St. P. Dom. James I, 1619-23, p. 330.

[45] The petition of Wardner and Moore was almost successful. Charles gave his approval and ordered a warrant prepared for his signature. The warrant was never signed. See P.R.O., St. P. Dom. 1634, pp. 280/73 and 74.

The news publishers, Bourne and Butter, were thus brought face to face with contemporary governmental methods of raising money. They must pay, and pay handsomely, for the privilege of publishing news. Bourne began his rounds borrowing where he could. The registers of the Stationers Company for April, 1636, reveal the fact that he mortgaged a number of his copyrights to his printer colleagues.[46]

At length on 20 December 1638 the privilege of printing corontos was granted to Butter and Bourne.

A warrant under the Signett whereby his Matie giveth power to Nathaniel Butter and Nicholas Bourne Stationers and to their assignes for the imprintinge and publishing all matter of history of Newes of any forraine place or kingdome frome the first beginning of the late German Warres to this present. And also for the translating, setting forth, imprinting and publishing in the English tongue all Newes, Novells, Gazettes, Currantos or Occurrences that concerne forraine parts for the terme of XXI years. They paying yearly during the said terme towards the repayre of St. Pauls church London the sum of 10 £.[47]

The new patent carried with it all the protections which were included in the recently announced Star Chamber Decree for the regulation of printing (11 July 1637).[48] The news publishers were guarded against competition from foreign importations (Items 1, 5, 6, 7). Like other patentees, they were supported by the state law-enforcing officers in suppressing all domestic printers who presumed to print newsbooks in violation of their patent. Item 3 of the Decree appointed the principal secretaries of state or their appointees as licensers for "all bookes of history, belonging to this State, and present times, or any other Book of State affaires" which included newsbooks.

The publishers lost no time, as is indicated by the first coronto issued under the new patent and entered on the Stationers' registers under the date 19 December 1638. The address to the reader in this first issue stated that "this intelligencer, the Curranto, having been long silenced, and now permitted to speak again, presents you here at the first with such things as passed some months since,

---

[46] Arber, *op. cit.*, IV, 360. See also, *Ibid.*, p. 330.

[47] Docquet, Charles I, 1637-38. December 20, 1638. (St. P. 38/17).

[48] See Chapter 6, p. 142. The decree is set out in full in Arber, *op. cit.*, IV, 528-36.

not because we conceive that they are absolutely Novel to you, but
first because there is Fraud in generalities, we thought fitt to ac-
quaint you with each particular; and secondly, that by these ante-
cedents, you may then better understand the Consequents, which
wee shall now publish weekly as heretofore."

Difficulties with the licensers continued to harass the publishers. Succeeding numbers appeared at irregular intervals. The
licensers were both dilatory and erratic. No regular publication date
could be maintained in the face of officials who sometimes from
sheer negligence and other times from perversity failed to certify
the copy. In the last issue of the newsbooks published by the partners which is preserved in the British Museum, Butter unleashes
his disgust:

> The Printer to the Reader: We had thought to have given over print-
> ing our foreign avisoes, for that the licenser (out of apartiall affection)
> would not oftentimes let pass apparent truth, and in other things (often-
> times) so crosse and alter, which made us almost weary of printing,
> but he being vanished, (and that office falled upon another, more under-
> standing in this Forraine Affairs, and as you will find more candid.)
> We are againe (by favour of his Majestie and the State) resolved to go
> on printing, if we shall finde the World to give a better acceptation of
> them, (than of late) by their Weekly buying them. It is weel known
> these Novels are well esteemed in all parts of the World, (but heere,)
> by the more judicious, which we can impute to no other but the dis-
> continuance of them, and the uncertaine days of publishing them,
> which, if the posts fail us not, we shall keepe a constant day every weeke
> therein, whereby every man may constantly expect them, and so we take
> leave January the 9th, 1640.[49]

The underwriters of the privilege must have been disappointed
with the reception which greeted the revival of newsbooks on foreign affairs. Continental news was no longer of such pressing importance as it had been in 1622. The affairs in Germany had settled
down for a long siege. On the other hand, events at home were
absorbing the interest of the public. Ship money, subsidies, Papism,
and Presbyterianism were discussed on every side. The country was
working itself into a state of civil war. The occasional pamphlet of
domestic news which was allowed to appear was soon sold out; the
heavy and censored productions of the firm of Butter and Bourne

---

[49] Burney collection (British Museum). Butter evidently attempted to
continue the series by himself after 1640 but after a sporadic issue, dropped
the series 10 December 1642. Folke Dahl, *op. cit.*, p. 91.

lay on their hands. With the opening of Long Parliament in November, 1640, the widespread discontent came to a head. England waited breathlessly for news from Westminster. The corontos of foreign news died a natural death; the "diurnals" of Parliamentary proceedings were about to be born.

During the reigns of James I and Charles I the right of the crown to control the publication of news was firmly established. On the other hand, the practical difficulties of even such a potent authority as the king to put his recognized powers into execution were apparent. The licensing system was impractical and inefficient; the Stationers Company, avid in its pursuit of pecuniary advantage, could not be trusted; the ecclesiastical officers were in the prevailing state of public opinion a handicap rather than an assistance. If news was suppressed, rumor took its place. Only "official" news could counteract the rumors, but who could be trusted to guide this hydra-headed monster, public opinion? The question perplexed the Stuart statesmen of the early seventeenth century as it was to perplex the leaders of the Commonwealth.

PART 3

Control of the Press
DURING THE PURITAN REVOLUTION

1640-1660

CHAPTER 8

Chaos in the Printing Trade

On 3 November 1640 the Parliament, afterwards known as the Long Parliament, held its opening session at Westminster. For the ensuing twenty years the government of England was to fluctuate between anarchy and dictatorship, experimenting with and discarding various popular and democratic forms and culminating in 1660 with the restoration of a modified monarchy. During these twenty years the press of England was subjected to varying types and degrees of control ranging from almost complete freedom under the early years of the Long Parliament to the strict regulation under the Council of State. It was a period of experimentation in both politics and journalism. Governments set up by popular opinion sought vainly for a formula by which that same popular opinion might be regimented for the self-perpetuation of the officials in power. The results were largely negative. In fact, the period of the Interregnum demonstrated to the intelligent scientists of government that none of the historical methods for the control of the press and public opinion could be depended upon to work successfully over any extended period of time.

Revolt Against the Stationers Company

The most effective single agency for the regulation of the press under the Tudors had been the Stationers Company, the corporate and monopolistic body of printers.[1] Resting directly upon the royal prerogative and subject immediately to royal command, the official printing craft organization had been the most successful enforcement agency of the sixteenth- and early seventeenth-century governments. At the opening of the Long Parliament, however, the Stationers Company as an agency of control was being undermined both from without and from within.

Parliament's first step was to question and then to curtail the prerogative powers of the crown. As the center of authority shifted from the crown to Parliament, the position of those agencies based upon the prerogative became precarious. The officials of the Stationers Company owed their positions to the king, but as the power of the crown weakened, they readily shifted their allegiance to Parliament. Such a shift, however, could not be made without confusion and without weakening the power and authority of the Company. For three years, 1640-1643, while the adjustment was taking place, the printing organization was without a rudder.

The Star Chamber, the royal enforcement agency, was abolished 5 July 1641,[2] followed by the destruction of the Court of High Commission.[3] The printing craft was freed from its royal master, but was being subjected to the control of both Houses of Parliament and its various committees. The shift was naturally accompanied by confusion and chaos. With the controls of the king, Council, Star Chamber, and High Commission abolished or curtailed, the printers of the realm found themselves for the first time free to print what they pleased. By the time Parliament had settled down to the business of governing the country, it found the printers loath to give up their recently developed revenues, and the Company found it increasingly difficult to revive its controls over member printers.

Another source of confusion to the printers was the division or conflict of authority between various units of Parliamentary government. The House of Commons and its committees, the House of Lords and its committees, the courts of common law, and finally the religious groups all sought to impose their wishes on the Stationers Company. Conflicting orders were issued; printers arrested by a committee of the Commons were freed by order of the

---

[1] See above, Chapter 3.
[2] 17 Car. 1, cap. 10.
[3] 17 Car. 1, cap. 11.

Lords; and occasionally jurisdiction was disputed between two committees of the same house. Master and journeymen printers, depending upon their craft for a living, threw up their hands in despair and proceeded to print what pleased or profited them regardless of orders from the government or the property rights of their fellow craftsmen.

Another cause for the breakdown of the authority of the Stationers Company was the internal conflict between the officers and the monopolists on one side and the journeymen printers and apprentices on the other. The crown had traded valuable monopolistic grants in return for the assistance of the officers of the Company in suppressing obnoxious printing. These grants had been protected by the king through the Star Chamber and the High Commission. With the fall of the king and the abolition of the two judicial agencies, the privileged position of the officers of the Company and of the wealthy printers became exceedingly vulnerable. Occasional outbreaks of opposition from the unprivileged printers had occurred during the early seventeenth century, but the combined efforts of the crown and the officials of the Company had been able to cope with these.

By 1640 the internal affairs of the Stationers Company had been concentrated in the hands of a group of wealthy stationers. The master and wardens, instead of being elected by the membership at large as provided in the charter, were chosen annually by the Court of Assistants. This court, or "Table" as it was called, consisted of a self-perpetuating group of monopolists in the printing trade. They controlled the funds of the Company; they participated in the publication of the various stocks to the exclusion of other printers; and by the system of patents and monopolies managed to get control of most of the valuable printing properties. The journeymen and apprentices after securing their freedom found themselves unable to make an honest living. Either they must work for the monopolists at a starving wage or they must engage in surreptitious printing of forbidden or patented works.

With the overthrow of the royal authority the unprivileged printers hastened to Parliament with their grievances. A memorial of these grievances is preserved in a tract entitled *Scintilla, or A Light broken into darke Warehouses. With Observations upon the Monopolists of Seaven severall Patents, and Two Charters Practised and performed, By a Mistery of some Printers, Sleeping Stationers, and combining Book-sellers. Anatomised and layd open in a Breviat, in which is only a touch of their forestalling and ingrossing of Books in Pattents, and Raysing them to excessive prises.*[4] The memorial was addressed to Parliament, but that body was too busy with the king and church to take up the matter.

The dissatisfied radical elements in the Company continued, however, to embarrass the reigning officials in the Court of Assistants. On 28 June 1645 there appeared on the streets of London an anonymous paper in which the journeymen posed a number of questions concerning the financial status of the Company:

What the English Stock is worth in value, which was fourteen thousand pounds at least?

What the Latine Stock is now worth, It was at first seven thousand pound, the addition to it of four thousand pound?

What the Irish stock is worth, which was three thousand pound?

What the Grammar produced: three hundred pound we paid towards it.

What became of the money we gave to defend us in the Latinestock Shute [i.e. suit]?

What is become of the Livery Fine?

What is become of the Renter-Wardens Fines?

What is become of Master John Nortons gift?

What is become of Master Standeshes gift?

What is become of Master George Bishops gift?

What is become of all the Pole-money and what left?

What is become of Master John Adams his gift?

What has become of the corn-money?

What has become of the 75. pound of M.B.

Whether the suspicion of corruption was justified, we have no way of knowing at present.[5]

The controversy over the powers of the Court of Assistants and the rights of the journeymen and apprentices stirred the Com-

---

[4] The author was undoubtedly George Wither. The tract appeared in September, 1641. It is reprinted in Edward Arber, *Transcript . . .* (1875), IV, 35-36.

[5] According to Mr. Charles Robert Rivington's notes on the history of the Stationers Company read at a meeting of the London and Middlesex Archaeological Society 12 December 1881, all the plate of the Company was sold in August, 1643, to repay a loan from Mr. Miller. The original loan had been used to meet the Company's proportion of the forced loans which Charles I had levied in the absence of a Parliamentary grant.

pany to its foundations. The proposal by the committee of the House of Commons to grant to eleven stationers an exclusive right to print Bibles brought the matter to a head. The excluded stationers and printers immediately petitioned the Commons to withdraw the grant and to issue it in favor of the entire Company.[6]

The complaints which reached the ears of Parliament became so loud and frequent that the Committee on Examinations was forced to call in the master and wardens who were ordered to call a meeting ("common hall") of the entire membership of the Company. The leaders of the dissatisfied group including Master Featherstone, Master Sparkes, Master Thompson, Master Partridge, and Master Underhill appeared with their grievances. At a second meeting on 1 April 1645, a committee of twelve men of the Company was chosen to adjust the ordinances and settle the question of the powers of the court. Denied access to the account books, the committee reported that the entire Court of Assistants should be asked to resign and a new election held. The original investigating committee was then enlarged by five members from the official group, and the haggling over the number of and nomination of new assistants began. In the meantime the printing of the Bible was begun with the approval of the committee with the understanding that all members of the Company would be given an opportunity to participate in the venture. After several months of squabbling, the master and wardens refused to call a common hall. The committee then on its own responsibility issued a call,[7] in spite of an appeal by the entrenched officials to the mayor to stop the proceedings. In the face of this opposition the meeting was held on June 23. The conservative elements must have marshalled their forces for their 224 adherents out of a total membership of about 500 were able to rout the reformers. Robert Mead was re-elected master and John Parker and George Miller named new wardens. The Court of Assistants retained the right to elect its own members, and the printing of the Bible went forward under the original subscribers. The leaders of the unsuccessful reform group were called before the common council of the city of London for censure.[8]

[6] British Museum E. 669 f. 6.

[7] B.M. E. 288 (44).

[8] Arber reprints a number of the documents describing the controversy, *op. cit.*, II, 583ff. The following note appears in the city council minutes

Piracy and Counterfeiting

One of the immediate effects of the curtailment of the king's prerogative powers by the Long Parliament was confusion followed by discord in the ranks of the printing monopolists. The legality of the original grants by the crown was questioned, and the unprivileged printers, long excluded from the rich pastures where wealthy printers and stationers had fattened, hastened without legal formality to transform the reserved areas into common feeding grounds.

On 22 March 1641 the question of the printing patents was brought to the attention of the House of Commons by means of a petition from Thomas Cowper and eight others for the reversion of the patent in Bibles. Cowper had proceeded to print Bibles without authority from the Stationers who, upon discovery of his piracy, had proceeded to seize and sequester all his stock. He appealed to Parliament, claiming that "through the printers desire for gain, and to the great prejudice of the Commonwealth, they had raised the prices of bibles to double what they could very well afford for." [9]

The workmen printers of London, attracted by the clamor between rival stationers claiming the Bible patents, entered the fray with the petition of their own addressed to Parliament which they printed and distributed throughout London. The workmen complained of their subjection to the patentees; they protested the control of the affairs of the Company by a few wealthy stationers, and requested the cancellation of all printing patents heretofore granted to stationers and booksellers who were not printers. Among these

(Repertory 57 part 2, fol. 146b) "Item, This day upon the humble petition of the Master Wardens and assistants of the Company of Stacioners London therby intymatinge That certaine persons members of their societie Doe endeavor (to the greate disturbance of the said company) in undue manner to possesse the Cominalltie of their said Company That the choyce of master and wardens and removeinge of the present assistants is solely in their power And to that purpose have complotted for a Common hall to bringe their designe to passe and that master ffetherstone master Sparkes master Tompson Master Partridge and Master Underhill are Actors of the said innovacon. This courte takinge not only to the distracon and confusion upon the said Company But upon the good and peacable government of all other Companies Doth order that the said parties be cummoned to appeare before this Courte on Tewesday next (1 July 1645) to answer the contempt of said petiocioners."

[9] Cal. St. P. Dom., 1640/1, p. 508.

were the patent for Bibles originally granted to Christopher Barker, the patent for law books first granted to Richard Tottle and lately confirmed to John More, the patent for Latin, Greek, and Hebrew Bibles held by Roger Norton, and the patent of Thomas Symcock for printing of all things on one side of a sheet.[10]

The petition concluded:

We beseech your Honours to consider, that none of the aforesaid Patentees were at all acquainted with the Mystery of Printing, or ever served any time to any Printer: yet have they and their assigns, hitherto enjoyed their said Patents (being the sole livelihood of Printing) to the great prejudice of us the said artists, and the whole state in generall; for if it may stand in your Honours good liking, to make void these Patents, the Commonwealth shall be farre better served with these and all other Bookes, they shall be better Printed, and on better paper, and yet shall be sold one shilling in foure shillings cheaper than they are now and every Workman in the said Art shall have a competent livelihood, to maintain them, which were are not now as yet able to have, by reason of the aforesaid Patents.

Complaints of authors whose works were being issued promiscuously by printers must have reached the ears of the committee on printing for the House of Commons on 29 January 1641/2 ordered that printers refrain from printing anything "without the name and consent of the author." This is one of earliest recognitions of the rights of authors by the English Parliament.[11]

Further hearings were held by a committee of the Commons on the position of the printing monopolists,[12] but no action was taken. The office of king's printer was vacated and in its place the Commons and Lords each appointed an official printer.[13] A new

[10] B.M. 669 f. 4 (79); Robert Steele, *Tudor and Stuart Proclamations* (Oxford, 1910), No. 2026.

[11] Commons Journal, II, 402 (January 29, 1641/2); B.M. E. 207 (2).

[12] Commons Journal, III, 123 (10 June 1643).

[13] The king's printers printed for the Parliament, but as war became imminent the printing was given to J. Hunscott, later by the Clerk of the House of Lords to J. Wright, by the Clerk of the Commons to Husband and Franck, and as regards Oxford printing by the king to Leonard Lichfield, printer to the University. In 1649, Scobell, Clerk of Parliament, handed the printing to Cotes, and afterwards to Husband. In 1650, Husband and Field are the official printers, Field being the actual printer. T. Newcomb's name appears in 1653, while W. Du-Gard was Cromwell's printer, and H. Hills, for Hills, Calvert, and Brewster, was printer to the Council of State. Hills is "printer to the Lord Protector" on 21 December 1653, sharing the office with Du-Gard, and later

edition of the Bible with notes to conform with Puritan standards had been ordered by the House of Commons, and upon the announcement of its completion the Company of Stationers petitioned the House for the patent for the benefit of the entire membership.[14]

By 1643 the old monopolists and master printers had become desperate. Parliament had granted no redress. Journeymen were opening printing shops of their own. The old Star Chamber decrees regulating the number of apprentices and printing establishments were disregarded. Property in copies was nonexistent; piracy and counterfeiting were rampant; and entries in the Stationers' Register had dwindled.

In April of 1643 there appeared a pamphlet [15] setting forth the grievances of the stationers and requesting a complete reorganization of the control of printing. The pamphlet, attributed to Henry Parker, pointed out the inability of the Stationers Company to control printers who were nonmembers and then proceeded to set out reasons for continuing property rights in copies. The author avoided using the word "monopoly" in his discourse. The several requests of the Stationers were: (1) power to regulate number of apprentices, (2) authority to regulate number of printing establishments, and (3) authority to preserve property rights in printed matter.

Parker agreed that unless some right in copies was recognized the art of printing would decay. "As the case now stands," he insisted, "Stationers are so farre from having any encouragement to make them active and alacrious in the service of the State, that they cannot serve it without discouragement; and they are abridged of their ancient Right, Propriety in Copies being now almost taken away and counfounded; if one Stationer preferre any Complaint against another, the Complainant shall be sure to have his Copy re-printed out of spite, and so the ruine of himself and family, is

---

with Field, February, 1665. J. Field becomes printer alone on the fall of Richard Cromwell. J. Streator appears 12 October 1659 as "Printer to Parliament," Hills and Field 31 October as "Printers to the Committee of Safety," Hills as "Printer to the Army," 22 December, Streator and Macocke as Printers to Parliament, A. Roper and T. Collins as Printers to the council of State, 17 March 1660, Husband and Newcomb as printers to the Commons, Macocke and Tyton as Printers to the Lords, on the Restoration and finally, Christopher Barker and John Bill are reinstated as king's printers by 30 May 1660.

[14] B.M. 669 f. 6 (107); Steele, *op. cit.*, No. 2360 (January, 1643).

[15] *Remonstrance of the Stationers*, B.M. E. 247.

made the reward of his zeal and forwardness." To offset the charge
of monopoly, Parker pointed out that the ownership of certain valuable properties was requested for the entire membership of the
company and not for individual printers. The rebuttal on this point
(that in the past the common property of the Company had been
monopolized by the officials) was not mentioned in Parker's discourse.

Finally the ordinance on printing upon which a committee
of both houses had been working for some time was passed 14 June
1643. In answer to the Stationers' complaints, it decreed that "no
person or persons shall hereafter print, or cause to be reprinted any
Book or Books, or part of Book or Books heretofore allowed of and
granted to the said Company of Stationers for their relief and maintenance of their poor, without the license of the Master, Wardens
and Assistants of the said Company; nor any Book or Books lawfully
licensed and entred in the Register of the said Company for any
particular member thereof, without the license and consent of the
Owner or Owners thereof." [16]

Its general rights recognized, the Stationers Company continued to petition Parliament for the special privileges formerly enjoyed by royal patentees, particularly the printing of Bibles and of
law books.[17] Piracy and counterfeiting continued in spite of the
Ordinance and the efforts of the searching parties organized by
the Company.

Enforcement by the Stationers Company

The period between the fall of the Star Chamber and the enactment of the printing ordinance of 1643 was, as has been pointed out,
a period of confusion and discord among the printers of London.
With the keystone of the enforcement structure destroyed, the entire
edifice collapsed. Insurgent printers, long suppressed by Star Chamber and High Commission, openly published partisan attacks on
both king and Parliament. Political and religious controversialists
suddenly found the press open to them. The unprivileged printers,
who had chafed since the days of Elizabeth under the restrictions
of the monopolists, took immediate advantage of the destruction of

---

[16] C. H. Firth and R. S. Rait, *Acts and Ordinances of the Interregnum,*
1642-1660 (London, 1911), I, 184.

[17] See *Diary or Exact Journal* for 26 August 1644.

enforcement agencies. Piracy and counterfeiting were openly practiced. Patents were infringed on all sides, and whenever a printer
issued a work which proved profitable he was sure to see the market
flooded with reprints.

Under these conditions neither the Stationers Company nor
Parliament was in a position to restore "order." The Company was
torn by internal bickering, and both the Lords and Commons had
before them at the moment the more urgent problem of the conflict
with the king and an imminent civil war. The freedom which the
press enjoyed during this short period was due to the failure of
enforcement agencies and to the pressure of other issues rather
than to any belief on the part of the Parliamentarians that the press
should be free. In fact, Parliament turned its attention to the regulation of the press at the earliest possible moment.

Both Houses of Parliament upon assuming the sovereign powers of the crown turned to the Stationers Company for assistance
in controlling the press. On 6 April 1641 the Commons ordered the
master and wardens of the Company before it and charged them
with seeking out the printer of a speech purporting to have been
made by Mr. Maynard, a member of the House.[18] A few months
later (5 June 1641) the Commons again authorized the Company
in general terms "to take the best Course they can to suppress and
hinder . . . this licence of Printing."[19] The printers, however, dis-
gusted with the corruption among the officials of the Company, refused even that measure of cooperation which they had given
under the Star Chamber decrees. When Nicholas Bourne, master of
the Company, called at the printing establishment of Richard
Herne to discover the publisher of a "scandalous" pamphlet, the
printer threatened with oaths to kill Bourne if he set foot inside his
house. Herne asserted that he knew who printed the offending
pamphlet and furthermore that he had a right to print it.[20]

The House of Commons, dissatisfied with the enforcement by
the Company, sought to control the printers through its own committees and their pursuivants. On 9 March 1643 the House of
Commons gave authority to the Committee on Examinations to

---

[18] Commons Journal, II, 116.
[19] Ibid., p. 168.
[20] Ibid., pp. 268-69 (24 August 1641).

search, apprehend, and commit irregular printers.[21] Under this grant the committee appointed thirteen searchers, Felix Kingston, Samuel Main, George Miller, John Bellamy, William Lee, Jr., John Partridge, Christopher Meredith, Robert Dawlman, Matthew Walbanck, Richard Coats, Joseph Hunscott, and John Raworth, all stationers of London.[22] This method too proved ineffective until at last in 1643 an attempt was made to revive the old alliance between the government and the printing patentees.

The House of Lords experienced similar difficulties. Early in March, 1641, a committee appointed to examine "the business of printing and selling unlicensed books and pamphlets" reported the arrest of several culprits and recommended the punishment of these as a monition to the others. It also recommended that the Stationers Company continue its searches as authorized under its charter.[23]

The company, however, was no more successful executing the orders of the Lords than it had been in following the commands of the Commons. On 21 October 1641 the officers of the Company appealed to the Lords for assistance in suppressing a printing establishment erected by Walkadyn, a marker of cloth, Ashton, a draper, and Thomas Winter. The operators of the printing shop had resisted the Company searchers "with guns and ordnance."[24]

Finally on 26 August 1642 both Houses of Parliament joined in a Declaration designed to suppress the flock of seditious and scandalous pamphlets aimed at the members of the sovereign body. In addition to setting up a temporary licensing system, the Declaration ordered the entry of all publications in the Register book of the Stationers Company, and the officers of the Company were given authority to continue their searches and seizures.[25]

Even with so express an authorization, the searchers for the Company encountered resistance. William Ashton, whose press and printing materials had been seized by Company searchers, swore out a warrant for the arrest of the master and his assistants and had them called for trial before the common-law courts. The Lords,

[21] *Ibid.,* pp. 996-97; B.M. E. 538 (1).
[22] B.M. E. 538 (1).
[23] Lords Journal, IV, 180, 182.
[24] *Ibid.,* p. 398.
[25] *Ibid.,* V, 321; B.M. E. 114 (32).

upon petition of the Company, hastily issued an order staying the
prosecution of the officials.[26]

The Ordinance for the Regulation of Printing (14 June 1643)
provided for, among other things,[27] the cooperation of the Stationers
Company in the enforcement in return for Parliamentary recognition of the ancient rights of the Company and its officers. The Company searchers were authorized to seize the printing materials of
all "irregular" printers, and to carry them to the Stationers' Hall
where they were to be made unserviceable for printing. Authority
was also given to seize and apprehend all printers found engaged
on unlawful or unlicensed works and to bring the culprits before
either House of Parliament for punishment.

The enforcement campaign of the Company of Stationers
under the Ordinance of 1643 was conducted with two objectives
— to protect the property rights of the company and its membership from piracy and counterfeiting by the host of printers which
had sprung up since the abolition of the Star Chamber, and secondly to assist the government by way of repayment in suppressing
dangerous and seditious publications. The old alliance of Tudor
days was again in force.

But even the combined activity of the Lords, Commons, and
Stationers Company could not suppress the printers of London who
for three years had enjoyed a comparative freedom from regulation.
The propertied Stationers who sought to enforce the government
orders encountered resistance in the form of organized piracy. No
sooner did a Stationer report an irregular printer than he found his
most valuable printing properties reprinted and on sale in the
shops of London.

The most persistent government searcher was the stationer,
Joseph Hunscott, whose activities cover the entire period of the
Interregnum. Hunscott was admitted to the livery of the Stationers
Company 5 February 1638,[28] and his fee of twenty pounds was
remitted because "he hath done the company good service in many
businesses." In 1641 he was made beadle and charged with the
duty of enforcing the company regulations. He was one of the Stationers named as searcher by the Committee on Examinations (13

---

[26] *Ibid.*, VI, 42.

[27] The licensing provisions are discussed below, pp. 186ff.

[28] Court Book C, f. 153.

March 1643), and he was deputed as official searcher by the Company under the Ordinance of 1643.[29]

Hunscott must have spent most of his time ferreting out secret and irregular printing. In May, 1643, he seized the press which William Ashton had set up in an obscure place in the parish of St. Giles-in-the-Fields. The next day Hunscott and the master of the Company were served with warrants for their arrest, charging them with unlawfully appropriating the property of a citizen of London. Only the intervention of the House of Lords saved the searchers from a trial before the law courts.[30]

The lot of Company searcher was far from tranquil. Hunscott and his fellows were bodily ejected when they appeared at the dwelling house of Henry Tooley and William Hicks to search for imported Bibles.[31] The Company on 7 February 1644 agreed to stand the charges for the defense of Hunscott against suits brought against him in connection with his seizures.[32] The harassed beadle was resisted on every side and reported to the House of Lords 8 July 1645 that although he had repaired to all printers and showed them the warrant from the house that nevertheless numerous printers continued to avoid the orders.[33]

One of the most recalcitrant of the irregular printers was Robert Eeles. Acting as a pursuivant for a committee of the House of Lords, he had seized a press belonging to William Larner. Equipped with this press he proceeded to print patented and copyrighted works of the wealthy booksellers. The Stationers Company referred to him as "a common printer and seller of unlicensed books" and did their best to ruin him. He was the object of attacks both by the Stationers and by other irregular printers whom he had betrayed. The master of the Company, upon leaving Westminster Hall one day, spied Mrs. Eeles, a street vendor, selling pamphlets. He searched her for seditious pamphlets upon which she cursed

---

[29] Court Book C, f. 269b.

[30] Historical Manuscripts Commission, 5th Report, p. 85; Lords Journal, VI, 42.

[31] Historical Manuscripts Commission, 6th Report, App., p. 17; Lords Journal, VI, 25.

[32] Court Book C, f. 214.

[33] Historical Manuscripts Commission, 6th Report, App., p. 19.

the master in far from lady-like language and then sued out a warrant for his arrest on the charge of battery.[34]

The Company searchers were themselves not above emulating the method employed by Eeles in securing a press. Warden Thrale was in 1653 called before the Court of Assistants for appropriating a press on the ground, he claimed, it had been used in printing offensive literature.[35] He was ordered to restore the press to its owner.

---

[34] Lords Journal, VIII, 463, 684, 688; Historical Manuscripts Commission, 6th Report, p. 154.

[35] Court Book C, f. 280b.

CHAPTER 9

Parliament and the Press

The collapse of the king's authority, the abolition of the Star Chamber and of the Court of High Commission, and the chaotic condition of the printing trade presented Parliament with the immediate problem of regulating the press. The men who assembled at Westminster in 1640 for the dual purpose of reforming religion and circumscribing the powers of the crown were primarily political and religious reformers, interested in their particular and individual brands of "truth" and unaware of any great philosophical principles of freedom of discussion. No sooner had Parliament settled down to the business of dealing with the king and bishops than its attention was diverted by a continuous stream of complaints by individual members against the publication of critical, subversive, or seditious pamphlets. Added to this stream were the complaints of the Stationers Company against piracy and unauthorized printing which had formerly been dammed up behind the walls of the Star Chamber and High Commission. And finally Parliament as a whole was aghast at the monster, public opinion, which it had raised up and which in turn was threatening to destroy it. The immediate problems of Parliament in relation to the press were the elimination of chaos and piracy in the printing trade, suppression of sedition, protection for religion, control of news of Parliamentary activity, and last a program of active propaganda in defense of the Parlia-

179

mentary position. Efforts to solve these problems took place simul-
taneously in the House of Commons and in the House of Lords and
resulted finally in the Ordinance of 1643.

The House of Commons Takes Control

In answer to the complaints of ministers, stationers, and members, the House of Commons on 17 May 1641 appointed a committee "for printing" to which were referred all complaints as well
as the duty of drafting legislation to remedy the abuses.[1]

This committee grew out of three previous committees which
had been charged with investigating particular irregularities in the
printing trade. The committee appointed to prosecute Archbishop
Laud for treason was charged 5 February 1641 with examining the
authority under which the primate and his appointees had suppressed certain books.[2] The next day a special committee of sixteen
men was appointed to suppress the publication of a speech made
by the king's solicitor on ship money before a joint conference of
the two Houses.[3] A special committee on printing members' speeches
continued to meet during the month of April. It consisted of some
of the leading figures in Parliamentary history such as Mr. Glynn,
Mr. Maynard, Mr. Corbett, Sir John Colpeper, Sir Edward Deering, Sir John Evelyn, Mr. Richard Moore, and Mr. Nicholls.[4] In
the meantime a subcommittee of the Grand Committee for Religion had been appointed and was on 13 February 1641 enlarged
and made a committee of the Commons "to examine all abuses
in printing." [5] The evident overlapping of the committees became
apparent to the House, and on 17 May 1641 they were combined
under the chairmanship of Sir Edward Deering. Three new members, Mr. Selden, Mr. Grimston, and Mr. Rouse, were added to the
committee in July.[6]

The combined Committee on Printing continued to hold hearings at which complaints referred to it by the House were presented. Among such complaints were those against the publication
of a speech under Sir John Holland's name,[7] the book *The Protestation Protested*,[8] the pamphlets *The True Relation of the French*

---

[1] Commons Journal, II, 148.   [2] *Ibid.*, p. 79.

[3] *Ibid.*, p. 80.   [4] *Ibid.*, p. 136.   [5] *Ibid.*, p. 84.

[6] *Ibid.*, p. 221. [7] *Ibid.*, p. 190 (28 June 1641). [8] *Ibid.*, p. 206 (10 July 1641).

Ambassage and *The Brownists Conventicle*,[9] and a number of published sermons.[10]

Parliament in the meantime was being harassed on all sides by the publication of pamphlets, newsbooks, sermons, protestations, and petitions. The Presbyterians and the Independents were making bids for both Parliamentary and public support. The royalists and high churchmen found presses willing to print their attacks. The House commanded the Stationers Company to redouble its efforts at suppression; members of the House were forbidden to supply notes of proceedings to printers; [11] and the committee on printing was urged to find a speedy remedy.[12]

To add further to the confusion, a book by the chairman of the committee on printing entitled *A Collection of Speeches made by Sir Ed. Deering, Knight and Baronet in Matters of Religion* gave immediate offense to the Presbyterian party in the House. The book was ordered burned by the hangman, and Sir Edward was disabled to sit in Parliament and committed to the Tower.[13] The Stationers Company was ordered to assist in the burning,[14] and as an afterthought was ordered the following day (5 February 1642) to search for copies of the book.[15] Deering was ordered to turn over all material which he held as chairman of the committee on printing [16] to his successor, Mr. White.[17]

The House of Commons continued to refer obnoxious publications to the committee on printing, but evidently the results were not gratifying for on 19 February 1642 the House inquired "Why do they not find a remedy?" [18] and again on 7 April 1642, they are ordered to "bring in Tomorrow, the Order they are appointed to prepare, to hinder this liberty of printing." [19]

The House itself decided to proceed against a number of printers of the irritating pamphlets and newsbooks. John Franck, printer, was called before the bar for printing *The Message of the House in reply to His Majesty's last Message*. John Wright, the stationer, and Gregory Dexter, printer, were cited for publishing

---

[9] *Ibid.*, p. 206 (12 July 1641).   [10] *Ibid.*, p. 221 (23 July 1641).

[11] *Ibid.*, p. 220 (22 July 1641).   [12] *Ibid.*, p. 324.   [13] *Ibid.*, p. 411.

[14] *Ibid.*   [15] *Ibid.*, p. 414.   [16] *Ibid.*, p. 419.

[17] *Ibid.*, p. 472.   [18] *Ibid.*, p. 441.   [19] *Ibid.*, p. 514.

The Humble Petition and Declaration of both Houses. William Humphreyville, Robert Ward, and Robert Wood were also ordered to appear.[20] The charge against these printers and publishers was printing "without license." These defendants were able to escape conviction and punishment by showing that no licensing provisions were in force since the destruction of the Star Chamber.

Parliament decided to act at once. A special committee composed of Mr. D'Ewes, Mr. White, Mr. Grimston, Mr. Whistler, and Mr. Cane was charged with drafting an ordinance.[21] The ordinance itself was read in the House 24 August 1642 [22] and passed. With the concurrence of the Lords the following *Special Order of both Houses concerning Irregular Printing, and for the suppressing of all false and Scandalous Pamphlets* was published:

Whereas there hath beene of late great disorders and abuses by Irregular Printing, to the great scandall of Religion and Government, and a Bill is in preparation for the redresse of those mischiefs, which by reason of the present distractions cannot be so speedily perfected and passed as is desired; It is therefore Ordered by the Lords and Commons in Parliament, that no person or persons shall Print, publish, or utter, any Booke or Pamphlet, false or scandalous, to the proceedings of the Houses of Parliament, or either of them, nor shall Print, utter or publish, any Booke or Pamphlet, with the name of the Clerke of either House of Parliament set thereunto, or with any expression pretence of Order from both or either of the said Houses without special Order from the said Houses, or either of them, or of the Committees of them, or either of them concerning Printing; and the same to be entred in the Register Booke of the said Company, according to the ancient customs, and the Master and Wardens of the company of Stationers, London, and the Vsher of the Black-rod, and Serjeant of the commons House of Parliament and their Deputies, are hereby authorized and required, to make diligent search from time to time, for all such Bookes and Pamphlets, to bee hereafter Printed, and the same to seize, and take, together with the presses, and other printing Materials, wherewith the same shall be printed; and carry them to the common-hall of the said company, there to remaine till either House of Parliament shall otherwise dispose thereof; And all his Majesties Officers shal upon request, ayde and assist to apprehend offenders in the premises, and to bring them before the Lords or Commons House of Parliament, or the Committee appointed for Printing, upon whose report of the Fact, such course shall be taken

[20] *Ibid.,* pp. 500-501.
[21] *Ibid.,* p. 624 (June, 1642).
[22] *Ibid.,* p. 734.

with the said Offenders, as shall be just. And for that purpose the said Committees are to set at such times and places as they shall thinke fit.[23]

This first Parliamentary ordinance for the control of printing followed the traditional methods formerly employed by the crown. The regulation was couched in the form of a royal proclamation; the alliance with the Stationers Company was revived; and the royal law-enforcing officers were goaded into action. No licensing system was set up, probably because the committee on printing was still in the process of working out the details.

The Commons next turned its attention to providing a positive antidote for the scurrilous publication of the independents and other radicals. An appropriation was made 2 June 1643 for the printing and dispersal of pamphlets in several counties.[24] Members of the House were also prohibited from sending pamphlets and "false news" into the country.[25] The House had already provided for an official report of the votes,[26] and these printed reports were ordered dispersed "with all care and diligence."

To counteract the "false and scandalous" rumors which were circulating about the country, a Proclamation was issued 8 October 1642 threatening punishment for those who go about asserting that they (the Commons) "intend to assesse every mans pewter and lay excizes upon every commodities." [27] On 21 April 1643 another special committee of eight members was appointed "to consider of an Order to prevent the spreading of false Rumours." [28] Disbursements for 1642 included at item of £75, 4d. for printing and distributing "official" information.[29]

By June, 1643, the Committee on Printing was ready with a draft bill. On June 10 it was voted by the Commons, on June 14 concurred in by the Lords, and on June 16 the licensers were appointed.[30]

---

[23] B.M. E. 114 (32). Dated August 26 and 27, 1642. Robert Steele, *Tudor and Stuart Proclamations* (Oxford, 1910), No. 2255; Commons Journal, II, 739; Lords Journal, V, 322.

[24] Commons Journal, II, 611.

[25] *Ibid.*

[26] *Ibid.*, pp. 500-501 (28 March 1642).

[27] Steele, *op. cit.*, No. 2274; Commons Journal, II, 801.

[28] Commons Journal, III, 54.

[29] Calendar of State Papers, Domestic, 1641-43, p. 428.

[30] For the terms of the act see below, pp. 186ff.

The House of Lords and the Press

Even more than the Commons, the House of Lords considered itself the legitimate heir to those prerogative powers which the crown had exercised for the control and regulation of printing. What little objection was voiced to the shift in authority from crown to Parliament came not so much from those who were subject to the regulations as from a few hardy souls whose thinking had carried them beyond the mental borders of their times. The public at large for the most part acquiesced in the principle of the control of the press by Parliament. The legitimate printers and stationers were among the supplicants for such control. The arguments which took place among members of Parliament were directed not toward an analysis of the basis upon which Parliamentary authority to regulate the press rested but upon the immediate problems of what controls would be effective in suppressing the unprecedented flood of printed discussion of religious and political questions.

The House of Lords lost no time in completing the shift from royal to Parliamentary authority. Early in 1641 Dr. Bray, one of the licensers appointed by the Ecclesiastical Commission, was summoned to appear before the House, charged with licensing the publication of Dr. Pocklington's sermons. Dr. Bray confessed that he licensed the books, but pleaded that he had not read the manuscript with proper caution. He agreed to make a public recantation of his error at St. Margaret's church.[31]

On 4 March 1641 upon presentation by the Stationers Company of a list of printers of unlicensed works, the House of Lords appointed a committee on printing "to examine the whole business." [32]

This committee, after questioning several culprits produced by the Stationers Company, reported back to the House that three of the printers should receive exemplary punishment while the others should be dismissed with an admonition. John Wells, Stephen

[31] John Nalson, *An Impartial Collection of the Great Affairs of State* . . . (London, 1682-83), I, 787; Edward Arber, *Transcript* (1875), V, lxxviii.

[32] Lords Journal, IV, 175. The following were members of the committee: The Earl of Bath, Earl of Clare, Earl of Monmouth, L. Viscount Saye and Seale, L. Bp. of Chester, Ds. Robarts, Ds. Pawlett, Ds. Perpointe, L. Bp. of Lincolne, L. Bp. of Sarum, L. Bp. of Exon, L. Bp. of Elye, Ds. Howard de Charl, Ds. Dunsemore, Ds. Herbert de Cherb, Ds. Seymour (or any five of them).

Buckley, and Henry Walker were called before the House for a hearing. No proof was adduced against Buckley who was dismissed, but Walker and Wells were committed to the Fleet.[33] Upon their own petition and apology, the two printers were released two weeks later.[34]

The Lords Committee relied largely for enforcement on the officers of the Stationers Company. Repeated charges to these officials to search and suppress printing appear in the Journals, but still the flood of unlicensed pamphlets continued. Late in October, 1641, the Committee on printing, enlarged by five new members, was ordered "to consider how the Press may be regulated and that Printing of such Books may be suppressed." [35] The judges were also asked to prepare a draft bill on the same subject.[36] In the meantime prosecutions were undertaken against the printers, William Gage, Bernard Alsopp, and the Wilsons, father and son.

On 25 April 1642 the Lords appointed a select committee to meet with a committee of the Commons. It was suggested in the committee that perhaps a remedy could be found in the law. Upon solicitation the judges replied that in their opinion the printing of libels was a publication of them and the printer liable.[37] Thomas Walker, who at the order of the Lords, was already in the Tower, was transferred to Newgate for trial. The result of the joint meetings of the committees of the two houses was the Declaration of 24 August 1642.[38]

Neither the Stationers Company nor the courts of law seemed capable of controlling the vast number of pamphlets which found their way into circulation. The Lords were particularly irritated by the publication of a *Petition of London with an Answer of the House* before the matter had come up for consideration. A special committee on pamphlets was appointed 17 December 1646 for the purpose of suppressing these printed discussions.[39]

The pamphlets, however, continued to appear. Among the more irritating to the Lords were *Another happy Victory Obtained by his Excellency the Earl of Essex, The Complaint of the Com-*

---

[33] *Ibid.*, p. 182.   [34] *Ibid.*, p. 186.   [35] *Ibid.*, p. 396.   [36] *Ibid.*, p. 652.
[37] *Ibid.*, V, 37.   [38] *Ibid.*, p. 321. See above, p. 182.
[39] *Ibid.*, pp. 496-97. The following were members: Comes Northumb, Comes Holland, Comes Sarum, Comes Exon, Comes Bollingbrooke, L. Viscount Saye and Seale, L. Grey de Warke, L. Howard de Este.

mons, The Propositions for Peace presented to the King, and the *Continuation of the News.* The printers of *Continuation,* Leach and Coles, were ordered to attend the House and were committed to the Fleet.[40] The printers, Richard West, Thomas Alsopp and Bernard Faucett, Richard Herne, and Pecke, were all committed to the Fleet "to remain until the Pleasure of this House be further known." [41] A few days later the Lords issued an order that all those printers in gaol should be released upon their presentation of good security that they would behave in the future. They were also ordered to refrain from printing anything concerning Parliament without a special order under the the hand of the clerk of either House.[42]

The case of the printer, Richard Herne, illustrates the difficulties encountered by the House of Lords in its attempts at prosecution. Herne was brought before the House 12 January 1642 and confessed to printing *His Majesty's gracious Answer etc.* He was imprisoned at the pleasure of the House; [43] but in February it was discovered that he was issuing pamphlets in spite of his confinement. He was again summoned before the Lords (9 February) and charged with printing *An Abstract of the Bill against the Biship etc.* Herne denied the printing in spite of the testimony of Joseph Hunscott, the Stationers' searcher, that he bought a copy "of women" at Herne's house. The five mercury women (hawkers of pamphlets) were produced and admitted that they had sold the pamphlets.[44] Herne continued to deny that he had printed the papers, and the next day his servants were called who testified "that divers particular pamphlets have been printed at Herne's the printer since his being in the Fleet." Herne was sent back to confinement.[45]

On 14 June 1643 the Lords concurred in the Ordinance for the regulation of abuses in printing which had been sent up from the Commons.[46]

Parliamentary Licensing

With the enactment of the Ordinance for the regulating of printing (14 June 1643), the transition from control by the crown

---

[40] *Ibid.,* p. 533.   [41] *Ibid.,* p. 547.   [42] *Ibid.,* p. 554.

[43] *Ibid.,* p. 547.   [44] *Ibid.,* p. 597.

[45] *Ibid.,* p. 598.   [46] *Ibid.,* VI, 95.

under its prerogative powers to jurisdiction by Parliament was completed. It is significant that the movement which sought to curtail the powers of the crown did not seek to abolish the controls but merely the source from which the controls emanated. Parliament substituted itself and its appointed committees for the Star Chamber and High Commission. The methods for control and regulation of the press which were evolved by the Tudor monarchs were retained under Parliamentary auspices. Parliament replaced the crown as the master of the printers and publishers. The old alliance with the Stationers Company whereby that body agreed in return for the protection of its monopolies and property in copies to assist in the enforcement was continued. The licensing system was revived although with Parliamentary and Presbyterian licensers in place of the royal and Episcopal censors.

Under the terms of the Act, all books, pamphlets, and papers were required to be licensed by persons appointed by Parliament and to be entered in the Register at Stationers' Hall. No order or declaration of either House was to be printed without permission from one or both Houses. Searchers were to include the officers of the Stationers Company, the Gentleman Usher of the House of Peers, appointees of the Committee on Examinations, as well as justices of the peace, captains, and constables. Printing materials and equipment used in printing of unlicensed works were to be seized and disposed of according to the orders of either House of Parliament. Apprehended printers were to be referred to either House or to the Committee on Examinations. Punishment was at the discretion of these bodies.[47]

Six days after the passage of the Act for the Regulation of Printing the list of licensers was announced: for books of divinity, any two of a list of twelve names; for law books, any two of a list of four names; for Phisick and Surgery, the President and four censors; for books of common or civil law, Sir Nathaniel Brent or any other three doctors of civil law; for books of heraldry, etc., any three heralds; for books of philosophy, history, poetry, morality and arts, Mr. Brent, Mr. Langley, and Mr. Farnaby; for mathematics, almanacks, and prognostications, Mr. John Booker; for declarations, ordinances, fast sermons, and other things agreed on by one or

[47] C. H. Firth and R. S. Rait, *Acts and Ordinances of the Interregnum, 1642-1660* (London, 1911), I, 184.

other House of Parliament, the House or its committee for printing; for small pamphlets, portraitures, etc., the clerk of the Stationers Company.[48] The classification for purposes of licensing follows closely the earlier classifications of the Star Chamber decrees.[49]

The two Houses of Parliament, with the assistance of the Stationers Company and the Common Council of the City of London[50] proceeded valiantly to put the Printing Act of 1643 into execution. The entries in the Stationers' Register immediately increased.[51] Each House, acting independently, undertook to exercise judicial jurisdiction over violations of the Act. This jurisdiction was frequently exercised by the House itself, but on occasions the function was delegated either to a standing or to a select committee. Complaints from persons or groups aggrieved by a particular publication were frequent. Punishments, however, were light. Before long the failure of either House or its committee to act as a brake on the increasing number of publications devoted to the discussion of domestic affairs became apparent.[52]

On one occasion the two Houses of Parliament engaged in a jurisdictional dispute. John Wright, who had been appointed official printer by the House of Lords, was requested by the clerk to print the *Ordinance for the Excise*. The House of Commons, however, issued an order to Wright forbidding the printing, and upon his refusal to comply he was ordered to appear before the lower house.[53] The printer appealed to the House of Lords. A message was dispatched to the Commons demanding the release of the printer on the ground that "all things that are agreed upon last in the House are to be printed by order of this House."[54] A committee

---

[48] B.M. E. 55 (9); Firth and Rait, *op. cit.*, I, 186; Arber, *op. cit.*, V, liii-liv.

[49] See above, pp. 62, 143.

[50] The Common Council of the City of London enacted an ordinance (9 October 1643) "for the prohibiting of all persons whatsoever, from crying to sale about the streets of the city, any pamphlets, books or papers whatsoever." The Marshalls and Constables were charged under the pain of indictment with the enforcement of the ordinance. B.M. E. 538 (1).

[51] G. E. B. Eyre and C. R. Rivington, *Transcript* . . . (London, 1913), I (Reg. E.).

[52] Parliament's trouble with the publishers of newsbooks is discussed in Chapter 10.

[53] Commons Journal, III, 180-81 (24 July 1643).

[54] Lords Journal, VI, 147-48.

of the Commons was appointed to confer with the Lords, but without further ado the printer was discharged.[55]

The House of Commons subdivided the burden of enforcement and adjudication among its various committees, reserving to itself however the more flagrant violations or prominent culprits. The Committee on Sequestrations was ordered to suppress the sale of pamphlets printed at the king's headquarters at Oxford.[56] The Committee on Examinations received most of the assignments to prosecute printers of "scandalous" pamphlets.[57] Peter Coles's presses were sequestered by this committee and released only after posting a £1000 bond.[58] This committee was also charged with examining the publishers of the pamphlets *Civicus*[59] and *Justiciarus justificatus*.[60]

The Committee on Printing continued to function, and to it were referred the squabbles among the printers and stationers. The duty of discovering the author and printer of Milton's pamphlet on divorce was assigned to this committee.[61]

The Committee of Both Kingdoms was assigned the duty of suppressing unofficial discussions of foreign or Scottish affairs. Robert Bostock was prosecuted before this committee for the publication of the pamphlets *Truth's Manifest* and *A Short and True Relation of some main passages, wherein the Scots are particularly concerned*.[62] Other obnoxious publications were referred to the Committee for Complaints for investigation and suppression.[63]

A special committee was appointed by the House of Commons whenever a particularly irritating publication appeared. This committee of thirty-two members was first appointed 3 February 1647 and given authority "to send for witnesses, parties, and papers, and to commit such as they find faulty."[64] A group of five of the com-

---

[55] Commons Journal, III, 184, 192; Historical Manuscripts Commission, 5th Report, p. 97.

[56] Commons Journal, III, 315.

[57] *Ibid.*, p. 549.

[58] Cal. St. P. Dom., 1641-43, p. 513.

[59] Commons Journal, IV, 164.

[60] *Ibid.*, p. 505.

[61] *Ibid.*, III, 606.

[62] Cal. St. P. Dom., 1645-47, pp. 15, 144, 330, 343.

[63] Commons Journal, IV, 682, 431-32; V, 223.

[64] *Ibid.*, V, 72-73.

mittee was given power to act with Mr. Challoner as chairman.[65]
Another special committee of ten members was appointed 27 November 1647 to investigate and suppress unlicensed newsbooks.[66]
This committee had power to imprison licensers, authors, printers,
and publishers, and to seize pamphlets and burn them, to destroy
and take away presses and type, and to search for parties, witnesses,
papers, and records.[67]

While the House of Commons was busily engaged in revising
the political and religious institutions of the kingdom, the House of
Lords found itself on the defensive. Unable to take the lead in the
political realignments, it occupied itself in maintaining its dignity by
a campaign of suppression of both factual reports and criticisms of
itself and its policies. The prosecutions brought by the House itself
were directed against the publishers of pamphlets and newsbooks.
Among those prosecuted were Thomas White, Robert White, Richard Royston, Marchmont Needham, Richard Overton, Robert Eeles,
George Smith, and Henry Walker. The abolition of the House of
Lords late in 1648 relieved this body of further difficulties with
the press.[68]

As the position of Parliament shifted from that of a critic of
the established order to that of defender of its revisions in government and religion, the attacks upon these innovations increased in
number and virulence. Neither the Parliament itself nor its committees were equal to the task of suppressing printed criticisms. On
3 September 1647 a committee of three was appointed to propose
a new ordinance transferring the onus of enforcement to the Committee of the Militia of London. The Act as finally adopted (20
September 1647) provided for additional penalties for violation.
The author or authors of an unlicensed publication were to be fined
forty shillings or imprisoned forty days. The printer was to be fined
twenty shillings or spend twenty days in prison and to lose his
printing materials and presses. Booksellers or stationers were sentenced to ten shillings or ten days in jail. Hawkers and peddlers

---

[65] *Ibid.*, p. 82.

[66] *Ibid.*, p. 371. See below, p. 214.

[67] *Ibid.*

[68] *Ibid.*, VI, 166, 168. The suppression of newsbooks by the House of Lords
is discussed below, pp. 210-11.

were to forfeit their wares and be whipped as common rogues.[69] The Committee for Examinations of the House of Commons was charged with the enforcement of the Order. It was given power to make searches, to demolish presses, and to commit prisoners.[70]

Still the flood of pamphlets,[71] newsbooks, and diurnals continued. The royalist writers, employing both Oxford and London printers, launched scathing attacks upon Parliamentary leaders. The religious independents objected in print to the Presbyterian influences in England. The Parliamentary writers contradicted both themselves and each other. In such a state of affairs the control of the nation passed from Parliament to the Army. Chaos produced military rule and eventually a dictator, Oliver Cromwell.

Liberty of the Press

The theory held by Parliament during the civil wars—that the press should be strictly regulated and that the Houses of Parliament, instead of the crown, were the proper sources of the authority to regulate—was based on both precedent and expediency. The civil wars represented a conflict in political and religious symbols with the latter predominating, and it was impossible for the leaders of the revolt to dissociate themselves from the intellectual climate of the age. Only a few individuals were able to grasp those principles which became current only after a century or more of experimentation. The basic opposition of the Puritan reformers to the control of the press by the crown was directed not against the fundamental principle of "control," but against the kind of control which discriminated against their particular religious or political tenets.

Implicit in the theory of the Reformation was the principle that there was a definite, discernible, and discoverable truth in religious doctrine, the presentation of which could not fail to convince the unbeliever. Freedom to present these truths would result in conversion. It took only a few years for the Puritan leaders to realize that "truth" is not always victorious even where given a free field.

---

[69] Firth and Rait, *op. cit.*, I, 1021.

[70] B.M. E. 409 (3).

[71] An analysis of the pamphlets preserved in the Thomason collection in the British Museum shows that although only 22 pamphlets were published in 1640, more than 1,000 were issued in each of the succeeding four years. The record number of 1,966 appeared in 1642.

The inevitable deduction was that the dissemination of information and argument should be closely guarded for the preservation of both the ideals and offices of those in positions of authority. Thus, Parliament soon found itself theoretically in the same position as that occupied by the Tudor and Stuart monarchs. The press must be controlled in the interests of the state and of religion.

The principle of freedom of enquiry, of discussion, of dissemination of arguments and information, owes its inception to a few philosophic minds and its early growth to its espousal by the rapidly developing minority groups. Men like Henry Robinson and John Milton could conceive of universal freedom of the press; minority groups like the Independents and the Levellers seized the banner and marched behind it.

The cycle of the Reformation was almost complete. The discussions and arguments which grew out of the original attack on Rome sired a variegated breed of religious conclusions, the very existence of which depended upon continuous proselyting. Samuel Hartlib, friend of Milton, predicted as early as 1641 that ". . . the art of Printing will so spread knowledge that the common people, knowing their own rights and liberties will not be governed by way of oppression. . . ." [72] Public opinion and the control of public opinion were rapidly becoming factors of more practical importance than any law written in Scripture or on the tables of the heart.[73] The publication of pamphlets at the outbreak of the civil war sponsoring the several and distinct brands of religious truth led to the publication of other pamphlets engaged in a counterattack. Soon pamphlets began to deplore the publication of pamphlets. A dim realization of the function and theory of public opinion was discernible. Truth was still absolute, but its power to perpetuate itself without repressive assistance began to be doubted.

The repressive measures of Parliament and the enforcement by the Stationers Company presented new targets for the pamphleteers. One of the first to attack was William Walwyn, a religious and political writer, whose efforts on behalf of the sectaries and religious toleration inevitably led him to oppose the regulation of

---

[72] A description of the Famous Kingdom of Macaria" (London, 25 October 1641).

[73] William Haller, *Tracts on Liberty in the Puritan Revolution* (1934), I, 28.

printing.[74] Walwyn, although not a sectary, protested the exclusion from toleration of the Separatists by the Apologists and Presbyterians alike. He boldly criticized the clergy for wanting the power lately wrested from the prelates.

His attack on the printing regulations appeared in a pamphlet entitled *The Compassionate Samaritane* which was printed some time in June or July, 1644.[75] The tract was published anonymously and without license or imprint. Addressing himself to Parliament, Walwyn granted the theoretical necessity for some sort of regulation of printing in the interest of the state but deplored the extension of the licensing system to include all dissenting discussion. Not yet prepared to champion either complete religious toleration or liberty of the press, the pamphleteer nevertheless objected to the narrow and bigoted interpretation of both the Scriptures and the Printing Act by the Puritan divines. Walwyn was one of the first to point out the inconsistency and impracticability of the licensing system. He was not yet prepared to adopt complete freedom as an inescapable alternative. He concluded his memorial by demanding the repeal of all statutes against Separatists and "that the Press may be free for any man that writes nothing highly scandalous or dangerous to the state."

Walwyn's arguments are epitomized in these excerpts:

. . . In the beginning of Your Session when our Divines (as they would have us call them) wrote freely against the Bishops, & the Bishops made complaint to You for redresse: some of You made answer, that there was no remedy, forasmuch as the Presse was to be open and free for all in time of Parliament: I shall make bold as a Common of England to lay claime to that privilege, being assured that I write nothing scandalous, or dangerous to the State, (which is justly and upon good grounds prohibited by Your Ordinance to that effect) only I humbly desire You to consider whether more was not got from You by that Ordinance then You intended, and that though it was purposed by You to restrain the venting and dispersing of the Kings writings and his Agents, yet it hath by reason of the qualifications of the Licensers wrought a wrong way, and stopt the mouthes of good men, who must either not write at all,

---

[74] Walwyn's writings are discussed by Haller, *op. cit.*, I, App. A.

[75] *Ibid.*, p. 125. A second edition appeared 5 January 1645. A copy of the first edition is preserved in the library of Yale University. Walwyn reaffirmed his position on the press in his "Just Defense" (May, 1649) reprinted in Haller, *op. cit.*, III, 350-98.

or no more then is suitable to the judgments of interests of the Licencers . . . (Walwyn, A4-A5)

. . . And that men may not vindicate themselves by writing, their
next interest is to be masters of the Presse, of which they are lately become by an Ordinance for licensing of Bookes, which being intended by
the Parliament for a good & necessary and (namely) the prohibition of all
Bookes dangerous or scandalous to the State, is become by meanes of
the Licencers (who are Divines and intend their owne interest) most
serviceable to themselves (scandalous bookes being still disperst) in the
stopping of honest mens writings, that nothing may come to the Worlds
view but what they please, unlesse men whill runne the hazard of imprisonment, (as I now doe) so that in publike they may speake what
they will, write what they wil, they may abuse whom they will, and
nothing can besaid agains them. (Walwyn, 37-40)

Whereas William Walwyn arrived at a theory of liberty of the
press through his efforts to secure religious toleration, Henry Robinson, another pamphleteer of the same period, espoused freedom of
discussion and the right of private judgment as a necessary adjunct
to the economic principles of private enterprise and private property. Robinson, strangely for his times, managed to keep clear of all
religious groups and movements and devoted his writings toward
establishing a model economic commonwealth. Like many of his
own and succeeding ages, he soon discovered the practical inade-
quacies of theology. Every economic, social, or political conflict was
able to find adherents who could square its tenets with the will of
God. The result was to discredit all theology and to lead Robinson
to espouse the doctrine of free conscience as the most practicable
method of hurdling these irritating theological questions. "No man
can have a natural monopoly of truth, and the more freely each
man exercises his own gifts in its pursuit, the more of truth will be
discovered and possessed." [76]

Having embraced the economic theory of laissez faire, it was
but a step for Robinson to come to the conclusion that freedom of
the press was a theoretical correlative as well as a practical solution of the problem. In his pamphlet *Liberty of Conscience* published in March, 1644, without author's name, license, or imprint, he
expressed this conclusion:

But farre more rarely shall you finde a man to give preheminence
in point of his Religion, each thinking his owne to be the truest; this

<hr>

[76] Haller, *op. cit.*, I, 69.

combat therefore must be fought out upon eaven ground, on equal termes, neither side must expect to have greater liberty of speech, writing, Printing, or whatsoever else, then the other: But it will be again objected, that if such a tolleration as this be granted, the whole Kingdome will be quickly pestered with a greater confusion than that of Babel; to which I answer, That the confusion will not be such as is so much imagined and feared, though it may seem greater at first then afterwards, when every man hath associated himselfe with such as are of his owne opinion; . . .[77]

Of a different intellectual stratum from that of the foregoing pamphleteers was John Milton, the poet. Highly educated, steeped in classical knowledge, of a philosophical bent of mind, and endowed with a facility for majestic presentation either in prose or poetry, the great literary genius found himself drawn into the swift current of events, and like his contemporaries unloosed himself in the production of anonymous and argumentative pamphlets.

The immediate occasion for Milton's interest in liberty of the press was his difficulties with the Stationers Company and the authorities over his pamphlets on divorce. This first pamphlet growing out of Milton's difficulties with his wife was published in August, 1643. It was anonymous and unlicensed. A second edition appeared 2 February 1644, also unlicensed but with the author's initials (J.M.). This was followed by a second tract on divorce (15 July 1644) which was properly entered on the registers of the Stationers Company and was licensed under the hands of Mr. Dounham and Mr. Parker, wardens. The ire of both the Westminster Assembly and Parliament over the publication of these obnoxious pamphlets aroused the officials of the Stationers Company to exculpate themselves. In a memorial to Parliament they pointed out that the blasphemous and pernicious opinions were being aired in unlicensed and unregistered pamphlets as objectionable to the printers as they were to Parliament. Milton's pamphlet on divorce was mentioned as an illustration of objectionable publication, and the author was cited before the Committee on Printing but evidently was not prosecuted.

Milton carefully prepared his answer to the Stationers Company, to the Westminster Assembly, and to the Committee on Printing. It appeared 24 November 1644 as *Areopagitica; A Speech of*

[77] Pages 17-18. Copy in Union Theological Seminary; reprinted in Haller, *op. cit.,* III, 105-78.

Mr. John Milton/For the Liberty of Unlicensed Printing/to the Parliament of England.[78] The pamphlet carried neither booksellers' nor printers' name and was unlicensed and unregistered. Regardless of the incident which led to its publication,[79] the *Areopagitica* stands today as the "most perfect literary expression of the ideal of freedom produced during the struggle of 1644." [80] It gave to succeeding generations the benefits of an argument, the effect of which has expanded as the literary reputation of its author has increased.

In its own day and upon its own contemporaries the *Areopagitica* had very little effect. It was published in only one edition (was not republished until 1738 with the exception of an abridgment in 1693) and went unmentioned by most of the writers and public men of the times.[81]

A fact which has tended to detract somewhat from Milton's reputation as a defender of liberty of the press was that during the whole of the year 1651 he acted as official licenser or censor of newsbooks. Both the semi-official *Mercurius Politicus* and the *Perfect Diurnal* were licensed under his hand.[82] Masson, the biographer, expresses surprise that his hero and author of the *Areopagitica* should be found in such a capacity,[83] but explains by asserting that Milton in addition to his other secretarial work for the Council of State acted as co-editor with Marchmont Needham of *Mercurius Britannicus.* The evidence so far adduced is unconvincing. Either Milton had by 1651 changed his mind on the subject of licensing the

[78] David Masson in his *Life of Milton* (1858-80), III, 275, claims that this pamphlet was the first appeal for the liberty of the press. The writings of Walwyn and Robinson seem to dispute this statement.

[79] J. G. Muddiman (J. B. Williams), *History of English Journalism* . . . (London: Longmans, Green, 1908), p. 61, claims "it was clearly provoked by Milton's own personal inconveniences with the licenser and nothing else; for it contains no advocacy of any real liberty of the press and no plea for toleration."

[80] Haller, *op. cit.*, I, 75.

[81] Haller, who made an investigation into the contemporary publications, writes: "It appears incredible that Milton's great plea for freedom of the press should have failed of any mention whatever in the thousands of pages printed at the time and abounding in specific references to hundreds of other publications." Haller, *op. cit.*, I, 135. Unlike Overton, who was thrown in prison, Milton was merely cited by the Stationers Company before the House of Lords and the prosecution promptly dismissed.

[82] See below, p. 225.

[83] Masson, *op. cit.*, IV, 324.

press or he had never intended by his *Areopagitica* that this freedom, enjoyed by serious and scholarly books, should be extended to newsbooks of ephemeral as well as explosive contents.[84] The latter explanation is the more probable one. Milton is not inconsistent unless one reads into *Areopagitica* a broader statement on the principle of freedom of the press than is to be found in the words themselves. Milton began by attacking the principle of licensing but soon found himself carried into the main stream of freedom of the mind with the result that his pamphlet stands as a literary monument to intellectual liberty but leaves much to be desired as a statement of the principles of freedom of the press. Milton wanted freedom of discussion for serious-minded men who held honest, although differing, opinions. He was not willing to extend this same freedom to men of lesser standing with less serious purposes. To him, both Roman Catholic literature and ephemeral journalism were beyond the pale, and unlike Walwyn, he by-passed the problem of freedom of the press as related to the safety of the state. Since Milton failed to advocate universal freedom of the press, it is no inconsistency to find him later censoring newsbooks. *Areopagitica* is a literary classic; it is an invaluable contribution to political thinking on the subject of intellectual liberty; it is not, however, a comprehensive statement of the principles of liberty of the press.

A fourth member of the group of pamphleteers who were laying a rational basis for a theory of freedom of discussion was Richard Overton, printer. Through the writings of the early group of radicals whose works he printed on his secret press, he became initiated into the principles of the Separatists. His excursions into theology led him to translate the law of God into the principles of democracy. The process begun by the Reformation which developed into the theory of individual liberty and liberty of the press is well illustrated by Overton's career. He began with the assertion of the natural supremacy of reason in matters of religion and then moved on to proclaiming the natural equality of human rights.[85]

Overton and his co-worker William Larner operated a secret press in Coleman street (1643-1645), the Martin Mar-Priest Press

---

[84] W. M. Clyde, *Struggle for Freedom of the Press* . . . (London: Oxford University press, 1934), pp. 19, 172-73, 261, espouses the latter position.

[85] Haller, *op. cit.,* I, 97.

(1645-1646), the Goodman's Fields Press (1645), and a press in Bishopgates street (1646).[86]

On 8 April 1645 Overton published his own pamphlet, *The Arraignement of Mr. Persecution,* in which the author anticipates the allegorical method of Bunyan. Opposing religious uniformity on the rationalist's ground of political advantage and natural right, the printer-author boldly attacks the Presbyterian party for attempting to displace the prelates as censors of the press. In a few words Overton reduced the licensing system to an absurdity.[87]

The pursuivants of the Stationers Company were unable to locate Overton's press. During the summer months he continued to issue radical pamphlets, and when Lilburne was imprisoned by the House of Lords in June, 1646, he printed his famous declaration of the rights of man, *A Remonstrance of Many Thousand Citizens* (July 7), followed by *An Alarum to the House of Lords* (July 31). When called before a committee of the Lords, Overton refused to answer, resting upon his constitutional and natural rights. He was then brought before the House itself where he again refused to answer, declaring "He was not bound to answer to any Interrogatories to accuse himself, he being a free-born subject." [88] He was committed to prison at Newgate, from which, Prynne-like, he issued an account of his sufferings.[89]

As Haller has pointed out, "What was notable in Overton's tracts was the vigor and clarity with which, in accents that hark forward to Tom Paine and the Declaration of Independence, they marshalled the dogmas of natural liberty in support of popular government, of toleration and freedom of the press, of abolition of tithes, monopolies and imprisonment for debt." [90]

The outstanding defender of Liberty of the Press during the

---

[86] H. R. Plomer, "Secret Printing During Civil War," *The Library,* new series, V (October, 1941), 374-403.

[87] *Arraignement of Mr. Persecution,* pp. 24-25.

[88] Lords Journal, VIII, 457.

[89] *A defiance against all Arbitrary Usurpations or Encroachments, either of the House of Lords, or any other, upon the Soveraignity of the Supreme House of Commons* (September 9, 1646) was followed by *An Arrow against all Tyrants and Tyrany, shot from the prison at Newgate into the Prerogative Bowels of the Arbitrary House of Lords* (October 12) and by *The Commoners Complaint* (February 10, 1647).

[90] Haller, *op. cit.,* I, 114.

Puritan Revolution was John Lilburne. Like Burton, Bastwick, and Prynne, he had suffered under the Star Chamber for publishing seditious tracts,[91] and like his three compatriots, he went to trial seeking not justice but publicity. While in jail he wrote and published an account of his sufferings. At the opening of Long Parliament he was set free and began a long and intense career as a pamphleteer, espousing the common man's growing consciousness of interest and power in a competitive society.[92]

Lilburne naturally gravitated into that group of social and religious radicals who were seeking to avoid the return of the old type of church-state. Gradually and almost imperceptibly this group drifted down the stream of religious toleration, made tentative landings in the territory of political democracy, and dimly discerned in the distance the principle of freedom of discussion and of the press.

The champion of toleration and of the press unloosed himself in a pamphlet, *A copie of a letter to Mr. William Prynne Esq.* (January, 1645), issued without license or imprint and probably printed by Richard Overton.[93] Demanding freedom of the press as the privilege of a free-born English subject, Lilburne challenged the apostles of Presbyterianism to an open and public debate.[94] "For if you had not beene men that had been afraid of your cause, you would have been willing to have fought and contended with us upon even grounds and equall terms, namely that the Presse might be open for us as you."

In retaliation, Prynne had the pamphleteer summoned several times before the Committee on Examinations, and finally the House of Lords placed him under arrest. Here was another opportunity to propagandize by publicizing his sufferings.[95] His three months incarceration gave him time to prepare his next blast which appeared 10 October 1645 as *Englands Birthright Justified.*[96] The

---

[91] *A Christian Mans Triall*, 1638. Republished in 1641.

[92] Haller, *op. cit.*, I, 14.

[93] Reprinted in Haller, *op. cit.*, III, 179.

[94] John Lilburne, *A copie of a letter*, pp. 2, 3.

[95] *Copy of a Letter . . . to a Friend*, 25 July 1645.

[96] Reprinted in Haller, *op. cit.*, III, 257. The pamphlet in the Thomason collection in the British Museum carries neither license, imprint, nor separate title page. It was probably printed by Overton on the press which was later seized by Joseph Hunscott, agent of the Stationers Company.

author lists as one of his grievances,

> The third monopoly . . . that unsufferable, unjust and tyrannical Monopoly
> of Printing, whereby a great Company of the very same malignant fel-
> lows that *Canterbury* and his Malignant party engaged in their Arbitrary
> *Designes* against the Peoples and *Parliaments* just Priviledges (who
> turning with every winde, doe endeavour by all possible means as well
> as now as then to sell and betray the Kingdom for their own gaine) are
> invested with an Arbitrary Unlimited *Power,* even by a generall Ordi-
> nance of Parliament, to print, divulge and disperse whatsoever Books,
> Pamphlets and Libells as they please, though they be full of Lyes, and
> tend to the poysoning of the Kingdome with unjust and Tyrannical
> Principles.[97]

Lilburne was imprisoned by order of the House of Lords and
shifted to the Tower where he remained until August, 1648. Here
he again dramatized himself as suffering in the interests of the common man, his rights and his privileges.[98]

With Parliament manned by a group of bigoted religionists, no
avenue was open to the dissenter but an appeal to the public
through the press for the creation of an opposition party. In such
manner as this the Leveller party was born.[99] It took form during
the early months of 1647 in support of a series of petitions to the
House of Commons demanding the enactment of revolutionary
constitutional changes to accord with the principles and reforms
which Lilburne, Walwyn, and Overton had been advocating.

The contribution of the Leveller party to political theory included (1) a written constitution, (2) limited powers, (3) separation of powers, and (4) freedom of the press. These principles
were enumerated in a series of petitions to Parliament beginning
with the Large Petition of 11 September 1648. The Petition of 18
January 1649 contains the most complete statement of the position
of the Levellers on freedom of the press.[100]

After calling the attention of Parliament to the fact that
it owed its ascendancy to "unlicensed" printing, the petition boldly

---

[97] Lilburne, *op. cit.,* p. 10.

[98] See "England's New Chaines Discovered" (1648-49) reprinted in
William Haller and Godfrey Davies, *The Leveller Tracts, 1647-1653* (New
York: Columbia University press, 1944), pp. 156-70.

[99] For a history of this movement and its bearings on Democracy, see T. C.
Pease, *The Leveller Movement* (Baltimore: Williams and Wilkins, 1916).

[100] Steele, *op. cit.,* No. 282; B.M. 669 f. 13 (73); Commons Journal, VI,
120.

recommends the revocation of all ordinances against free printing. The conclusion is an astute piece of political reasoning which succeeding ages have failed to improve.

As for any prejudice to Government thereby, if Government be just in its Constitution, and equal in its distributions, it will be good, if not absolutely necessary for them, to hear all voices and judgments, which they can never do, but by giving freedom to the Press, and in case any abuse their authority by scandalous pamphlets, they will never want Advocates to vindicate their innocency. And therefore all things being duly weighed, to refer all Books and Pamphlets to the judgment, discretion, or affection of Licensers, or to put the least restraint upon the Press, seems altogether inconsistent with the good of the Commonwealth, and expressly opposite and dangerous to the liberties of the people, and to be carefully avoided, as any other exorbitancy or prejudice in Government.[101]

Nowhere in the literature of liberty can be found a more comprehensive or more logical statement of the argument for liberty of the press. The answer of Parliament was to pass an ordinance enlarging the crime of treason to include seditious publications,[102] and to have the chief Leveller, John Lilburne, tried for treason. The jury, however, refused to convict and Lilburne was released.[103] The Levellers won in the courts but lost the country to a military dictatorship.

---

[101] *Ibid.* For other petitions of the Levellers see B.M. 669 f. 15 (50). *The Second Part of England's New Chaines Discovered* (24 March 1649) by the Leveller authors is reprinted in Haller and Davies, *op. cit.*, pp. 171-89.

[102] Steele, *op. cit.*, No. 2847; B.M. 1060 (26); Commons Journal, VI, 209.

[103] The best account of the famous trial is to be found in Pease, *op. cit.*, pp. 286-300.

CHAPTER 10

Parliament and the Newsbooks

Reporting Parliament

The government of England had long been the particular province of the king and the nobility under the Tudor and early Stuart monarchs, but the intense religious and political questions of the middle of the seventeenth century succeeded in arousing an absorbing interest in public affairs on the part of the middle and lower classes. Affairs of government might not be within the scope of the average man, but religious salvation was every man's business, and when the government interfered in, or blocked, the contemporary gropings for religious light, the conduct of that government became an individual matter. As the breach between the king and Parliament widened, the desire of the subjects to participate in governmental problems naturally increased. The public demand for information and discussion of the vital issues led inevitably to the publication of domestic news, just as a few years before the prevailing interest in the religious wars on the continent had produced the corontos of foreign news.

Another factor in the evolution of domestic news was the attempt by the different factions or parties to present their cases before the country. Parliament, in particular, was anxious to enlarge its body of supporters. The various religious groups were seeking

representation as well as support. Argument and discussions were
heard on all sides. For the first time changes in religion and government were sought by an appeal not to the king but to the country.

A third element which led to the publication of domestic news
was the breakdown of the royal regulations for the control of printing. The licensing system collapsed late in 1640. The licensers
appointed by the Ecclesiastical Commission continued to do occasional licensing until 1642, but no attempts were made to enforce
the regulations. The king's power was gone, and Parliament had not
yet settled into the position of authority. In such a situation the
impecunious printers who had chafed under the Star Chamber
restrictions were more than anxious to supply the demand for news.
The bars were down; the supply was open; and the demand seemingly insatiable.[1]

One of the first publishers of domestic news was Samuel Pecke
who on 29 November 1641 issued a newsbook under the title of
Heads of Several Proceedings in Both Houses of Parliament.[2] The
first number was printed by John Thomas; later issues were printed
by various printers including Nathaniel Butter and William Cooke.
With No. 4, the title of the newsbook became *Diurnal Occurrences,*
and still later the *Perfect Diurnal.*[3] Ten years earlier neither Pecke
nor his printers would have dared to issue a periodical of domestic
news. As it was, nothing happened to either editor or printers. The
king had weightier matters on his mind, and Parliament was not
yet firmly in the saddle.

[1] An analysis of the items on the Thomason collection in the British Museum shows that the peak of newspaper production during the Puritan Revolution was reached in 1645, when the number of newspapers published was 722.
The following is a tabulation of newspapers found in the collection:

1641	4	1648	612	1655	350
1642	167	1649	554	1656	104
1643	402	1650	284	1657	25
1644	673	1651	356	1658	103
1645	722	1652	494	1659	253
1646	503	1653	460	1660	164
1647	407	1654	483		

[2] A volume of Parliamentary proceedings had been published by William
Cooke as early as June, 1641 (Burney collection).

[3] *Times Handlist,* p. 20; R. S. Crane and F. B. Kaye, *A Census of British
Newspapers and Periodicals, 1620-1800* (Chapel Hill: University of North
Carolina press, 1927), No. 295; Stanley Morison, *The English Newspaper*
(Cambridge: University press, 1932), lists eight variations in title.

The initial publication of a periodical of domestic news was followed by a host of imitators. With the Star Chamber gone, the Stationers Company was helpless against piracy. The imitators carried such confusing titles as *A Continuation of the True Diurnal, A True Diurnal of the Passages in Parliament, The True Diurnal Occurrences, A Perfect Diurnal of the Passages in Parliament.*[4]

In addition to the almost identical titles, the same title was frequently counterfeited. William Cooke's *Diurnal Occurrences in Parliament* was counterfeited by F. Cowles and T. Banks, while the latter's *A Perfect Diurnal of the Passages in Parliament* was duplicated in turn by Cooke. None of the diurnals was licensed or entered in the register of the Stationers Company. A few carried the authorization of a clerk of Parliament such as "Jo Browne, Cler. Parliamentor,"[5] or "Averred by R. P. Clerke."[6] The *Times Handlist* identifies thirty distinct publications for the year 1642.[7]

For five months (November, 1641-March, 1642) the competing publishers of the diurnals of domestic news remained unmolested. Half-hearted attempts at order and authenticity were made by the Commons, such as the licensing of several news pamphlets on foreign affairs by members of Parliament.[8] On 20 March 1641 the Committee on Printing appointed Sir Edward Deering as licenser,[9] but no attempt seems to have been made to license the diurnals.

The Stationers Company was ordered 6 April 1641 to suppress the publication of a speech by a member of the House of Commons,[10] and an order given that "none but the Printer appointed by this House shall print" the proceedings. John Ashton, a bookseller, was reprimanded for publishing the *Protestation* of 3 May 1641.[11]

News pamphlets must have continued to appear during the summer of 1641, for on July 22 the House forbade its members to

---

[4] *Times Handlist*, p. 20.

[5] *A True Diurnal*, No. 10, 1642.

[6] *The True Diurnal Occurrences*, January 31–February 7, 1642.

[7] A bibliography of the diurnals is badly needed. A beginning has been made in the check lists of *The Times* and of Crane and Kaye.

[8] Butter continued to exercise the patent on foreign news as late as 23 July 1641. G. E. B. Eyre and C. R. Rivington, *Transcript* . . . (London, 1913), I, 29.

[9] Commons Journal, II, 108.

[10] *Ibid.*, p. 116. No appointment of an official printer is recorded.

[11] *Ibid.*, p. 136.

give out copies or notes of the proceedings.[12] An attempt at official reporting was made on 30 July 1641 when the Commons ordered the vote on the *Protestation* to be printed and attested under the clerk's hand.[13] On 21 March 1642 both houses listed the abuse of printing as one requiring immediate suppression.[14] A week later, 28 March 1642, a resolution was adopted suppressing all unlicensed diurnals.[15] The printers, John Wright, Gregory Dexter, William Humphreyville, Robert Ward, and Robert Wood, were ordered to appear as delinquents. Eight diurnals ceased publication.[16]

During the early months of 1642, both Parliament and the king were preparing for civil war. Both sides sought public support and were at the same time extremely sensitive to criticism or adverse propaganda. Parliament voted to pay for the dispersal of "books" of favorable content and at the same time spurred on the Committee on Printing to suppress pamphlets of false news.[17] A committee was appointed to prevent the publication of any aspersion on Parliament, and a proclamation on false rumors was issued October 8.[18]

In the meantime the diurnals were reviving. Late in May, 1642, they began to appear one by one, the first being *The Heads of All Proceedings in both Houses of Parliament,* dated May 30 and printed for J. Smith and A. Coe. *A Perfect Diurnal* by Samuel Pecke was revived sometime in June while a duplicate, issued under the hand of the clerk to the House of Commons, appeared 18 July 1642, printed for Robert Williams.

A third *Perfect Diurnal,* a competing newsbook issued first by

---

[12] *Ibid.,* p. 220.

[13] *Ibid.,* p. 230. No copy survives.

[14] B.M. E. 141 (4).

[15] Commons Journal, II, 500-501. "Resolved that what Person soever shall print . . . sell any Act or Passages of this House under the name of a *Diurnal,* or otherwise, without the particular Licence of this House, shall be reported a high Contemner and Breaker of the Privilege of Parliament, and so punished accordingly."

[16] The suppressed diurnals were *A Continuation of the True Diurnal of Passages in Parliament, A True Diurnal of the Passages in Parliament, The Diurnal Occurrences in Parliament, A Perfect Diurnall of the Passages in Parliament, Irelands True Diurnall, The True Dirunall Occurrences* (John Hammond), and *Diurnall Occurrences.* (I. G.)

[17] Commons Journal, II, 611. A note of the disbursements, for a *Diurnal of Parliamentary Occurrences* and for other articles purchased, with the price is preserved in Calendar of State Papers, Domestic, 1641-43, p. 428.

[18] Robert Steele, *Tudor and Stuart Proclamations* (Oxford, 1910), No. 2274.

John Thomas, appeared soon afterwards. Although sixteen different varieties of diurnals were issued by the end of October,[19] none was entered in the register of the Stationers Company.

The House of Lords now entered the fray. After chastising Richard West, printer, for printing the *Propositions for Peace* as though authorized by the clerks of both Houses,[20] they called in the publishers of *The Continuation of the News*,[21] Francis Coles and Francis Leach. The printers sought to exculpate themselves by saying that Pecke, the scrivener, had furnished them with the copy.[22] Pecke was ordered to appear, but apparently could not be found. The two printers therefore, together with Bernard Alsopp and Thomas Fawcett, who confessed to printing scandalous pamphlets, were committed to prison in the Fleet. Two days later their release was ordered provided they entered into a bond as security for their good behavior.[23] The printers either objected to the recognizance on principle or were unable to find sureties, for they remained in prison. On 1 February 1643, the two newsbook publishers and Samuel Pecke, the editor, petitioned for their release.[24] The Lords took no action but on April 24 they presented another petition praying for their discharge on bail.[25] After more than three months in jail, they were released upon security "not to print anything concerning the Parliament without special order of Parliament."

The House of Lords with the aid of the Stationers Company's beadle, Joseph Hunscott, continued valiantly to hunt out the seditious printers. John Norton was arrested 24 January 1642; Richard Herne was taken 8 February, and Thomas Badger and Richard Lowndes were ordered to appear on the same date.[26] Henry Walker was arrested 16 March for further publications much to the consternation of the Lords who had assumed that he was still behind bars.[27]

---

[19] *Times Handlist*, pp. 20-21.

[20] Lords Journal, V, 519.

[21] The correct title was *Continuation of Special and Remarkable Passages*. This diurnal was begun in August, 1642, and continued until February, 1646.

[22] Lords Journal, V, 533.

[23] *Ibid.*, p. 554.

[24] Historical Manuscript Commission, 5th Report, p. 70.

[25] *Ibid.*, p. 82; Lords Journal, VI, 16.

[26] Lords Journal, V, 570, 593, 596.

[27] *Ibid.*, p. 651.

Not all Parliament's troubles were concerned with the inaccurate or unauthorized publication of its proceedings. The royalist press at Oxford began early in 1643 to issue pamphlets and newsbooks presenting the king's side of the conflict. *The Oxford Diurnal* appeared early in January,[28] and the more famous *Mercurius Aulicus* under the editorship of Peter Heylin and Sir John Berkenhead issued its first blasts against the Parliamentary cause soon after the beginning of the new year. *Mercurius Rusticus*, by Bruno Ryves, D.D., entered the fray in May, 1643, and began flaying Parliamentary principles and their adherents. The House of Commons was aroused but was unable to suppress either the printing at Oxford or the circulation within London. The Committee on Examinations was given power to prosecute printers and vendors of newsbooks, and the most enterprising Stationers were appointed as searchers.[29] Unable either to get along with the newsbook publishers of their own faction or to suppress the circulation of opposition propaganda, Parliament turned to new measures.

Censorship of Newsbooks, 1643-1647

One of the reasons for enacting the *Ordinance for the Regulation of Printing* (14 June 1643) was to regulate the reporting of Parliament. Reports of proceedings of Parliament were to be licensed by either House or the committee on printing, while pamphlets and newsbooks were to be licensed by the clerk of the Stationers Company, Henry Walley.[30]

The immediate effect of the Ordinance was to bring some semblance of order among the newsbooks and diurnals. True, the act failed to suppress the royalist journals, *Mercurius Aulicus*[31] and *Mercurius Rusticus,* but the more flagrant counterfeits and confusing titles were eliminated. From June to April, 1644, Walley exercised meticulous care in his new position. All the regular newsbooks were licensed under his hand,[32] including *Certain Informations from*

---

[28] A copy of the first issue is in the Yale University library.

[29] 13 March 1643, B.M., E. 538 (1); Commons Journal, II, 996.

[30] See below, pp. 187-88.

[31] There was constant leakage of news from Parliament to *Aulicus* much to the consternation of the Lords. Lords Journal, VI, 254. Copies of the royalist newsbook were occasionally seized in London. *Mercurius Britannicus*, No. 4.

[32] Eyre and Rivington, *op. cit.,* I, 58ff.

several parts of the Kingdom, edited by William Ingler and printed by George Bishop and Robert White; [33] *The Parliament Scout,* edited by John Dillingham and printed by George Bishop and Robert White; [34] *The Kingdom's Weekly Intelligencer* edited by "R. C." and printed by George Bishop and Robert White; [35] *The Weekly Account,* printed by John Greensmith and others; [36] *The Perfect Diurnal,* edited by Samuel Pecke and published by Francis Coles and Lawrence Blaiklock; [37] *Mercurius Civicus,* printed by John Wright Sr. and Thomas Bates; [38] *Mercurius Britannicus,* edited first by Captain Thomas Audley and later by John Rushworth and printed by George Bishop and Robert White; [39] *The True Informer,* edited by Henry Walley (the licenser) and printed by Thomas Bates and John Wright Sr.,[40] and *The Scottish Dove* edited by George Smith and printed by Laurence Chapman and Lawrence Blaiklock.[41] The licensed newsbooks carried the legends "Printed according to order" or "This is licensed and entered according to order."

The principal printers of newsbooks formed a tightly knit little group. Occasional journals were issued by other printers but few were successful.[42] The competition between the publishers must

[33] First entered in the Stationers' Register 24 June 1643, Eyre and Rivington, *op. cit.,* I, 58. The fee for each registration was sixpence. The last issue was entered February 15, 1643/4.

[34] First registration 26 June 1643. Continued until 30 January 1645.

[35] First registration 3 July. "R. C." says J. G. Muddiman's, *History of English Journalism* (London: Longmans, Green, 1908), stands for Richard Collings. The newsbook continued until 9 October 1649.

[36] No. 1 is dated July 3-10, 1643, and registered July 8. Only one number is known. The title was appropriated by Matthew Walbanck and Bernard Alsopp on September 6. Philip Lane was publisher. With the issue of 5 May 1647, the name became *The Perfect Weekly Account.* The newsbook continued until 21 June 1648.

[37] First registered 22 July; continued until 8 October 1649. Laurence Chapman became associated with Coles and Blaiklock in the printing in March, 1644.

[38] Begun in May but first registered 12 July 1643. Continued until 10 December 1646.

[39] First registered 5 September 1643; continued until 18 May 1646.

[40] First registered 12 September 1643; continued until 22 February 1645.

[41] Registered 19 October 1643; continued until 26 November 1646.

[42] *Wednesday's Mercury* printed by Humphrey Blunden lasted less than a month. *The Scottish Mercury* appeared in only one number (13 October 1643),

have been intense when on Mondays the ten or more newsbooks appeared on the streets of London.[43] However, the Stationers Company attempted to keep order among the printers, and consequently although titles or catch words were frequently similar they were seldom identical. Humphrey Blunden issued a newsbook under the title, *Kingdom's Weekly Intelligencer* (13 November 1643), but he was promptly squelched. He changed the name in the next issue to *The Complete Intelligencer*.[44]

Walley's career as exclusive licenser of all newsbooks continued until 4 March 1644. On that date the authorization for printing *Mercurius Britannicus* was under the hand of the Lord General of the Parliamentary forces, the Earl of Essex. The shift in licensers was evidently purely a precaution for military purposes. It was not long, however, until Walley, who continued to license all other newsbooks, found himself in trouble. Parliament took offense at a passage in a newsbook criticizing a member, Sir Richard Onsloe, and discharged the licenser 11 April 1644. John Rushworth, clerk assistant to the House of Commons, was given the position of censor of newsbooks.[45] Under his supervision the licensing of newsbooks becomes irregular. Rushworth was a busy man and must have been irked by the tiresome duty of reading innumerable proof sheets. The printers, also, found it difficult to get action out of the nimble clerk and secretary. Entries in the register now come in batches of twos and threes, and on 21 August 1644, seventeen issues of *The Weekly Account* are entered under one date. Either the sheets had been held back by the licenser, or the printer had neglected to enter them in the register.[46]

---

as did *The Compleate Intelligencer and Resolver* (2 November) and the *Informator Rusticus* (3 November) printed by Robert Austen and Andrew Coe. *Britanicus Vapulans* appeared in two numbers (2-9 November). See *Times Handlist*, pp. 21-23.

[43] At the instance of the Stationers Company, the Common Council of the City of London enacted an ordinance suppressing the hawkers and mercury women who sold unlicensed pamphlets and newsbooks. Guildhall Mss. 669 F 7 (49).

[44] Eyre and Rivington, *op. cit.*, I, 84, 86.

[45] Commons Journal, III, 457-58. The Lord General continued to license *Mercurius Britannicus*.

[46] Eyre and Rivington, *op. cit.*, I, 129. The entire year's issues of a newsbook printed by George Bishop were entered on the register on one date, 4 March 1645, *Ibid.*, p. 151.

Rushworth finally in despair received Parliament's approval of the appointment of Gilbert Mabbott as his deputy for the licensing of newsbooks (26 March 1645).[47] His troubles were increased by the particular sensitivity of the House of Lords. Robert White, printer of the *Kingdom's Weekly Intelligencer*, was called to the bar [48] of the upper house 18 June 1644 for aspersions on Lord Stanford. The newsbook had been duly licensed and registered. White avoided the wrath of the House by naming Captain Audley as the author of the offending article. There is no record of any punishment imposed on either printer or author other than censure.

A few months later White was again in difficulties with the House of Lords, this time for an article in the *Parliament Scout* defaming the honor of the Lord General. The author (not named) and printer were apprehended by the agents of the Stationers Company and imprisoned by order of the Lords.[49]

Audley who was now licensing *Mercurius Britannicus* under authority of the Lord General again found himself before the upper House 13 March 1645, this time for a passage which attacked the king. The records of the House do not indicate the disposition of the case.[50]

Under the deputy, the licensing entries continued as erratic as they had been under Rushworth. Poor Mabbott was torn between satisfying the Commons, the Lords, the Army, and the publishers. The Lords particularly continued to haunt both Rushworth's deputy and Audley. On 4 August 1645 they complained of a passage in *Mercurius Britannicus* and after questioning Audley, who licensed the newsbook, and White the printer, Marchmont Needham, the editor, was called in. All were committed to prison, but later released with an admonition. Audley was forbidden to do any further licensing, and thereafter *Britannicus*, like the rest of the newsbooks, was licensed by Mabbott.[51]

---

[47] *Ibid.*, p. 158. The Lord General either by himself or through Thomas Audley continued to license *Mercurius Britannicus*. An entry in the register on 10 November 1645 establishes the fact that although newsbooks may have been read and allowed before publication, they were not entered in the register until some time afterward.

[48] Lords Journal, VI, 595, 597.

[49] *Ibid.*, VII, 164, 165.

[50] *Ibid.*, pp. 267, 272.

[51] *Ibid.*, pp. 525, 528, 539. Needham was again in trouble with the Lords

The same four men, White the printer, Needham the writer, Rushworth the official licenser, and Audley the deputy, were called before the Lords again on 21 May 1646. This time Needham appeared. He confessed the authorship of all numbers of the *Britannicus* after No. 52. He was sent to the Fleet without trial (23 March) while the Lords went further into the business.[52]

A week later he was bailed under the condition that he refrain from writing any more pamphlets without leave of the House.[53] Audley, when he appeared, denied licensing the newsbooks and was relieved.[54] George Smith, author of *The Scottish Dove* (licensed and registered), was forced by the Lords to apologize to the French ambassador for references to the French king, and copies of the newsbook were ordered burned.[55]

Even the mercury women were not beneath the notice of the House of Lords. Abigail Rogers, who sold pamphlets and newsbooks, was imprisoned upon refusal to name the person from whom she obtained her wares. After a week in jail she obtained a release on the ground that she was with child.[56]

The House of Commons was no less zealous in its persecution of the newsbook writers and publishers than was the House of Lords. Prosecutions were begun against the publishers of *The Scottish Dove* [57] and *Mercurius Rusticus*.[58]

Wholesale arrests were ordered in October, and the newsbook publishers, John Field, Laurence Chapman, Edward Griffin, and Francis Leach were apprehended. Lawrence Blaiklock and Samuel Pecke were called to appear, but all were dismissed with warnings.[59] Unable to stem the publications or to control their contents, the House of Commons on 9 March 1647 discharged Mr. Rush-

---

23 October 1645, but he managed to escape. *Ibid.*, p. 567. Audley reappears as licenser of *Mercurius Britannicus* on 4 October 1645. Eyre and Rivington, *op. cit.*, I, 196. He drops out 26 March 1646, but appears again 9 May 1646.

[52] Lords Journal, VIII, 321, 325.

[53] *Ibid.*, p. 241.

[54] *Ibid.*, p. 373.

[55] *Ibid.*, p. 504 (24 September 1646).

[56] *Ibid.*, pp. 615, 645.

[57] Commons Journal, IV, 664.

[58] *Ibid.*, p. 682.

[59] *Ibid.*, pp. 693, 694, 703 (14 October 1646).

worth and his deputies.[60] Sir Nathaniel Brent undertook to license
a few numbers but after a few weeks his name too disappears.
Two issues of *Perfect Occurrences* were entered 12 April 1647, and
a batch of twenty diurnals was registered 28 June. With the exception of six issues of the *Kingdom's Weekly Intelligencer* (no
licenser's name), no further newsbooks were registered until 22
December. For the second time Parliament found itself unable to
accommodate itself to the new journalism even when it was placed
under the supervision of an official licenser. Once again the newsbooks were suppressed.

The Army Takes Control, 1647-1649

Ever since the Self-denying Ordinance (3 April 1645) the
breach between Parliament and the Army had continued to widen.
The devout among the soldiers wanted an assurance that they would
be allowed to enjoy liberty of conscience, and devout and profane
alike wanted to receive their pay in full. Unable to obtain satisfaction on these points, the soldiers organized themselves into
political groups composed largely of Independents as opposed to
the Presbyterians who held the political reins in London. The newsbooks were not slow to align themselves on one or the other side
of the dispute. As the pressure from the Army increased and the
published accounts of the negotiations accompanied by editorial
criticism multiplied, Parliament became frantic. A special committee of thirty-two members was charged with the task of suppressing these reports and criticisms.[61]

The energy of the House of Lords equaled if not exceeded
that of the Commons in the campaign of suppression. Henry Walker,
publisher of *Perfect Occurrences,* was summoned to appear for a
reflection on a minister.[62] A month later he was again censured
for reporting some proceedings of the House.[63]

---

[60] *Ibid.,* V, 109.

[61] *Ibid.,* pp. 72-73 (3 February 1647). The committee headed by Mr.
Corbett and Mr. Christopher Yelverton was given power to suppress all ballad
singers and vendors of pamphlets on the streets of London. The publications
which were particularly irritating included *A Warning to all Counties of England, A New-Found Stratagem,* and *A True Narrative Concerning the Army's
Preservation of the King's Majestic Person.*

[62] Lords Journal, IX, 37 (26 February 1647).

[63] *Ibid.,* pp. 131, 142 (9 April 1647).

After Rushworth had been relieved of his licensing duties (9 March 1647), Parliament itself and its committees attempted to carry on. Among the newsbooks which were discontinued as a result of Parliament's drive were *The Parliament Scout, Mercurius Civicus, Mercurius Britannicus, The True Informer,* and *The Scottish Dove.* Those which continued to print weekly numbers, apparently with Parliamentary approval, were *The Kingdom's Weekly Intelligencer, The Perfect Weekly Account, Perfect Occurrences, The Moderate Intelligencer,* and *A Perfect Diurnal.* From 12 April to 28 June 1647 none of these newsbooks was entered on the register of the Stationers Company.

After several months of hearings and deliberations, the committee of Parliament could recommend nothing better as a remedy for the abuses than the enactment of a new licensing act with more stringent penalties for violations. Accordingly, on 30 September 1647 the new Ordinance was passed by both Houses. The licensing was to be done by an appointee of one or both Houses of Parliament. Authors, writers, or editors were liable to a penalty of forty shillings fine or forty days in jail; the printers' punishment was twenty shillings or twenty days in jail; the stationers and booksellers were assessed ten shillings or ten days in jail; while the hawker or newspeddler was to be whipped as a common rogue.[64]

On the same day (30 September) Gilbert Mabbott was reappointed by the House of Lords as licenser of weekly pamphlets.[65] This appointment had been sponsored by General Fairfax who on 21 September had dispatched a letter to the House recommending Mabbott. The general's solution of the newsbook problem was to use every effort to suppress the unlicensed ones and at the same time to offset those which were undetected by permitting the publications of a few weekly sheets carrying the stamp of authority.[66]

The unfortunate Mabbott, appointed by the House of Lords, indebted to the Army for his appointment, and held responsible by the House of Commons, continued to fill the position as official licenser of newsbooks until 22 May 1649. The official newsbooks of this period (1647-1649) were *The Moderate Intelligencer, The*

---

[64] C. H. Firth and R. S. Rait, *Acts and Ordinances of the Interregnum, 1642-1660* (London, 1911), I, 1021.

[65] Lords Journal, IX, 456.

[66] *Ibid.,* p. 441.

Perfect Account, Perfect Occurrences, The Perfect Diurnal, and *The Moderate.*

In spite of the new Ordinance and the efforts at enforcement by the Stationers Company, unlicensed newsbooks appeared on the streets of London. Search was made in vain for the author (Needham) and printers of *Mercurius Pragmaticus.*[67] The presses of the printer of *Mercurius Melancholicus* were seized and destroyed.[68] The House of Commons made valiant efforts to capture the printers of the various counterfeits parading under the titles *Mercurius Pragmaticus* and *Mercurius Elenchichus.*[69]

The Committee on Printing summoned Mabbott (21 December 1647) for licensing *His Majesty's Declaration,*[70] and after much haranguing an appropriation of £30 was made for the employment of persons to prosecute the printers.[71] The Committee was ordered to sit "constantly" and the Committee on Examinations was directed to assist in the suppression.[72]

---

[67] *Ibid.,* p. 472.

[68] Calendar of State Papers, Domestic, 1645-47, p. 602. Which one of the three competing journals of this title was suppressed, it is difficult to tell.

[69] Commons Journal, V, 371.

[70] *Ibid.,* p. 395.

[71] *Ibid.,* pp. 420, 424, 427.

[72] B.M. E. 409 (3). Not mentioned in the Commons Journals. The following is the text of the order (24 February 1648): "It is this day Ordered by the Commons House of Parliament, That the Committee for Examinations, or any foure of them, have power to appoint such persons as they think fit, to search in any house or place where there is just cause of suspicion, that Presses are kept and employed in the printing of Scandalous and lying Pamphlets, and that they do demolish and take away such presses, and their materials, and the Printers Nuts and Spindles which they find so employed, and bring the Master-Printers, and Workmen Printers before the said Committee; And that the Committee or any foure of them have power to commit to prison any of the said printers, or any other persons that do contrive, or publikely or privately vend, sell, or publish any Pamphlets, scandalous to His Majesty, or the proceedings of both or either Houses of Parliament, or that shall refuse to suffer any Houses or Shops to be searched, where such presses or pamphlets as aforesaid are kept. And that the persons employed by the said Committee, shall have power to seize such scandalous and lying pamphlets as they find upon search, to be in any Shop or Warehouse, sold or dispersed by any person whomsoever, and to bring the persons that so kept, published or sold the same before the Committee; And that such persons as the committee shal comit for any of the offences aforesaid, shall not be released till the parties imployed for the apprehending of the said persons, and seizing their presses and materials, be satisfied for their paines and charges. And all justices of the Peace, Captains, Officers, and Constables, are required to be assisting in the appre-

In addition to its discussions with the Army, Parliament had for some time been conducting negotiations with Commissioners from Scotland. The publication of reports of these discussions together with critical comments on them spurred Parliament to further efforts at control. On 13 March 1648 another order was issued prohibiting the publication of reports of any proceedings of the governing body except by special direction from either House.[73]

Mabbott's load became increasingly heavy and his position more precarious as the breach between Parliament and the Army widened. He made a special report to the House of Commons in August, 1648, recommending certain changes in the licensing system.[74] An appeal to the House of Lords over Mabbott's head resulted in the licensing of *The Perfect Occurrences* by the upper house itself.[75] Theodore Jennings made his appearance as licenser along with Mabbott early in 1649,[76] and Edward Walley, judge advocate of the Army, entered the register 1 February 1649 as licenser of one of the newsbooks.[77]

No matter how seriously he accepted his duties, it was inevitable that Mabbott should offend at least one of his three sponsors, the Commons, the Lords, or the Army. During the summer of 1648 he discovered that Dillingham's *Moderate Intelligencer* had been running a line "Dieu nous donne les Parlyments briefe, Rois de vie Longue," and thereupon refused to license further issues. Furthermore to keep a going concern from dying and at the same

---

hending of any of the persons aforesaid, And in searching of their Shops, Houses, and Warehouses; And likewise all Justices of peace, Officers, and Constables, are hereby required, from time to time, to apprehend such persons as shall publish, vend, or sell the said Pamphlets: And it is further ordered, that this order be forthwith printed and published, to the end that notice may be taken hereof, that the contemners of this order may be left inexcusable for their offence."

[73] Commons Journal, V, 493.

[74] *Ibid.*, p. 695. The nature of these recommendations is unknown although there are indications that Mabbott requested that complete authority be placed in his hands.

[75] Eyre and Rivington, *op. cit.*, I, 306.

[76] The first publication licensed by Jennings was *A Collection of Notes on the King's Trial*, 20 January 1649. *Ibid.*, p. 307. This registration to Ibbitson, printer, on the first day of the trial was in the nature of a "blocking entry." See pp. 78-79. Two further collections of notes on the trial were licensed by Jennings on 23 January.

[77] *Ibid.*, p. 309.

time compensate himself, Mabbott took over the editorship of the newsbook himself with Robert White as printer. Dillingham complained to the House of Lords, now tottering on the brink of extinction, while the printer also petitioned that the right and title to the name *Moderate Intelligencer* be awarded to him.[78] The Lords, still somewhat devoted to the principle of monarchy, ordered Mabbott to cease his publications and restore the newsbook to Dillingham. White's petition was passed over in silence. When the licenser, instead of discontinuing his publication, changed its name to *The Moderate,* the House of Lords took the question of these competing names under advisement, but before a decision was reached the upper house was abolished.[79]

The trial and execution of the king during the early months of 1649 provided the most spectacular news event of the entire seventeenth century. Not only was it of unparalleled interest to the entire nation, but its political implications and overtones provided material for endless discussions. Parliament was frightened at the prospect of a possible reaction among the body of its supporters. The event itself could not fail to furnish all anti-Parliament factions with powerful ammunition. As early as 3 February the House of Commons charged a special committee of forty members with suppressing printing and preaching on the king's trial,[80] and a few days later all narratives of the trial and execution were gathered for perusal by the House. To offset the influence of these reports, the Committee was ordered to prepare a report of the event from Parliament's point of view.[81]

The division in political sentiment throughout the country and the impotence of Parliament to suppress unlicensed printing led the Army under General Fairfax to issue military orders in the hope of controlling the situation. The warrant addressed to Richard Lawrence, Marshall-General of the Army, set out and directed him to put into execution the following ordinances: (1) 28 September 1647, (2) 14 June 1643, (3) 9 March 1642, (4) 13 March 1642, and

---

[78] Hist. Ms. Comm., 7th Report, p. 33; Lords Journal, X, 345.

[79] *Ibid.,* p. 508. Another conflict over property rights in a title of a newsbook between Mabbott and Henry Walker is presented in W. M. Clyde, *The Struggle For Freedom of the Press* . . . (London: Oxford University press, 1934), pp. 146-49.

[80] Commons Journal, VI, 131.

[81] *Ibid.,* pp. 135, 143-44.

(5) 9 October 1643.[82] The deputies of the Marshall were authorized under the warrant to search for and seize all unlicensed printing presses with or without the consent of the Stationers Company. The oath of one "credible witness" was declared sufficient for a conviction before any justice of the peace, master in chancery, or the judge advocate of the Army. Half the fine was allotted to the apprehending officer and the other half to the poor of the parish where the offense was committed. This warrant together with the Treason Act of 14 May 1649 [83] constitutes the most stringent regulation of freedom of discussion of the Puritan Revolution. Any person writing against the government or the Army was guilty of treason and liable to execution. The democratic principles of the Levellers were abandoned both by Parliament and the Army for those of a dictatorship. In May the Council of State took over the executive reins of the government.

Under these circumstances Mabbott, the licenser of newsbooks, who imperceptibly had been swinging over to the position of the Levellers, found his duties intolerable and resigned 7 May 1649. Two weeks later he was discharged, and then to defend himself from criticism presented his reasons for resigning in *The Perfect Diurnal* (May 21-28):

1. Because many thousands of scandalous and malignant pamphlets have been published with his name thereunto, as if he had licensed the same, (though he never saw them) on purpose (as he conceived) to prejudice him in his reputation amongst the honest part of this nation.

2. Because that imployment (as he conceives) is unjust and illegall as to the end of its first Institution, *viz.* to stop the Presse for publishing anything that might discover the Corruption of Church or State in the time of Poperty, Episcopacy, and Tyranny, the better to keep the People in ignorance, and carry on their Popish, factious, trayterous and Tyrannical designes for the enslaving and distruction both of the bodies and soules of all the free people of this Nation.

3. Because Licensing is as great a monopoly as ever was in this nation, in that all men's judgements, reasons, etc. are to be bound up in the licensers (as to lycenceing) for if the author of any sheet, book or treatise writ not to please the fancie, and come within the compasse of the lycencers judgement, then he is not to receive any stamp of authoirty for publishing thereof.

4. Because it is lawfull (in his judgement) to print any Book, sheet,

---

[82] B.M. E. 538 (1).

[83] Commons Journal, VI, 209; Steele, *op. cit.*, No. 2847.

etc. without lycenceing, so as the authors and printers do subscribe their true names thereunto, that so they may be lyable to answer the contents thereof, and if they offend therein, then to be punished by such lawes as are or shall be for those cases provided.

No more effective indictment of licensing is to be found in the English language.

CHAPTER 11

Experiments in Control

of the Press, 1649-1660

The execution of Charles I was followed by the abolition of the monarchy and the House of Lords, and a Commonwealth was set up with executive authority placed in the hands of a Council of State. The power of the central government was based upon the Army. Opposition was widespread, in Ireland, in Scotland, and in England itself. Upon Cromwell's return from conquering the royalist combination in Ireland, he succeeded in quelling the mutinous elements in the English Army and in subduing the Scots. Quarrels between the Army and the Rump Parliament continued until finally Cromwell expelled both the House of Commons and the Council of State (1653). The reforms proposed by the succeeding "Little Parliament," a collection of Puritan leaders, produced a political reaction among the conservative and propertied classes. It drew up the Instrument of Government, a written constitution, under which Cromwell became Lord Protector.

The chaotic state of the central authority in government during the period of the Commonwealth and the Protectorate is nowhere more clearly reflected than in the attempts at the control and regulation of the press. Restrictions more despotic than those of the Star Chamber followed by periods with no discernible regulations, enforcement at one moment stringent and at the next completely absent, hand-in-glove cooperation with the Stationers Company and a few months later the complete exclusion of the trade organization from official duties, licensing and then no licensing, newsbooks with a wide latitude in reporting public affairs and then no newsbooks at all except "official" ones—all these conditions are to be found during the decade (1650-1660) preceding the restoration of the monarchy. These vagaries in regulation and enforcement peculiarly do not reflect the shifts in supreme authority from the Army to the Rump Parliament, to the Council of State, to Cromwell, but usually represent changes of attitude within the group or the individual who at the moment was to be found at the top of the pyramid.

One point, however, became clear to the authorities during the Commonwealth. Journalism, controlled or uncontrolled, had become a permanent social and political phenomenon. Once the public had become interested and aware of its craving for information, ways and means were inevitably found to satisfy this demand. The food may have been unwholesome or even tainted, but food was demanded. Gradually the problem had shifted from one of suppression of all information to one of determining what and by what means information should be doled out.

Neither the Independents nor the Presbyterians, the Royalists nor the Roundheads, Parliament nor the Army, the Council of State nor Cromwell, had any real solution for the problem of printed news. Each cried out for a measure of freedom while rising to power; each sought to buttress acquired authority through some measure of control. To what extent and in what directions this control should be exercised was the immediate question presented to each. Complete freedom was not considered as one of the possible solutions largely for these reasons: historical precedents were lacking, experimentation had not yet demonstrated the ineffectiveness of the traditional regulations, government was not yet considered an instrument of the people for their own well-being and therefore participation even by the middle classes although tolerated at times was not an accepted tenet of those in power, the sensitiveness of public officials to comment and criticism by the public at large, the inexperience of the channels of communication in delivering and the public in digesting a free and uncontrolled flow of information and comment on public issues, and lastly the age had not learned a restrained and civilized toleration of divergent points of view. All of those factors had to be modified before freedom of the press could be achieved.

A number of interesting problems in public opinion and its management is presented during the short period 1650-1660: How much did each reigning authority owe its ascendancy to the laxity of its predecessor's regulations and how much to the aggressiveness of its own propaganda? Was there any relationship between the instability of a government and its effectiveness in the control of the press? What weight can be assigned to each of the factors mentioned?

The Press Under the Commonwealth, 1649-1651

The regulations for the control of the press during the Commonwealth and the Protectorate were (1) military measures (9 January 1649 to September, 1649), (2) the Printing Act of 20 September 1649 (attempted enforcement to September, 1651), (3) the Printing Act of 7 January 1653, and (4) Cromwell's orders of 28 August 1655.

The regulations in force after the execution of the king (30 January 1649) included the warrant given by General Fairfax to the militia of London to suppress both the royalist and the Presbyterian press. These orders were supplemented on May 14 and again on July 17 by the Treason Act,[1] making it a capital offense to criticize or disparage the "government." The military warrant seems to have been suspended sometime in April, but whether from ineffectiveness or because of a change of heart induced by Lilburne's pleas for more freedom it is difficult to tell.[2] John Bradshaw, as president of the Council of State, made a show of legality by issuing a number of warrants for the arrest of printers, including William Larner and Samuel Sheppard.[3]

In spite of the Treason Act the number of royalist mercuries

---

[1] Commons Journal, VI, 209.

[2] Lilburne's *The Second Part of England's New Chains Discovered* was published in March, 1649.

[3] Calendar of State Papers, Domestic, 1649-50, p. 529.

increased. *Mercurius Elencticus* parodied the act in tantalizing fashion. *The Man in the Moon* by John Crouch opened its barrage on April 16 and continued a running attack on Parliament, the Army, and the Council of State until June, 1650. Additional battalions which now rushed to the front in the wave of reaction against the murder of a king included *Mercurius Pragmaticus*, *Mercurius Militaris*, *Mercurius Melancholicus*, and a revived *Mercurius Aulicus*.

The Council of State sent into action two groups of searching parties, one in charge of the Provost Marshalls and the other under the supervision of the Stationers Company. Provost Marshall Zachary Bishop was assigned the north side of the Thames while Provost Marshall Munk and his twelve assistants were ordered to patrol the area south of the river with orders to seize all mercury women who sold unlicensed newsbooks or pamphlets.[4] The master and wardens of the Stationers Company together with their assistants were given authority to seize all seditious books and pamphlets and to apprehend the printers under a special warrant from the Council of State.[5]

On 20 September 1649 the new Printing Act was passed by what :emained of Parliament.[6] Drawing upon the Tudor proclamations, the Star Chamber decrees, and previous ordinances of Parliament, the new act presented the most detailed list of regulations for the press of the entire seventeenth century. Printing was limited to the city of London and the two universities, with the exception of presses at York and Finsbury engaged in printing the Bible. No house was to be let to a printer without notice to the Stationers Company, nor were any implements of printing to be made, press imported, or type cast without such notice. Most stringent of all was the requirement that all printers must enter into a bond of £300.

All "scandalous" and "seditious" matter was prohibited and no seditious book was allowed to be sent by carrier or by post.

---

[4] J. G. Muddiman, *History of English Journalism* . . . (London: Longmans, Green, 1908), p. 111.

[5] Cal. St. P. Dom., 1649, p. 529.

[6] C. H. Firth and R. S. Rait, *Acts and Ordinances of the Interregnum, 1642-1660* (London, 1911), II, 246.

All books and pamphlets were required to be licensed (no licensers were named), and authors' and licensers' names were ordered to be prefixed to every publication. All unlicensed works which were seized were to be turned over to the secretary to the Council of State.

Newsbooks from henceforth were ordered suppressed and all previous licenses withdrawn. Official news of Parliament was to be licensed by the clerk, Army news by the Army, and all newsbooks entered in the Stationers' Register. Former laws against dispersing "false" news were ordered enforced.

Under the heading of copyright might be assigned those provisions prohibiting the importation of Bibles and the penalty of six shillings eight pence for every pirated copy of a book duly entered and registered in the Stationers' Register.

Enforcement of the provisions was entrusted largely to the Stationers Company.[7] Its appointees were to search for all unallowed books and presses and to inspect all imported books. Any two magistrates "upon just cause of suspicion" could issue a warrant for the inspection of all packs and packets. The Lord Mayor of London was entrusted with the task of suppressing all newshawkers, mercury women, and ballad singers.

Fines fixed by the act were: author £10, printer £5, bookseller £2, importer £5, buyer £1 (provided he concealed the book). Hawkers were to be sent to the house of correction. The act itself was to remain in force for two years until 20 September 1651.

Thomas Newcombe was the first printer to post bonds under the new act.[8] On October 9 three others joined him; the next day there were nineteen others listed; and by the end of the month forty-two printers had entered into recognizances to observe the law.

Under the new regulations all the licensed newsbooks were suppressed by the end of the year (1649).[9] Only the royalist jour-

---

[7] A special committee was appointed by the Council, 10 November 1649, to assist the Stationers Company in enforcement. The following were named: William Lee, Christopher Meredith, Richard Coates, John Wilson, Abraham Miller, John Wright, Edward Muttershead, Joseph Hunscott.

[8] Cal. St. P. Dom., 1649, p. 522 (22 September).

[9] A *Perfect Diurnal* was suspended October 8, *The Kingdom's Weekly Intelligencer* October 9, *The Moderate* September 25, *The Perfect Weekly*

nals remained and even these found it increasingly difficult to elude the searchers. In place of the licensed press there now appeared the official journals. *The Briefe Relation* under the supervision of Gaulter Frost, secretary to the Council of State, was the official journal of government affairs. *Several Proceedings In Parliament* by Henry Scobell was the Parliamentary journal. *A Perfect Diurnal of Some Passages and Proceedings of and in Relation to the Armies* was edited by John Rushworth, secretary to the Army, assisted by Samuel Pecke. A fourth official journal, *Mercurius Politicus*, joined the group in June, 1650, edited by Marchmont Needham, now on the payroll of Parliament, and licensed by John Milton, Latin secretary.

Only one problem remained—the suppression of the royalist mercuries. This seemingly impossible feat was accomplished during the months of May and June, 1650, with the assistance of two important figures in the history of the Commonwealth, Parliament Joan and Oliver Cromwell. Parliament Joan, a fat, middle-aged woman, was employed by Parliament as a spy and later undertook to sell counterfeit royalist mercuries on the streets of London for the purpose of identifying and apprehending the agents who dispersed the genuine article. Her methods were so successful that by the end of June not a single royalist newsbook could be bought in London. Cromwell, back from the Irish campaign, lent the support of his presence to the law-enforcing bodies engaged in apprehending and prosecuting the culprits.

But just as royalist journalism was being routed out, a new crop of *licensed* newsbooks, many of them with well-known titles, arose. On 28 June 1650 the *Impartial Scout*, edited by Daniel Border was revived. Henry Walker's *Perfect Passages of Every Daies Intelligence* came out as the *Weekly Intelligencer of the Commonwealth* on July 23, and even Samuel Pecke's *A Perfect Diurnal of Some Passages in Parliament* joined the group July 22. None of these newsbooks was entered in the register of the Stationers Company, but they were printed by bonded printers and so must have had the approval of authority. Why these journals were allowed to appear is not quite clear. Perhaps they were a part of a campaign for public support in the approaching war with Scotland, and it

Account October 10, *The Moderate Intelligencer* October 4, *Perfect Occurrences* October 12.

was felt that more satisfactory service could be performed by an apparently independent press than through "official" journals.

Failure of the Council of State (September 1651—August 1655)

The printing act of 1649 did not expire until September, 1651, but for several months it had not been enforced. The official journals, *A Perfect Diurnal,* licensed by John Rushworth and printed by Griffin and Leach, *Mercurius Politicus,* licensed by Milton [10] and printed by Thomas Newcomb, and *Several Proceedings,* licensed by Henry Scobell and printed by Robert Ibbitson,[11] continued their registration in the records of the Stationers Company even after the expiration of the act. On the other hand, *The Weekly Intelligencer, Perfect Passages, Faithful Scout* edited by Daniel Border and printed by Robert Wood, and *A Perfect Account* printed by Bernard Alsopp, were entered neither before nor after the expiration of the act of 1649. All seven of these newsbooks continued regular publication until Cromwell's order of suppression in September, 1655.[12]

Aside from these seven publications there were occasional attempts to establish new journals or to revive old ones. *Mercurius Pragmaticus,* edited by Samuel Sheppard and printed by James Moxon, made a valiant effort to survive, but after changing its name twice, it collapsed in the summer of 1651. Only one issue of each of the following newsbooks is known: *The True Informer,* 28 August 1651; *The Modern Intelligencer,* 3 September 1651; *Mercurius Scoticus,* 30 September 1651; *Mercurius Bellonius,* 4 February 1652; *The Dutch Spy,* three numbers, March, 1652; *Mercurius Phreneticus,* 19 July 1652; *The Loyal Messenger,* 10 August 1653; *The Loyal Intelligencer,* 30 January 1654; others lasting only a short period include *The Diary,* 29 September-3 November 1651; *The French Intelligencer,* 25 November 1651-18 May 1652; *Mercurius Democritus,* 8 April 1652-9 November 1653.[13]

[10] Milton's name ceases to appear along with those of the other licensers in January, 1652. (G. E. B. Eyre and C. R. Rivington, *Transcript* . . . London, 1913), I, 389). A satisfactory explanation of Milton's position as licenser had not yet been found. See above, pp. 196-97.

[11] *Several Proceedings* is not entered in the register between 9 October 1651 and 12 January 1653. (*Ibid.,* pp. 380, 406.)

[12] See below, pp. 230-31.

[13] For lists see Muddiman, *op. cit.,* App. D.

Whether the failure of these journals was due to economic causes or to suppressive measures by the government is difficult to ascertain. The printers and editor of the *Faithful Scout* were twice summoned to appear before the authorities for offending articles,[14] and James Cottrell, printer, was imprisoned by order of the Council for publishing an offending newsbook entitled *Mercurius Britannicus.*[15] Other than these, the records of the Council show few prosecutions during this period.

As early as 5 March 1652 work had begun on a new bill to replace the expired printing act of 1649. Two problems immediately arose, and the Council became the focus for pressure groups which were aligned on either side of the two issues. The first issue was that of freedom of the press with the Levellers and Independents on one side and the Presbyterians and Stationers on the other. The second problem was the status of the Stationers Company and the monopolists who were seeking a revival of their privileges.

On the issue of freedom of the press, the Levellers had late in 1651 made further complaints that "the liberty of Printing was even more restrained than ever (except to books maintaining the most tyrannous principles) as the Book entitled *The Case of the Commonwealth of England stated,* and the like which to the shame of these times were freely licensed." [16] Again in June, 1652, the adherents of Lilburne petitioned for a free press,[17] but it is noteworthy that the large Petition of July which contains a complete list of grievances did not mention liberty of the press.[18]

On the other side of this issue was the group of Presbyterian stationers and printers who protested the publication of "popish" as well as "sectarian" books. This group later identified as the "Beacon Firers" included Luke Fawne, Samuel Gellibrand, Joshua Kirton, John Rothwell, Thomas Underhill, and Nathaniel Webb. A printed protest compiled by these men was published 21 September 1652 as *A Beacon Set on Fire.*[19] The remedy suggested was a strict licensing system administered by "godly men," with sufficient

---

[14] Cal. St. P. Dom., 1651-52, pp. 444, 464.
[15] *Ibid.,* 1652/3, pp. 78, 88.
[16] Petition to Commons, B.M. 669 f. 15 (54).
[17] B.M. E. 669 f. 16 (50).
[18] B.M. E. 705.
[19] B.M. E. 657. 14.

penalties and enforcement at common law guaranteed by awarding
the penalty to the informer. A sequel, *A Second Beacon Fired by
Scintilla* (Michael Sparke), appeared in October decrying the leth-
argy of Parliament and of the enforcement officers.

With Lilburne out of the country, the lead in the opposition
was taken by the left wing of the Independent party including such
men as Colonel Pride, Lieutenant-Colonel Gough, Major Bridge,
Adjutant-General Merest, Captain Kiffen, and Isaac Grey. On 8
October they replied with *The Beacons Quenched* in which they
charged the Stationers with desiring to suppress the press in the
interest of Presbyterianism. Prayer and adequate answers to the
popish books were suggested as substitutes for the repressive measures advocated by the Stationers. The latter defended their position
in a second pamphlet [20] arguing that strict regulation was "the only
way to prevent the publishing of such books as tended to the dis-
honour of God and disturbance of the State."

A revival of the controversy in 1654 by the publication of
A Second Beacon Fired [21] led to the publication of John Goodwin's
able defense of freedom of the press in his pamphlet, *Fresh Discovery of the High Presbyterian Spirit*,[22] in which after disposing
of Biblical argument he poignantly demonstrated the absurdities inherent in a system of suppression. "The setting of Watchmen with
authority at the door of the press to keep errors and heresies out of
the world," he wrote, "is as weak a project and design, as it would
be to set a company of armed men about a house to keep dark-
ness out of it in the night season." Although not couched in such
elevated language as Milton's *Areopagitica,* Goodwin's pamphlet
stands as one of the great landmarks in the progress toward freedom of the press from government control.

The second problem which was presented to the Council of
State and to Parliament in the discussions concerning a new act
for printing was concerned with the monopolies held by the Stationers Company and its privileged members. On one side of this
issue were aligned those stationers and printers who claimed legal
title to valuable printing patents derived from grants dating back

[20] *The Beacon Flameing,* B.M. E. 683.30 (15 December 1652).
[21] B.M. E. 813. 1 (October, 1654).
[22] B.M. E. 821 (18 January 1655).

to the days of Elizabeth.²³ Opposed to these were the disenfranchised members of the printing craft, who since the revolt of 1645
had little to say in the government of the Company, and also those
printers who had received special grants from the Puritan Parliament. The principal item in the controversy was the printing of the
Bible. Mathew Barker, a leading member of the Stationers, claimed
the sole privilege of printing the New Testament through the grant
to his father from James I. If Parliament could grant exclusive
privileges to John Field (Acts of Parliament) and to William Du-
Gard (printer for a time to the Council of State), argued Barker
through his spokesman William Ball,²⁴ it could confirm his monopoly in the Bible.

One of the principal grievances of those who had revolted
against Charles I had been the manipulation of commercial monopolies by which the treasury had been replenished and favorites
rewarded. Most of these had been abolished by the Long Parliament, but the printing monopolies had been merely suspended during the confusion of the civil wars. Thus the question of the revival
of the printing patents was squarely presented to the Council and
to Parliament. Several hearings were held and action on the proposed new act postponed in order to permit discussion of this vital
problem. On 7 January 1653 the new act for the regulation of printing was passed by a vote of 22 to 17.²⁵

Of all the Parliamentary acts of the Puritan Revolution, the act
of 1653 most resembles the old Star Chamber decrees. Except for
the following changes, the Printing Act of 1649 was revived *in toto.*

The Council of State was given authority to determine the
number of printing houses, the number of apprentices, and the number of presses. (Under the Star Chamber decrees this power lay
with the Stationers Company and the Ecclesiastical Commission.)
The Council was also authorized to make such rules and regulations
concerning the government of printing which it decided were from
time to time necessary to combat the abuses. The Stationers Com-

²³ See above, pp. 74ff.

²⁴ *A Briefe Treatise Concerning the Regulating of Printing. Humbly pre-
sented to the Parliament of England. by William Ball.* B.M. E. 1295. 3. 24
November 1651. Reprinted in W. M. Clyde, *Struggle for Freedom of the
Press* . . . (London: Oxford University press, 1934), App. B.

²⁵ Commons Journal, VII, 244-45; Firth and Rait, *op. cit.,* II, 696. Reprinted Clyde, *op. cit.,* App. C.

pany, which had heretofore retained the right to make these rules, was ordered to assist in the enforcement.

All persons exercising the art of printing must have the permission of the Council of State and must have acquired the right by patrimony or served as an apprentice to a lawful master printer for a space of seven years. All printing was confined to the dwelling house of a master printer.

To satisfy the complaints of importers who accused the representatives of the Stationers Company engaged in searching incoming cargoes of appropriating such imported books to their own use, it was provided in the new act that such inspections should take place within forty-eight hours with adequate notice to the owners together with a remedy at law for loss or damage caused by the inspection.

On the issue of freedom of the press, Parliament sided with the Presbyterian Stationers and against the Independents and Levellers, but it was not prepared to take a position as defender of printing monopolies. The exclusive right to print was placed under the jurisdiction of the Council rather than under the Stationers Company, and amendments to confirm the Bible patent in Mathew Barker and to set the price for unbound Bibles were voted down.

The press of England operated under this act from 7 January 1653 until Cromwell as Lord Protector inaugurated his own system of control 28 August 1655. The Council of State instead of the Court of the Stationers Company became the chief regulatory body with the latter occupying the position of a semi-official enforcement agency. The work of the Council was subdivided among a number of committees to which were assigned the discovery and suppression of various offending pamphlets and newsbooks. Among those prosecuted under this arrangement were John Speed, author of *The Parliament's Catechism,* and John Clowes and Robert Austen, printers of *A Charge of High-Treason exhibited against Oliver Cromwell.*[26] The author, Lilburne, when he returned from exile a year later, was arrested and sent to the Tower, and in answer to the indictment laid against him published a pamphlet justifying his

---

[26] The Council of State ordered the publication of an answer in a pamphlet entitled *Sedition Scourg'd, Or a View of that Rascally & Venemous Paper,* etc.

position and castigating those spies who were the chief witnesses against him.

Little change in the publication of newsbooks followed the enactment of the printing ordinance of 1653. Mabbott as agent for the Army returned as licenser replacing Rushworth. Entries of newsbooks in the Stationers' Register continue with the same irregularity. *Severall Proceedings,* printed by Ibbitson and licensed by Malyn, secretary to Cromwell, was entered at the end of the fiscal year in a batch of fifty-two numbers, as were both *Mercurius Politicus,* printed by Newcomb and licensed by Thurloe, and *The Perfect Diurnal,* printed by Leach and licensed by Mabbott.[27] At least seven other newsbooks continued regular publication without either official registration or licensing but apparently with the tacit permission of the authorities. In July, 1653, however, the encroachments of these unofficial journals led to the announcement by Parliament that no news of Parliament could be published without a written license from the clerk.[28] Thereafter *Mercurius Britannicus* carried the only news of Parliament, but in the disturbed state of affairs the order was evidently incapable of enforcement. A few months later Parliament complained of the continued breach of its privileges through the unauthorized printing of news of Parliamentary proceedings.[29]

The Council of State found itself no more able to cope with the publication of newsbooks and pamphlets than did its predecessors. The Protector himself decided to take the matter into his own hands.

Cromwell and the Press

On 28 August 1655 Cromwell's orders for the control of the press were put into effect. Three commissioners for the regulation of printing, John Barkstead, lieutenant of the Tower, Alderman John Dethick and George Foxcroft, were charged with the following duties: [30]

    1. to secure names and location of master printers, their servants,

---

[27] Eyre and Rivington, *op. cit.,* I, 451.
[28] Commons Journal, VII, 288.
[29] *Ibid.,* p. 296.
[30] B.M. E. 1064. 58.

workmen and apprentices, to see how many presses each operated, and to inquire "of what fame, quality, conversation, or condition of every such master printer is and how he, and his servants and workmen stand affected to the present Government,"

2. to suppress and prosecute all unlicensed printers,

3. to prosecute all those printers who having entered into bonds may have broken the condition of the bond,

4. to suppress all news-books except those licensed by the Protector or his Council,

5. to execute the acts suppressing street hawkers and mercury women,

6. to send all offenders to Bridewell to undergo "corporal and pecuniary punishment," and to appoint deputies to assist in the enforcement.

Armed with these instructions the three lieutenants went to work. Within a month all the official as well as the unofficial newsbooks were suppressed. *A Perfect Account* ceased on 25 September; *A Perfect Diurnal*, 24 September; *The Weekly Intelligencer*, 25 September; *Several Proceedings*, 27 September; *The Faithful Scout*, 28 September; *Perfect Passages*, 28 September; and *Mercurius Fumigosus*, 3 October. Only *Mercurius Britannicus*, edited by Marchmont Needham and licensed by Thurloe remained. It was joined in the first week in October by a Monday edition under the same sponsorship entitled *The Public Intelligencer*. Needham continued to draw not only the profits from the venture but an annual subsidy from Cromwell's government. Newcomb printed both newsbooks which were registered regularly in the records of the Stationers Company.

With the suppression of the printed avenues of communication, news and discussion were driven underground where discovery was still more difficult. In October after the work of suppression had been completed Secretary Nicholas wrote in a private letter, "Cromwell's strictly prohibiting the printing of news is a sure sign that his affairs at home and abroad go not well. He has been tampering to bring in as many Swiss guards as, with his faction in the army, may secure himself." [31]

Cromwell's method of dealing with the newsbooks was undoubtedly successful. No other journal except Needham's two editions was allowed to appear. Whether or not Cromwell was

[31] Cal. St. P. Dom., 1655, p. 384.

more tolerant than his supporters is a moot question; the fact remains that the Protector brooked no public discussion or criticism in the form of newsbooks.[32] The system was so solidly grounded that even with the death of the Protector 3 September 1658, the controls continued until late in 1659. However Richard Cromwell, his successor, could not long withstand the forces which were swelling up within the country. With spectacular suddenness, the Puritan Revolution and its various systems for the control of the Press collapsed with the restoration of Charles II.

Conclusions

What, then, were the contributions of the period of turmoil and governmental experimentation commonly known as the Puritan Revolution toward the development of a theory and practice of freedom of the press? Historians are frequently prone to minimize the political innovations of the period 1640-1660 on the ground that the old order was essentially re-established under the third Stuart monarch, Charles II; but regardless of the effect of the Restoration, the experience of a nation over a period of twenty such eventful years could not be immediately obliterated. In the writings of the pamphleteers and in the demands of political and religious minorities are to be discovered the seeds from which later grew the doctrines of religious toleration, democracy in government, and liberty of the press.

Several of the steps toward the establishment of freedom of the press taken by the Puritan governments did in fact survive the Restoration. The Star Chamber was never re-established, and although the High Commission was restored, its powers over the press were drastically curtailed. A further permanent contribution of the period was the firm establishment of Parliament's jurisdiction over the control and regulation of printing. Charles II made several abortive attempts to revive the prerogative powers of the crown, but neither he nor his successors were able to oust Parliamentary jurisdiction. A third permanent effect of the Puritan governments was to disestablish the Stationers Company as the controlling

---

[32] Clyde attempts rather unsuccessfully to crown the Protector with the halo of defender of freedom of the press in answer to severe criticism made by Muddiman. See Clyde, *op. cit.*, Chapter X and Muddiman, *op. cit.*, pp. 150-57.

authority in the printing trade. Even Mr. L'Estrange, Surveyor of the Press under Charles II, could find little to recommend the revival of the old powers enjoyed by the Company under the Star Chamber decrees.

In addition to these permanent effects, the Puritan Revolution accomplished certain changes in the regulation of printing which although not adopted immediately after the Restoration were soon recognized as necessary concessions to the growing power of public opinion. The curtailment of the monopolistic grants to the Stationers Company and to the prominent and influential printers accomplished during the period 1640-1660 set a precedent which the Restoration government was never able successfully to overcome. The monopolies in foreign news such as those granted to Butter and Bourne were incapable of revival, and even distribution of domestic news could no longer be made a monopoly under the crown.

On the other hand, several of the methods of control which had been developed by the Puritan governments were soon adopted by the restored Stuarts. The official newspaper, the instrument of Cromwell, was seized upon as a practicable method of regulation as well as an effective means for the dissemination of propaganda. The practice of using the law courts instead of the Star Chamber and High Commission inaugurated under the Commonwealth was continued and expanded under the succeeding monarchs. And finally the maintenance of a semi-official alliance with the Stationers Company was retained as an important means of enforcement.

The failure of the Puritan Revolution to establish a firm foundation for freedom of the press in spite of the arguments of Milton, Lilburne, and Goodwin was due more to the inability of the people to accept and adjust themselves to such liberties than to the unwillingness of the governors to grant such rights. The lesson, that the control of the dissemination of information and opinion brings with it greater evils than those which it is designed to overcome, was dimly perceptible to the more advanced minds of the age but was scarcely grasped by the average Puritan. Only when his particular dogmas or theories were threatened with suppression was he an eager champion of freedom of discussion. The Puritan's insistence upon his constitutional rights when tempered with the tolerance of the Restoration provided the fertile ground in which the seeds of liberty of the press eventually germinated.

PART 4

Control of the Press
UNDER THE LATER STUARTS

1660-1714

CHAPTER 12

The Regulation of Printing Acts,
1662-1694

As soon as the more pressing matters of state pertaining to th
Restoration were disposed of, a new program for the control anc
regulation of the press was put into effect. All the orders, decrees,
and acts of the Puritan Revolution were repudiated, and theoretically at least the government took up where it left off in 1641.
The only surviving act of importance to the press was that abolishing the Star Chamber which had received the assent of Charles I.

The new program was not a re-establishment of those forms
of control which had existed under the early Stuarts, nor was it
a continuation of the devices adopted during the various phases
of the Puritan Revolution. No serious attempt was made to revive
the Star Chamber and its decrees, but instead the king with no
observable hesitancy permitted and even urged Parliament to assist
in regulating that which fifty years before had been a matter subject solely to the royal prerogative.

Although there was very little resistance to Parliamentary participation in the regulation of printing on constitutional grounds,
the king did not, however, give up those powers which his prede-

cessors had enjoyed. The royal proclamation was still retained as a method of legislating in the affairs of the press, and one of the first acts of Charles II was to issue a proclamation (13 August 1660) calling in and suppressing two books written by John Milton.[1] This was followed by an order against the publication of almanacks or prognostications without license.[2] Not only did the king exert his prerogative power to suppress and license, but he continued to retain the royal authority over copyrights.[3]

In spite of the exercise of these prerogative powers over the press, neither the king nor his advisers offered any objection to a concurrent and in some measure pre-emptive control by Parliament. The king did not release his powers; he merely added to them the support and assistance of Parliamentary legislation. On 10 June 1662, the "Act for preventing the frequent Abuses in printing seditious, treasonable, and unlicensed Books and Pamphlets, and for regulating of Printing and printing Presses" went into effect. This Act continued to be the basis for the regulation of the press in England for over thirty years, from 1662 to 1694 with the exception of the years 1679-1685.[4]

The operation of this Act of 1662 will be discussed under the following headings (1) regulation of the printing trade, (2) licensing provisions, (3) printing copyrights and patents, (4) enforcement methods, and (5) expiry of the Printing Act.

---

[1] B.M. 669 f. 25 (70); Robert Steele, *Tudor and Stuart Proclamations* (Oxford, 1910), No. 3239.

[2] B.M. 669 f. 26 (16); Steele, *op. cit.*, No. 3258. George Wharton, Esq., was named licenser.

[3] Proclamation 21, November, 1661, affirming the rights of Joshua Kirton and Nathaniel Webb in "the morning exercise of Cripplegate." P.R.O., St. P. Dom. 44 (80); Steele, *op. cit.*, No. 3337.

A further reaffirmation of the royal authority over the press was the proclamation (5 December 1662) ordering the reprinting and use by schoolmasters of the book of instruction, *God and King*. The price was fixed by royal command at sixpence. B.M. 700 f. 12 (1); Steele, *op. cit.*, No. 3371.

[4] The original act, 13 and 14 Car. II, c. 33, continued in force for two years (1662-64) when it was renewed by 16 Car. II, c. 8 (1664) extending the effect of the act "until the end of the next session of Parlyament." 16 and 17 Car. II, c. 4 extended the life of the Act to 1679. Parliament failed to reenact the law in 1679, but it was revived in 1685 (1 Jac. II, c. 17, sec. 15), renewed by 4 Gul. & Mar. c. 24, sec. 14. In 1694 the House of Commons refused to renew the Act. See below.

Regulation of the Printing Trade

The Printing Act of 1662 was based upon the same theories as were the Star Chamber decrees of 1586 and 1637 and the acts of the Puritan Parliaments of the Interregnum. Although the regulations of Charles II were issued from Parliament instead of from the Star Chamber, they followed the general lines of control as devised by Archbishop Whitgift under Elizabeth. Special privileges were offered to the stationers and printers in return for their cooperation in enforcing the state regulations. These regulations took the form of declaring who could print, import, or sell printed matter, what printed matter was specifically forbidden to be printed or imported, and what formalities must be complied with in preparing and offering for sale the printed matter which was permitted.

Printing was strictly limited under the Act of 1662 to the master printers of the Stationers Company of London and the printers of the two universities, Cambridge and Oxford.[5] There were operating in London at the time of the enactment some fifty-nine master printers,[6] but under the terms of the Act, no new master printers were to be created by the Company until the number was reduced by death or otherwise to twenty. Replacements to keep the number to twenty were to be "nominated, appointed and allowed" by the Archbishop of Canterbury and the Bishop of London. The number of master printers must have been quickly reduced, for a paper in the Public Record Office dated 1668 lists the names of only twenty-eight master printers, four of whom were accused of having set up printing shops contrary to the Act.[7]

Only four founders of type were permitted in the kingdom and replacements were likewise to be made by the Archbishop of Canterbury and the Bishop of London.

As a further safeguard all master printers and founders were required to become bound with sureties in the sum of £300 before a court of justice as a guarantee that they would engage in no unlawful printing.

---

[5] A further exception was the press permitted the Archbishop of York.

[6] St. Co. Ct. Bk. Lib. D, f 81.

[7] Cal. St. P. Dom. Charles II, 1667-68, p. 503. The Plague of 1665 is credited by L'Estrange with carrying off eighty members of the printing trade. Cal. St. P. Dom. Charles II, 1665-66, p. 20.

Each master printer was allowed no more than two presses, but past wardens of the Stationers Company were allowed three. The number of apprentices was by the terms of the Act limited to the following; those master printers who had been wardens were allowed three apprentices; master printers who were of the livery could have two; and all other master printers could keep one apprentice only.

To keep the journeymen printers from being seduced into illegal printing through want of employment, the Act provided that every master printer should employ at least one journeyman. On the other hand, any journeyman out of employment who was offered work by a master printer was required to accept upon pain of three months imprisonment. No journeymen except those who were Englishmen and free of the Stationers Company were allowed to work at the printing trade.

The importation of books printed abroad was as strictly regulated as was the printing at home. All importers were required to be members of the Stationers Company except in the case of special licenses granted by the Archbishop of Canterbury or the Bishop of London. The importation of books printed in English was prohibited, and all books printed in foreign languages were required to be landed at the port of London except by special dispensation from the archbishop. The officers of the customs were ordered to hold all consignments of books until they were inspected by an appointee of the archbishop.

In addition to defining who could print and who could import books, the Act of 1662 set definite restrictions on the retail sale of printed books. Booksellers were limited to members of the Stationers Company and to those persons specially licensed by the Lord Bishop of the diocese in which the retailer resided. All "haberdashers of small wares, ironmongers, chandlers, and shopkeepers" were specifically prohibited from engaging in the book trade. An exception was made in the case of the shopkeepers in and about Westminster Hall who had been in business before 1661.

The restrictions upon the kinds of writings which could be printed, imported, and sold were just as stringent as the restrictions on who could print, import, and sell. In the first place, nothing could be printed, imported or sold under the terms of the act, which was "heretical, seditious, schismatical, or offensive . . . to the Christ-

ian faith or to the doctrine or discipline of the Church of England."
Further, it was an offense to print anything offensive to any officer
of the government or to a corporation or to any private persons or
person. No prosecution under the latter clause seems to have been
recorded. Also, all printers were prohibited from reprinting any
book or copy which, either by royal patent or by entry in the registration book of the Stationers Company, had been assigned to a
particular printer.

Having designated who could print and sell books and having
specifically designated what kind of books could not be printed and
sold, the Act of 1662 established a set of imposing formalities with
which the authorized printers were required to comply.

In addition to the licensing requirements (discussed immediately following) the printer was required to set his own name on
every piece of printing issued from his shop and to learn the name of
the author of the writing to be divulged in those cases where the
licenser desired the author's name. All printed matter, including
"titles, epistles, prefaces, proems, preambles, introductions, tables,
dedications, etc. were required to be entered in the register of the
Stationers Company.

The printer was also required to reserve three printed copies
of the best and largest edition of every book, one for the royal
library and one for each of the two University libraries. This provision was undoubtedly difficult to enforce as both an order by the
Court of the Stationers Company [8] and a special re-enactment in
17 Car. II, c. IV, seem to have had little effect.

Licensing Provisions

The licensing provisions of the comprehensive Regulation of
Printing Act of 1662 have tended to overshadow the other sections
of the law in spite of the fact that the section setting up an official
censorship constituted only a small part of the complete program
of regulation. One of the earliest acts of Charles II was to appoint
Sir John Berkenhead as official licenser under the authority of the
royal prerogative. Berkenhead, who had begun *Mercurius Aulicus*
as a royalist organ during the civil wars, continued to license

---

[8] Ct. Bk. Lib. D. f. 146 (6 October 1668). See also Order B.M., # P. M. C.
18e (42).

popular and periodic publications from November, 1660, until the summer of 1663 when an official Surveyor of the Press was appointed. The royal prerogative was also the basis for a proclamation issued on 25 September 1660 appointing George Wharton as official licenser of almanacks and prognostications.[9]

The Act of 1662 made one important change; it established the licensing system under Parliamentary authority. It prohibited the printing of any book or pamphlet unless it "shall be first lawfully licensed and authorized to be printed by such person and persons only as shall be constituted and appointed to license the same."

The Act named the following official licensers: For books concerning the law, the Lord Chancellor, the Keeper of the Seal, the Lords Chief Justices, and the Lord Chief Baron, or their appointees; books of heraldry, titles of honor and arms, the Earl Marshal or his appointee; books of history and affairs of state, by the principal secretaries of state or their appointees; all other books including those on divinity, philosophy, science, and art, by the Archbishop of Canterbury and the Bishop of London, or their appointees. Books published by the University printing houses were required to be licensed by the Chancellor or Vice Chancellor of the respective University.

In an attempt to avoid the pitfalls into which previous licensing systems had fallen, the Act specified in detail the method under which a license could be issued. A not uncommon practice had been to present a manuscript for approval to the official censor and upon receipt of his authorization to change, add, or amend the manuscript before it was printed. The printer or author was required under the terms of the new Act to submit two written copies of each manuscript in the English language, one of which was to be delivered back to the printer or owner and the other to be preserved in the office of the licenser "to the end that such licenser may be secured that the copy so licensed shall not be altered without his or thire privity." [10]

The licenser also was required to testify under his hand on the

---

[9] Steele, *op. cit.*, No. 3258.

[10] See Order to Stationers Company to punish Robert Hayhurst (Hurst) for changing the licensed manuscript in the printed copy. Cal. St. P. Dom. W. & M., 1689-90, pp. 55, 123.

manuscript copy that nothing contained in the book was "contrary
to Christian faith or the doctrine or discipline of the Church of
England or against the state or government of this realme or contrary to good life or good manners." This certification was ordered
to be printed at the beginning of the book with the name of the
licenser.

Two of the licensing classifications set up in the Act of 1662
were bound to give trouble both to the government and to the
printers principally because most of the controversial and "dangerous" publications fell in either one or the other of these classifications. These two groups were "books of history and affairs of
state," the licensing of which was entrusted to the principal secretaries of state, and works on "divinity, philosophy, and all other
works" the perusal of which was assigned to the Archbishop of
Canterbury and the Bishop of London or their appointees. The licensers of the latter group were almost always the chaplains of
the Bishop of London and included such men as Dr. George Stradling, Dr. Frank, Dr. Brabourn, Dr. Midgley and Dr. Poplar. In
later years the Archbishop and Bishop both delegated their authority to the persons selected as licensers by the secretaries of
state.[11]

The licensers operating under warrant from the secretaries of
state were faced with an almost impossible task. During the first
period of the operation of the licensing provisions, 1662-1679,
practically all the licensing under the authority of the secretaries
was done by Roger L'Estrange. In spite of the latter's efforts probably no more than half the pamphlet literature which appeared
carried the official allowance.[12]

Henry Oldenburg, secretary of the recently formed Royal Society, was appointed licenser of books on affairs of state 4 February
1675,[13] but soon retired in disgust. A translation of *Les Amours du
Roy Tamerlain* had been submitted to him for his license which
was refused on the ground that it appeared to be a libel against the
king. Instead of retaining the manuscript, Oldenburg returned it

---

[11] L'Estrange and Bohun licensed both religious and secular literature.
Charles Blount, *Character of Edmund Bohun* (1693), p. 98.

[12] Mr. Madan asserts that at least half the publications of the Oxford
Press were issued without a license. *The Library*, 4th Series, VI (September,
1925), 121-22.

[13] Ct. Bk. Lib. D. f 257a.

to the publisher so as not to frighten off future supplicants. Evidently Secretary Williamson had upbraided the licenser for allowing a dangerous manuscript to leave his hands, for on 29 April Oldenburg requested to be relieved of his duties "because of the tenderness of the employment and the vast expense of time it requires." [14]

Following the revival of the Act on printing by Parliament in 1685, enforcement of the licensing provisions became even more difficult, and licenser followed licenser. James Fraser served from 1689 to 1692.[15] He lost his office for licensing Rev. Dr. Walker's book, *A True, modest, and faithful account of the author of Eikon Basilike*.[16] Fraser was followed by Edmund Bohun who fulfilled the duties for five months.[17] He was dismissed for licensing a pamphlet supporting the title of William III to the Crown of England by right of conquest.[18] Bohun was followed by a Mr. Heron who lasted only a few months and who was in turn succeeded by Edward Cook, a lawyer, who seems to have served up to the expiration of the Act in 1694.[19]

Printing Patents and Copyrights [20]

No picture of the restrictions on the press in the late seventeenth century is complete without a description of the patent and copyright systems which, continuing down to the close of the reign of Queen Anne, served both as a reward for compliance with the

[14] Cal. St. P. Dom. Charles II, 1676-77, pp. 76, 92.

[15] Cal. St. P. Dom. W. & M., 1689-90, p. 30; John Dunton, *Life and Errors* (1705), p. 208.

[16] Blount, *op. cit.*, p. 31.

[17] Cal. St. P. Dom. W. & M., 1691-92, p. 438; *Dictionary of National Biography*, II, 769.

[18] "An Account of Mr. Blunt's late book entitled, *King William and Queen Mary Conquerors*, ordered by the house of Commons to be burnt by the hand of the common hangman on Wednesday morning next, at 10 o'clock in the Palace Yard, Westminster, Lond." 1693. Historical Manuscripts Commission, 7th Report; House of Lords Ms., pp. 379-80; Lords Journal, XV, 192, 195, 197, 198. Bohun who later was appointed chief justice of South Carolina and died of the small pox in Charleston 5 October 1699 attributed his downfall to the "Whig intrigues." *Diary and Autobiography of Edmund Bohun*, edited by S. W. Rix, 1853.

[19] Dunton, *op. cit.*, p. 267.

[20] For the early history, see above, Chapter 3, pp. 74-82.

printing regulations and as a means identifying the interest of the individual printer-patentee with that of the government.

The printing patents were monopolistic grants by the crown as distinguished from copyrights which arose out of prior registration in the books of the Stationers Company. The royal grant might vest the ownership of a single book in the author, printer or stationer,[21] or it might reserve an entire field of the publishing business for the benefit of a particular person or group of persons.[22] The most important patent in reserved fields, aside from the grants to the Stationers Company, was that of royal printer or printer to the king which was based on a grant in 1635 and which after the Restoration had become the property of John Bill and Christopher Barker. In 1666 the patent was assigned to H. Hills and Thomas Newcomb and in 1689 became the property of Charles Bill and Thomas Newcomb.[23]

The patents held by the Stationers Company and known as the "stocks" were a continuous source of disaffection among the printers and journeymen who were not privileged to become partners in the lucrative business represented by these grants. At the same time the crown, under whose authority the "stocks" were held, was not above threatening the withdrawal of the grants as a penalty for noncompliance with the printing regulations.[24] In 1671 under pressure from the crown, the "stocks" of the Company were divided equally among the "legal" printers.[25]

---

[21] See grant of ownership in *The English Pilot to John Sellers,* hydrographer. B.M. C. 21 f. 1 (48). Also grant to Miles Dodson of exclusive right to print *God and King* for thirty-one years. Cal. St. P. Dom. Charles II, 1661-62, p. 52.

[22] One of the most obnoxious grants from the point of view of the printer-members of the Stationers Company was the patent to Sir Roger L'Estrange giving him exclusive right to print and publish "all narratives not exceeding two sheets of paper, mercuries, diurnals, playbills, quack-salvers, bills, etc." 15 August 1663, Cal. St. P. Dom. Charles II, 1663-64, p. 240. This patent is discussed below. Proc. B.M. C. 21 f. 1 (48); Steele, *op. cit.,* No. 3553 (8 November 1671).

[23] Steele, *op. cit.,* I, 477.

[24] "Particulars of His Mat[e] commands towards the regulation of the Press to be communicated to the Company of Stationers vizt. (3) That what member soever of the Co. of Stat. having an interest in the English stock, shall offend in manner aforesaid, shall have the profit of his stock sequestered for one year by the said Co. and disposed by them, to the poor of said Co." Ct. Bk. Lib. D. f 170 (5 September 1670).

[25] Ct. Bk. Lib. D. f 187.

A further license to the Stationers Company to print certain French comedies and Aesop's *Fables* for thirty-one years was issued in 1666. This patent contained an affirmation of the patents for primers, psalters, psalms, and almanacks granted to the Company by James I.[26]

The Printing Act of 1662 confirmed the rights of both the patentees under royal grants and of the owners of copyrights registered in the books of the Stationers Company. A penalty of six shillings eight pence was authorized to be assessed against the publisher of all pirated books, one half of which was to accrue to the crown and the other half to the proprietor of the copyright. In case the rightful proprietor did not sue for his share within the space of a year, the Act permitted any person to sue for the fine.

A committee was appointed sometime in 1666 to look into the matter of printing patents and in November issued a report declaring the law-patent a monopoly.[27] A warrant was issued in 1668 prohibiting all further printing of common-law books until the legality of the patent could be determined.[28] The question of the validity of the patent, which was particularly obnoxious to the booksellers and stationers,[29] was presented to the Court of Parliament in 1666 by Richard Atkyns,[30] where it was decided that the king through his prerogative powers could legally grant an exclusive patent for the printing of law books.[31] A reversion in the law-patent was granted to Edward Sayer of the Inner Temple in 1702 to begin after the expiration of Atkyns' term.[32]

---

[26] Cal. St. P. Dom. Charles II, 1666-67, p. 412. The Company was forced to defend its patent against Samuel Speed who was discovered printing a primer and a psalter, claiming a license from the Chaplain of the Archbishop of Canterbury. *Ibid.*, 1668-69, p. 280.

[27] *Ibid.*, 1666-67, p. 263.

[28] *Ibid.*, 1667-68, p. 481.

[29] See *The case of the Booksellers and Printers stated: with answers to the objections of the patentee.* 1666. B.M. C. 18 el (52).

[30] Atkyns was the scoundrel who in "The Original and Growth of Printing," (reprinted in Edward Arber, *Transcript* . . . (1875), I, 20) which he had published to promote his patent rights, sponsored the story that printing had been introduced at Oxford before Caxton's day. See above, pp. 22ff. Atkyns claimed the law patent through his wife who was the daughter and heir of George Moore. Atkyns did not exercise his patent rights but had leased them to a group of Stationers whom he was now suing for £1110 arrears.

[31] Atkyns case. Cart. 89.

[32] Cal. St. P. Dom. Wm. III, 1700-1702, p. 515.

The king in 1669 granted to John Seymour "for services during the late troubles and since the Restoration" the exclusive right to print all almanacks and prognostications for a term of forty-one years. The patentee was also given the power to search on suspicion.[33] A lengthy dispute over the right to print almanacks between the Company and Seymour was first decided in favor of the Company by Solicitor General North.[34] Seymour was compensated for the loss by special grants from the crown of certain classical and school books for forty-one years.[35] The Stationers also contested this grant but were estopped by an order from the Principal Secretary.[36]

A suit was then begun in the Court of King's Bench where it was decided in 1677 that the king had the authority to issue patents for almanacks or, for that matter, for any book or class of books, but that the patent to the Stationers antedated that to Seymour and was therefore superior in validity.[37] The Company's ownership of the patent for almanacks was further strengthened by a decision of Parliament (1681) confirming the validity of the original grant.[38] This decision in Seymour's case had far-reaching effects, for no longer could the crown threaten to withdraw a patent for failure to assist in enforcing the printing regulations. Once again, in 1709, the court was asked to rule on the validity of the almanack patent, but it refused to commit itself without further hearings.[39]

---

[33] Cal. St. P. Dom. Charles II, 1670, p. 735.

[34] Ct. Bk. Lib. D. f. 181b (20 August 1671). See also Cal. St. P. Dom. Charles II, 1663-64, p. 369. The Company based its claims on a grant from James I (1616) which claims it shared with both Oxford and Cambridge universities. See E. F. Bosanquet, "English 17th Century Almanacks," *The Library*, 4th Series, X, 361-97.

[35] Cal. St. P. Dom. Charles II, 1664-65, pp. 13, 34. See also *Ibid.*, 1668-69, p. 539.

[36] *Ibid.*, 1664-65, p. 119.

[37] Seymour's Case, 3 Keb. 792, 1 Mod. 256. The court reasoned: "There is no difference in any material part betwixt this almanack and that which is put in the rubrick of the Common Prayer. Now the almanack that is before the Common Prayer proceeds from a public constitution . . . so that almanacks may be accounted prerogative copies. . . . There is no particular author of an almanack; and then by a rule of law the King has the prerogative in the copy."

[38] Stationers Company *vs.* Lee (Leigh) 2 Cas. in Chan. 66, 76, 96. Not until late in the eighteenth century were these grants declared by the courts to be monopolies and illegal. Stationers Company *vs.* Carnan, 6 Bac. Abr. 7th ed. 509 (1781).

[39] Stationers Company *vs.* Partridge, 10 Mod. 105.

In 1678 the king attempted to placate the Stationers by a grant
of the exclusive right to print a list of seventeen classical titles for
a period of forty-one years in reversion after the term of thirty-one
years granted by the crown in 1666.[40] At the same time Roger Norton, king's printer, was given a patent for Latin Bibles and Latin
and Greek grammars.[41]

The patent for English Bibles,[42] probably the most valuable of
all printing rights, engendered a contest between Oxford University
and the London printers which lasted until 1705. The original agreement between the University and the Stationers Company whereby
the Company paid an annual fee of £200 for the rights of the
University in the English Bible and in other books expired 24
March 1672. A committee representing the Oxford Press met with
the Stationers Company and with Roger Norton, and an agreement
was reached,[43] but these arrangements did not prove satisfactory
for long. The Bible patents were contested in the courts in 1682 [44]
and in 1684 [45] and again in 1685.[46]

As for individual copyrights, as long as the Act for the Regulation of Printing was in force (to 1694) there was at least some
semblance of legality attached to the ownership of a copy which
had been entered in the Stationers' Register, but with the expiration
of that Act the Company found itself incapable of enforcing its own
ordinances especially against those stationers who were not members. Parliament on several occasions toyed with the idea of enacting new legislation along the lines of the recently expired Act but
could come to no agreement. In the meantime the stationers, printers, and binders continued to petition for relief.[47]

[40] Cal. St. P. Dom. Charles II, 1678, p. 569.

[41] Ibid.

[42] The patents for Greek, Latin, and Hebrew Bibles were held by Roger
Norton. Ibid., 1667, p. 496; Ibid., 1678, p. 569.

[43] Ibid., 1672-73, p. xxviii.

[44] Anonimous, 1 Vern. 20, Company of Stationers, 2 Chan. Cas. 66, 76, 96.

[45] Hills et al. vs. Oxford University 1 Vern. 275.

[46] Stationers vs. Parker, Skinner, 233. See also Cal. St. P. Dom. Charles
II, 1671, pp. 397, 444-45, 450-51, 458, 466-67, 486, 575; Ibid., 1671-72, pp.
xxvii, 25; Ibid., 1672-73, pp. xvii-xviii, 49, 56-57; Ibid., 1673-75, p. xxix.

[47] Commons Journal, XV, 313 (26 February 1707); Ibid., p. 316 (28 February 1707); Ibid., XVI, 240 (12 December 1709); Ibid., p. 291 (2 February
1710). The absence of any petition for protection on the part of authors and
translators is noteworthy.

The first Copyright Act was finally passed in 1709/10 (8 Anne, c. 21) after it became clear that no comprehensive legislation for the control of the press could be obtained from Parliament. It gave the copyright owner of works already in print a statutory right to exclusive ownership for twenty-one years and to authors or owners of manuscripts not yet in print an exclusive right to publish for a term of fourteen years from the date of first publication, with an additional term of fourteen years accruing to authors who were living at the expiration of the first term.

Evidence of ownership was, according to the terms of the Act, to be established by registration in the books of the Stationers Company. The fees for such registration and for certificates were set by the Act, and elaborate provisions were included to guard against the unwarranted enhancement of the price of books under the statutory monopoly. Thus some two hundred years after the introduction of printing, the first copyright law was enacted. Henceforth the protection of property rights in printed matter was divorced completely from any attempts at control of the content or quality of such printed matter. The sire of the Act of 8 Anne was the Printing Act of 1662; its progeny, the series of copyright acts in England and the United States including the current laws on the subject.

Enforcement of the Printing Acts

Any estimate of the success or failure of the enforcement of the printing regulations must await an intensive survey of the productions of the press in the latter half of the seventeenth century. This much, however, is evident, that in spite of the stringent regulations and the multiplicity of agencies of enforcement, there continued to flow from the presses a stream of publications which in that day and age were considered either seditious or offensive. While some of the publications seem mild enough to modern eyes accustomed to lively and often vituperative political criticism, it must be remembered that in the seventeenth century both the government and its subjects were inexperienced in either digesting the printed page or judging its effects. The reading public was not yet sufficiently aware of the fact that all printed matter is not necessarily authoritative, and the government, on the other hand, had not become accustomed to a public discussion of its acts nor had

yet discovered that unjust criticism frequently carries its own antidote. An ever-present fear of a political or religious uprising contributed to the seventeenth-century state of mind. Charles I had
lost his head; several political coteries had been supplanted during
the Interregnum; the Oates and Ryehouse plots confirmed the suspicions of the people during the reign of Charles II; James II was
forced to flee; and after the Revolution of 1688 the fear of a Jacobite
retaliation continued to disturb the British statesmen down to the
establishment of the Hanoverian line. Under these conditions it is
not surprising to see the extraordinary efforts put forth to enforce
the printing regulations.

It is also worthy of note that the stringency of the enforcement
of the regulations varied directly with the state of agitation of public opinion. For instance, very little effort was made to suppress
printed matter in the early years of the reign of Charles II when all
was harmony, but drastic steps were taken to suppress dissenting
opinion during the troubled years of 1675-1685.

The fountainhead of all agencies of enforcement was the king
and his Council. The Council occasionally acted directly but more
often instigated enforcement through such agencies as the principal
secretaries of state, the office of the Surveyor of the Press, and the
Stationers Company. The following discussion of the enforcement
of the Printing Act is presented under these headings: (1) by
direct action of king and Council; (2) by the principal secretaries
of state; (3) by the office of Surveyor of the Press; and (4) by the
Stationers Company.

Direct attempts by the king and Council to enforce the press
regulations were undertaken through two devices, the proclamation
and the Order in Council. At least twenty proclamations were issued
under the authority of the royal prerogative during the period of
the later Stuarts for the purpose of assisting in the suppression of
printed matter.[48] The proclamations varied from orders to enforce
the licensing provisions to commands to seize the author of, or to
suppress, a particular book. The following is a copy of a typical
proclamation issued by William III, 5 November 1696:

---

[48] Eight were issued by Charles II (Steele, *op. cit.*, Nos. 3516, 3570, 3595,
3622, 3624, 3625, 3699); three by James II (*Ibid.*, Nos. 3859, 3888, 3891);
three by William and Mary (*Ibid.*, Nos. 3997, 4016, 4101); two by William
(*Ibid.*, Nos. 4212, 4271); and four by Anne (*Ibid.*, Nos. 4369, 4372, 4400,
4539).

Whereas, We have been Inform'd, That a False, Scandalous and Seditious Libel, and Destructive to the Freedom and Liberties of Parliament, Intituled An *Account of the Proceedings of the House of Commons in Relation to the Recoining the Clipp'd Money, and Falling the Price of Guineas,* has been Printed and Dispersed; and whereas the Knights, Citizens and Burgesses in Parliament Assembled, have humbly besought Us to Issue Our Royal Proclamation, for Discovery of the Author of the said Libel: We therefore (with the Advice of Our Privy Council) have thought fit to Issue this Our Royal Proclamation, hereby Requiring and Commanding all Our Loving Subjects whatsoever, to Discover the Author of the said Libel, to the end that he may be dealt withal, and Proceeded against according to law. And we do hereby Promise and Declare that Whosoever shall Discover the Author of the said Libel, shall have and Receive as a Reward, for such Discovery, the sum of Five hundred Pounds; which said Sum of Five hundred Pounds the Commissioners of Our Treasury are hereby Required and Directed to Pay accordingly. And we do so also further Promise and Declare, that if any Person (other than the Author himself) who was any ways privy to, or instrumental, in the Printing or Dispersing the said libel, shall Discover the Author thereof, the Person making such Discovery, shall not only have the said Sum of 500 lbs., as aforesaid, but also Our gracious Pardon for his Offence; And we do hereby strictly Charge and Command all Our Loving Subjects (as they will answer the contrary at their Perils) that they do not anyways Conceal, but Discover the Author of the said Libel, to the end that he may be Proceeded against with the utmost Severity, according to law.[49]

Another direct method used by king and Council to assist in the suppression of objectionable printed matter was the Order in Council by which directions were given to various subagencies such as the principal secretaries, the Surveyor of the Press, the Lord Mayor of London, or the Stationers Company.

On 28 November 1666 the secretary of state was ordered by the Council to suppress *An Apology of the English Catholics.*[50] Sir Roger L'Estrange, the Surveyor of the Press, was given elaborate instructions to apprehend the parties responsible for the *Whore's Petition* in 1669.[51] The Lord Mayor of London was ordered by the Council in 1671 to round up the unauthorized printers.[52] On more than one occasion the Council felt it necessary to crack the whip

[49] B.M. C. 21, f. 2.
[50] Cal. St. P. Dom. Charles II, 1666-67, p. 296.
[51] *Ibid.,* 1668-69, p. 654.
[52] *Ibid.,* 1671, p. 447.

over the Stationers Company in order to induce compliance with the printing regulations. The Company was ordered to meet with L'Estrange for the purpose of devising new regulations; [53] it was enjoined to suppress hawkers; [54] it was advised to admit certain well-disposed printers to its court of assistants; [55] and finally in 1670 the threat of quo warranto proceedings against the Company's charter was used to secure adoption of a new set of by-laws designed to facilitate the enforcement of the printing regulations.[56]

Although the king and Council stood as the fountainhead of enforcement activities, the principal secretaries were responsible for carrying out the general orders under the Printing Act. The efficiency with which these officers dispatched their duties varied with the personality of the secretary and his subordinates. Lord Arlington was very active; Joseph Williamson was more adept than any of his predecessors; Sir Leoline Jenkins did no more than was necessary.

The duties of the principal secretary in connection with the regulations for printing, aside from licensing books on affairs of state [57] and the supervision of newspapers,[58] were to direct the messengers of the press, to organize searches, to issue warrants of arrests and releases, to hold examinations, and to order commitments and prosecutions, and to direct the Surveyor of the Press.

As general head of the intelligence service and as supervisor of the posts, the principal secretary was in an advantageous position to smell out violations of the printing regulations. In this business he was assisted by the corps of correspondents stationed throughout the kingdom and abroad and by employees in the post office. In addition, the secretary directed the activities of his deputies who in this instance were known as "messengers of the press." These men carried on investigations, made searches and seizures, and assisted in examinations.

During the years 1662 to 1666 the duties of detective were assigned to Roger L'Estrange as Surveyor of the Press, but begin-

---

[53] *Ibid.*, 1668-69, p. 446.
[54] St. Co. Ct. Bk. Lib.
[55] Cal. St. P. Dom. Charles II, 1680-81, p. 316.
[56] *Ibid.*, 1676-77, p. 590. See above, p. 65.
[57] See above, p. 242.
[58] See above, pp. 243-44.

ning in 1667 the messengers were directly responsible to the secretary. These messengers included John Wickham, Ralph Rutter, Andrew Crooke, John Wilson, and Robert Stephens. During the later years of the century John Gellibrand was appointed inspector of printing presses, and he together with Robert Stephens conducted most of the work of investigation. Armed with particular or general warrants issued by the secretary, these messengers made intensive searches in public and private houses for surreptitious printing, seized papers and persons, and carried them before the secretary.

The messengers were undoubtedly subjected to seductive offers by printers and stationers in return for immunity. These bribes were particularly attractive since the messengers were political appointees without any assurance of salary. In October, 1668, John Wickham, who together with Sam Mearne of the Stationers Company had seized a printing press belonging to Elizabeth Calvert, was accused of delivering back the press and selling the unlicensed books which he had seized.[59] Stephens, the most persistent of the lot, was also accused of accepting bribes.[60]

The authority of the principal secretary to issue general and special warrants for searches and seizures, which during the following century was successfully disputed,[61] continued throughout the later Stuart period as the most efficient implement of enforcement of the printing regulations. The legal status of these powers may be debated, but the fact remains that the occupants of the secretary's office exercised the authority to commit without cause in cases of treason and seditious libel,[62] to issue general warrants for the arrest of all persons who might be connected with a particular named event, and finally to search and seize papers with or without particularization. As to the last named power, the Printing Act of 1662 specifically provided that "one or more messengers under his majesty's sign manual or under the hand of one or both of his Majesty's

[59] Cal. St. P. Dom. Charles II, 1668-69, p. 37.

[60] Ibid., 1680-81, p. 440.

[61] See below, pp. 374ff. Also F. M. G. Evans, "The Principal Secretary of State," University of Manchester, Historical Series, XLIII, Chapter XI.

[62] The right of the secretary to commit in cases of treason and seditious libel was recognized by the courts in Rex vs. Kendal, 1696 (13 State Trials, p. 1013), and in Rex vs. Derby, 1709 (12 State Trials, p. 1299). After 1765 by a resolution of the Commons the cause of commitment was required to be shown and the right to seize papers withdrawn.

principal secretaries of state" might search the premises of any suspect and seize any papers there found.[63]

The wording of the warrants issued by the secretary varies all the way from complete particularization to the most general phrases. An example of the former is the warrant dated 23 July 1666 to Lewis Dormay to apprehend George Wither, Henry Eversden, Sarah Anderton, Elizabeth Goslin, and Margery Hickes for dispensing a seditious pamphlet entitled *Sighs for the Pitchers*.[64] A more common type of warrant was the one issued to Roger L'Estrange as Surveyor of the Press to "seize all seditious books and libels and to apprehend the authors, contrivers, printers, publishers, and dispersers of them, and bring them before him to be proceeded against according to law" and to "search any house, shop, printing room, chamber, warehouse, etc. for seditious, scandalous or unlicensed pictures, books, or papers, to bring away or deface the same, and the letter press, taking away all the copies and to search for and proceed against all printers, authors, publishers, or dispersers of the same." [65]

That the authority of the secretary to issue these general warrants was not necessarily based upon the provisions of the Printing Act is demonstrated by the number of warrants issued between 1679 and 1685 when the Act was not in operation.[66] However, of these only one is in the nature of a general search warrant.[67]

The warrants issued after the expiration of the Printing Act in 1694 continued but with greater particularization. They are usually issued for the arrest of named persons or for the search of specified premises, but warrants of the most general character are not lacking.[68]

---

[63] 14 Car. II, c. 33.

[64] Minute Entry Book 23, p. 220.

[65] Ent. Book 5, p. 177.

[66] See Cal. St. P. Dom. Charles II, 1680-81, pp. 179, 318; *Ibid.*, 1682, p. 591; *Ibid.*, July-September 1683, pp. 240, 409.

[67] *Ibid.*, 1682, p. 591.

[68] The Duke of Shrewsbury requested the Solicitor-General's opinion about the legality of the warrants in 1695, and a few days later warrants were issued to John Gellibrand, messenger of the press, to seize seditious and treasonable books, papers, and printing presses and persons in whose custody they are found. H.O. Letter Book (Secretary's) 5, p. 139. 9 May 1695. Cal. St. P. Dom., 1694-95, p. 465. The legality of these warrants was again questioned in 1697. *Ibid.*, 1697, p. 257.

Along with the authority to issue warrants of search, seizure and arrest, the principal secretaries during the seventeenth century exercised the right to conduct examinations of the suspects brought before them by their order. Even before the Act for the Regulation of Printing, Secretary Nicholas is found examining in private Zachary Crofton who confessed to writing two obnoxious books and who was thereupon imprisoned in the Tower.[69]

Printers and booksellers were frequently kept in prison for several months under no other judicial authority than the order of the secretary issued after a private examination or no examination at all.[70] Occasionally the examination was held by a deputy at a distant point and the results transmitted to the secretary.[71] That such examinations and commitments contributed to the agitation in favor of the Habeas Corpus Act of 1679, there can be no doubt.

One of the methods of enforcement employed by the secretaries from 1662 to 1668 was to require a bond or recognizance from those printers, booksellers, or hawkers who were accused of violating the provisions of the Printing Act. The Act itself provided that all persons who in the future were permitted to operate printing houses must enter into a bond for £300 not to print any unlicensed works.[72] The secretaries, however, extracted these recognizances from booksellers as well as from printers who were suspected of having some connection with unlicensed printing.[73]

Throughout the period of the later Stuarts the principal secretaries and their servants acted as detectives, searchers, arresting officers, examiners, and committing authorities in cases involving not only seditious but merely objectionable publications. The only limitation on their authority was that set out in the Printing Act, i.e., the houses of peers were immune from any searches.

As early as July, 1661, a proposal had been made to the Council for the erection of an office under the jurisdiction of the secretary

---

[69] Cal. St. P. Dom. Charles II, 1660-61, p. 546.

[70] See petition of Peter Lillicrap, printer, *Ibid.*, 1663-64, p. 213. See also cases of John Brudenell, stationer (*Ibid.*, p. 255); Richard Moon, bookseller (*Ibid.*, p. 297); Thomas Leach, printer (*Ibid.*, p. 425).

[71] *Ibid.*, 1667, p. 290.

[72] 14 Charles II, 3.

[73] See notes on bonds in Cal. St. P. Dom., 1661-62, pp. 572, 609; *Ibid.*, 1663-64, pp. 216, 225, 272, 278, 339, 582; *Ibid.*, 1665-66, pp. 386, 409; *Ibid.*, 1666-67, p. 286; *Ibid.*, 1677, pp. 388, 390, 395; *Ibid.*, 1667-68, p. 378.

of state charged with the supervision and control of the press.[74]
Sir Roger L'Estrange who had performed journalistic services for
the crown prior to the Restoration published a pamphlet justifying
the creation of such an office [75] and humbly petitioned that the
duties be assigned to him. In recognition of his services the king
granted him the monopoly in newsbooks [76] and appointed him
Surveyor of the Press, 15 August 1663. The following is a copy of
one of the numerous warrants issued to L'Estrange:

> His Ma[te] taking notice of ye many ill consequences that arise from
> ye printing, publishing, & dispersing of unlawful books & pamphlets to ye
> disturbance of ye government & of ye public peace of ye nation, His
> expresse pleasure & command is, that taking with you a constable you
> doe from time to time make search for & seize authors, contrivers, print-
> ers, binders, stitchers, & publishers, dispensers, & concealers of treason-
> able, schismaticall, seditious or unlicensed books, libells, pamphlets, or
> papers, & to bring them in safe custody before one of his Ma[te] principal
> sec. of state, to ye end they may be proceeded against according to law,
> together with all copys exemplaryes of such Books libells, pamphlets
> or paper as aforesaid. And in ye due execution hereof all justices of ye
> peace, constables, & other his Ma[te] officers & Subjects are to be aid-
> ing & assisting to you, as there shall from time to time be occasion, etc.
> [24 May 1664].[77]

Armed with these warrants, the Surveyor entered enthusiastic-
ally upon a career of control and suppression which lasted for almost twenty years. His own experiences during the Protectorate led
him directly to those printers who, either because of economic
circumstances or religious or political inclinations, were engaged in
producing unlicensed or seditious publications.

The theory of regulation under which L'Estrange proceeded
was that if printing were limited to a few chosen and well-affected
persons the productions of their presses could be controlled by an
officer of the crown who was responsible not to the Stationers Company and its hierarchy but to the king and Council. Throughout his
career the Surveyor was opposed to the traditional Elizabethan
method whereby the privileged Stationers Company assumed con-

---

[74] Cal. St. P. Dom. Charles II, 1661-62, p. 44.

[75] *Considerations and Proposals in order to the Regulation of the Press,*
June, 1663.

[76] L'Estrange's activities as a news publisher are discussed in Chapter 14.

[77] Entry Book Chas. II, 1664. Vol. 21, p. 21, and Vol. 16, p. 130.

trol of all printing in return for its monopolies. The stationers and printers were not to be trusted, argued L'Estrange, for the reasons that they are both parties and judges, their interest lies in the violation of the regulations, and they have failed to enforce the regulations in the past.[78]

Throughout the entire period of his stewardship, 1663-1680, the Surveyor of the Press, who according to Dunton would wink at unlicensed books if the printer's wife would but smile on him,[79] conducted and directed searches, made seizures and arrests, supervised examinations, directed prosecutions, and battled with the officials of the Stationers Company.[80] In spite of his ultimate failure to enforce the printing regulations, the Company never again regained the power and privileges which it formerly enjoyed.

The most successful agency for the regulation of printing during the sixteenth and early seventeenth centuries had been the Stationers Company, but by 1660 government officials were aware of the constantly decreasing effectiveness of the methods employed by the corporate group. The reasons for the failure of the Stationers Company to maintain successful surveillance of the printing trade were (1) the growing discontent within the trade, especially between the booksellers and the printers; [81] (2) the constantly increasing distinction between the prosperous officials of the Company who were also proprietors of the profitable printing monopolies and the poorer membership who found it difficult because of the monopolies to make an honorable livelihood; (3) the Presbyterian and Puritan sentiment among the Stationers which led them to oppose the cavalier government and the established religion; (4) the growing resentment against the printing patents, especially against those held by nonmembers of the Company, and finally (5) the reluctance of individual members to forego the profitable fields represented by the popular literature which the public was demanding and which the government was seeking to suppress.

The Stationers Company was authorized to assist in the enforcement of the printing regulations both by the Printing Acts and

[78] *Considerations and Proposals* . . . , pp. 24-28.

[79] Dunton, *op. cit.*, p. 265.

[80] A letter written by L'Estrange to Secretary Williamson illustrates his methods. 24 April 1668, Cal. St. P. Dom. 1667-68, pp. 357-58.

[81] See demand by printers for separation from the stationers. Cal. St. P. Dom. Charles II, 1660-61, pp. 372-73.

by royal proclamations.[82] That the officials of the Company were not giving satisfactory assistance was evident early in 1666,[83] and from this date until 1676 the Surveyor of the Press supported by the king and the principal secretaries conducted interminable negotiations with the Company for the purpose of improving enforcement of the regulations. Early in 1668 the king ordered the Company to admit to its court of assistants three members favorably disposed to the crown,[84] but this new blood was apparently unable to revivify the efforts of the Company.

In 1669 the Company was ordered by the crown to meet with the Surveyor of the Press to adopt new by-laws directed toward the enforcement of the printing regulations. After several months of dalliance the Company agreed to consider the regulations proposed by L'Estrange, and finally under the threat of quo warranto proceedings directed against the Company's charter the following regulations were adopted:

1. That all members of the company become bound in recognizance not to vend, publish, disperse, bind or stitch up, print, cause, or suffer to be printed any book, pamphlet, or paper whatsoever without a lawful license first had and obtained.

2. That no printer transgressing (*ut supra*) shall be allowed the printing of any of the books granted to the company by his Majesty's charter for a space of three years.

3. To what member soever of the company having an interest in the English stock shall offend in manner aforesaid shall have the profit of his stock sequestered for one year by the said company and disposed by them to the poor of the said company.[85]

A few weeks later the bylaws were further amended to permit the entrance into membership of the booksellers in and about Westminster Hall and all "forraigners in the printing trade." But having adopted these bylaws, the Company continued to delay the execution on the ground that a new charter with further powers over their membership was necessary.

In 1671 the Company adopted further concessions:

(1) To print the License & Licenser's name to every book; (2) To put

---

[82] Steele, *op. cit.*, No. 3516 (24 July 1668).

[83] Cal. St. P. Dom. Charles II, 1666-67, p. 430.

[84] *Ibid.*, 1667-68, p. 409. The men admitted were Roger Norton, Samuel Mearne, and Thomas Roycroft. Still further additions were made by royal command in 1681 (Cal. St. P. Dom., 1680-81, p. 316).

[85] St. Co. Ct. Bk. Lib. D. f. 174, 5 September 1670.

the printer's name at length to all books printed and to all papers; (3) If any book be divided to severall houses, the license to be showed, and the houses names to Mr. L'Estrange or his deputy at the beginning of its printing; (4) Not to permit any new printing house to be set up, contrary to the Act; (5) To reduce the presses and Apprentices in every house, according to Act of Printing; (6) All super numerary and illegal printing houses to be suppressed, unless the master, do enter into bond, as the Printers are to do, at the deducement; (7) No particular narration or history of the late warres to be printed without a new license; (8) To prefer the employment of journey freemen before foreigners; (9) The Stock work to be equally distributed amongst the legal printers; (10) To withdraw the Pençons from such as shall be found guilty of printing, binding and stitching or disposing illegal books, pamphlets, and papers.[86]

Again the execution was put off, and the officials of the Company continued to temporize, until finally L'Estrange under directions from Secretary Williamson presented terms for their acceptance which by vote of 14 July 1676 they promised to debate at the next general court.[87] On 6 March 1675, the bylaw that printers of seditious and libelous works be disfranchised was passed.[88]

The reasons for the unwillingness of the Stationers Company to cooperate with the authorities in the traditional manner are not difficult to discover. Armed with the protection of the court decision in Seymour's case, they were no longer afraid of losing existing patents and monopoly rights. In the second place the majority group within the Company was more anxious to take advantage of the pecuniary returns incident to the trade in popular literature than it was in maintenance of the established order. Not a little of the responsibility for the failure to enforce the regulation of the Printing Acts in the later part of the seventeenth century can be laid at the door of the Stationers Company.

[86] St. Co. Ct. Bk. D. f. 187, 3 August 1671.

[87] Historical Manuscripts Commission, Report IX, Pt. II, p. 76. Meetings between L'Estrange and the Company took place on August 28, 31, September 4, 7, 1671. According to the statement of the Surveyor of the Press he "told them plainly that the King would be trifled with no longer; Parliament was at hand, and if the Byelaw was not confirmed before it met they would be pestered with libels, and the blame would lie at their door. Upon this, a leading member sprang up and accused him of wishing to make the company slaves, and spoke disrespectfully of the King; but on L'Estrange's threatening to report the words, they were apologized for by others of the members."

[88] St. Co. Ct. Bk. Lib. D. f. 258b.

An analysis of the methods employed in enforcing the Printing Act by the king and Council, by the secretaries of state, by the Surveyor of the Press, and by the Stationers Company made it evident to the statesmen of the time that the fundamental basis of regulation was unsatisfactory. The subsequent failure to continue the Act was due not to any philosophical conclusion concerning the advisability of a free press but primarily to an inability to devise an enforceable system of regulation capable of achieving the results desired.

Expiry of the Printing Act

The renewal of the Regulation of Printing Act in 1692 was accompanied by extended discussions in both Houses of Parliament. The House of Commons received a petition from a number of independent booksellers, printers, and bookbinders charging that the Act prevented the free exercise of their trade.[89] In the House of Lords where the printers presented a similar petition attacking the Act "because it subjects all Learning and true Information to the arbitrary Will and Pleasure of a mercenary, and perhaps ignorant, Licenser; destroys the Properties of Authors in their Copies; and sets up many Monopolies," an amendment abolishing the licensing provision if the names of the author and printer were attached was adopted.[90] The booksellers, bookbinders, and Company of Stationers objected to any amendments abridging their monopolies or rights in copies. At a conference with the Commons it was apparent that no agreement on amendments could be reached, and the bill was passed in its original form.[91]

---

[89] Commons Journal, X, 817 (February 17, 1693).

[90] Lords Journal, XV, 280 (March 8, 1693).

[91] House of Lords Mss., IV, 379. Much of the disagreement both within and between the Houses of Parliament over renewing the bill was due to the publication under license from Bohun of *King William and Queen Mary Conquerors* (1693), a book which antagonized the Whigs.

T. B. Macaulay in his *History of England* (London: Dent, 1906), III, 181-88, gives an extended account of the incidents which led to the refusal of Parliament to reject the Licensing Act in 1692. According to the eminent Whig historian, the argument began with the licensing of a book which questioned Charles I's authorship of *Eikon Basilike.* The irate Tories succeeded in supplanting the Whig licenser Fraser with Edmund Bohun, a Tory who had adjusted himself to the presence of William on the throne on the theory of "conquest." Macaulay elaborately sets out to prove that the literary dilettante,

Two years later (1694) the Printing Act again came up for renewal, and this time the Lords again voted to continue the law with minor amendments. The Commons ordered a new draft to be prepared which they received 2 March 1694/5.[92] Again the Stationers Company petitioned that their property rights should be safeguarded,[93] and a group of independent printers complained that unless the Act were continued the printing trade would be "open to all Persons; which may not only be of dangerous Consequence to the Government, but will be ruinous to the said Trade." [94]

In spite of these petitions the House of Commons opposed the re-enactment of the law and supported its position in a lengthy document which was sent up to the Lords. All of the eighteen reasons for refusing to renew the Act were reasons of expediency rather than of conviction on moral or philosophical grounds. The authorship is attributed to the philosopher, John Locke, who had written but not published a paper along similar lines. Locke had important connections in Parliament, and these men undoubtedly had access to his writings. Unlike Milton, Locke grounded his arguments principally on the unnatural monopolies of the Stationers Company, on the vague and general terms of prohibition, and on the adequacy of prosecutions at common law. Nothing was said about the universal principle of freedom of the press.[95]

The Commons followed Locke's reasoning if not his exact words by emphasizing the commercial restraints contained in the Act.[96] Of the eighteen reasons advanced for refusal to continue the Act, thirteen were directed against the restraints on the printing

Charles Blount, an extreme Whig, deliberately bated the serious Bohun by writing and presenting for license an anonymous work entitled *King William and Queen Mary Conquerors* with the express purpose of getting the official into hot water. According to Macaulay, "The republican (Blount) succeeded in personating a high Tory. The atheist succeeded in personating a high Churchman." The publication of this book and the succeeding storm both in Parliament and out drove the Tory licenser from office. Macaulay's thesis is based on the authorship of Blount, which is generally accepted by bibliographers. See Leslie Stephen in *Dictionary of National Biography*, II, 786-89.

[92] Commons Journal, IX, 228, 254.

[93] *Ibid.*, p. 288.

[94] *Ibid.*, p. 289.

[95] See P. K. King, *Life and Letters of John Locke* (1858 ed.), pp. 202ff. Also B. Rand, *Correspondence of Locke and Clarke* (1927), p. 39.

[96] The document is found in Lords Journal, XV, 545-46 (18 April 1695).

and allied trades; only one was directly concerned with the licensing provisions; two belittled the attempts to suppress seditious publications; and two called attention to defects in the methods of enforcement.

In its attack on the commercial restraints, the Commons pointed out that the monopoly system under letters-patent as confirmed under the Act legalized property rights where none should have been granted and by legalizing these grants enhanced the price of books without adding to their quality. The general patent to John Streator was particularly irritating to the merchant-class members of the House. The copyright system under which registration in the records of the Stationers Company established exclusive rights was also attacked as was the provision that booksellers must be members of the London Company. Four separate reasons were advanced for abolishing the system of controlling imports of books, showing the difficulty of detecting imported books, the inconvenience of inspection methods, and the absurdities in limiting importations to the port of London. A separate point was made of the unwarranted restrictions in the act against the exercise of the printing trade in general, and in particular the restrictions on journeymen, on binders, on letter-founders, and on press-builders.

On the licensing provisions of the Act, the Commons objected first to the fact that the licensing had not been satisfactory in suppressing the kind of matter which should be suppressed, and secondly to the bribery which resulted from the failure to provide adequate compensation for the licenser.

Of the main purpose of the Act, the suppression of objectionable printing, the Commons observed that the results were unsatisfactory and that no test was set out to determine what books could be classed as "offensive." The provisions for search and seizure were criticized, and finally it was argued that since no penalties were provided in the Act, excessive penalties had been inflicted by the judges. As Macaulay has observed [97] "on the great question of principle, on the question whether the liberty of unlicensed printing be, on the whole, a blessing or a curse to society, not a word is said."

Modifications of the original Printing Act were presented to the Commons on at least four occasions between November, 1695,

---

[97] Macaulay, *op. cit.*, III, 328.

and 16 February 1698,[98] but the House could come to no agreement. One of the modifications provided for the licensing of news, leaving all other publications without censorship, but the bill failed to pass.[99]

The new century saw a number of attempts to revive the Act,[100] some of them sponsored by printers who complained of the lawlessness in the trade following the withdrawal of patent and copyright protection,[101] but in spite of anxious messages from the throne,[102] none of these attempts was successful.

To sum up, the reasons which prompted a majority of the members of Parliament to reject the Act for the Regulation of Printing were surprisingly enough the practical reasons arising from the difficulties of administration and the restraints on trade. The government was gradually settling down under a two-party system. Both parties had already enjoyed periods of ascendancy, and both were aware of the part which the press played in bringing them to power. Each was afraid to trust the other with the administration of a licensing act. And too, the last years of the Act had demonstrated that the officially appointed censors could not be trusted. A Whig was likely to turn Tory, and a Tory, Whig. The work was too arduous for a leader in the party and too dangerous for an underling.

---

[98] See Commons Journal, XI, 340, 354, 567, 685, 706; *Ibid.*, XII, 3, 99, 104.

[99] *Ibid.*, XI, 767 (April 3, 1697).

[100] *Ibid.*, XIV, pp. 249, 278, 287; *Ibid.*, XV, 316; *Ibid.*, XVII, 251, 261, 265, 293, 347, 360, 389, 406, 422, 434, 441.

[101] *Ibid.*, XIV, 338, 339 (15 February 1703).

[102] Lords Journal, XIX, 512, 625.

CHAPTER 13

Judicial and Parliamentary

Restrictions

The printers and publishers of the later Stuart period, already burdened with the restrictions of the Regulation of Printing Acts, were forced to contend with additional controls devised both by the courts and by Parliament. The criminal courts, armed with legal doctrines bequeathed by the Star Chamber and supported by frequent charges from the throne, extended the law of treason and of seditious libel until hardly a printer of the period escaped prosecution. The judges of the first two reigns following the Restoration (Charles II and James II) almost always sided with the crown in its contests with Parliament and public opinion and consequently have been severely criticized by later writers. The names, Scroggs and Jeffries, have become synonymous with vicious oppression. As a matter of fact neither Scroggs nor Jeffries applied a different law than that applied by their Whig successors, nor did they apply it more vehemently. Their explosions from the bench were certainly to be condemned, but their reputations have suffered unduly, largely because they sought to uphold a system of government which later generations have discarded. The judges of the succeeding period were scarcely less lenient nor did they apply a different rule of law. They escaped censure because their acts were supported both by Parliamentary and public opinion.

Like the courts, Parliament was anxious to keep printers and publishers in their proper places. Throughout the period, Parliamentary leaders objected to publicity. Curiously, the Revolution of 1688 made no observable change in this attitude, but the Revolution did foster those conditions which later made suppression of Parliamentary news impossible.

The Law of Treason

The law of treason is in most systems of jurisprudence the keystone of the legal structure which supports the state. In spite of the violent political and religious stresses to which the English state was subjected in the seventeenth century, resort to its extreme penalties was rare. More rare still were the instances in which printers and publishers were convicted as traitors for publishing matter inimical to the welfare of the state. In the sixteenth century only one printer, William Carter, was put to death,[1] and in the seventeenth century only two, John Twyn and William Anderton, were executed for treasonable publications.

Nevertheless, the law of treason was during the entire seventeenth century a real and present threat to freedom of expression. The few instances in which conviction and execution occurred served to remind the printers and publishers of the fate which awaited those who violated the law. The Twyn and Anderton cases were prosecuted more as examples to the printing trade than as a punishment to the culprits themselves. It was not until the end of the eighteenth century when the prosecution failed to obtain convictions [2] that the law of treason vanished as a threat to freedom of the press.

The law of treason in England is based on the statute 25 Edward III (1352) which defined the crime as (1) compassing or imagining the king's death, (2) levying war against the king, or (3) adhering to his enemies. Throughout the sixteenth and seventeenth centuries this definition was expanded by temporary enactments of Parliament each designed to cover a particular situation.

---

[1] See above, pp. 89ff.

[2] Trials of Hardy and Tooke. 24 State Trials, p. 199; 25 State Trials, p. 1 (1794).

The earliest of these statutes (26 Henry VIII, c. 13, 1534) recognized the fact that writings might endanger the security of the throne and in 1547 the words "by printing" were first used in a treason statute.[3] Soon after the Restoration, Parliament enacted a new treason law designed to fill the gaps in Edward III's statute by making it treason to intend any bodily harm tending to the death of the king, his deposition, a levying of war in the realm, or a stirring of any foreigners to invade the realm, provided that such intention was declared by printing, writing, preaching, or malicious or advised speaking.[4] These special additions to the definition of treason seem to have been seldom used against printers.

For some time it had been apparent that, strictly construed, the three clauses of 25 Edward III did not offer a complete protection for the security of the monarch and of the state. Hence there arose during the latter part of the seventeenth century that judicial extension of the statute known as *constructive* treason. Although all three clauses of the statute were extended by judicial decision, the first clause (compassing or imagining the king's death) was made to apply more particularly to writing and printing. Compassing or imagining the death of the king, being a mental state, could be proved only by overt acts. Anything, such as a writing showing an intent to murder the monarch, was such an overt act.[5] To levy war was treason, but to intend to levy war was not treason under the statute. The judges, however, soon ruled that to intend to levy war, as shown by written or printed matter, was an overt act showing an intent to compass the king's death. While mere scandalous words when spoken were not treasonable in Coke's day,[6] such words when written or printed became treasonable in the latter half of the seventeenth century.

The changed political and social conditions after 1660 were largely responsible for the changes in the judicial construction of the treason statute. Written, spoken, and printed discussions of public affairs had become widespread and had shown themselves

---

[3] 1 Ed. 6, c. 12. Subsequent acts of the same nature were 1 & 2 Phil. & Mary c. 10; 1 Eliz. c. 5; 13 Eliz. c. 1.

[4] 13 Ch. II, St. 1, c. 1, Sec. 1. This act was in force only during the life of Charles II.

[5] Rex *vs*. Owen, 1616, 1 Rolle Rep. 185.

[6] Pine's case, 1629, Cro. Car. 117.

capable of unseating a monarch. Words which when printed showed
an intent not to kill the king but to restrain him or defame him,
were held to be overt acts under 25 Edward III.[7] After the Revolution of 1688 spoken words and unpublished writings were again
held inconclusive as overt acts, but the law on written or printed
words remained the same.[8]

John Twyn was the first printer to suffer under these extensions
of the law of treason. Roger L'Estrange, Surveyor of the Press, and
his two assistants, Thomas Mabbs and John Wickham, searched
Twyn's home and succeeded in carrying off the corrected proofs of
a book entitled *A Treatise of the Execution of Justice*. This book
contained such seditious matter as that the supreme magistrate is
accountable to the people and that the people are entitled to revolt
and take the government into their own hands. That Twyn printed
the sheets, corrected some, and sold some, there is little doubt. A
jury, containing three members of the printing trade, found the
printer guilty of treason under the Statute of 25 Edward III.[9] The
judges held that the printing constituted an overt act showing an
intent to levy war and therefore to threaten the king's life. The
persistent refusal of the printer to reveal the name of the author
or to implicate others served only to irritate the judges. He was
(February, 1664) hanged, drawn, and quartered.[10]

William Anderton was apprehended by Robert Stephens, messenger of the press who, trailing two suspected journeymen-printers,
was led to the Anderton home. Here he was attacked by the printer's
wife and mother-in-law. The messenger, however, found a press
hidden in a secret room and, after beating off the women, carried
off copies of two books, *Remarks upon the present confederacy and
late Revolution in England* and *A French Conquest neither desir-*

---

[7] Twyn's case, 6 State Trials, p. 514; Sidney's case, 9 State Trials, p.
818. A further extension of the law of treason in the case of spoken words
is discussed in W. S. Holdsworth, *History of English Law* (Boston: Little,
Brown, 1924), VIII, 316.

[8] Charnock's case, 2 Salk, 361 (1696).

[9] Twyn was not tried under 13 Ch. II, 1 as the time limit for prosecution
under that statute had expired.

[10] 6 State Trials, p. 533; J. F. Stephen, *History of Criminal Law in England*
(London, 1883), I, 411. Holdsworth, *op. cit.*, VIII, 314. *An Exact Narrative
of the Tryal and Condemnation of John Twyn* (London, 1664). The sheets
which were seized are preserved among the State Papers, Dom. Charles II,
1664-65, pp. 88, 76.

able nor practicable.[11] The indictment for treason charged that these books were intended to incite rebellion and the return of James II. Again the judges acquiesced in the extension of the law of treason by ruling that a printed book which *tended* to incite rebellion was an overt act sufficient to establish an intent to compass the king's death. Anderton, who persisted in refusing to name the authors of the books, was found guilty and after some delay was hanged 12 June 1693.[12]

Twyn and Anderton were the only printers to be executed for high treason in England during the later Stuart period.[13] Why were there so few, especially during the hysterical periods of political and religious unrest of the seventeenth century? According to Professor Veeder, the "forced construction of the various treason statutes was too cumbersome as an instrument of suppression." [14]

---

[11] Lord Macaulay describes the first book as "perhaps the most frantic of all the Jacobite libels. In this tract the Prince of Orange is gravely accused of having ordered fifty of his wounded English soldiers to be burned alive. The governing principle of his whole conduct, it is said, is not vainglory, or ambition, or avarice, but a deadly hatred of Englishmen and a desire to make them miserable. The nation is vehemently adjured on peril of incurring the severest judgments, to rise up and free itself from this plague, this curse, this tyrant, whose depravity makes it difficult to believe that he can have been procreated by a human pair."

Of the second tract, Macaulay says that it exhorted the people to rise in insurrection. They are assured that a great part of the Army is with them. T. B. Macaulay, *History of England* (London: Dent, 1906), III, 235.

[12] 12 State Trials, p. 1246, *Proceedings on the King and Queen's Commission of the Peace*, B.M. 515. 1. 2 (149); *An Account of the Conversation, Behavior and Execution of William Anderton printer*, B.M. 515. 1. 2 (150).

[13] William Newbolt and Edward Butler, printers, were convicted of treason in the last decade of the century for printing and publishing "King James' Declaration." Both apparently were pardoned. See 15 State Trials, p. 1404, quoting from the Harleian Mss.

[14] *Select Essays in Anglo-American Legal History* (Boston: Little, Brown, 1909), III, 463. Lord Macaulay, however, makes the bald statement that "the overt acts which it imputes to the prisoner undoubtedly amount to high treason. To exhort the subjects of the realm to rise up and depose the King by force, and to add to that exhortation the expression, evidently ironical, of a hope that it may not be necessary to inflict on him any evil worse than banishment, is surely an offense which the least courtly lawyer will admit to be within the scope of the statute of Edward the Third. On this point indeed there seems to have been no dispute, either at the trial or subsequently." Macaulay, *History of England*, III, 235-36. (This is Macaulay at his Whig best).

Macaulay also belittles Anderton's refusal to implicate the authors by stating that "his natural courage was kept up by spiritual stimulants which the nonjuring divines well understood how to administer." (p. 237). He fur-

Other reasons for the small number of treason trials were the fact that juries were difficult to handle, the death penalty was in many cases considered too drastic, and the procedure was often too detailed. A further impediment to prosecutions based on the publication of seditious matter was the passage of the act for regulating trials for high treason in 1695-1696.[15] Under this act persons indicted for high treason were allowed copies of the indictment (five days before trial) and of the panel of jurors (two days before trial), were permitted to be defended by counsel, and could compel attendance of witnesses. In addition the problem of evidence was settled by requiring two witnesses to the same overt act or to two overt acts of the same nature.

The result of this act was to force the seventeenth-century religious and political leaders to adopt other means of suppression and control, means such as seditious libel where the statutory definitions were no impediment.

Seditious Libel

No single method of restricting the press was as effective as the law of seditious libel as it was developed and applied by the common-law courts in the later part of the seventeenth century. Hardly a year passed without one or two major prosecutions, and Luttrell's *Diary* for the year 1684 records sixteen trials for this offense between April 30 and November 28.[16]

Printers and publishers were being constantly harassed by the official searchers whose job it was to seek out all seditious printing and turn it over to the crown prosecutor.[17] Although not a capital

ther dispatches the executed printer and his adherents by the statement that the "Jacobites . . . represented him at once as a poor ignorant artisan who was not aware of the nature and tendency of the act for which he suffered, and as a martyr who had heroically laid down his life for the banished King and the persecuted Church." (p. 237.)

[15] 7, 8 William III, c. 3.

[16] Stephen, *op. cit.*, II, 313.

[17] Printers and publishers who were prosecuted for seditious libel 1660-1714 included Simon Dover (1664), Thomas Brewster (1664), Nathan Brooke (1664), Richard Royston (1668), Nathaniel Thompson (1679), William Badcock (1679), Benjamin Harris (1679), Francis Smith (1680), Henry Carr (1680), Jane Curtiss (1680) (1682), Joanne Browne (1681), Thomas Snowden (1682), Nathaniel Thompson (1688), William Paine (1682), John Farwell (1682), Richard Janeway (1681), Nathaniel Crouch (1680), James

offense, the penalties were often severe including indefinite imprisonment, heavy fines, and large bonds for good behavior.

The beginnings of the law of seditious libel as it was applied during the later Stuart period are to be found in the prosecutions before the Star Chamber in the late sixteenth and early seventeenth centuries. The abolition of this court by the Long Parliament in 1641 did not abolish the law under which printers and publishers were prosecuted. These rules were adopted in almost every respect by the common-law courts and in some cases were even extended, and although they may sound harsh to modern ears they were accepted without question by the seventeenth-century mind. As both Stephen and Holdsworth have pointed out [18] the crime of seditious libel depends on the contemporary view of the relation between the ruler and the subject. In the seventeenth century the ruler retained many of the characteristics of the feudal overlord. He was the fountainhead of justice and law. His acts were beyond popular criticism. "If the ruler is regarded as the superior of the subject, as being by the nature of his position presumably wise and good . . . it must necessarily follow that it is wrong to censure him openly, that even if he is mistaken his mistakes should be pointed out with the utmost respect, and that whether mistaken or not, no censure should be cast upon him likely or designed to diminish his authority." [19]

In the later part of the eighteenth century this view of the relation between the sovereign and his subjects was being supplanted by the theory that the ruler is the agent and servant who has been delegated certain powers and can be censured by every member of the public who merely exercises in his own person the right which belongs to the whole of which he forms a part.[20] Much of the disagreement over the rules governing seditious libel in the eighteenth century can be attributed to the growth of the latter doctrine.

The prominence of the law of seditious libel in suppressing political discussion in the late seventeenth century can be traced

---

Ostwood (1680), Jane Tulchre (1714). See W. H. Hart, *Index Expurgatorius Anglicanus* (London, 1872).

    [18] Stephen, *op. cit.*, II, 200; Holdsworth, *op. cit.*, VIII, 338.

    [19] Stephen, *op. cit.*, II, 299.

    [20] Holdsworth, *op. cit.*, VIII, 338.

to the fact that the law of treason was too limited as well as too cumbersome [21] to control the almost hysterical state of public opinion during the succession of crises preceding the establishment of the Hanoverian line. No government after 1660 was so stable that it could disregard the attacks which were being constantly made upon it, and with the expiry of the Regulation of Printing Act seditious libel was for a time almost the only remedy against factious attacks upon the government.

In these circumstances it is not surprising to find the common-law courts giving the widest meaning to the term "seditious" as applied to written and printed matter. In fact, during the entire period any reflection on the government in written or printed form was a seditious libel. In arriving at this rule of law the judges were assisted by the Regulation of Printing Acts under the authority of which they declared that it was illegal to publish anything whatever about the government, and therefore it was additionally reprehensible to publish anything damaging to the government.[22] Peculiarly, neither the expiration of the Printing Act in 1694 nor the Revolution of 1688 made any change in the law as stated by Chief Justice Scroggs. In 1704 Chief Justice Holt established this all-inclusive definition of seditious libel on a more permanent basis by declaring

. . . this is a very strange doctrine to say that it is not a libel reflecting on the government, endeavouring to possess the people that the government is maladministered by corrupt persons, ... To say that corrupt officers are appointed to administer affairs is certainly a reflection on the government. If people should not be called to account for possessing the people with an ill opinion of the government, no government can subsist. For it is very necessary for all governments that the people should have a good opinion of it. And nothing can be worse to any government than to endeavour to procure animosities as to the management of it; this has always been looked upon as a crime, and no government can be safe without it.[23]

Only a few examples of the type of publication upon which

---

[21] See above, pp. 268-69.

[22] Rex *vs.* Carr, 1680, 7 State Trials, p. 1114; Rex *vs.* Harris, 1680, 7 State Trials, p. 929. Although Chief Justice Scroggs was later impeached for arbitrary acts in connection with these cases, it was never alleged that his statement of the law was wrong.

[23] Rex *vs.* Tutchin, 14 State Trials, p. 1095.

prosecutions were based are necessary to illustrate the scope of the law. In 1679 Benjamin Harris was indicted and tried for seditious libel for publishing the following:

"We in the country have done our part in chusing, for the generality, good members to serve in parliament; but if (as our last two parliaments were) they must be dissolved, or prorogued, whenever they come to redress the grievances of the subject, we may be pitied but not blamed. If the Plot takes effect (as in all probability it will) our parliaments are not then to be condemned, for that their not being suffered to sit occasioned it." [24]

Another example of seditious publication is No. 4, Vol. II, of *The Weekly Pacquet of Advice from Rome, or the History of Popery,* in which Henry Carr (Care), the publisher, wrote:

There is lately found out by an experienced physician, an incomparable medicament called, *The Wonder-Working Plaister,* truly Catholic in operation; some what akin to the Jesuits Powder, but more effectual. The virtues of it are strange and various. It will make justice deaf as well as blind; and takes out spots out of the deepest treason more cleverly than Castile-soap does common stains. It alters a man's constitution in two or three days, more than the Virtuosos Transfusion of Blood in seven years. It is a great alexipharmic, and helps poisons, and those that use them. It miraculously exalts and purifies the eye-sight, and makes people behold nothing but innocence in the blackest malefactors. It is a mighty cordial for a declining cause, stifles a plot as certainly as the itch is destroyed by butter and brimstone. In a word, it makes fools wise men, and wise men fools, and both of them knaves. . . .[25]

Coming at the time of public apprehension over the Oates plot, Carr's newspaper undoubtedly inflamed public opinion. The jury found the publisher guilty of seditious libel, and Chief Justice Scroggs in addition to imprisoning Carr ruled that the periodical should cease publication.[26] This ruling was later presented by a committee of the House of Commons as one of the bases for im-

[24] *An Appeal from the Country to the City for the Preservation of his Majesty's Person, Liberty, Property, and the Protestant Religion.* 7 State Trials, p. 927 (1679).

[25] 7 State Trials, pp. 1112-13.

[26] The rule in Carr's case was "Die Mercurii proxima post tres Septimanas Sanotae Trinitias, Anno 32 Car. II. Regis. Ordinatum est quod Liber intitulat 'The Weekly Pacquet of Advice from Rome, or the History of Popery,' vel non ulterius imprimatur vel publicetur per aliquam personam quamcunque. Per Cur." *Ibid.,* p. 1114.

peaching the chief justice. The articles of impeachment were, however, dropped with the proroguing of Parliament in 1680.[27]

One of the legal problems which arose in connection with seditious libel was the question of seditious or malicious intent. In the criminal indictment it was customary to allege that the accused had published the libel with the most vicious intentions. Falsely, seditiously, maliciously, and factiously were common terms. As pointed out by Holdsworth, "naturally the use of these common forms tended to give rise to the view that the crime was, not so much the intentional publication of the seditious words, as their publication with a seditious and malicious intent." [28] This problem was no problem at all under the Star Chamber where the judges acted without a jury, but the common-law judges were disturbed by this question for more than a hundred years. Was it necessary to prove that the publisher maliciously intended to produce sedition, or was it sufficient to prove that he merely intended to publish the matter? The judges of the seventeenth century adopted the latter point of view, holding that proof of the publication of the matter was in itself sufficient to establish an intent to publish it, and that further proof of a false and seditious intent was unnecessary.[29]

Another problem closely connected with the question of intent was the province of the jury. Who determined whether the publication was seditious or not, and who determined whether there was any malice? The Restoration judges solved this by ruling that the court should decide both questions as a matter of law. The jury merely determined matters of fact; such as, did the defendant actually publish these words.

Following this line of reasoning Chief Justice Scroggs directed the jury in Carr's case that if it found that he published the newspaper he must be found guilty of the crime of seditious libel.

"If you find him guilty and say what he is guilty of, we will judge whether the thing imports malice or no. Sir Francis Winnington hath told you there are some things that do necessarily imply malice in them. If this thing doth not imply it, then the judges will

---

[27] 8 State Trials, p. 163.

[28] Holdsworth, *op. cit.*, VIII, 342.

[29] Rex *vs.* Barnardiston (1684), 9 State Trials, p. 1334; Rex *vs.* Carr (1680), 7 State Trials, p. 1111.

go accordingly to sentence; if it doth, so that it concerns you not one farthing, whether malicious or not malicious — that is plain." [30] This rule that the jury's duty was to determine whether the accused published the offending matter and that the judge would determine both whether the matter was offensive and whether there was malice carried over into the eighteenth century until it was changed by act of Parliament in 1796.[31]

A third problem in the law of seditious libel which became acute in the next century was the question of the truth of the published matter. The seventeenth-century judges were not unduly troubled by this question as most of the writings and printed matter on which indictments were based were of such a nature that their truth or falsity could not readily be established. Where, however, the defendant attempted to justify his words, he was promptly silenced.[32] Occasionally evidence was admitted at the trial to show the falsity of the publication, and upon at least one instance the defendant was challenged to prove the truth of his charges,[33] but in the majority of prosecutions neither the court nor the jury considered the truth of the alleged seditious matter as pertinent to the case.

The case which was frequently cited in the next century as authority for the rule that truth was a defense to seditious libel was the *Case of the Seven Bishops*.[34] This case, which was tried at the height of the religious and political upheavals preceding the overthrow of James II, arose over the publication of a statement by the seven bishops justifying a refusal to publish the king's declaration of liberty of conscience and questioning the legality of his power to suspend the laws against nonconformists. In that case there is no doubt that both the malicious intent and the question of truth were left to the jury, but as both the eminent legal historians, Stephen and Holdsworth, contend, the case is useless as a precedent. The public excitement, the overwhelming legal talent employed by the bishops, and the cowardly attitude of the judges all served to make

---

[30] 7 State Trials, p. 1128.

[31] See below, p. 391. Fox's Libel Act, 32 Geo. III, c. 60.

[32] Rex *vs*. Keach, 6 State Trials, p. 701 (1665).

[33] Trial of Thompson, Paine, and Farwell, 8 State Trials, p. 1359 (1682).

[34] 12 State Trials, p. 183.

the case a *cause célèbre* but of very little value as a legal precedent.[35]

By the end of the century it was apparent that prosecutions for seditious libel were becoming less effective in controlling public discussion of state affairs than they had been under Charles II and James II. The trial of John Tutchin in 1704 for publishing in his subsidized periodical, *The Observator,* the charges that French gold was bribing national leaders, that Parliament had authority to set up a king, and that there was corruption among the navy managers amply demonstrated the difficulty of getting convictions. The jury returned a verdict of guilty of composing and publishing but not writing the offensive matter. A motion was made in arrest of judgment that the original writ was faulty in dating it October 23 when it should have been October 24, and after a lengthy legal argument the case was dropped and never tried again.[36]

Restrictions by Parliament

The early seventeenth century witnessed attempts by Parliament on one hand to extend the freedom of speech of its members and on the other to suppress all reflections on either its members or its policies by outsiders.[37] Throughout the period of the Interregnum (1640-1660) the legislative body (or what remained of it) continued to exercise sovereign powers over public discussions of all kinds, adding at the same time to its own authority all those rights enjoyed by the crown under the prerogative.[38] With the Restoration, Parliament entered upon a new phase in its relation to oral, written, and printed discussions of political and religious questions. Its own privilege of freedom of speech and debate were secured by a provision in the Bill of Rights,[39] and for the remainder of the century the problem was one of restrictions *by* Parliament rather than restrictions *on* Parliament. Under the guise of privilege both Houses claimed the power to punish any conduct of which they disapproved. These powers, as Holdsworth has suggested, were "almost as vague and elastic as those comprised in in the preroga-

---

[35] Holdsworth, *op. cit.,* VIII, 344; Stephen, *op. cit.,* II, 315.

[36] 14 State Trials, pp. 1095-1200.

[37] See above, pp. 112-16.

[38] See above, pp. 179-201.

[39] I Will. & Mary, sess. 2, C. Sec. i 9.

tive."[40] However, after 1688 the common-law judges, now freed from domination by the crown, proceeded to make inroads on the powers of Parliament, but even the great Chief Justice Holt was unable to restrict Parliament's claim to punish publishers of seditious and schismatical writings.[41] The legal distinction between contempts of Parliamentary authority and seditious libel was still nebulous in 1700, and under these conditions it is not surprising to find both Houses claiming the right to punish all criticisms and discussions of its proceedings regardless of whether these publications were a libel on the House or a mere criticism of Parliamentary policy.

Examples of the suppression of libels on Parliament are common throughout the period 1660-1714. Whenever the attention of the House of Lords was directed to an obnoxious publication, the procedure was to appoint a committee to examine the printer or publisher and then to order the offending publication burned by the common hangman and the publisher or author held in confinement until he submitted to the House. In 1675 the attention of the Lords was called to a pamphlet entitled *A letter from a person of quality to his friend in the country.*[42] A committee of thirty-five Lords was ordered to make an investigation and report to the House. After examining a woman hawker, the Surveyor of the Press, L'Estrange, the officers of the Stationers Company, and Mr. Starkey, the bookseller, the committee was forced to report that it was unable to discover the author or the printer.[43]

A typical example of the methods employed by the House of Lords in relation to printed libels on its members is the case of William Carr who was charged with the publication of a libel on Lord Gerard of Brandon. The committee for privileges which conducted the examination reported to the House which, after ordering the paper to be publicly burnt, fined Carr £1,000, sentenced him to stand in the pillory, and committed him to prison during the king's pleasure.[44]

---

[40] Holdsworth, *op. cit.*, VI, 257.

[41] *Ibid.*

[42] The contents of this pamphlet of thirty-four pages are printed *in extenso* in Parliamentary Register (Lord's Proceedings), Vol. 25, pp. 129-60.

[43] Historical Manuscripts Commission, 9th Report, Pt. II, p. 66; Lords Journal, XIII, 13, 17.

[44] Lords Journal, XII, 173, 174, 176 (1667).

The Lords continued zealously to guard the reputation of its members throughout the seventeenth century. In 1697 John Salisbury, the printer of the *Flying Post,* was called before the House for a reflection on the Duke of Bolton, but he escaped with a reprimand.[45] In 1701 the House again attempted to suppress a number of pamphlets which it was charged were "loading them with abominable crimes," but it is impossible to determine the results of these efforts from the available records.[46]

Unlike the Lords, the House of Commons was more concerned with reflections on its policies than with libels on the reputation of its individual members. While both Houses were active in attempting to suppress what were considered seditious, scandalous, and schismatical publications, it was in this field that the House of Commons took the lead. Any publication reflecting on the proceedings of the House was considered a breach of privilege and was punished as such. Enforcement activities increased in proportion to the controversial nature of the subject under discussion. A typical entry in the Journals of the House is the following:

A complaint being made to the House of a printed paper dispersed abroad, intituled *Mr. Duncomb's Case,* reflecting upon the Proceedings of this House;

One of which Papers was produced, and delivered in at the Table; and there read;

Resolved; That a printed Paper intituled *Mr. Duncomb's Case* is false, scandalous, and malicious; and highly reflecting upon the Proceedings of this House, and the Honour of the Commons in Parliament assembled.

Ordered, That the said printed Paper be burnt, by the Hands of the Common Hangman upon Saturday Morning next in the Palace-Yard; And the Sheriffs of *London* and *Middlesex* do see the same performed.[47]

The House of Commons frequently issued orders to the sergeant at arms to arrest the distributors of seditious pamphlets,[48] and occasionally sought the assistance of the crown in apprehending printers and publishers.[49] Whenever the offending publications

---

[45] *Ibid.,* XVI, 138, 139.

[46] See Cal. St. P. Dom., 1700-1702, p. 456.

[47] Commons Journal, XII, 147 (7 March 1689).

[48] *Ibid.,* VII, 331.

[49] *Ibid.,* X, 111.

were seized, they were ordered to be publicly burned.[50] Among those ordered burned were *A Short History of the Convention; or New-christen'd Parliament*,[51] *An Account of the Proceedings in the House of Commons in relation to the Recoining the clipp'd Money, and the Falling Price of Guineas*,[52] *An Inquiry into the Causes of the Miscarriage of the Scots Colony at Darien*,[53] and Defoe's *The Shortest Way with Dissenters*.[54]

At the opening of the eighteenth century the Commons became actively interested in maintaining what it considered to be religious orthodoxy. In addition to suppressing a number of pamphlets on religious subjects,[55] it proceeded to impeach the famous preacher Henry Sacheverell for his doctrines as expressed in his published sermons.[56] The fall of the Whigs and the ascendancy of the Tories are ascribed to these attempts to control the discussion of religious doctrine.

Among the newspapers which were prosecuted by the House of Commons were the *Flying Post* (1697), the *Observer* (1703), and the *Daily Courant* (1712). John Salisbury, printer of the *Flying Post*, was arrested by order of the House of Commons for publishing "we hear that when the Exchequer Notes are given out, upon the Capitation fund, whoever shall desire specie will have it at 5 & half per cent. of the Society of Gentlemen that have subscribed to advance some Hundred thousands of pounds."[57] The majority in the Commons was irritated by an article appearing in the *Observator* for December 8-11, 1702, entitled "Some further remarks on occasional conformity." John How, the printer, Benjamin Bragg, the publisher, and John Tutchin, the author, were arrested and later released, but a few months later another article on the same subject in the February 9-12, 1703, issue again aroused the House, but this time the three men absconded.[58]

The publisher of the first daily newspaper ran afoul of the

---

[50] *Ibid., passim.*   [51] *Ibid.*, X, 11 (1689).   [52] *Ibid.*, XI, 572 (1696).

[53] *Ibid.*, XIII, 123 (1700).   [54] *Ibid.*, XIV, 207 (1702).

[55] *Of the Sacramental Test, Ibid.*, XVI, 57 (1708); *The Rights of the Christian Church asserted against the Romish and all other Priests, Ibid.*, XVI, 385 (1710); *A Defense of the Rights of the Christian Church, Ibid.; Tractatus philosophico-theologious de Persona, Ibid.*

[56] 15 State Trials, p. 1 (1709-10).

[57] Commons Journal, XI, 765.

[58] *Ibid.*, XIV, 269-70, 336-37.

House of Commons in 1712 by publishing in the issue of April 7 a memorial to the House. A committee was appointed to investigate, and received testimony from Samuel Buckley, the publisher, that he had copied the offending article from a Dutch paper. Upon a divided vote the publisher was taken into custody.[59]

Parliamentary Reporting [60]

The efforts to punish contempts of Parliamentary privilege in published reflections on its membership and on its proceedings did not keep the legislature from expending a large part of its time in the suppression of published reports of its proceedings. As Parliament extended its sphere of influence in the affairs of state after the Revolution of 1688, the problem of handling the news of its deliberations as well as of its decisions became increasingly important.

On the side of secrecy were the precedents of several centuries, all pointing to the value of privacy as a defense against the encroachments of a powerful monarch. Except for the short interim in the early days of the Puritan Revolution, no published reports of Parliamentary proceedings had been permitted. In 1640 the votes and proceedings began to appear in the diurnals, and in 1641 Parliament for the first time gave these published reports its official sanction.[61] The experiment, however, was dropped as soon as the legislature was firmly established in the seat of authority. Historical and customary precedents also prohibited all strangers from attending the sessions of either House. So careful was Parliament of its privilege of freedom of debate that it required all speeches to be oral and prohibited readings from notes or manuscripts for fear that these written papers might be used later against the speaker.[62]

For some time after the Restoration, Parliament maintained its traditional attitude toward all reporting of its proceedings, but near the end of the reign of Charles II the highly controversial question of the succession made it necessary to allay widespread rumors and also on occasion to appeal to the country for support. The effect

---

[59] *Ibid.*, XVII, 175, 182; *Parliamentary History of England,* edited by William Cobbett (London, 1806-20), VI, 1124.

[60] For early history see above, Chapter 10.

[61] See above, pp. 202-4.

[62] *Parliamentary History of England,* IV, 620.

of events on the development of Parliamentary reporting is discussed under the headings: (1) restrictions on published reports, (2) official or sanctioned publications, and (3) prosecutions of newsletter writers.

One of the first acts of the House of Lords in 1660 was to prohibit the publication of "any Act, Ordinance, Order, Vote, or other Proceedings that have been agitated in the House without order from the same, upon paine of having such proceedings prosecuted against them as shall be just." [63] This order remained in effect in the House of Lords throughout the later seventeenth century and seemed to have caused little trouble in comparison to the difficulties which the House of Commons encountered in enforcing similar regulations.

In 1675 it became necessary to make some efforts to enforce the prohibition against printing the reports of cases tried before the Lords.[64] The House of Lords, like the courts, claimed the exclusive right to control the publication of all reports of its judicial proceedings, and on this basis in 1697 it ordered the arrest of John Churchill, a printer, for publishing "Cases in Parliament resolved and adjudged upon Petitions and Writs of Error." The printer was released with a reprimand, but to prevent such a scandal from recurring, it was resolved that it was a breach of privilege for any person to print anything relating to its proceedings, judicial or otherwise.[65] This standing order of 1697 was the basis for the restrictive practices of the House of Lords during the entire eighteenth century.

The House of Commons, like the House of Lords, claimed the right to regulate all reports of its proceedings. An order prohibiting published reports "without the Order of this House" was made 3 July 1661.[66] Occasionally special permission was given to a member to publish his speech in order to confound rumors or to correct

---

[63] Lords Journal, XI, 79. Order published by John Bill and Christopher Barker, London, 1660.

[64] Ibid., XII, 713.

[65] Ibid., XVI, 391. "Resolved, that it is a breach of the Privilege of this House, for any Person whatsoever to print, or publish any thing relating to the Proceedings of this House, without the leave of this House; and that the said Order be added to the Standing Orders, and set on the Doors of this House."

[66] Commons Journal, VIII, 249.

misinterpretations.[67] Surprisingly few printers or publishers were prosecuted for violation of this order of 1661 prohibiting the publication of proceedings. Although neither the official *London Gazette* nor the publications of the newspaper-monopolists ventured into the field of Parliamentary reporting, independent printers occasionally issued pamphlets which touched on legislative matters. The House of Commons, however, was too busy suppressing unfavorable attacks on its actions to bother with the prosecution of the occasional factual report. The printer, Richard Janeway, was arrested for publishing *An Address agreed upon by a Committee of the House of Commons,* but he seems to have been released soon afterwards.[68]

The problem of the official publication of Parliamentary debates was thoroughly discussed in the House of Commons during this period with the result that the final actions of that body were officially made public. These final actions are usually termed "the votes and proceedings." At the opening of the first Parliament under Charles II, both Houses appointed official printers who were given exclusive rights to issue all Parliamentary publications. The House of Lords 26 April 1660 appointed Francis Tyton and John Macocke,[69] and the Commons a few weeks later gave the Speaker authority to name the official printer.[70] Henry Hills and John Field seem to have enjoyed the prerequisites of the office for a few months but on August 24 Hills and Field were called in and deprived of whatever rights they had held.[71]

Such great care was exercised by the Commons over the official reports of its proceedings that even the Speaker himself was required to have a special permit from the House before publishing his own speeches.[72]

The traditional reluctance of the House of Commons to take the country into its confidence is illustrated by the debate on the motion to print the *Address on Grievances* and the king's answer in

[67] *Ibid.,* VIII, 142 (29 August 1660); *Ibid.,* p. 83 (2 June 1660); *Ibid.,* X, 310 (16 December 1689).
[68] *Ibid.,* X, 105.
[69] Lords Journal, XI, 46.
[70] Commons Journal, VIII, 14.
[71] *Ibid.,* pp. 134, 165.
[72] *Ibid.,* p. 142.

the session of 1673. It was argued that although the Commons might authorize the publication of its own address, it had no right to publicize the king's answer. It was further argued against the motion that, since newsbooks were prohibited from publishing Parliamentary matter, all appeals to the people should be avoided, and again that the publication of the *Address* would make it appear that the Commons did not trust the king. In support of the motion the argument was advanced that nothing in the proposed publication was disparaging either of the king or the Commons and that it would increase public respect for the king by ending the disputes about quartering of soldiers. The vote was evenly divided, 105 to 105, with the Speaker casting the deciding vote against publication.[73]

The question of the official publication of the votes and proceedings of the House of Commons was raised for the first time in 1680. At that time popular sentiment against Roman Catholics and against the Catholic heir to the throne, the Duke of York, was running high, and in spite of the opposition of Charles II the House of Commons presented a bill to exclude James from the throne. Popular support for the bill was strong, and in self-protection against charges of Papism the Commons voted 30 October 1680 to print the votes of the House "the same being first perused and signed by the speaker." [74] At the opening of the next session of Parliament in 1681, a similar motion requiring publication of the votes was adopted on the ground that such publication "prevented all misrepresentations of us to the world by false copies of our votes." [75] Sir Francis Winnington revived the argument presented in the Long Parliament that the people having selected the members of Parliament ought to be informed of what action was taken by their representatives. The objection was that such action was undignified.[76]

The votes as authorized for publication by the Speaker were formal, curtailed, and carefully censored. Remarks by members on propositions before the House were not included. Other publishers

---

[73] *Parliamentary History* . . . , IV, 583-84.

[74] Commons Journal, IX, 643.

[75] *Ibid.,* p. 708 (24 March 1681).

[76] *Parliamentary History* . . . , IV, 1306-8 taken from Williams, *Votes and Proceedings,* 1680-81.

could reprint the votes upon paying a gratuity to the official printers.[77]

A few years later during the reign of William and Mary the question of the official publication of the votes of the House of Commons was again raised, and this time (22 January 1688/9) the majority voted to cease publication.[78] In March the question was revived and the arguments for and against publication were presented at length. The reasons against publication were that it was contrary to precedent, that action by the Commons was not final and might appear to be contradicted by the Lords or by the king, that the vote was frequently rescinded which fact might give the public an erroneous impression of the House, that the public is less interested in the votes than in the reasons which are not published, that the votes without the reasons are meaningless, that publication of the votes might threaten freedom of debate, and finally that since the Lords do not publish, why should the Commons.

The reasons presented in favor of publication of the votes were that the people were entitled to the information, that an accurate publication of the votes would counteract inaccurate and unofficial reports which were being surreptitiously dispersed in the coffee-houses, and that threats to freedom of debate by the king would in no way be affected by publication since the king was informed of the proceedings of the house through other channels.

Sir Richard Temple summed up the arguments against publication by pointing out that

This matter is of more moment than at first it semed to be; little benefit and great inconvenience may come from it. I dislike all innovations. In a great assembly, what is done must be with great reason; there ought to be no innovation. All that can be proved for printing it is to rectify Coffee-houses, and for beyond the sea. I saw, at Oxford Parliament, another thing gained, upon commissions that gentlemen had from their country about the Exclusion Bill. I hope we shall not imitate Holland, to go to our principals for Instructions; it may be of dangerous consequence to alter the government. I hear of balloting-boxes; they have had them in Scotland, but they are weary of them, as precluding all debates. This strikes at the essential privilege of Parliament, when you have advanced in a Bill, and then reject it, and the people know not the reason of that. I would have sending the Votes to Coffee-houses redressed; but

---

[77] Michael MacDonagh, *The Reporters Gallery* (London: Hodder and Stoughton, 1913), p. 101.

[78] Commons Journal, X, 12.

it is far less inconvenience than that your Resolutions should go about from yourselves with approbation; I never heard any good reason for it, nor any good success of it when done. It will prove a levity without doors, to alter your Vote already made, and your Reasons not known.[79]

Sir Thomas Littleton stated the arguments for publication:

I am for printing your Votes, and I see no inconvenience by it; it will be great if you do not print them. England has from the clerks all you do, but not the truth of what you do; and it is fit England should know both. In former parliaments, when they were invading and undermining the people, they were ashamed of it; but we are now under a king that preserves our liberties, and there is no reason but the people should know it. It is fit the people should know the good things transacted betwixt the king and this house. Such a union may have great influence both abroad and at home. I am for printing them.[80]

The vote was 145 for publication and 180 against.[81] In October of the same year (1689) the House quietly voted again and this time the majority approved printing the votes.[82] From this date to 1702 the House of Commons authorized the publication of its acts, taking the precaution, however, of prohibiting all reprints such as had occasionally appeared in newsbooks.[83] Official publication of the votes was authorized, but republication in newspapers was still prohibited.

In 1702/3 the conflict between the House of Commons and the House of Lords over the Bill for Preventing Occasional Conformity seems to have impinged upon the dignity of both Houses with the result that the Commons withdrew its standing order authorizing publication of its votes.[84] The House of Lords thereupon broke a long-standing precedent by authorizing for the first time in its history the publication of its official acts. The Commons was thus forced to release its votes for publication in order to meet the unfavorable publicity contained in the published votes of the Lords.[85]

From 1680 on, except for these short intervals in 1689 and 1703,

---

[79] *Parliamentary History* . . . , V (9 March 1688/9), 166.
[80] *Ibid.*
[81] Commons Journal, X, 45.
[82] *Ibid.*, p. 273.
[83] *Ibid.*, p. 358; *Ibid.*, XI, 2.
[84] *Ibid.*, XIV, 208 (25 February 1702/3).
[85] *Ibid.*, p. 231 (23 November 1703).

the House of Commons has permitted the official publication of its decisions.[86]

In its new constitutional status arising from the establishment of a limited monarchy following the Revolution of 1688, Parliament continued to shroud itself in secrecy, not as a protection against the king who was now subservient to it but as a guard against too much interference from the public. The struggle between Parliament and the king now gave way to a struggle between Parliament and the people. The seventeenth- and early eighteenth-century Parliamentarians accepted the theory that they were *representing* the people but at the same time they refused to acknowledge that they were *responsible* to the people. Not being responsible to the public, there was no reason to inform it of matters under discussion or of reasonings on these matters. On this basis both Houses of Parliament came to the conclusion that all reports of its proceedings in the public prints were a breach of privilege. The official publication of votes was sufficient; newspapers and pamphlets should not meddle with Parliamentary affairs.[87]

During the early years of Charles II the printed newspapers were effectively controlled by the monopolists, Muddiman, L'Estrange, and Williamson. None of these dared risk the withdrawal of his monopoly by publishing news of Parliament. As long as the Printing Acts were in force the propertied printers were reluctant to arouse the animosity of Parliament by reporting its proceedings.

Except for the short-lived experiments during the Puritan Revolution, the first accounts of Parliamentary news containing more than the mere recital of legislation enacted were published in the written newsletters which circulated in the London coffee-houses. Muddiman was circumspect in his written newsletters and seldom mentioned the proceedings in Parliament. The newsletter writers of the last decade of the seventeenth century were far more bold, perhaps because of their adherence to one or the other of the political parties which were contending in the halls of Westminster. The writers of these letters were mainly clerks and scriveners in and about Westminster hall, and they collected their news and gossip from the clerks and messengers in the service of the government,

[86] See Report of Select Committee on Publication of Printed Papers (H. of C.), 1837.

[87] MacDonagh, *op. cit.*, pp. 88-89.

many of whom were not averse to the then universal practice of augmenting their income by peddling information on government affairs. In 1689 the House of Commons was sufficiently irritated by the newsletter writers to warn them not to report its proceedings.[88]

One of the most successful of the letter publishers of this period was John Dyer who, according to the diarist Luttrell, was twice in trouble for publishing Parliamentary news as early as 1693.[89] Late in 1694 Dyer was summoned to appear before the House of Commons for publishing reports of its proceedings in his newsletters. He appeared before the bar and upon his promise not to offend again was released.[90] Dyer, who was attached to the Tory party, was undoubtedly encouraged to issue his reports by party leaders within the House, for he continued to include Parliamentary news in his letters, and as a result was arrested in 1695,[91] 1696,[92] 1697/8,[93] and 1698.[94] He absconded in 1698 and remained in hiding until the storm had blown over; afterward he went back to work again. Lord Mohun, who was mentioned in a newsletter, took matters into his own hands and severely beat up the newswriter.[95] In 1702/3 the Commons again charged Dyer with "misrepresenting the proceedings of the House," and ordered his arrest, but again he was not to be found.[96] The following year (3 January 1703/4) the lower house repeated its order that "no News-Letters-Writers, do in their Letters, or other Papers that they disperse, presume to intermeddle with the Debates or any other proceedings of this House." [97]

The proceedings of the sedate House of Lords were not immune from the newsletter writers who, in the political squabbles of the early years of Queen Anne, discovered that the prohibition of

[88] Commons Journal, X, 281 (8 November). The warning was repeated 28 October 1690. Ibid., p. 454.
[89] Narcissus Luttrell, Brief Historical Relation of State Affairs from September 1678 to April 1714 (Oxford: University press, 1857), III, 166-67, 237.
[90] Commons Journal, XI, 192, 193.
[91] Cal. St. P. Dom., 1695, 30.
[92] Commons Journal, XI, 710.
[93] Ibid., XII, 48.
[94] Luttrell, op. cit., IV, 206.
[95] Parliamentary History . . . , V, 863.
[96] Commons Journal, XIV, 207 (February 25).
[97] Ibid., p. 278.

1697 [98] against discussing the proceedings of the Lord referred only to printed reports and not to handwritten newsletters. In 1707 several persons were arrested in coffeehouses for distributing letters which purported to be a report of the minutes of the proceedings. The Lords were shocked and ordered an immediate investigation. One of the letters picked up in the coffeehouses was traced to a William Rowland who admitted that he had a regular business of writing newsletters containing House proceedings. Where did he get his material? the investigating committee asked. From two men, Bond and Kelsey, who turned out to be managers of coffeehouses. Bond, whose coffeehouse was located near the Court of Requests, at first denied any connection with the newsletter but later admitted that he furnished the writers with information for a fee of 18 pence a week. Where did Bond get his information? From members of the House of Commons and from clerks who frequented his establishment.

Another newsletter was traced to Robert Guest who admitted to the Lord's committee that his house was rented to two letter publishers, Allen and Horton. Cree, who wrote the letters, testified that the information was gathered by Allen who in turn admitted buying it from coffeehouses. The investigation and subsequent proceedings lasted from February to April, 1707, and at the end of that period all defendants were discharged upon payment of fees and promising not to offend further. [99]

In spite of the efforts of both Houses of Parliament to control the newsletter writers, news of Parliamentary discussions was being circulated. Word of mouth was of course the principal means, but written as well as printed accounts eluded detection. The division within Parliament into political groups each striving to gain ascendancy through public support made it difficult to enforce the rules, and as long as a strong minority either openly or surreptitiously encouraged the circulation of Parliamentary news, complete suppression was impossible. Coffeehouse discussions were the most difficult to suppress; next came the newsletter writers, and finally the ephe-

---

[98] See above, p. 280.

[99] Details of the investigation of the newsletters is to be found in the Manuscripts of the House of Lords, VII, 51-52, and in the Lords Journal, XVIII, 230, 233, 234, 244, 305, 307, 309.

meral printed matter such as pamphlets and newspapers which were more readily traced through the printing types.

To summarize the status of Parliamentary reporting at the end of the seventeenth century, it is found that both Houses adopted rules early in the reign of Charles II prohibiting published reports of both votes and debates, the Lords in 1660 and the Commons in 1661. The early resolution of the Lords was reiterated in 1697 and was applied specifically to reports of judicial proceedings before the upper house. The Commons, however, rescinded its action in 1681 to the extent that it permitted the *official* publication of its votes as censored by the Speaker, but continued its prohibition against unofficial reports of the votes as well as against all publication of its debates. This policy continued unchanged (with the exception of a short period in 1688) until 1702 when a special prohibition was ordered against republishing the official report of the votes in newsletters or in newspapers. At the opening of the eighteenth century, the Lords prohibited all reports both official and unofficial; the Commons permitted the publication of the official report of its votes but not of its debates and allowed this official version to be republished but not in newsletters or newspapers.

CHAPTER 14

Regulation of Newspapers, 1660-1714

Monopolies in News

The change in government accompanying the restoration of Charles II was accomplished with surprisingly few innovations in the methods for controlling and regulating the publication of news. One of the first acts of the Council of State after the dissolution of the Long Parliament was to discharge Marchmont Needham from his position as editor of the *Publick Intelligencer* and *Mercurius Politicus,* the two official newsbooks of the Protectorate. Henry Muddiman, who had ingratiated himself with General Monck, had begun the publication of the newsbooks, the *Parliamentary Intelligencer,* 26 December 1659, and *Mercurius Publicus,* 5 January 1660; and these two new publications supplanted Needham's newsbooks as the official mouthpieces of the Council of State.

As the Council's control over the government increased, the competing newsbooks of the Protectorate were suspended. Needham's two publications came to an end 9 April 1660; *The Faithful Scout* suspended 6 January 1660; *Occurrences from Foreign Parts* continued until 13 March 1660. In the meantime Muddiman's two semiweekly newsbooks became the exclusive media for the dissemination of news.[1]

Muddiman's newsbooks were firmly entrenched by the time the Council of State was dissolved and Charles II restored to the crown. The *Parliamentary Intelligencer,* the Monday edition, was changed by Muddiman 1 January 1661 to *Kingdom's Intelligencer* while the Thursday edition, *Mercurius Publicus,* continued with the same name. For the first few months after the Restoration Muddiman's newsbooks were entered in the Register of the Stationers Company under authority of the king's Council.[2]

With the dissolution of the Council of State Muddiman's position as exclusive purveyor of news became less secure. The Council's authority to him expired with the Council itself, and his sole claim to the news monopoly rested upon his association with General Monck and Secretary Nicholas. In the meantime several ephemeral publications appeared but soon suspended. Among these attempted newsbooks were *Mercurius Fumigosus, London's Diurnall, Mercurius Phanaticus, A Perfect Diurnall, Mercurius Honestus, The Phanatic Intelligencer, Mercurius Aulicus.* These appeared between February and June, 1660, but rarely lasted more than one or two numbers.

Muddiman's chief competitor for his privileged position as news distributor was Oliver Williams. In 1637 Charles I had granted a patent to Captain Robert Innes for the establishment of an office of intelligence "whither masters or others having lost goods, women for satisfaction whether their absent husbands be living or dead, parents for lost children, or any others for discovering murders or robberies, and for all bargains and intelligences." The patent which ran for a term of forty-one years and which had lain dormant was purchased from Innes' widow by Oliver Williams in 1657. Williams had set up several offices scattered throughout London and had proceeded to publish a *Weekly Information from the Office of Intelligence.* The whole scheme soon collapsed because of the restriction

---

[1] *Parliamentary Intelligencer,* No. 14, 26 March to 2 April 1660 was the first number issued "by the order of the Council of State" and in it announcement was made of Needham's discharge and the appointment of his successors. The entry in the Stationers' Register is dated 9 April 1660, G. E. B. Eyre and C. R. Rivington, *Transcript* . . . (London, 1913), II, 257. Muddiman's newsbooks were printed by John Macocke.

[2] Eyre and Rivington, *op. cit.,* II, 264, 267, 268, 280.

in the patent that no definite fees could be charged. After Needham's dismissal Williams revived his office of intelligence and commenced a semiweekly periodical, *A Particular Advice*, 30 June 1659, Fridays,[3] and *Occurrences from Foreign Parts*, 5 July 1659. With the final dismissal of Needham by the Council of State Williams appropriated the titles, *Mercurius Politicus* and *Publick Intelligencer* (July, 1660).[4]

With the return of the king, Williams thought his position strong enough to attack Muddiman in his newsbooks. Muddiman replied, attacking the validity of the Innes patent, which he claimed went no further than the establishment of offices of information and could by no stretch of the imagination be extended to include printed newsbooks. In July, 1660, the Privy Council issued orders for the suppression of all printed newsbooks other than Muddiman's *Parliamentary Intelligencer* and *Mercurius Publicus*.[5]

As the conduct of government became settled in the hands of the royalists, Sir John Berkenhead, the former writer of *Mercurius Aulicus*, was appointed by the Council to supervise the newsbooks. On 5 November 1660 Muddiman's *Publick Intelligencer* was entered under a license by Master Berkenhead,[6] who seems to have continued in the position as official censor until the enactment of the Printing Act of 1662.

As a reward for his services, Muddiman was given at the intercession of Secretary Nicholas the privilege of free postage for his letters and correspondence.[7] This privilege of free postage, together with the strict supervision of his printed newsbooks, led Muddiman to engage in an extensive correspondence which developed into his written newsletters. These letters were sent to subscribers all over England with or without the printed gazettes. In the meantime Nicholas had been supplanted by Lord Arlington as secretary of

---

[3] The name of this periodical became *An Exact Accompt*, January, 1660. John Cranne, an Anabaptist printer and preacher, was the writer.

[4] Williams also began, 21 February to 16 March 1660, the first daily, *A Perfect Diurnal*, reporting the proceedings of the House of Commons.

[5] J. G. Muddiman, *The King's Journalist* (London: John Lane, 1923), p. 130.

[6] Eyre and Rivington, *op. cit.*, II, 282.

[7] St. P. Dom. Charles II, 160, No. 149, Para. 1, and 139, No. 61. See also Hickes' *Narrative* set out in Appendix d of J. G. Muddiman's *The King's Journalist*.

state, and Muddiman as well as Joseph Williamson, who had been under-secretary to Nicholas, were transferred to the new appointee. For three years, 1660-1663, Muddiman remained the sole journalist of England supplying both printed and written news.

Muddiman's three-year monopoly in news distribution was brought to an abrupt end (August, 1663) with the grant of a patent to Sir Roger L'Estrange in recognition of the latter's services to the crown. The Regulation of Printing Act had been adopted by Parliament (May, 1662) and had conferred on the principal secretaries of state the major responsibility for the control and regulation of the press.[8] With Secretary Nicholas out of the way, L'Estrange had succeeded in convincing his successor, Lord Arlington, that a single supervisor of printing with unlimited powers of search and seizure could make a clean sweep of recalcitrant printers and objectionable printing. As compensation for these services, L'Estrange requested and was granted a patent for the exclusive publication of "all narratives or relacons not exceeding two sheets of paper and all advertisements, mercuries, diurnals, and books of public intelligence."[9] In return for these monopolies L'Estrange as

---

[8] See below, pp. 252-55.

[9] The following is a copy of the warrant directing the drawing of the grant (15 August 1663) State Papers Domestic, Charles II, 78, No. 96: "Charles R, whereas in contempt of our laws and authority many treasonous [sic], seditious, and unlicensed pamphletts, libells, & papers are dayly printed, vended & dispersed by the obstinate & implacable enemies of our Royall person & government, for redresse and remedy, hereof, Our will & pleasure is That you prepare a grant for our Royall signature for the erecting and constituting of an office for the surveying of the Imprimery, & Printing Presses, & for the preventing of the inconveniences aforesaid. And it is our will & pleasure that you prepare a grant for Our Royall signature of ye said office unto Roger L'Estrange, Eq. of whose loyalty & abilities wee. are well assured, & him to authorize and appoint to bee Our surveyor of all the imprimery and printed Pictures & also of all Books and papers whatsoever hereafter to be imprinted or reprinted, except Books concerning the Common Laws of this Realm, or Books of History concerning the State of this Realme or any other books concerning affairs of state or concerning Heraldry, Titles of Honor & Armes or the Office of Earl Marshall or Books of Divinity, Physick Philosophy Arts & Sciences and such other books and papers as are granted by our Letters Patent to our proper & Peculiar printers & usually claimed & imprinted by them by virtue of the said letter patent. To have and to hold the sd office or offices of our sd. Surveyor & licencer for & during the term of his natural life to bee exercised by himself or his sufficient deputie or deputies which sd. deputy or deputies are from time to time to bee approved by the late Archbishop of Canterbury & Lord Bp. of London or one of them and by our principall secretaries of State or either of

Surveyor of printing agreed to act as sole licenser under both secretaries of state and the ecclesiastical authorities.

Late in August, 1663, the office of Surveyor of the Press was finally set up and given over to L'Estrange. Muddiman's two newsbooks immediately ceased publication and their places were taken by *The Intelligencer* (31 August 1663) and the *News* (3 September 1663).[10] Both newsbooks were published "With privilege" and were edited and licensed by L'Estrange and printed by Richard Hodgkinson.

L'Estrange typified the seventeenth-century official attitude toward printed news. He decried the public demand for more information concerning affairs of state but condoned the publication of such news provided no untoward reactions were precipitated. As both publisher and censor, responsible to the crown through the secretaries of state, he held his monopolistic privileges only on condition that he exercised discretion. His income, on the other hand, depended largely on the popularity of his wares. On more than one occasion he was forced to expand his services to satisfy public demand.[11] At no time since the reign of Charles I was the press of England so effectively controlled as it was by L'Estrange during the years 1663-1665.

In the meantime, Muddiman who was also attached to the office of Lord Arlington, continued his system of correspondence

them with a sole privilege of writing, printing & publishing all Narratives or relacons not exceeding two sheets of paper & all advertisements, Mercuries, Diurnals & books of publick intelligence. And likewise of printing or appointing to be printed all Ballads, Maps, Charts, Portraitures, & Pictures not formerly printed & all Breifs & Collections, Bills of lading, Play-bills, & Quicksalver Bills, of customs & excise bills, Post-office bills, auditors bills, Ticquets & all forms or blanks of bonds, bills, indentures, & warrants, with power to search for and seize all unlicensed Books & papers & all seditious, treasonable, schismaticall & scandalous books & papers & to seize & apprehend all & every the offendors thein and to bring them before one of our principal secretaries of state or the next justice of peace, to bee proceeded ag'st according to law together with all other privileges and powers necessary or conducing to Our Service in ye Premisses. For which this shall be our warrant given at Our Court at Whitehall. The 15th day of August 1663, in the 3rd year of our reigne. By his Mate Command, Henry Bennet. To our Attorney or Solicitor General, Charles R."

[10] *The Intelligencer* was the Monday edition and the *News* the Thursday edition. They were numbered and paged separately through No. 18, after which the two were numbered consecutively.

[11] When war broke out with Holland in 1665, L'Estrange was forced to double the size of the *News* (27 April).

and newsletters by means of his privilege of free postage. Williamson, under-secretary for Arlington, who employed Muddiman in
his official correspondence work, looked with envy on the profits to
be made from both L'Estrange's newsbooks and Muddiman's newsletters. A carefully planned attack was launched by the ambitious
under-secretary first against L'Estrange and then against Muddiman.

Under-secretary Williamson's first step in undermining L'Estrange's monopoly in printed news was to refuse to furnish the
publisher with information. In his letter refusing to cooperate, the
under-secretary, who was attending the court at Oxford to avoid the
plague, made an offer to the Surveyor of printing to take over the
publication of the newsbooks in return for an annuity of one hundred pounds.[12] The terrified L'Estrange dispatched several letters
to Lord Arlington [13] and made a personal appeal to the king. In
the meantime, Williamson sent word to Muddiman to come to
Oxford to edit a competing newsbook. The *Oxford Gazette,* a semiweekly, made its appearance 16 November 1665, edited by Muddiman and printed by Leonard Litchfield, the University printer. A
reprint was immediately produced in London by Thomas Newcombe. By this time L'Estrange was desperate and to compete
with the *Gazette* issued an enlarged and revised newsbook which
he called *Publick Intelligence* (28 November 1665). The *Gazette,*
however, had the advantage of the most important stock in trade
of newsbooks, that is, news. In the end L'Estrange was forced to
relinquish his monopoly in return for £100 out of the profits of the
Gazette together with a salary of £200 of the Secret Service fund
as compensation for his duties as Surveyor of printing. With No. 24
(5 February 1666) the *Gazette* was transferred to London and
thereafter was known as the *London Gazette.*

Having successfully acquired control of the printed newsbooks,
Williamson now turned his attention to the written newsletters from
which Muddiman had derived most of his living. While the letter-
writer was in Oxford editing the *Gazette,* Williamson entered into
an intrigue with James Hickes, a clerk in the post office, for the purpose of securing a list of Muddiman's correspondents.[14] Upon the
return of the court to London Muddiman was dismissed from his

---

[12] Cal. St. P. Dom., 1665-66, p. 15.

[13] Cal. St. P. Dom., 1665-66, pp. 17, 20, 22.

[14] Cal. St. P. Dom., 1665-66, pp. 61, 62, 64, 77.

position as editor of the *Gazette* and his place taken by Charles Perrot.[15] Williamson hired a clerk to take over the written newsletter business and ordered Hickes to stop all letters to Muddiman. The latter now attached himself to the office of the other secretary of state, Sir William Morice. After much bickering in which Williamson and Hickes attempted to disparage the reputation of Muddiman, the latter under the protection of Morice issued a printed newsbook, the *Current Intelligence*, 7 June 1666, which was sent to his correspondents along with his written newsletters. Saddled with payment both to L'Estrange and Perrot, the *Gazette* was suffering from Muddiman's competition when in September, 1666, the printers of both newsbooks were burnt out in the great fire of London. When the debris was cleared away and the *Gazette* revived, Muddiman contented himself with his newsletters leaving the field of printed news to Williamson and the *Gazette*.

Aside from Williamson's *Gazette* the only other newsbooks which were suffered to appear were several trade and advertising publications which were set up after the fire. L'Estrange made an attempt which lasted only one number.[16] Thomas Bromhell was more successful with his *City Mercury* (10 June to 24 October 1667) which contained advertisements and news of trade. Others which appeared were *The Mercury, The London Mercury, Weekly Advertisements,* and another *City Mercury*. These publications carried no political news and were published largely within the confines of the City of London. Neither Williamson nor L'Estrange, as far as can be determined, made any effort to suppress them.

Beginnings of a Party Press, 1679-1695

For thirteen years, from the great fire in London in 1666 to 1679, England was again without printed domestic news. The official newspaper, the *London Gazette*, was issued regularly but it contained only royal proclamations, foreign news culled from other official gazettes, and advertisements.[17] As long as L'Estrange received his £ 100 under his arrangement with Secretary Williamson,

---

[15] It is impossible to tell whether Muddiman resigned his position as editor or was requested to retire. See J. G. Muddiman, *The King's Journalist,* p. 186.

[16] *Public Advertisements,* 25 June 1666.

[17] Several advertisement sheets were published during this period, but these were concerned solely with trade.

he continued active in suppressing any attempts to print domestic news or to interfere with his patent.

The country, however, was not without means of securing information. As the official *Gazette* declined in content, Muddiman's newsletters increased in popularity. They were to be found in all important country houses as well as in the taverns and coffeehouses of London. Williamson's attempts to supplant these letters with his own correspondence proved futile, and Muddiman continued supreme in the field until he ceased writing in 1689.[18]

There were other ways besides the Press in which news and rumors were published. During the Interregnum the coffeehouses had become important centers of social, literary, and political life, and from them news, comments, and rumors were speedily disseminated. "People generally believed," [19] says Clarendon, "that those houses had a charter of privilege to speak what they would without being in danger to be called in question."

In 1666 the problem of the coffeehouses was called to the attention of the king. Clarendon recommended their suppression but Coventry, fearful of the loss of the license fees, pointed out "that it had been permitted in Cromwell's time, and that the king's friends had used more liberty of speech in those places than they durst do in any other"; and that he thought it would be better to leave them as they were.[20] However, in 1675, the coffeehouses were suppressed by royal proclamation.[21] This raised such an outcry that the order was recalled on condition that the coffeehouse keepers entered into recognizances to prevent scandalous papers or libels from being brought to their houses, or read there, and to give information within two days of any scandalous reports circulated there.[22]

Political, religious, and dynastic problems furnished the impetus for the emergence of the first party newspapers in 1679. The question of the succession divided the nation into two camps, each of which rushed into print in an appeal to the country. Charles II

---

[18] Muddiman's career during this period is adequately described by J. G. Muddiman in *The King's Journalist* (London, 1923), Chapters X, XI, XII.

[19] *Life of Edward Earl of Clarendon* (1843 ed.), p. 1190.

[20] *Ibid.*

[21] Robert Steele, *Tudor and Stuart Proclamations* (Oxford, 1910), No. 3622; Cal. St. P. Dom., 1675-76, pp. 496-97, 500, 502.

[22] Steele, *op. cit.*, No. 3625.

was without legitimate children, and his brother, the Duke of York, later James II, was an avowed Roman Catholic. The declining years of the Restoration monarch revived all the old animosities between Protestants and Catholics and created a state of mind in which the vicious seeds of the Popish plot were planted.

In 1678 Titus Oates, who had just returned from an extended tour of the continent, testified that he had discovered a malignant plot among the Roman Catholics to murder the king, fire London, and massacre its inhabitants. Unfortunately the magistrate before whom this testimony was given was found murdered a few days later. The country was beside itself with alarms and fear. The agitation did not burn itself out until some twenty-two laymen and priests had been executed.

History has proved Oates to have been a forger and a perjurer, but the men and details behind his plot have never been thoroughly exposed. There is evidence that a group of prominent men opposed to the succession of James, including the Earl of Shaftesbury, directed the maneuvers of the infamous Oates. Regardless of the sponsorship, a group of newsbooks began to appear late in 1678 stirring up animosity against the Catholics and opposing the succession of the king's brother.[23]

The first newsbook directed against the Duke of York and his adherents appeared 3 December 1678, edited by Henry Care and printed by Langley Curtiss. This weekly sheet was entitled *The Pacquet of Advice from Rome; or, The History of Popery* with a subtitle *The Popish Courant*.[24] The second publisher of anti-Jacobite newsbooks appeared on the scene soon after the lapse of the Regulation of Printing Act 26 May 1679. The following month Benjamin Harris began the publication of *The Domestic Intelligence* which later became *The Protestant Domestic Intelligence*. These newsbooks continued to feed the flames ignited by the Oates and Shaftesbury plots, and in the almost hysterical state of public opinion Charles II was forced to prorogue Parliament. Thus the licensing provisions expired, and the enforcement officials found themselves helpless. The publications of Care and Harris were imitated by

[23] J. G. Muddiman has no doubt but that the entire press campaign of these years was directed by Shaftesbury. *The King's Journalist*, p. 211.

[24] According to Mr. Muddiman this newsbook was at first licensed, but the Stationers' Register shows no entry until 20 December 1682. *Ibid.*, p. 212.

Poor Robins Intelligence, The Weekly Packet of Advice from Germany, Smith's *Current Intelligence,* and Nathaniel Thompson's *True Domestic Intelligence.* Most of these including several which seem to have lasted only a few numbers were supporters of the Protestant party.[25]

Public feeling fired by the newsbooks ran so high that Charles II was forced to act. He discovered much to his surprise that the prorogued Parliament had failed through an oversight to re-enact the Regulation of Printing Act.[26] Calling the judges of the kingdom together, the king inquired what were his powers under his prerogative to regulate the newsbooks. The judges replied:

"That His Majesty may by Law prohibit the Printing and Publishing of all News-Books and Pamphlets of News whatsoever, not licensed by His Majesty's Authority, as manifestly tending to the Breach of Peace, and disturbance of the Kingdom." [27]

Armed with this opinion the king issued a royal proclamation ordering the suppression of all newsbooks except those properly licensed by authority.[28] Reverting to Tudor and early Stuart precedents, the machinery of the crown was put into action. The part played by the judiciary in punishing the writers, editors, and publishers of these propaganda newsbooks has been discussed in the chapter immediately preceding.[29]

On the side of the Government, the Tories (as they came to be called) issued, in addition to the *London Gazette,* a number of newsbooks in opposition to the Shaftesbury Protestant press. Although not as numerous as the Whig papers, these included *Heraclitus Ridens* printed by Benjamin Tooke, *The Weekly Discovery,* also printed by Tooke, *The Observator,* edited by L'Estrange, and the *Loyal London Mercury.*

Muddiman, whose newsletters were Tory in tone, was faced with

[25] The *Times Handlist* lists at least fifteen newsbooks, for the year 1680, most of them lasting only a few numbers.

[26] Whether the failure to re-enact this law was due to oversight on the part of the crown officers or to a fear that Parliament would reject has never been ascertained.

[27] No official report of this opinion of the judges has been found although it is reported in the *London Gazette,* No. 1509, May 3-6, 1680, and is referred to by Chief Justice Scroggs in the case of Henry Care, 7 State Trials, p. 1127.

[28] Steele, *op. cit.,* No. 3715 (12 May 1680).

[29] See above, pp. 269-75.

competition from Jasper Hancock, the principal Whig newsletter writer of the time. The establishment of the Penny Post [30] in opposition to the Duke of York's patent as postmaster general facilitated the circulation of these letters. A host of imitators including Amy, Smallridge, Combs, and Cotton soon arose; but the Privy Council took matters into its own hands and in December, 1679, ordered them all suppressed. This, however, was not accomplished until 1683 and then only with the help of the new Tory administration in the city of London.[31]

With juries, sheriff's office, and House of Commons all packed with Whigs, the king in 1681 followed the advice of the high Chief Justice of the Common Pleas, Francis North, and allowed L'Estrange, through his *Observator,* to counteract the influence of the Protestant pamphlets and newsbooks on their own level. When the Oxford Parliament insisted again on bringing in the Exclusion Bill to keep James from the throne, Charles appealed directly to the people through a Declaration which was read in every parish in the land. One by one the Protestant and Whig newsbooks ceased and by November, 1682, all was again in order.

James II succeeded to the throne of England upon the death of his brother in 1685. Quiet on the newsbook front continued for another two years. The Regulation of Printing Act was revived by a complacent Parliament, and no newsbooks other than the *London Gazette* were allowed to appear. Some news-sheets and pamphlets opposing the government were, however, printed in Holland and smuggled into the country. Public discussion was driven underground, and Whig coffeehouses reverberated with wild rumors and seditious argument. On two occasions the king issued proclamations against the circulation of seditious literature. On 10 February 1688 an order for the suppression of seditious and unlicensed books and pamphlets was again issued.[32] The selling of books was strictly limited to the members of the Stationers Company, and peddlers of literature were ordered to cease. A second proclamation (26 October 1688) was designed to restrain the spreading of "false news." All subjects were warned not to write, print, nor speak any false

---

[30] Cal. St. P. Dom. Charles II, 1679-80, p. 313; *Ibid.,* 1683, p. 374.

[31] Muddiman, *op. cit.,* pp. 221ff.

[32] Steele, *op. cit.,* No. 3859.

news whatsoever, or to meddle with affairs of state in their common discourse.[33]

The Revolution of 1688 which brought in William and Mary
witnessed a revival of Whig newsbooks. The Act for the Regulation
of Printing continued in force, and under it warrants were issued for
search and seizure of seditious printing, this time on the Tory
side.[34] James Fraser was appointed deputy licenser by the Earl of
Shrewsbury,[35] and the Stationers Company was ordered "to make
often and diligent searches in all such places you or any of you shall
know or have any probably reason to suspect, and to seize all unlicensed, scandalous books and pamphlets, and to do such other
things as the Act of Parliament in the case directs." [36]

In March, 1693, John Gellibrand was appointed inspector of
printing presses and charged with suppressing all Tory and Jacobite
literature.[37] Gellibrand together with Robert Stephens kept a sharp
watch over all printing, and until the Act for the Regulation of
Printing expired only licensed and innocuous publications were
allowed to appear. The licensed newspapers of this period, 1688-
1694, consisted of the *London Gazette,* the *Orange Gazette,* the
Athenian Gazette and Mercury, edited by John Dunton and the
Account (1694), the parent of the Tory newspapers which arose
after the expiration of the Printing Act.

The important change which took place in the status of the press
following the Revolution of 1688 was the relinquishment by the
crown of all prerogative rights governing the press. One searches
in vain in the documents of the period for an official statement to
this effect, but nevertheless William and the succeeding monarchs
made no claims to prerogative rights over printing. From then on
Parliament was supreme in the control of the press.

It is also worthy of note that although freedom of speech and
debate in Parliament was guaranteed in the Bill of Rights in 1689,
no mention was made in that historic document of freedom of the
press. Parliament on several occasions following the accession of
William and Mary re-enacted the Act for the Regulation of Print-

[33] *Ibid.,* No. 3888.
[34] Cal. St. P. Dom., 1689-90, pp. 2, 3, 7, 55, 121.
[35] *Ibid.,* pp. 30, 74.
[36] *Ibid.*
[37] *Ibid.,* 1693, p. 85.

ing, and it was allowed to expire only because the members of Parliament became divided in their political attachments.

After 1694

On the day in 1694 when the Regulation of Printing Act expired there was only one responsible newspaper published in London, the *London Gazette*. Charles Perrot who had edited this publication for the principal secretaries of state had been replaced by Robert Yard in 1671. Yard continued as editor until 1702 filling the official newspaper with government announcements and foreign dispatches. Domestic news was left to the host of ephemeral publications which sprang up during the last years of William III. These publications although independent commercial ventures in their beginnings were soon absorbed by the eighteenth-century political coteries.[38]

From 1695 until almost the end of the reign of Queen Anne, there was comparative freedom for the publishers of domestic news. The old regulations had been found ineffective and new ones had not yet been devised. The licensing and trade regulation provisions of the Printing Acts were gone. Neither William nor Anne was in a position to revive the old prerogative powers of the crown. The political leaders also were loath to make use of the judicial controls which had been found useful in the time of Charles II.

The summer of 1694 saw the emergence of a number of important journals of domestic news. Benjamin Harris began another short-lived publication on May 14 before emigrating to the American colonies to become the publisher of the first American newspaper. George Ridpath, the Whig writer, began his career with the *Flying Post* late in May of the same year, and was joined by the Tory journalist Abel Roper and the indefatigable Abel Boyer. These early political journalists seem to have had their troubles not only with the opposition but with their own supporters. The story of subsidization belongs with the history of the eighteenth century.[39]

At the close of the seventeenth century several important trends in the liberation of the press can be discerned. The prerogative powers of the crown were gone forever. The licensing require-

[38] See below, pp. 335-45.
[39] See below, Chapter 16.

ments had been abolished, and the printing trade was at last free from commercial regulation. The power of the Stationers Company as a trade monopoly had been finally smashed. The Commons had acquiesced in the publication of its votes although it still refused to permit reports of its debates.

On the other hand, many confining regulations remained and new devices of control were under consideration. The law of seditious libel as developed under Charles II was continued by the Revolution judges. The House of Lords still objected to the publication of its votes. Political groups were raising funds for the subsidization of writers and newspapers, and the government was seriously considering a new system of regulation through taxation.

PART 5

Control of the Press
IN THE EIGHTEENTH CENTURY

1714-1776

CHAPTER 15

Control Through Taxation

The eighteenth century in England was an age of increased social intercourse. Politics, literature, and the press took on a tone of urbaneness and sophistication. The directness and earthiness of the Tudors were gone, along with the sophistry and rationalizing of the Stuarts. In their places there arose an attitude in the public mind which sought to disguise all unpleasant facts, to achieve ends by indirectness, and to keep public business politely but firmly in the hands of a chosen few. In politics it was an age of control by party groups, each seeking to maintain itself and to undermine the other through secret manipulations and party deals.

In its relations with the press the government discarded the direct methods of control as practiced by the Tudor statesmen. It did not even seek to justify its regulation as the Stuarts had attempted to do in the preceding century. The rhetoric of the times called for tactical expressions of political belief in the freedom of the press, that is, in freedom from the Tudor and Stuart types of control; but in actual practice, it was universally recognized by political leaders that the stability of government as well as their continuance in office demanded some form of control over the media of communication.

The eighteenth-century statesmen saw no reason to revive such obviously unsavory methods of control as state licensing and printing-trade regulation. There were other methods, more subtle, more indirect, and therefore less dangerous. Taxation, subsidization, and prosecution under due process of law—these were the methods employed by the state to control and regulate the press during the period between the death of Anne and the Declaration of American Independence.

The First Stamp Tax

Toward the end of the seventeenth century, it became obvious that the system of licensing and trade regulation was incapable of maintaining order in the field of periodical publications. The Regulation of Printing Act was allowed to lapse, and attempts to revive the act in the Parliamentary sessions of 1695-1696, 1696-1697, and 1697-1698 were rejected by the House of Commons. The Act had proved unworkable, and the Commons would have none of it.[1]

The House of Lords continued to dally with variations of the Act, and in the session of 1698-1699 passed a bill providing for registration of all presses with the Stationers Company and requiring each piece of printing to bear the names of the printer and publisher, but again the Commons refused to concur. The House of Lords itself rejected a similar bill in the session of 1702, and bills of the same tenor failed to pass the Commons in 1703-1704 and 1713.[2]

The consideration given to this proposed legislation shows that Parliament was not at all convinced that the press should be freed. That it remained temporarily free was due, not to political or philosophical conviction, but to the quarrel between the two houses of Parliament in the early years of the eighteenth century and to the failure to agree upon a suitable system of regulation.

The impetus for a substitute method for the control of the press came from two quarters, from the printers and publishers themselves and from the government. For more than two centuries the trade printers had been accustomed to some form of regulation. The wealthier and more conservative members of the craft were uneasy now that the Stationers Company had been stripped of its

---

[1] See above, pp. 206ff.

[2] M. A. Thomson, *Constitutional History of England, 1642-1801* (London: Methuen, 1938), IV, 300.

powers and the government no longer protected copies or told them what they could print.

As early as 1693 the printers had submitted to Parliament a petition "For reviving and continuing the act for the regulation of printing." [3] The failure to revive the act, said the publishers, would result in "the impoverishment and ruin of hundreds of English families, and the enriching of the Dutch printers and Booksellers." A similar petition from the printers was presented to the House of Commons in 1698.[4] Again in 1703 the free workmen-printers petitioned for the revival of at least those provisions of the Regulation of Printing Act which limited the number of printing houses and the number of apprentices.[5] It is evident from these petitions that the printers and publishers were interested in restoring some sort of order in the printing trade by maintaining existing printing monopolies, but that on the other hand they were not anxious to revive the licensing system.

The principal impetus in the search for a substitute for the Regulation of Printing Act came from the government. The queen, the ministry, and the clergy were continuously scandalized by the flood of pamphlets and newspapers meddling in matters of state and church. Anne first attempted to control the stream of printed matter by issuing proclamations from the throne. The first of these (26 March 1702) after reciting the medieval statutes against spreading of false news, pointed at the increase in heretical, seditious and scandalous publications since the expiration of the Acts for the Regulation of Printing. The queen pre-emptorily ordered that "the publication of false news or of books of this kind is to stop." [6] As was to be expected, the Proclamation had little effect. Additional orders from the throne were issued on 24 February 1704,[7] 25 May 1704,[8] 20 December 1705,[9] and 15 March 1714/5.[10]

[3] Lincoln's Inn Collection, M.P. 102/309.

[4] *Ibid.*, M.P. 102/311.

[5] *Ibid.*, M.P. 102/307.

[6] Robert Steele, *Tudor and Stuart Proclamations* (Oxford, 1910), No. 4315. B.M. Copy, 21 h 3 (232).

[7] Steele, *op. cit.*, No. 4369.

[8] *Ibid.*, No. 4372.

[9] *Ibid.*, No. 4400.

[10] *Ibid.*, No. 4539.

In the final years of her reign, Whig criticism of her foreign policy forced Anne again and again in her messages to Parliament to call for help in the control of the press. A bill was finally introduced in June, 1712, but it reached only second reading. The queen reiterated her request at the next session, but the more pressing questions of peace and the succession postponed for the time being all proposals for regulating the press. It was also obvious that opposition to the bills came not from the Whigs alone but from the London printers who, although willing to accept registration of presses and apprentices and to append their printers' marks to each publication, were opposed to the clause requiring the author's name to appear on every piece of printing.[11]

The eventual method of control devised by Anne's ministers and adopted by Parliament was neither precipitous nor accidental. In searching for additional sources of revenue to help pay for Marlborough's foreign wars, the queen's ministers (probably Robert Harley) included almanacks and calendars along with a large group of consumer's products as suitable items for taxation. The revenue act of 1710 (9 Anne, cap. 23) for the first time [12] imposed a tax on printed matter. All calendars and almanacks for one particular year and printed on one side of a sheet of paper were to pay one penny per copy. For almanacks for one year on more than one side of one sheet, the tax was two pence, and for almanacks covering several years, the above rates were to be paid for each year.

Henry St. John, Viscount Bolingbroke, is credited with the discovery that a tax on publications would serve the double purpose of providing revenue and at the same time serve as a substitute for

---

[11] *The Printers Proposal for a regulation of the press.* Lincoln's Inn Collection, M.P. 102/306. The reason for their opposition to the last clause, according to the printers, was that it would "very much discourage the publication of many excellent treatises, through the excess of modesty in some, who will rather stifle their performances than suffer their names to appear in print, though to a work deserving of the greatest applause, and on the other hand, some very good books will be lessened in the esteem of many readers, through a prejudice to its author."

[12] C. H. Timperley in his *A Dictionary of Printers and Printing* . . . (London: Bohn, 1839), p. 584, under date of 1701 reports a bill for laying a stamp-duty of a penny on every number of a periodical publication. It appears that the proposal should have been dated 1711. See also James Grant, *The Newspaper Press* (London: Tinsley brothers, 1871), I, 95, and Alexander Andrews, *History of British Journalism* (London: Richard Bentley, 1859), I, 94.

the Regulation of Printing Act.[13] Which motive was uppermost in the minds of the ministers or the members of Parliament is almost impossible to tell, but it appears that the principal objective of the first Stamp tax (10 Anne, cap. 18, 1712) was the control of "licentious, schismatical, and scandalous" publications. Defoe had warned the government in the preface to Volume VII of his *Review* (1711) that the tax would not suppress criticism of the government but would drive it underground. The ministers, however, felt that they could not lose. If the Stamp tax produced revenue, well and good; if it discouraged periodical publications, so much the better.

That the Stamp tax of 1712 was an expedient substitute for the lapsed Regulation of Printing Acts in the control and regulation of the press is established by the circumstances surrounding the passage of the act. The queen, acting on the request of the ecclesiastical Convocation, had in her speech to Parliament on January 17, 1711/12, recommended that some remedy be provided for the "great license . . . taken in publishing false and scandalous Libels such as are a reproach to any government. This Evil seems too strong for the Laws now in force: it is therefore recommended to you to find a Remedy equal to the Mischief."[14] A proposal to increase the revenue of the Stamp Office by taxing weekly newspapers and pamphlets had been circulated the year before, pointing out that a tax would probably reduce the circulation of newspapers from 45,000 to not above 30,000.[15]

The immediate occasion for the new tax was the publication by Samuel Buckley in the *Daily Courant* of a reflection on the conduct of the Dutch in the war. Parliament was incensed and on 12 April 1712 resolved itself into a committee of the whole to consider the license of the press. The committee reported on April 22 with a series of twelve resolutions embodying the provisions of the Stamp Act as finally passed.[16]

---

[13] J. M. Thomas in "Swift and the Stamp Tax of 1712" (*Publications of Modern Language Association,* n.s. XXIV (1916), 247-63) successfully disposes of the charge that Swift was the author of the suggestion for a tax on publications.

[14] *Ibid.,* pp. 258-59.

[15] Cal. of Treas. Papers, 1708-14 (cxxix, undated 1709-10), p. 235.

[16] William Cobbett, editor, *Parliamentary History* (London, 1806-20), VI, 1125; Commons Journal, XVII, 196. See also, "The History of the Proceedings

It is obvious that the bill was designed to check the publication of those newspapers and pamphlets which depended for their sale on their cheapness and sensationalism. As stated by Collet Dobson Collet in his *History of the Taxes on Knowledge:* [17]

Was there no way by which, without the necessity of constant contention, private men might be prevented from using the Press to make their opinions public? The pamphleteers were not rich, but they were often persons of education, and not penniless. When only a few copies of their writings were wanted they could pay for them, but now that reading was become more common, and that great numbers of copies were printed, the cost had, to a great extent, to be paid by the readers. If these sheets could be taxed their distribution might become difficult, and when any one attempted to evade the tax he could be punished, not as a libeller, but as a smuggler, and the character of what was printed would not come under discussion, as it generally would under a trial for libel. At the time we are recording, 1709, these considerations appear to have very much occupied the minds of the members of the House of Commons.

The new tax bill was not enacted without opposition from the printers, publishers, and paper makers of the realm. The manufacturers of paper objected to the tax on the ground that its main purpose was not revenue but suppression of newspapers and pamphlets.[18] The printers pointed out that the effect of the tax would be to destroy all newspapers and that if the purpose of the act was to prevent libels, a suitable remedy could be found by requiring all publications to carry the name of the publisher.[19] It was further argued that, "nothing will contribute more to the spreading and publishing seditious libels, than the said tax; because it is to be feared, that many of the poorer printers, to prevent their families from starving, will be tempted to print whatsoever shall be offer'd

of the Second Session of this Present Parliament" (London), B.M. 8132 d 65 (2), and "The History and Defense of the Last Parliament" (London, 1713), B.M. 809.

[17] (London, 1899), I, 7.

[18] "Case of the manufacturers of paper, the Stationers, Printers, etc. of this kingdom relating to several duties on paper and printing, now voted in the House, Humbly represented to the Honourable House of Commons," Lincoln's Inn Collection, M.P. 102/282, undated. Also "The Case of the poor paper makers and printers, further stated." *Ibid.*, M.P. 102/284, undated.

[19] "The Printers case; humbly submitted to the consideration of the Honourable House of Commons," Lincoln's Inn Collection, M.P. 102/305.

them, by any person who will be at the charge of the impression tho' at never so great a hazard." [20]

On 16 May 1712 the first tax on newspapers (10 Anne, cap. 18) was passed without a division in the House of Commons, and on May 22 a message was received from the Lords that they had agreed to the bill without amendment.[21] The Act contained four general provisions affecting the press: (1) the tax on newspapers and pamphlets, (2) the tax on advertisements, (3) the tax on paper, and (4) registration and enforcement provisions.

(1) Beginning August 1, 1712, all newspapers and pamphlets were to be taxed at the following rates:

For newspapers and pamphlets printed on a half sheet or less, one halfpenny sterling.

For newspapers and pamphlets larger than a half sheet and not exceeding a whole sheet, one penny sterling for every printed copy.

For newspapers and pamphlets larger than a whole sheet and not exceeding six sheets in octavo (or twelve sheets in quarto, or twenty sheets in folio), two shillings for every sheet in "one printed copy." It will be noted that no distinction was made between periodical publications such as newspapers and single issues such as pamphlets.

The fact that printed books larger than six sheets octavo, etc., were exempted entirely from the tax indicates that the principal objective of the government was the suppression of the small ephemeral publications which were sniping at the policies of the ministry.

Also exempted from the newspaper and pamphlet tax, no matter what their size, were school books, books of piety and devotion, daily accounts of bills of goods imported and exported, weekly bills of mortality, and single advertisements published by themselves. *The Weekly Pacquet* (of prices), for example, was completely exempted from the tax.

(2) The use of advertising to give publicity to demand and supply had increased with the growth of newspapers, and by 1712 the advertisements in the *Daily Courant* averaged nine to ten.

[20] *Ibid.*

[21] Commons Journal, XVII, 196, 198, 200, 203, 212, 216, 217, 218, 226, 227, 234.

Once again the purpose of the tax was to diminish the possibility of profit in periodical publications and thus render them more amenable to ministerial control.

The tax on advertisements applied to all newspapers published weekly or oftener, including the London *Gazette*, the official newspaper, and amounted to twelve pence sterling for each advertisement. This tax did not apply to books or pamphlets, to trade publications, or to single advertisements published separately.

(3) The duties on paper contained in the first Stamp Act had been preceded by an ad valorem tax of 25 per cent on imported papers passed by Parliament under William III (8-9 William III, cap. 7, 1696). The new act (10 Anne, cap. 18) changed the basis of the tax to the ream and included domestic as well as imported papers. For imported papers the tax ranged from one shilling per ream for German foolscap to sixteen shillings per ream for Imperial Fine.[22] The tax on domestic paper ranged from four pence per ream for ordinary brown paper to one shilling six pence for Demy Fine.

(4) That the real purpose of the Stamp Act was not revenue but suppression of the press is clear from the miscellaneous provisions for the administration and enforcement of the taxes. All newspapers and pamphlets printed in London were required to be registered at the Stamp office, and each publication was required to contain the name and address of the publisher for ready identification with a penalty of 20 pounds for noncompliance. Failure to pay the tax also resulted in loss of all copyrights. Such was the inconspicuous beginning of the elaborate "Security System" which was erected on the Stamp Act in the late years of George III.

Effects of 10 Anne, Cap. 18

A survey of available sources of information on the journalism of the years immediately following the enactment of the first stamp tax supports the following conclusions:

1. A sizable number of newspapers were immediately killed by the Act.

2. Approximately the same number were able to survive the first year of taxation as were killed by the Act.

[22] The duties on imported papers were raised again August 2, 1714, by 12 Anne stat. 2 cap. 9.

3. Within a year the publishers devised methods of avoiding the tax, and the government found it impossible to enforce collections.

The effect of the Stamp Act on the newspapers of the last years of the reign of Queen Anne has been commonly judged in the terms of quotations from two contemporary observers, Addison and Swift.

Addison's comments in the *Spectator* (No. 445, August, 1712) were as follows:

This is the Day on which many eminent Authors will probably Publish their Last Words. I am afraid that few of our Weekly Historians, who are Men that above all others delight in War, will be able to subsist under the Weight of a Stamp, and an approaching Peace. A Sheet of Blank Paper that must have this new Imprimatur clapt upon it, before it is qualified to Communicate anything to the Publick, will make its way in the World but very heavily. In short, the Necessity of carrying a Stamp, and the Improbability of notifying a Bloody Battle, will, I am afraid, both concur to the sinking of those thin Folios, which have every other Day retailed to us the History of Europe for several years past. A Facetious Friend of mine, who loves a Punn, calls this present Mortality among Authors, The Fall of the Leaf.

Addison was, of course, giving his opinion as to the probable effect of the Act and was not reporting the actual results of the tax. See below for the effect of the tax on his own publication, the *Spectator*.

Swift wrote to Stella (*Journals,* 5 August 1712): "Do you know that all Grub-street is dead and gone last week? No more ghosts or murders now for love or money! I plied it close the last fortnight, and published at least seven papers of my own, besides some of other people's, but now every single half-sheet pays a halfpenny to the queen. The *Observator* is fallen; the *Medleys* are jumbled together with the *Flying Post;* the *Examiner* is deadly sick; the *Spectator* keeps up and doubles its price. I know not how long it will last. Have you seen the red stamp the papers are marked with? Methinks the stamping is worth a halfpenny."

Here again is a hasty and undoubtedly exaggerated picture of the effect of the stamp tax. Grub Street was not dead; newspapers could still be purchased for money if not for love. While listing several suspensions, Swift failed to mention the newspapers which continued to publish their regular editions after August, 1712.

From a study of the existing files of the newspapers of the period, it can be concluded that at least five newspapers were suspended because of the stamp tax (*Observator, Medley, Plaindealer, Supplement,* and *Protestant Postboy*) and at least four newspapers were able to survive the Act (*The Examiner, Flying Post, Daily Courant,* and *Evening Post*). Also surviving were the official *London Gazette,* the monthly publications larger than six pages such as *Present State of Europe* and *Present State of Great Britain,* and the commercial publications such as the *Weekly Pacquet,* all of which, with the exception of the *Gazette,* were exempted from the newspaper and advertising taxes. Existing files do not permit a definite conclusion regarding the fate of eight additional journals.[23] They may have been suspended before August, 1712, but there is no available evidence that they were victims of the tax.

The problem of the effect of the tax on the three periodicals, Steele's *Tatler,* Addison's *Spectator,* and Defoe's *Review,* is equally difficult. While these publications are classed generally as literary periodicals as distinct from newspapers, they contained news features as well as editorial comment on current political affairs. As to the *Tatler,* the problem is not complex. There is no doubt that Steele discontinued his publication 2 January 1711 for no other reason than that he was tired of his original plan and had become interested in the production of a daily essay paper.[24] More controversial is the effect of the Stamp tax on the *Spectator* which began publication on 1 March 1711 and continued for 555 numbers to 6 December 1712, to be revived for 79 numbers from 18 June to 20 December 1714. The publishers met the tax in August, 1712, by doubling the price of the publication. One student concludes that the *Spectator* was suspended on 6 December 1712, because "it has ceased to be a profitable business venture." [25] The newspaper stamp tax had reduced the circulation by forcing an increase in subscription price, but what, according to Mr. Lewis, killed the *Spectator* was the advertising tax. The number of advertisements after August, 1712, was approximately half the number which appeared before

---

[23] *Historian, Hermit, Night Post, Rambler, Rhapsody, Bristol Postboy, Liverpool Courant,* and *Weekly Worcester Journal.*

[24] W. J. Graham, *English Literary Periodicals* (New York: Nelson, 1930), p. 66.

[25] Lawrence Lewis, *The Advertisements of the Spectator* (New York, 1909), p. 65.

the tax.[26] It is more than probable that the tax on newspapers and advertisements contributed to the suspension of the *Spectator*, but it is impossible to establish the Stamp Act as the sole cause of its discontinuance.

The effect of the tax of 1712 on Defoe's *Review* is almost as uncertain as the effect on the *Spectator*. The author extended Volume VIII to 16 months to conclude the year on August 1, the date the tax was to take effect. The tax was met by the publication of a new series, Volume I, printed on only a single leaf (two pages) and in smaller type. Subject to only a halfpenny tax this publication must have been reasonably successful as it was increased from a biweekly to a triweekly with No. 43. It is generally agreed that Defoe dropped the *Review* to take on the publication of the *Mercator*.[27]

Beginning in August, 1712, the newspapers, including the *Daily Courant* and the triweeklies which survived the tax, all carry the red stamp, a rose and a thistle joined by the stalks and enclosing the Irish shamrock, the whole surmounted by a crown. Since the records of the Stamp office do not go back before 1749, it is impossible to determine the revenue produced by the tax. Steele in No. 555 of the *Spectator* claims the income was above £20 a week, an amount which would be produced by a daily circulation of from 1,600 to 1,700 copies.

Within a year, however, the newspaper proprietors by careful reading of the original draft of the law discovered a number of loopholes in the Act, and by 1713 evasion of the tax was almost general. The first loophole noticed was the phrase "in one printed copy" in the provision for a three-shilling tax on newspapers and pamphlets larger than a whole sheet (four pages). Comparing this section with the phraseology of the preceding section which provided for a tax of one penny "for every printed" copy larger than a half sheet and not larger than a whole sheet, the publishers concluded that the first was a tax of three shillings *per impression*. It was carefully pointed out to the Stamp office that whereas single sheets paid a penny *per copy*, newspapers and pamphlets more than a single sheet paid only three shillings *per edition*.

---

[26] *Ibid.*, pp. 69-71.

[27] A. W. Secord, *Defoe's Review* (New York: Columbia University press, 1938), intro. pp. xviii, xix, xxii-xxiii.

The immediate effect of this discovery was the expansion of newspapers to a sheet and a half, or six pages.[28] Even the official *London Gazette* published six pages and omitted the stamp in its edition of May 5-9, 1717. In order to fill six pages the editors of weekly newspapers adopted a number of devices such as larger type, deeper headings, heavier leading, wider margins, and more significant, began to include critical essays and feature material of the type made popular by the *Tatler* and the *Spectator*. The daily papers found it impossible to expand to six pages and continued to pay the tax. The period of 1713 to 1725 was the heyday of the weekly taxless journals at the expense of the taxable daily and tri-weekly newspapers. The weekly newspaper then became the organ of political intrigue and party passions, while the dailies barely survived. The direct ancestor of the modern weekly political review owes its birth to the accident of draftsmanship of the tax law of 1712. Six pages had to be filled to avoid the tax; news was scarce or stale; and the political essay or editorial was invented to fill the white space.

Following the discovery of the loophole in the statute, the Stamp office made little effort to enforce the tax, and many pamphlets as well as newspapers of less than six pages carried no stamp. It was also argued by the printers that even the halfpenny tax on half-sheets was illegal since here again the act failed to specify "for every printed copy."

The tax on advertising also fell into abeyance because of difficulties of enforcement. The statute provided that the tax was to be paid "by all and every person and persons who shall print or publish, or cause to be printed or published, any advertisement or advertisements." When called to account for failure to pay twelve pence for each advertisement, the publishers insisted that the tax should be collected from either the author or the printer; the printer insisted it was the responsibility of the publisher, and the author or editor shifted the liability to the printer or publisher.

[28] Stanley Morison misconstrues the method by which the tax was evaded but describes the effect of the evasion on the typography and format of the newspapers of the period. *The English Newspaper, 1622-1932* (Cambridge: University press, 1932), p. 86. F. K. Hunt, *The Fourth Estate* (London, 1850), I, 204, assumes that the Act provided different rates for newspapers and for pamphlets and that the tax was avoided by registering newspapers as pamphlets.

The result after 1714 was general noncompliance with the tax. As many daily and weekly newspapers appeared after 1714 as were published before 1712. According to Crane and Kaye,[29] 65 newspapers and periodicals appeared during the year 1711, 51 in the year of the tax, 1712; 45 in 1713, 54 in 1714, and 67 in 1715.

More specifically the tax of 1712 fell most heavily on the printers and writers who supported the government and who were therefore more or less compelled to pay the tax. While the Tory party seemed willing to sacrifice the presentation of its own side of political controversies in order to kill off the literature of the opposition, the ministers were somewhat astonished to discover that the loyal journals were suffering under the tax and that the opposition publications were avoiding it.[30] Swift came to this same conclusion a few years later when he wrote concerning the tax: "For the adverse party, full of rage and leisure since their fall, and ·unanimous in defence of their cause, employ a set of writers by subscription, who are well versed in the topics of defamation, and have a style and genius levelled to the generality of readers; whilst those who would draw their pens on the side of their prince and country, are discouraged by this tax, which exceeds the intrinsic value both of the materials and the work." [31] The tax was undoubtedly a direct cause of the widespread subsidization of newspapers and political writers, discussed in Chapter 16.

Another result of the operation of the first Stamp tax was the stimulation of the growth of the provincial press in England. Prior to 1694, a country press was impossible under the Printing Act, and country readers satisfied their appetite for news with the London newsletters and newspapers. The earliest provincial newspapers dated from the opening of the eighteenth century, but none seems to have survived the first impact with the Stamp Act of 1712.

---

[29] R. S. Crane and F. B. Kaye, *Census of British Newspapers and Periodicals* (Chapel Hill: Univ. of North Carolina press, 1927), pp. 183-86. See also J. R. Sutherland, "Circulation of Newspapers and Literary Periodicals 1700-1730," *The Library*, 4th Series, XV, 110.

[30] Timperley, *op. cit.*, pp. 601-2.

[31] *History of the Last Four Years of the Queen*, Book III. Andrews, in his *History of British Journalism*, I, 109, is evidently of a different political bias when he writes: "The Stamp Act may perhaps, on the whole, be regarded as having had a wholesome effect in purging the newspaper press and confining its management to men of character and respectability."

The application of the tax after 1714 to four-page dailies and tri-weeklies and the exemption from the tax of the six-page weekly periodicals, operated to the advantage of the country press. Evidently country subscribers were unwilling to pay the increased subscription price of the London dailies and tri-weeklies and turned to the taxless provincial weekly for their summaries of London news. The *Times Handlist* mentions at least twenty-two provincial weekly newspapers established between 1714 and 1725.[32]

Later Stamp Acts

Soon after Robert Walpole had entrenched himself as First Lord of the Treasury and Chancellor of the Exchequer, he turned his attention to the modification of the tax structure. The loopholes in the existing newspaper tax were pointed out to him, and he lost no time in presenting the problem to Parliament. Walpole was more conscious of the power of the press in creating and maintaining public support than any of his predecessors in office, and he therefore devoted a large part of his energies to the direction and control of this important medium of political activity.

As early as 1717 John Toland had called the government's attention to the loopholes in the tax on newspapers and pamphlets, pointing out that the failure to enforce the law resulted in the vilification of the administration and also a loss of revenue. Professing to be a zealous advocate of "liberty of the press," Toland decried the "licentiousness under which seditious insinuations were spread and public ministers abused with impunity. He urged an amendment to the Stamp Act to stop up the loophole whereby the six-page papers were evading the tax, and in addition, he recommended that the evening newspapers, which were being published on post days and which were culling their news from the morning journals, be prohibited altogether.[33]

Charles Townshend, secretary of state, is credited with the suggestion that a complete census be taken of the newspapers issued in London together with a statement of their political affiliations. The politically-minded Walpole immediately fell in with the plan, and in 1723 Samuel Negus, an impecunious printer, agreed to gather the data. His report listed thirty-four presses as issuing matter

---

[32] *Ibid.*, pp. 217-18.
[33] B.M. Add. Ms. 429, ff. 49, 50.

favorable to King George, three as "non-jurors," four as Roman
Catholics, and thirty-four as "High Fliers" or opposed to the existing administration.[34]

The fact that the opposition press was at least equal to the
administration supporters prompted Walpole to urge the enactment of a statute closing the loopholes in the stamp tax.[35] In February, 1724, a committee of the House of Commons presented a bill
which was passed in the form of 11 George I, cap. 8 and provided
for a tax at the rate on one penny per sheet and one halfpenny per
half sheet on all journals, mercuries, or other newspapers. The
preamble to the act recites the methods which had been used to
avoid the tax of 10 Anne.

Under the new stamp tax, a distinction was made for the first
time between newspapers and pamphlets. In Anne's reign it was
the political pamphlet which caused the greatest irritation to the
ministers, and a tax of three shillings was placed on all publications
of six pages or more. The failure of the law to specify three shillings
per copy, however, nullified the tax and even made it profitable for
newspapers, which had not been singled out for special consideration, to expand to six pages in order to pay only three shillings per
edition. In 1724, however, the political pamphlet had given way to
the political periodical, and the new tax law permitted pamphlets
to continue to be published under the old rate of three shillings
per impression, but the loophole was closed to newspapers. 10 Anne,
cap. 18 was pointed primarily at pamphlet literature and only incidentally at newspapers; 11 George, cap. 8 was directly aimed at
newspapers and made no attempt to remedy the evasions as practiced by the publishers of pamphlets.

The direct effects of this new tax on newspapers, which went
into effect 25 April 1724, are even less obvious than the effect of
the first tax in 1712. In 1724 there were 82 periodicals and newspapers issued in London; in 1725, 76; and in 1726, 64. The number
did not rise to 82 again until 1734.[36] Only 9 new periodicals were

---

[34] The Negus report is printed in Timperley, *op. cit.*, p. 630. Negus was
rewarded by a carrier's place in the Post Office.

[35] The writer finds it impossible to agree with Mr. Laurence Hanson's
statement (*Government and the Press, 1695-1763* [London: Oxford University
press, 1936], p. 13.) that "The motives which prompted the government to
introduce these new scales seem to have been solely pecuniary."

[36] Crane and Kaye, *op. cit.*, pp. 184-86.

published in 1726 as compared to 16 in 1725 and 17 in 1724. However, none of the established journals seems to have suspended because of the new tax. Most of them survived by increasing the price and decreasing the size of the newspaper. The standard journal was reduced from a six-page folio to a four-page quarto.[37]

Compliance with the new tax seems to have been quite general after its enactment, but within a few years stampless newspapers were again being hawked on the streets of London. The first recorded yield of the tax was £16,500 for the year 1749. One method of evasion as practiced by the *London Journal* was a system of predates whereby the periodical was classified as a pamphlet rather than a periodical, but this ruse does not seem to have been general.[38]

To aid in the enforcement of the tax, Parliament in 1743 made it a crime subject to three months in jail to hawk or sell unstamped newspapers, and informers were to be rewarded with 20 shillings.[39] In spite of these penalties, it was still possible to buy unstamped papers on the streets of London. The most obvious result of the tax was to make newspaper publishing less profitable as a business and consequently more susceptible to political bribery and subsidy.

Except for closing of loopholes and improving enforcement methods, the publication taxes, including the stamp tax, the advertising tax, the tax on paper, and the pamphlet and almanack taxes, continued at the rates set up earlier in the century. The first important change in the newspaper tax took place under William Pitt's coalition ministry in 1757 at a time when the government was searching for new sources of revenue to finance the Seven Years' War. The theory of the government in raising the newspaper tax was that in time of war an anxious public was willing to pay an increased subscription price for news of the military and naval engagements. The new revenue act, 30 George II, cap. 19, increased the stamp tax by one halfpenny on all newspapers of four pages (one sheet) or less. A four-page newspaper now paid a stamp tax of three halfpence. The tax on advertisements appearing in daily

---

[37] Stanley Morison, *The English Newspaper, 1622-1932*, gives an excellent discussion of the effects of the tax on newspaper typography.

[38] See *Notes and Queries*, Ser. XI, Vol. 7, (May 10, 1913), p. 375.

[39] 16 George II, cap. 26 (1743). See also *Cal. Treas. Books and Papers, 1742-45*, p. 242.

and weekly newspapers was increased to two shillings. It is estimated that the yield of this tax between 1758 and 1763 was approximately 43,000 pounds annually. Some fifteen periodicals ceased
publication in 1757 and six in 1758.

The Seven Years' War which had extended to the American
continent was also responsible for the act of Parliament establishing
a stamp tax in the American colonies.[40] The Act provided for a tax
of one halfpenny on every newspaper and pamphlet of a half sheet
or less and a penny per sheet for each publication up to six sheets in
size. A two-shilling tax was to be paid on every advertisement appearing in a newspaper or pamphlet, and publishers of almanacks
and calendars were to pay a stamp duty of four pence for every
copy. Stamp offices were ordered to be set up in each of the American colonies to administer the tax. The immediate and violent opposition to the new tax by the American colonists forced the Rock-
ingham ministry to repeal the American stamp tax on 1 May 1766,[41]
less than a year after its original enactment.

Once again the London publishers found a means of avoiding the increased taxes contained in the revenue act of 1757. It
would seem that the draftsmen of legislation on stamp taxes should
have profited from the unfortunate experience with the original
act of 1712, but nevertheless, the act of 1757 failed to make provision for taxation of newspapers larger than one sheet. The newspaper publishers once again were quick to take advantage of the
deficiency in the tax law by expanding their publications to six
pages and paying a tax of only three shillings for an entire edition.
It took a new act of Parliament (13 George III, cap. 65, 1773) to
remedy the situation by declaring the tax rate of 1757 applicable to
all newspapers regardless of the number of pages. During the three
years between 1773 and 1776 the tax was one pence for a two-
page newspaper, three halfpence for four pages and two pence for
a six-page paper. Unfortunately there are no accounts of the returns
of stamp tax between the years 1764 and 1794.

The American war for independence was responsible for the
next increase in the stamp tax on newspapers which was passed by
Parliament in 1776 under the sponsorship of Lord North. By an
act of 16 George III, cap. 34, the rate on newspapers was raised

---

[40] 5 George III, cap. 12.
[41] 6 George III, cap. 11.

by an additional halfpenny per copy to three halfpennies for a two-page paper and two pence halfpenny for a four-page newspaper. The six-page newspapers continued to pay the two pennies originally set up in 1773.

In 1789 the stamp tax was again raised, this time to two pence for a two-page newspaper and to two pence halfpenny for a four-page paper.[42] The tax on larger papers continued under the rates set up in 1773. To cover the additional tax the newspaper publishers immediately raised the price to four pence per copy. As the government had hopefully expected, the hawkers and dealers in newspapers found it increasingly difficult to sell their papers at the increased price, but not to be outdone they developed the practice of renting out the paper to readers for a limited period of time. Not only did the newsdealers rent out papers but they also returned the unsold copies at the end of the day to the Stamp office for rebates. This method of evasion was outlawed by the above act under a penalty of £5. Under the new tax law, allowances for unsold copies were abolished and instead a 4 per cent discount was set up to take care of overprinting and spoilage. Finally, the act raised the advertisement tax to two shillings, six pence.

The stamp tax continued to be one of the most effective fetters on the periodical press of England during the late years of the reign of George III. Increases in the tax were made in 1794,[43] and 1804,[44] until in 1815 [45] the tax on newspapers amounted to four pence per copy. The tax was reduced to one penny in 1836 [46] and finally abolished in 1855.[47] The advertisement duties were repealed in 1853 [48] and the paper duties in 1861.[49]

Throughout the eighteenth century, the newspaper stamp, advertisement, and paper taxes operated as an effective control over the periodical press. By making it difficult to operate newspapers at a profit, the government forced the publishers to accept subsidies and political bribes.

---

[42] 29 George III, cap. 50.
[43] 34 George III, cap. 72.
[44] 44 George III, cap. 98.
[45] 55 George III, cap. 185.
[46] 6 and 7 William IV, cap. 76.
[47] 18 and 19 Victoria, cap. 27.
[48] 16 and 17 Victoria, cap. 63, s.5.
[49] 24 and 25 Victoria, cap. 20, s.4.

CHAPTER 16

Control Through Subsidization

"Published by Authority"

The history of the subsidization of the press in England in the eighteenth century must necessarily begin with an account of the development and eventual decline of the official government newspaper, the *London Gazette*. Established in 1665 as the *Oxford Gazette* while the court was in residence in that city to escape the plague, the publication was removed to London in 1666 and has continued as the official government newspaper from that day to this.[1]

Because of the nature of its original establishment (by Joseph Williamson as under-secretary of state) and because it was from the beginning concerned principally with two types of news, official news of the court and foreign news, it was natural that the responsibility for, and jurisdiction over, the publication should be centered jointly in the secretaries of state. The financial accounts of the *Gazette* became part of the records of these offices, the editors and employees were attached to the office of one or the other of the principal secretaries, and the profits were divided between the two.

[1] See above. The best account of the early history of the *Gazette* is to be found in Laurence Hanson's *Government and the Press, 1695-1763* (London: Oxford University press, 1936), Chap. IV.

The secretaries themselves were, of course, responsible to the chief minister.

In the late seventeenth and early eighteenth centuries, the contents of the *Gazette* included both foreign and domestic news, but its principal fare was the announcements of various government departments, which today would be described as routine and official "government releases." In this newspaper are to be found the king's speeches to Parliament, royal proclamations, resolutions of the Privy Council, promotions and the activities of the court.

Foreign news came from the offices of the secretaries of state in the form of official reports from overseas representatives of the government. For almost a century the *London Gazette* continued to give the best account of foreign affairs of any English newspaper, relying largely on the already far-flung foreign service of the government. It was not until the eighteenth century that the privately owned press was able to compete with the official *Gazette* in the field of foreign news.

In the field of domestic news, the *Gazette* was handicapped from the beginning. Its coverage of provincial news was dependent upon the diligence and news-sense of the country postmasters, most of whom were lacking in both requirements. In payment for their "correspondence" the provincial postmasters received free copies of the newspaper. Early in the eighteenth century private publishers of domestic news soon outstripped this loose and inefficient system of country coverage.

The *Gazette* was especially inefficient in its coverage of London news. In reporting the events of the day as they occurred in the metropolis, the official newspaper relied largely on government sources and even in this area its attachment to the foreign office did not put it too closely in touch with government activities and policies on domestic affairs. Its most conspicuous failure, however, was in the field of political reporting. Chained to the current ministry, it was impossible for the *Gazette* to enter the arena of political controversy with any degree of impartiality, and added to its well-known attachment to the group in power was the difficulty of finding a person to direct its political activities who would be acceptable to the ministry and who at the same time could give a fairly accurate account of the political activities of the day. The result was that the privately owned press pre-empted the field of political reporting, and the *Gazette* finally contented itself with dull and dreary official announcements.

Throughout the reign of Queen Anne attempts were made by the ministry to establish the *Gazette* not only as the official organ of the government but as a political tool in the hands of the coterie in office. Charles Delafaye, who succeeded Robert Yard as editor upon the latter's retirement in 1702, had previously acted as French translator for the newspaper, and although he seems to have possessed some qualifications as an editor, he soon found it impossible to exercise his talents without irritating some important officer of the government. In 1704 he offended Admiral Graydon and Prince George, Lord High Admiral, in his account of the avoidance of a naval battle with the French, and Lord Marlborough, himself, complained of the treatment which his reports were receiving in the official newspaper. The Duke finally lost his temper and requested that his reports from the scene of action be published in the *Post Man*, instead of in the *Gazette*. Evidently Delafaye gave up the attempt to make a "newspaper" of the *Gazette*, and the writing and editing devolved more and more on junior clerks in the office.

The decline of the *Gazette* as a news medium can be traced in the circulation figures of this period. Professor Sutherland estimates that in 1704 the circulation was approximately 6,000.[2] His estimates for the other London newspapers of this period are: *Daily Courant* 800, *London Post* 400, *English Post* 400, *Post Man*, 3,800, *Post Boy* 3,000, *Flying Post* 400. In June, 1710, 8,500 copies of each issue of the *Gazette* (the account covers six issues) were printed; 5,400 were sold; 1,087 were complimentary copies to government officials, representatives abroad, and postmasters, and 2,000 remained on the printer's hands.[3] By 1717 the sales had dropped to 2,000, and Hanson concludes that this remained the usual circulation for the rest of the century.[4] Moreover, these circulation figures represent only the number of copies distributed and do not take into account the fact that the official *Gazette* after a cursory reading found its way into official files, whereas the un-

---

[2] J. R. Sutherland, "Circulation of Newspapers and Literary Periodicals, 1700-1730," *The Library*, 4th Series, XV (1934-35), 110.

[3] P.R.O., S. P. Dom. Anne, 44 Vol. 12. (89), printed in appendix IV, p. 141 of Hanson's *Government and the Press, 1695-1763*.

[4] Hanson, *op. cit.*, p. 85.

official London newspaper of this period was passed from person to person and on many occasions was read aloud to groups in coffee houses and other gatherings.

The decline of the *Gazette* prompted Robert Harley, chief minister, to take some action to re-establish the prestige of the newspaper as an instrument of the government. In this matter he sought the counsel and advice of Jonathan Swift, the eminent Tory political and literary figure. The first step was to get a new editor. The post was offered to John DeFonvive, the talented French Protestant who was writing the *Post Man,* and who was generally recognized as the most competent journalist in England not excepting Defoe. His reasons for declining the position are worth quoting in part:

". . . the writing of the Gazette, though judged trifling by such who never tried the difficulties thereof, requires more learning than some imagine, and a great deal of care to avoid blunders and contradictions; and as it must take up a man's whole time, it ought to have a suitable encouragement, and I dare say that the committing the writing of it to a young clerk and the revising to the four undersecretaries, which was done upon the pretence of saving copy money, has been one of the chief causes of the decay of the Gazette." [5]

DeFonvive with an annual income of £600 from the *Post Man* was unwilling to exchange his editorial freedom for the promise of a salary for life of less than £400.

After trying several minor reforms in an attempt to revive the reputation of the *Gazette,* Harley finally concluded that it would be necessary to introduce new blood. The position as editor of the *Gazette* was offered to Richard Steele in May, 1707, at a salary of £300 a year. The literary essayist was already recognized as a sprightly writer, but he was at this time not an experienced journalist. He entered upon his new duties with youthful enthusiasm, studying his competitors in the private publishing field and submitting a series of reforms by which he hoped to "raise the value of the paper written by authority, and lessen the esteem of the rest among the generality of the people." [6] He soon discovered that his youthful zest was no match for the traditionalism of a government

---

[5] Portland Mss., VIII, 187, Historical Manuscripts Commission.
[6] Richard Steele, *Epistolary Correspondence* (1809), I, 220.

bureau, and it was not long before he encountered the same restraints which plagued his predecessors. News from government representatives abroad and from postmasters at home was irregular and late; Marlborough and the Admiralty resented his attempts to brighten their reports; the work took his whole time with nothing left over for his own literary labors. He continued to draw his salary until September, 1710, at which time the editing of the *Gazette* was again taken over by clerks.

Swift came forth with a recommendation to Harley, this time for Dr. William King, a man of affairs as well as of letters and an unquestioned Tory. In December, 1711, he was appointed editor of the *Gazette* at £ 200.[7] Unfortunately King had neither the temperament nor the physical stamina to stay up until three or four in the morning correcting proofs, and in July, 1712, he resigned. He died the following December.[8]

As his successor Swift recommended Charles Ford,[9] who reluctantly accepted at £ 200 a year. He edited the *Gazette* without enthusiasm until the end of the reign two years later. The inability of the succession of literary figures to re-establish the reputation of the *Gazette* convinced both Swift and Harley that a government newspaper "published by authority" was no longer an effective medium of communication between the government and the people.

Shortly after the accession of George I, the Whigs appointed Samuel Buckley, eminent publisher of the *Daily Courant,* as editor of the *Gazette* (September, 1714). Buckley was an experienced and intelligent journalist and made one last effort to revive the publication as a news medium, but even he was unable to instill newssense and regularity in government correspondents.[10] In 1717 the editor received a patent for the office as editor for life and thereafter devoted most of his time and talents to his private publishing ventures including the *Daily Courant.*

---

[7] Jonathan Swift, Journal to Stella, 29 December 1711.

[8] *Dictionary of National Biography*, XI, 161-63.

[9] A biographical sketch of Ford is contained in the introduction to *The Letters of Jonathan Swift to Ford* (1935) by David Nichol Smith.

[10] Buckley was supported in his request for news from foreign representatives of the government by the Secretary of State, but even such an important official was unable to obtain regular news reports from his foreign staff. See Ragnhild Hatton, "The 'London Gazette' in 1718: supply of news from abroad," *Bulletin of the Institute of Historical Research*, XVIII (1941), 108-11.

The Whigs had come to power with the aid of unofficial journals and newspapers and therefore were not unduly concerned about reviving the *Gazette* as a political tool. With Buckley's death in 1741, the editorship passed to one of the under-secretaries and from that time continued to be a perquisite of that office.

As long as no serious competition was permitted under the Regulation of Printing Acts of the seventeenth century, the official London *Gazette* was able to maintain a respectable readership, but early in the eighteenth century it became apparent that a newspaper, written, edited, and published by governmental appointees could not compete for public favor with the privately edited and financed newspapers. Harley made a last desperate effort to revive the reputation of the *Gazette,* but with the advent of the Whigs under George I, the paper was allowed to seek its own level as an official record of events, and other means were sought to inform and influence the English public.

Talent for Hire

The subsidization of literary figures to perform political services became a common practice during the reigns of Anne and George I. As the changes in political and social climate engendered by the Revolution of 1688 began to permeate increasingly larger sections of the population, political leaders realized that their tenure in office no longer depended exclusively on royal favor. Popular support could maintain a minister in office in spite of opposition by the crown. Under these conditions it became apparent that the political group which could enlarge and maintain its standing with the literate and educated public would survive in office.

Government ministers realized as early as King William's reign that under the new theories of government originally set out by the philosopher John Locke public support by substantial sections of the upper and middle classes was essential. Public support in turn depended on the information, arguments, and opinions which reached the eyes and ears of leading groups in the kingdom. Political pamphlets, coffeehouse discussions, newspaper articles, all contributed to the formation of a public attitude on questions of policy and consequently affected directly the fortunes of political leaders.

How to communicate a favorable picture of a political group or of an announced public policy to the literate population was a problem to which the best political minds of the time addressed themselves. No longer was it possible for the group in office to eliminate or even to control public discussion of political issues. The arena was set and each group sought out its most effective combatants. Facility in political writing became a marketable accomplishment.

Although political lights like Bolingbroke were themselves effective partisan writers, it was inevitable that the leaders should turn to the current literary figures for help. In some instances this help was solicited by the party heads but just as frequently the writers themselves sought to market their wares. Along with the changes in political methods had come changes in the economic status of men of literature. In previous ages an accomplished writer maintained himself in his profession largely by securing the financial support of some wealthy patron. By the opening of the eighteenth century, this system of patronage was already breaking down, and by the end of the century it had practically disappeared. The time had not yet arrived when an author could depend solely on the income from his writings as sold to the public, and therefore he sought other employment related to his accomplishments. Political writing offered a tempting return either in the form of public office or in outright subsidy.

It is impossible to assess accurately the moral and ethical values involved in the financial arrangements which were made by leading literary figures of the early eighteenth century with political leaders. Biographers of the political essayists of the period have frequently attempted to unravel the negotiations between writers and politicians, but final ethical judgments in most cases have been largely subjective. Certain of the political essayists wrote only for that party which they honestly and conscientiously supported; others were ready to offer their talents to the highest bidder. Some of the party shifts by literary figures can be accounted for on the basis of conscientious change, others can be explained only on the basis of higher offers or disappointment over lack of adequate rewards. The participation of literary figures in the political journalism of the age can be presented by a brief review of the careers of such men as Daniel Defoe, Jonathan Swift, Joseph Addison, Richard Steele, Henry Fielding, Tobias Smollett, and Samuel Johnson.

Daniel Defoe was one of the first writers of this age to devote his talents to the service of political propaganda.[11] In the later years of William's reign he apparently used his pen in behalf of the Whigs and in return received several appointments such as government accountant, 1695-1699, and trustee for the government lottery, 1695-1696. His political pamphlets, all anonymous, won him the friendship of leading Whigs and his long poem, *The True-Born Englishman*, (1701) in defense of William, endeared him to the king.

When it was discovered that he was the author of *The Shortest Way with Dissenters*, (1702) an ironical attack on the church, he fled but was shortly discovered and imprisoned. While in prison he evidently offered to employ his talents in support of the Tory leader, Robert Harley, and the following November (1703) the queen pardoned Defoe on Harley's recommendation. It is impossible definitely to charge Defoe with betraying his principles by his appeal to Harley since there was at this period no great difference between a moderate Whig and a moderate Tory. For the next few years Defoe was engaged in editing *The Review* which was undoubtedly subsidized by Harley and Godolphin. In addition to his literary activities, Defoe also acted as a secret service agent for the Tory leaders. He received no regular income from the government but was paid erratically as shown by Defoe's letters to Harley preserved in the Portland manuscripts [12] and in spite of his requests the writer was never given a lucrative government office.

After Harley's fall from office (February, 1708) Defoe continued in the service of Godolphin and at the same time wrote for the moderate Whigs. As a moderate, it is not surprising to find the author supporting the policies of moderates both in the Whig and Tory groups. With the return of Harley to office in 1710 Defoe resumed his pamphleteering on behalf of the commercial policies of the Tory leader and in 1710 obtained control of the *Edinburgh Courant* and the *Scots Postman*, evidently with money supplied by

---

[11] The best source for Defoe's political activities is James Sutherland's *Defoe* (London: Methuen, 1937).

[12] Portland Mss., IV, *passim*, Historical Manuscripts Commission, 15th Report, Appendix, Part IV, London, 1897.

Harley. Even after the death of the queen and the dismissal of Harley, Defoe continued to issue pamphlets in behalf of his patron, but he soon realized that his future lay in becoming an earnest Whig. His official duties on behalf of the Whigs consisted of toning down as far as possible the Tory newspapers which were then being published, including the *Mercurius Politicus* and Mist's *Weekly Journal*. Defoe's connection with the *Weekly Journal*, for which he began to write in the summer of 1717, became common knowledge. He was accused of being the author of an offensive letter in that journal, but the government allowed the matter to be forgotten as his partial control of the newspaper was useful to the Whigs and a prosecution might bring to light many awkward facts.

In 1719 Defoe collaborated in a new journal, the *Daily Post*, and in 1720 he had a hand in the *Whitehall Evening Post*. There is no doubt that he was paid directly by the government for these political services, but existing records do not reveal the details of this payment. Defoe was no charlatan in spite of the fact that he readily shifted his political allegiance. He was pre-eminently a writer and a theorist and was willing to accept financial support from whatever leader or party would espouse his moderate position. However, he was not above planting items in opposition newspapers or engaging in secret negotiations between publishers and politicians. He represented a new type of political journalist who sought to further the interests of his political views by whatever means were at hand.

Another literary figure to become involved in the political journalism of the times was Jonathan Swift. Following the publication of his *Discourse on the Dissensions in Athens and Rome* (1701), Swift was welcomed as a promising Whig writer by Somers, Halifax, and Sunderland, who promised him liberal preferments. Although urged to write against the Occasional Conformity Bill, Swift's strong church inclinations made it difficult for him to agree with the Whigs although he knew that his chances for advancement lay with that party. His failure to give full support to their church policy was probably the cause for withholding preferment, and as it became evident that Whiggism meant alliance with dissent, Swift's distrust of the leaders deepened into aversion. In October, 1710, he held a conversation with Harley, the Tory leader, and almost immediately thereafter began writing in behalf of the moderate Tories. From 2 November 1710 to 14 June 1711, he wrote the political notes in the *Examiner* as well as several pamphlets. Although he evidently had received promises of political patronage, these promises were never carried out. During this period he was the acknowledged avenue of liaison between the Tory leaders and the paid political writers. Swift was undoubtedly sincere in his political convictions and his writings expressed his convictions. His frustrations arose from the failure of the political leaders to compensate him properly for his activities in their behalf.[13]

The transition from individual patronage of authors to political employment is well illustrated by the career of Joseph Addison, the celebrated essayist. One of his earliest publications was a poem (1695) "to the King" with a dedication to Lord Somers. He received in return an annual pension of £300 presumably for travel in order to qualify him for a diplomatic position. In 1704 the essayist was sought out by Godolphin to produce a poem to celebrate the battle of Blenheim for which he received a commissionership of appeals (1704-1708). A year later he was given an under-secretaryship of state as a reward for the success of his poem, "Campaign." Addison continued to produce occasional anonymous political pamphlets, and in 1709 he was given an additional post as keeper of the records with an increase in salary to £400 a year. Addison's advancement in political circles induced a swarm of impecunious writers to attempt to imitate his example and seek financial security through political writings and consequent political patronage.

Addison's journalistic support in the *Whig Examiner* failed to maintain the ministry in power, and with the fall of the Whigs in 1710, he lost his offices. However, the death of Queen Anne and the triumph of the Whigs a few years later led to his appointment as secretary to the lords justices and when Sunderland became lord-lieutenant he received his old secretaryship. Upon Sunderland's retirement within the year, Addison was made one of the lord commissioners of trade. During this period he published the *Freeholder* (55 papers from 23 December 1715 to 9 June 1716), a political periodical in defense of orthodox Whig principles which had come under attack as the result of the rebellion in Scotland. Addison's last

---

[13] The best source on the political activities of Swift is *Dictionary of National Biography*, XIX, and bibliography.

political appointment was as secretary of state under Sunderland (1717), and in March, 1718, he retired because of failing health and was rewarded with a pension of £1,500.

A competent although not a brilliant official, Addison devoted all his personal and literary powers to the needs of his party. There is no doubt that his political services were made possible by reason of his literary accomplishments and that his preferments and pensions were the direct result of his activities as a political journalist in support of Whig leaders and Whig policies. Like Swift among the Tories, he stood as adviser to the minor writers of his party and became a mediary between them and the Whig leaders, and thus like Swift extended the practice of subsidizing literary men for their political writings.[14]

Richard Steele, like his contemporaries, sought to maintain himself and his family by performing literary services for political leaders. As early as 1707 he sought appointment from the Tories, and Harley conceived the idea that this young and sprightly writer might be the answer to the dull and uninfluential London *Gazette*. He was appointed editor in May, 1707, with a salary of £300 a year. His failure to cope with the official handicaps of that publication led him to seek a more lucrative and less onerous appointment, and he was rewarded in 1710 with a commissionership of stamps. He retained this post after Harley, the Tory, came to office, probably through the intervention of Swift.

After 1712 Steele became actively embroiled in party strife. He published Whig periodicals, pamphlets and newspapers, and championed the Hanoverian succession. In order to enter more actively in Whig politics he resigned his commissionership of stamps in 1713 and devoted his talents to the *Guardian*. His assistance to the party through this journal led Whig leaders to support his candidacy for Parliament to which he was elected on 25 August 1713. He became even more zealous in his political writings in the *Englishman* which succeeded the *Guardian* in October and which he continued to publish until he took his seat in the House of Commons. Thereafter the writer confined himself largely to political pamphlets rather than to periodical journalism.

---

[14] The best account of this phase of Addison's career is to be found in D. H. Stevens, *Party Politics and English Journalism, 1702-1742* (Menasha, Wisconsin: Collegiate press, 1916).

After the death of Anne, Steele received several political appointments, but in spite of the income from these offices he was almost always short of funds. He held such offices as Justice of the Peace, deputy-lieutenant for Middlesex, surveyor of the royal stables at Hampton Court, and finally the lucrative appointment as supervisor of the theater royal of Drury Lane. Steele gave himself over wholeheartedly to the practice of politics and undoubtedly enjoyed the strenuous conflicts of early eighteenth-century partisanship. Like many of his contemporaries, his principal income was derived directly from his activities as a political writer and partisan journalist.

The practice of subsidizing literary figures in return for party support declined somewhat under Walpole who, during his long tenure of office, concluded that professional journalists and newspaper publishers were more useful for party purposes than the contemporary men of literature. However, under George II, both Henry Fielding and Tobias Smollett received compensation from political leaders for their support.

Fielding, who edited the *True Patriot*, was charged by Smollett in 1745 with being in the pay of the government at that time, but there seems to have been no basis for the insinuation. Fielding had been encouraged by his friends in the ministry who furnished him with political news and who probably bought a number of copies for free distribution, but there is no evidence that he was directly employed by them.[15]

During the next few years, Fielding issued an occasional anonymous political pamphlet and in 1747-1748 issued the *Jacobite's Journal* under the pseudonym of John Trott. His services to the government were recognized by appointment to the office of Justice of the Peace. In addition, the Duke of Bedford gave him leaseholds to qualify as a property owner and presented him with a yearly pension "out of public service money."

Still later in the century, Smollett flirted occasionally with political leaders but received no valuable preferments.[16] The great Samuel Johnson undoubtedly had hopes of receiving political favors

---

[15] The best source for this aspect of Fielding's career is W. L. Cross, *The History of Henry Fielding* (New Haven: Yale, 1918), 3 vols.

[16] See *Dictionary of National Biography*, XVIII, and L. L. Martz, *The Later Career of Tobias Smollett* (New Haven: Yale, 1942).

and finally convinced himself that he should accept a pension of
£300 "for past favors." There is no evidence that Johnson ever
sought to peddle his literary talents to the highest bidder, and his
political writings were never inconsistent with his settled political
convictions.

By the time of George III political writing was almost entirely
in the hands of journalists. Writers were discovering that they could
not devote their talents to literature and at the same time engage
in political journalism. As the century progressed and literacy became more widespread, writers were able to support themselves
almost solely by their literary efforts. As they became financially
independent, they tended to abandon the political field to the professional newspaper writers and editors.

Pension Newspapers

The anonymous pamphlet was the chief weapon in the political
warfare of the late seventeenth and early eighteenth centuries, but
by the end of the reign of Anne the political leaders were turning
more and more to the regularly published periodical as a means
of influencing public opinion. Astute political leaders became aware
that there was a growing public whose knowledge of politics and
current affairs was derived principally from newspapers and coffeehouse discussions. Literary lights who could turn out metered verse
in celebration of a military victory or in honor of a new court favorite were discarded in favor of accomplished prose writers like
Swift and Addison, and these in turn gave way during the reign
of George I to the political journalist such as Thomas Gordon, Samuel Buckley, and Thomas Arnall.

As has been pointed out, the press control system of the
eighteenth century rested on four supports: (1) the stamp tax which
eliminated a large number of marginal newspapers and rendered
those which survived financially unstable and therefore susceptible
to subsidization, (2) the system of subsidization as represented
by ministerial writers and the ministerial press, (3) strict control
of public discussions of the proceedings in Parliament, and (4)
active prosecution of the laws of seditious libel. Although the increasingly heavy stamp duties on newspapers and periodicals were
applied to both opposition and ministerial press alike, the latter

was able to obtain such advantages as ready access to news sources
and free distribution through the postal system as well as direct
financial assistance from the Treasury.

The early history of the subsidized press is largely a biography
of Daniel Defoe. Robert Harley, who rescued him from a prison
sentence for seditious libel, seized the opportunity to enlist this
able journalist and set him up as editor of a regularly published
periodical. *The Review* first appeared on 19 February 1704 and
continued without interruption until 1713 in spite of the numerous
other duties of its editor. That the paper was subsidized by the government is no longer open to doubt since the publication of the Portland papers by the Historical Manuscripts Commission.[17] Defoe,
the political journalist, has presented an intriguing moral problem
for his literary biographers, but Laurence Hanson appears to
have evolved a reasonable explanation of the writer's political
creed and journalistic morality. The key, says Hanson, to the understanding of Defoe's relations with various government ministers
lies in this—"he knew that he was a great writer who could write
to more effect on most topics than any of his contemporaries, and
that he saw no reason why the world should be deprived of the
fine writing which he could give it. He could and did write on both
sides in many controversies. He wrote both for and against the
Septennial Act. He espoused both parties in the Bangorian controversy. His justification, if there were need of it, would be that his
pamphlets represent the best work on both sides." [18]

As a ministerial writer Defoe loyally supported Harley and
his policies. After his patron's dismissal in 1708 he attached himself
to Godolphin, but was back in Harley's service upon his return to
office in 1710. Defoe's own justification of his shifting support was
set out in his pamphlet, *An Appeal to Honour and Justice*
(1715) and reads very much like the creed of a modern political
journalist: "It occur'd to me immediately, as a principle for my
conduct, that it was not material to me what Ministers Her Majesty
was pleas'd to employ, my duty was to go along with every ministry,
so far as they did not break in upon the constitution, and the laws
and liberties of my country; my part being only that of a subject,

---

[17] Portland Mss., IV, *passim*, Historical Manuscripts Commission, 15th Report, London, 1897.

[18] Hanson, *op. cit.*, p. 94.

(viz.) to submit to all lawful commands, and to enter into no service which was not justifiable by the laws." [19]

It has been estimated that from 1707 to 1714 Defoe received at least £400 a year from Harley.[20] Hanson has published the details of amounts paid the writer during the last four years of the reign of Anne from the Secret Service accounts in the Public Record office.[21]

By 1710 the political influence of the *Review* was declining as the knowledge of its ministerial support became more widespread. The *Examiner,* which first appeared on 3 August 1710, written and edited by Matthew Prior, William King, and Francis Atterbury, was supported by the Harley ministry. In October Swift began to write for the paper, which by 1711 had become the chief ministerial advocate, leaving such matters as trade and finance to the declining *Review.* Bolingbroke's rise in the government is credited to his sponsorship of the *Examiner* and his activities in enlisting some of the more accomplished writers of the time as its contributors. As director of the chief ministerial organ, Bolingbroke was able to advance his own political theories as those of the party, and on the basis of popular support created largely by the *Examiner,* he was able eventually to assume control of the government.[22]

A third ministerial newspaper was the *Post Boy* edited by Abel Roper. This three-times-a-week periodical was established in 1695 and from 1702 to 1709 was edited by Abel Boyer. After 1709 it was a definite supporter of ministerial policies with contributions by both Swift and Bolingbroke, and it could not have survived the stamp taxes without government patronage.[23]

The Whig opposition soon realized the influence exerted by the ministerial outlets and proceeded to support both financially and with contributed writings an opposition press. The *Whig Examiner* was begun in September, 1710, edited by Joseph Addison, and was followed after five numbers by *The Medley, a Letter to the Whig Examiner,* under the direction of Arthur Mainwaring, whose prin-

[19] Shakespeare Head Edition of novels and selected writings of Daniel Defoe, II, 208.

[20] Stevens, *op. cit.,* p. 57.

[21] Hanson, *op. cit.,* p. 96.

[22] Stevens, *op. cit.,* p. 31.

[23] *Ibid.,* p. 71; Hanson, *op. cit.,* p. 98.

cipal objective was to expose the authorship of articles appearing in the Tory press. Swift's style was so conspicuous in the *Examiner* that he was forced to retire and install Mrs. Manley as leader writer.

A short-lived lull in journalistic warfare occurred at the end of 1711, but early in 1712 the battle between the subsidized periodicals was on again. The *Examiner* was revived and carried the attack to the enemy under the guerrilla leadership of William Oldisworth, with Swift hovering in the background. *The Medley* was again called into action by the opposition and was refitted with Grub Street mercenaries. The forces of the government were strengthened by the appearance of the *Mercator* in 1713, sponsored by the ministry and edited by Defoe whose release from prison was arranged for the purpose of supporting the economic provisions of the Treaty of Utrecht.

To the Tories and particularly to Robert Harley should go the credit for developing the subsidized newspaper as an effective instrument in political warfare. During the reign of Anne it became apparent that the official publication, the *Gazette,* was almost useless as a medium of government propaganda, and that the political pamphlet could not by itself be relied upon to reach the masses. It was also apparent that the effectiveness of a ministerial paper depended in large part on keeping its dependency on the government secret.

The Whigs who came to power with the accession of George I were well aware that the time had passed when a government could suppress an opposition press through legal means, and they relied on the policies developed by the Queen Anne Tories for their control of public discussion of political issues. The stamp taxes were retained and strengthened, the prosecutions for libel were renewed, Parliamentary reporting was strictly circumscribed, and the subsidization of newspapers both directly and indirectly reached its zenith under the long administration of Robert Walpole.

Whig newspapers founded during the early years of George I with ministerial support were the *Grumbler,* Addison's *Freeholder,* and Ambrose Phillips' *Freethinker.* Samuel Buckley, who was rewarded with the *Gazette,* continued his Whig support in the *Daily Courant* for which he received substantial subsidies.

An ingenious technique for controlling the opposition press was devised by the Whigs with the help of Defoe. Because of his

long association with Tory writers and journals he was hired by
the Whigs to continue his outward appearance as an opposition
writer but at the same time to use his influence with Tory editors
to tone down some of the more vociferous and violently anti-admin-
istration writings. On this assignment Defoe joined the staffs of the
Tory papers, *Mercurius Politicus,* Dormer's newsletter, and Nathaniel Mist's *Weekly Journal.* His job was to extract the venom without killing the viper. At the same time there is no doubt that Defoe
was writing political pamphlets in support of the Tories and particularly in defense of Robert Harley, and it is therefore not surprising that the Whigs were somewhat suspicious of the loyalty of their
undercover man. His talents as a political journalist were too valuable for the Whigs to pass over, and consequently he was supported
in the publication of a new Whig journal, the *Whitehall Evening
Post.* Grub Street journalists soon discovered that Defoe was the
principal writer both for the Whig *Post* and the Tory *Journal.* The
government concluded that Defoe's services as saboteur in the editorial offices of Mist's *Journal* were not proving very effective, and
it was even conceivable that he was himself the author of some of
the more offensive articles appearing in that very popular opposition newspaper. To save himself once again from prosecution Defoe
ceased to be actively interested in the *Journal* and devoted himself
to the moderate Whig views as expressed in the *Post.*

The Whig ministry found itself in dire need of journalistic
support with the bursting of the South Sea bubble in 1721. The
opposition press gleefully made the most of the financial fiasco and
did not neglect to point out the part played by the Whigs in de-
feating the commercial clauses of the Treaty of Utrecht. Loudest
in its demand for a full investigation was the London *Journal,* begun
in August, 1719, by two dissatisfied Whigs, John Trenchard and
Thomas Gordon. Its denunciations of the financial crisis appeared
under the signature "Cato." The newspaper's circulation increased
with its vehemence, and it is reported that ten thousand copies of the
12 August 1721 issue were sold. The obvious purpose of the *Journal*
campaign was to unseat a government and to secure the election
of a new Parliament. In spite of the talent available on its side,
the government concluded that the simplest way to deal with the
Journal was to buy it off. Negotiations were begun through Benjamin Norton Defoe, bastard son of Daniel, but the publisher himself

soon took over and demanded £800 a year. The figures as preserved in the Public Records Office show that the publisher contended that seventeen thousand copies were printed at a cost of £1,768 per annum. Editorial costs were £600 for a total cost of £2,368. Revenues included £3,120 from the sale of fifteen thousand copies and £200 from advertisements. The publisher pointed out that a change in editorial policy would reduce the circulation to about eight thousand copies, halve the advertising revenue, leaving a net profit of only £124.[24] In September, 1722, Gordon and Trenchard were dismissed, Cato's letters ceased to appear, and the paper entered the service of the government. The exact terms of the transfer are unknown. Articles by such ministerial writers as Benjamin Hoadley began to appear, and as its uncritical support became evident to the readers, it declined in popularity as predicted by its proprietor.

The *Craftsman,* which was started in 1726 by Bolingbroke and the Pulteneys, presented a much more difficult problem for the government propagandists. Its staff, which included Swift, Gay, and Amhurst, were competent writers and well-informed on current political questions. Political controversy was maintained at a high level, and the periodical soon became the leading spokesman for the opposition to Walpole. Within a few years the coteries surrounding the *Craftsman* became the nucleus of the anti-Walpole factions.[25]

The long administration of Robert Walpole witnessed the peak in secret subsidization of newspapers. The chief minister saw little political value in financial assistance to the chief literary figures of his age and concentrated his support on publishers of daily and weekly organs as part of his broad plan for political control. A few publishers were heavily subsidized, a number received occasional assistance, and the opposition was either bought off or prosecuted in the courts. Administration newspapers as well as party materials were distributed free of charge through the post office while opposition papers, even when they paid their way, were held out or delayed. Walpole's methods of dealing with the press have been described by Escott. "He supplied the selected scribe with a copious and minute brief. With his own hand he wrote down all the details

[24] St. P. Dom. Geo. I, XXX, 5, 12, 34; LXVIII, 172.

[25] William Coxe, *Memoirs of Sir Robert Walpole, Earl of Oxford* (1798), I, 320, 361-64.

necessary for an exact understanding of the situation and issues. Next the minister set forth, in their exact order of importance, the arguments which should, he thought, be deduced from the facts in support of his case. Then followed the objections which his antagonist might raise, the answers which would dispose of them, or the statements by which they might be anticipated." [26]

Samuel Buckley, proprietor of the *Daily Courant*, performed the greatest service and received the largest rewards. In addition to the perquisites of the office of Gazetteer, he received direct subsidies as well as favors from the post office and the news sources in the government. In 1713, for instance, the government was paying for 750 double *Courants* sent to the post office every post day; in 1732 for 850, and in 1733 for 900. In 1734 the number, judging from the sum paid to the publisher, must have been over 2,000.[27] In return he gave wholehearted support to administration policies in his publications and, in addition, acted as spy and informant against opposition publishers. The State Papers contain many references to correspondence between Buckley and Charles Delafaye, government liaison officer for press affairs, relative to raids on seditious printers. Government writers such as Dr. Bland, Dr. Hare, Horace Walpole, and Mathew Concanen were frequent contributors to the *Courant*.

Other newspapers receiving ministry support in 1731, according to accounts published in the *Craftsman* and the *Grub Street Journal*, were the *London Journal, Read's Journal,* the *Free Briton,* the *Weekly Register,* the *Hyp Doctor,* and the *Flying Post.* Subsidization was largely through the free distribution of copies through the post office. It was estimated by the *Craftsman* at this time that the cost of the system of subsidization was approximately £20,000 a year.[28] Later evidence indicates that this estimate was slightly high, especially after the consolidation and economy measures instituted by Walpole in 1735.

The *London Journal* had lost its sparkle when it changed sides in 1722, but it continued to receive the support of the ministry in

[26] T. H. S. Escott, *Masters of English Journalism* (London: Unwin, 1911), p. 83.

[27] Calendar of Treasury Books and Papers, 1731-34, pp. 210, 262, 401, 578.

[28] *Craftsman*, No. 265, 31 July 1731; *Grub Street Journal*, No. 86, 26 August 1731.

spite of its mediocrity. The liveliest of the ministerial pension papers was the *Free Briton* published by William Arnall (or Arnold) under the pseudonym of Francis Walsingham. He received his journalistic training on the *London Journal,* and beginning in 1729 he devoted his talents to answering the charges of the Craftsman group. His paper was distributed free by the post office, and in addition the proprietor and editor received direct subsidies from Walpole's treasury. Between 1730 and 1736 he received at least £12,500 for copies of his paper.

Another newspaper which was bought out by the ministry was the *British Journal* in which had appeared the Cato letters after the subversion of the *London Journal.* On the death of Trenchard, Thomas Gordon, co-editor, entered into an arrangement with Walpole not only to divert the *Journal* to the support of the government but to act as a sort of general supervisor of the pensioned press. In addition to postal subsidies, the proprietor received appointment as Commissioner for Wine Licenses, and as a result was pointed out by his contemporaries as one political writer who achieved financial security through the use of his talents.

The actual payments in the form of subsidies to newspapers during Walpole's administration are recorded in the Treasury accounts between 1729 and 1736 and also in the findings of the Secret Committee of 1742.[29] This committee was appointed to obtain evidence of the wasteful use of public moneys but had available to it only the treasury books and was not permitted to examine the private accounts of the minister or the secret service records. Much of the funds used for political purposes during this period cannot be traced since payments were usually made to a subordinate in the treasury who signed the receipt and who then turned the cash over to the ultimate recipient. Walpole admitted to the Committee that he spent £5,000 a year on newspapers. The final report of the Secret Committee listed £50,007 8s. to this account which does not vary substantially from a tabulation of the figures in the treasury books.

The Louther account books found among the treasury papers cover the years 1714-1740 and show the following payments between the dates of 18 April 1730 and 18 February 1740: William

---

[29] See Cal. Treas. Papers, 1739-41, p. xii; *Ibid.,* 1729-45, *passim;* also Commons Journal, XXIV, 295.

Arnall, £12,510, 8s. 4d; Samuel Buckley, £2,086, 74s. 10d.; John Walthoe, printer, £19,981, 19s. 10d.; William Wilkins (mostly for *London Journals*) £6,013, 18s. 9d. The treasury accounts themselves show payments as follows during the period 4 December 1729 to 6 February 1736: William Arnall received £9,115 for *Free Britons,* John Walthoe was paid £22,649, 10s. 8d. for *Courants, Daily Gazette* and other printing; *The Corn-Cutter's Journal* received £1,222, 10s. between 1 October 1733 and 28 June 1735.

For a period of ten years Walpole paid out between £5,000 and £10,000 a year, not a large sum by present standards and not as large as was currently suspected by contemporary opposition, but large enough to assure the ministry of a favorable press.

In 1735 the ministry sought to reduce its expenditures for press support and consequently the *Daily Courant, Free Briton,* and the *London Journal,* chief recipients of financial support, were consolidated into one publication, the *Daily Gazetteer.* A government which could establish newspapers could also disestablish them. Osborne of the *Journal* wrote the political leaders on Saturdays, Walsingham (Arnall) of the *Free Briton* on Thursdays, and the editors of the *Daily Courant* filled out the rest of the week. The paper was for a time distributed free to the coffeehouses and of course was circulated post free.

As the chief journalists of Walpole's early career either died or retired, they were replaced by a younger generation of writers who failed to keep up the close political relationship with the chief minister which had been enjoyed by such men as Buckley, Arnall, and Osborne. Whether Walpole felt so secure in his position that he did not need the assistance of these journalists or whether he felt that their contribution to his support was so slight as not to warrant the expense is not clear, but nevertheless it is evident that the chief minister's support of the political journals declined after 1735. The result was apparent in the political discussions in the contemporary newspapers. Important matters of state were not mentioned or treated only sketchily. Also contributing to the decline of the *Gazetteer* as the official ministerial organ was the spread of the knowledge that it was subsidized and therefore ready to do the minister's bidding. Walpole's cabinet reluctantly concluded that its paid writers and post free newspapers were no match for the talents of the opposition. As Hanson has pointed out: "It needed new persuasives to convince the government that in engaging with an enemy so much better equipped than itself it was waging a barren warfare. Money could not buy the talent which ties of friendship had given to the Tories." [30] The fall of Walpole in February, 1742, terminated the practice of regular financial support for the ministerial press. The less aggressive ministries which followed were well aware of the scandal that was created by the report of the Secret Committee, and even though during the rest of the century occasional sums were supplied to newspaper proprietors, there was no attempt to revive the system of regular subsidization. Political conversion, personal friendships, and promise of government posts were the principal bait held out by the Pelhams. In the later years of the reign of George II, Henry Fielding made a valiant attempt to establish an independent political newspaper, *The Champion*, and there is some grounds for concluding that he relinquished this opposition newspaper in 1741 in return for some favors. His *Jacobite's Journal* (1747) presents a neat political problem. Ostensibly published in support of the Tories, its espousal of Jacobite principles did more to harm that party than to help, and lends credence to the charge that the paper was on the ministerial pension list.[31]

With Fielding out of the way with his appointment as a magistrate, the only other opposition writer of note, William Guthrie, was bought off with a pension of £1,200 a year. Even the *Craftsman* found itself in difficult financial circumstances due to increased stamp taxes and renewed enforcement, and the editor, Thomas Cooke, in 1748 made several overtures for government support. The last opposition to the Newcastle ministry, James Ralph, who in former years had been associated with the *Daily Gazetteer* and with Fielding's *Champion*, published the *Remembrancer* in 1748, but by 1751 he was flirting with a group of politicians formed after the death of the Prince of Wales. The Bedford faction, however, made a higher offer and Ralph supported its interest in the *Protester*. The ministry finally agreed to buy him off with a pension of £300 a year.[32]

By the 1760's the system of pension newspapers had ceased to exist. Thereafter newspapers were dependent on subscriptions, copy

---

[30] Hanson, *op. cit.*, p. 117.

[31] G. M. Godden, *Henry Fielding* (1910), *passim*.

[32] Hanson, *op. cit.*, p. 121.

sales, advertising, or support from a political party or faction.[33] Direct government subsidy was temporarily abandoned to be revived by Shelbourne, Fox, and Pitt after 1782.[34] The stamp taxes made newspaper publishing a risky business, but in spite of the handicaps a few papers continued to exist without government support, and with the increase in advertising the way was open for the establishment of the great organs of the late eighteenth century such as the *Morning Chronicle* (1770), the *Morning Post* (1772), and the *Times* (1785).

---

[33] For subsidies to the *Briton* under George III, see below.

[34] An excellent account of subsidies after 1782 is to be found in Arthur Aspinall, *Politics and the Press, 1780-1850* (London: Home and Van Thal, 1949), pp. 66-108.

CHAPTER 17

Reporting Parliament

At the beginning of the eighteenth century the reporting of proceedings in both Houses of Parliament was severely restricted. The Commons permitted the publication of an official report of its votes but not of its debates and further restricted the re-publication of its votes in newspapers and newsletters. The Lords prohibited all reports, official and unofficial, of both its votes and its debates.[1] By the end of the eighteenth century both Houses had retreated under public pressure; and although the restrictive rules were never officially repealed, not only were newspapers permitted to report the proceedings in Parliament but steps were taken to give reporters access to both Houses. What were the causes of this significant change? In the first place, by the end of the eighteenth century Parliament's constitutional position had changed. The House of Commons had become more representative of the people and as such felt a greater responsibility to the electorate, particularly to the London electorate. Also, party activity had developed to the place where appeals for public support were vital to the continuance of a group or ministry in power. An additional factor was the growth of the great London dailies in the last quarter of the century. These newspapers and their managers were able with the support of their London readers to impress upon

---

[1] See below, pp. 279-88.

Parliament the necessity for some sort of report to the public. The present chapter seeks to trace the development of the freedom of the press to report Parliamentary proceedings.

Early Reports of Debates

One of the first attempts in the eighteenth century to publish the proceedings of both Houses of Parliament was made by Abel Boyer in his monthly publication, *The Political State of Great Britain.* Beginning in 1703 it contained monthly reports of proceedings in spite of the standing orders of Parliament, and it continued without serious interruption until Boyer's death in 1729. The editor justified his circumvention of the orders against reporting on the ground that he postponed publication of his reports until after each session had adjourned and also that he was writing history and not a report of current affairs. He was clever enough to tinge his reports with the politics of whatever party was in power, and by the time his publications were released to the reading public most of the controversy and irritation had evaporated. In spite of the editor's care he was called before the House of Lords (5 March 1711), and he and his printer were kept in custody for six days, after which they were released upon payment of fees and promise to offend no more.[2] This was the only instance in which Boyer was in trouble with either House during the twenty-six years of his editorship. Aside from orders against individual pamphlets criticizing judgments of the Lords [3] this was the only prosecution by the upper house for the seventeen years preceding the accession of George I.

In deference to Boyer's enterprise it should be pointed out that his reports of the debates were quite accurate although far too scanty in comparison with later standards. He obtained his information from petty officials and messengers of both Houses and on occasions sat in the gallery during debates. The following is an example of his reporting of a debate: [4]

---

[2] Lords Journal, XIX, 243, 246, 248, 252, 253.

[3] *Ibid.,* XVII, 442; XX, 328, 330, 340, 344. An attempt was made to continue the *Political State* after Boyer's death in 1729, but competition from both the monthly, *The Historical Register,* and from the weekly newspapers caused its end in 1735.

[4] *The Political State of Great Britain,* I, 41-42, January, 1711.

This Resolution being taken, Sir Thomas Hanmer moved, That in the said Address they should represent to Her Majesty, That the most effectual Way to give Spirit to Her Friends, and defeat the restless Malice of Her Enemies, would be by Discountenancing all Persons of such Principles, and Avoiding all Measures of such Tendency, as might weaken Her Majesties Title and Government: This Motion occasion'd a small Debate, in which Mr. Lechmere said, That they ought likewise humbly to caution her Majesty against such Measures and Principles as might weaken the Settlement of the Crown in the Illustrious House of Hanover, and advance the Hopes of the Pretender. No Member offering to second Mr. Letchmere, Mr. Harley stood up and said, 'That tho' the Protestant Succession was already sufficiently establish'd and secured by several Acts of Parliament, so that it seem'd needless to add any thing to them; yet, since a Motion was made in Favour of the Illustrious House of Hanover, it would look strange, both at Home and Abroad, if the same should drop: Whereupon it was resolv'd, That the Cause offer'd by Mr. Lechmere should be inserted in the Address, which was done accordingly. On the last Day of November, Sir Thomas Hanmere reported the said Address, which he had himself drawn up, and which, with an Amendment, was approv'd, being as follows: . . . .

The London newspapers, both daily and weekly, avoided the displeasure of Parliament by omitting all references to debates during this early part of the eighteenth century. Occasionally a provincial newspaper would carry an item taken from one of the circulating newsletters, but the House of Commons moved promptly in such cases.[5] The House of Lords was even more vigilant than the Commons and proceeded against an advertisement of the life and works of a member of the House.[6] When James Read in his *Weekly Journal or British Gazetteer* inadvertently included the name of the Earl of Stratford in a list of "conspirators concerned in the late plot" the House proceeded immediately against him.[7] Publishers of individual trials or of collections of trials before the Lords were still required to obtain special permission before publication.[8] Late in 1722 a few intrepid publishers of newspapers and pamphlets discovered what they thought was a loophole in the

[5] See case of the *Exeter Mercury or Weekly Intelligence, The Protestant Mercury or Exeter Post Boy* for printing a resolution of the House of Commons, November, 1718. Commons Journal, XIX, 30, 42, 43, 44, 53, 54.

[6] Lords Journal, XXI, 659, 660, 667 (22 January 1721/22).

[7] *Ibid.*, XXII, 128, 129, 143.

[8] See *Ibid.*, XXIV, 339, 352 (6 February 1733/34).

House of Commons rules on the publication of debates. A number of papers appeared on the streets of London with a report of proceedings before a committee of the House. This loophole was immediately closed by the House on 23 January 1723 with the passage of the following resolution:

> That no News Writers do presume in their Letters or other Papers that they disperse as Minutes, or under any other Denomination, to intermeddle with the Debates, or any other Proceedings, of this House, or any Committee thereof.[9]

The Magazines

The first attempt to give a contemporaneous account of the proceedings of Parliament in the eighteenth century was made by the audacious printer, Edward Cave (1691-1754).[10] While in school at Rugby he was accused of robbing a henroost, but succeeded in extricating himself only to be expelled for obstructing the discipline of the school. In London he became a journeyman printer and later obtained a place at the post office. He began to send news to various country newspapers, and it was not long before he included news items on proceedings in Parliament in his notes.

In 1728 the House of Commons was informed that a printed report of its proceedings had appeared in the *Gloucester Journal*, published by Robert Raikes at Bristol. Raikes was ordered to appear before the House, where he testified that he obtained his intelligence from Edward Cave of the post office. Both publisher and correspondent were imprisoned and fined and then released on their promise to offend no more.[11] However, within a year Raikes was recalled to London to explain the publication of an item in the 11 February 1729 issue of the *Journal*. This item was a mistake, said the publisher, inserted without his knowledge by his workmen. The item was traced to Robert Giddins, also a postal clerk. Both the clerk and John Stanley, the distributor of written newsletters were fined, reprimanded, and then discharged.[12]

[9] Commons Journal, XX, 99. For case of Henry Parker, printer, for publishing a report of the Committee to examine the Harburgh Lottery, see *Ibid.*, XX, 133, 141, 143, 145, 149, 153, 154, 160, 161.

[10] The best biography of Cave is to be found in C. Lennart Carlson, *The First Magazine* (Providence: Brown University, 1938), pp. 3-28.

[11] Commons Journal, XXI, 85, 104, 108, 115, 117, 119, 127.

[12] *Ibid.*, pp. 227, 238, 249, 263.

In January 1730/31 Cave published the first issue of the *Gentle-man's Magazine*, which became so popular that by 1739 its sale was more than 10,000 copies. Some of the chief literary men of the day, including Dr. Johnson, wrote for the magazine. The first attempt to report Parliament was made in the No. 5, May, 1731, issue in the following manner: [13]

> The Debates relating to this Bill were to this effect, viz., Those who were against it apprehended that great Difficulties would arise in translating the Law out of Latin into English, and might multiply Law Suits, in regard to the interpretation of English Words. And a certain Lord, and great Lawyer, said That if the Bill passed, the Laws ought also be translated into Welch, since many in Wales did not understand English. To which the Duke of Argyle reply'd, That the Meaning of the Law had been long understood by the Interpreters (Judges) thereof, and would surely be so when translated: That our Prayers were in our native Tongue, that they might be intelligible, and why should not the Laws, wherein our Lives and Properties were concern'd, be so for the same Reason? and added, that he was glad to hear that the said Lord had nothing else to say against the Bill than a Joak. Other Lords instanc'd, That in the Reign of Edward III. an Act of Parliament passed for having the Laws in English and not in French (as they were then) for the ease of the People. After which a Debate arose about Law Proceedings being wrote in a plain legible Hand, and not in Court Hand, wherein the Earl of Isla said, That in Scotland they were come to that pass, that the Sheriffs knew nothing of the Contents of the Writs they executed; and therefore mov'd, that the Proceedings in the Exchequer in Scotland, which were in the English manner, might be also wrote in a plain legible Hand, which was agreed to; as likewise that Records be wrote in the same Hand a [*sic*] Acts of Parliament are engrossed; and that the Time allowed the Lord Chancellor and Judges for translating the Law into English, be till the Year 1733.

In the same issue the editor included the king's speech to both Houses as well as the list of acts approved. In 1732 Cave became bolder and in July began reporting the debates of the adjourned session, following the practice of Boyer's *Political State*.[14] To avoid prosecution he omitted names of speakers, referring, for example, to Sir Robert Walpole as Sir R——t W——le.

Dr. Johnson has described Cave's reporting methods: "Cave had interest with the doorkeepers; he and the persons employed under him got admittance; they brought away the subject of dis-

---

[13] *Gentleman's Magazine*, I, No. 5, pp. 213-14, May, 1731.
[14] *Gentleman's Magazine*, II, No. 7, pp. 864-67.

cussion, the names of the speakers, the side they took, and the order in which they rose, together with notes of the various arguments in the course of the debate." [15]

In the hope of avoiding prosecution under the standing orders of Parliament, Cave took a number of precautions. First, he gave only short abstracts of the bills during the sitting of Parliament; second, he postponed publication of debates until recess time; third, he omitted the full names of speakers; and, finally, he attempted to present as accurate a picture of Parliamentary proceedings as was possible under existing restrictions.

The *London Magazine*, chief competitor of Cave's *Gentleman's Magazine*, first appeared in April, 1732, and began immediately to print earlier and more complete reports of Parliamentary debates. It was published by an important syndicate of London booksellers with John Wilford as principal editor. Notes of speeches were obtained in the same manner as by Cave, and this raw material was rewritten in final form by Thomas Gordon, the translator of Tacitus. In their first issues both magazines followed closely the pattern set by Boyer in his *Political Register*, but by 1737 the popularity of the Parliamentary section of the publication had caused the editors to extend themselves by printing more and longer speeches. Of the two magazines the *London* was undoubtedly the first out with the debates. Both the *London* and the *Gentleman's* pirated from each other and from the *Political Register*. Since the reporting of the debates was begun only after the session ended, the news was frequently from three to twenty months late. The *London Magazine* avoided much of the delay by publishing special supplements during the recess in order to complete the report before the opening of the next session, a practice which was adopted shortly thereafter by Cave. As monthly magazines, both the *London* and *Gentleman's* avoided the heavy stamp duty which was applied to weekly and daily newspapers. They were able to sell a monthly copy of from 48 to 64 pages for six pence, of which only one penny, the same as paid by daily newspapers, went for a stamp tax.

On 13 April 1738, the publication of the speech of the king to Parliament caused the House of Commons to propose and adopt the following resolution:

[15] Sir John Hawkins, *The Life of Samuel Johnson, LL.D.* (2d ed.; London, 1787), p. 95.

That it is an high Indignity to, and a notorious Breach of the Privilege of this House, for any News Writer, in Letters, or other Papers (as Minutes, or under any other Denomination), or for any Printer or Publisher of any News Paper, of any Denomination, to presume to insert in the said Letters or Papers, or to give therein any Account of the Debates, or other Proceedings, of this House, or any Committee thereof; *as well during the Recess as the Sitting of Parliament;* and that this House will proceed with the utmost Severity against such Offenders.[16]

This resolution was a severe blow to both magazines as Parliamentary reports were undoubtedly their most popular feature. The monthlies no longer had any advantage over daily or weekly journals. Immediately the search was on for a loophole. The *London Magazine* first hit upon a device (May, 1738), that of reporting the proceedings of an imaginary political club. The subjects reported were those discussed in Parliament, and members of the club were given classical names such as Scipia Africanus, Tullius Cicero, M. Cato, etc. A code was inserted in a supplement giving the true identity of each member. Cave's solution of the problem appeared in the June issue of *Gentleman's.* The editor and his literary advisers, one of whom was Dr. Johnson, hit upon the ingenious technique of reporting an imaginary legislature of the state of Lilliput, with two branches, the House of Hurpes and the House of Clinab. Intriguing anagrams were employed to identify current political figures. Walpole became Walelop; Pultney, Pulnub; Halifax, Haxilaf. To make certain that no one missed the association, an anagrammatic key was issued with the magazine.

Both magazines published individual speeches, those in the *London* prepared by Gordon and those in the *Gentleman's* by William Guthrie. The *Gentleman's Magazine* gained fame in later years when it was discovered that Dr. Johnson wrote many of the speeches which appeared in that magazine between 1738 and 1743. Guthrie furnished much of the raw material which he collected from clerks, messengers, and members themselves. Johnson produced the finished form of the speech. It is apparent that many of the speeches of this period were reproduced from scanty notes

---

[16] Commons Journal, XXIII, 148. No resolution was necessary in the House of Lords since that body was a court of record and therefore theoretically always in session.

or no notes at all. After 1741 Johnson seems to have done the job himself without Guthrie's assistance.[17]

In the competitive race between the two monthlies, the *London* was undoubtedly first with its report of the political club. It gave a more complete account but reported fewer speeches than the *Gentleman's*.

The Tory attack on Sir Robert Walpole in 1741 focused the nation's attention on the proceedings in Parliament. Both the Tories and the Walpole supporters were fighting for their political lives, and public support was essential if either was to survive. The circulation of both the magazines soared to unprecedented heights, the *Gentleman's* achieving a circulation of fifteen thousand copies. Both publications grew bolder as time went on. They finally were called to account in April, 1747, this time by the House of Lords. The March, 1746, issues of both the *Gentleman's* and the *London* magazines had printed a brief account of the trial of Simon Lord Lovat for high treason in connection with the Jacobite rebellion of 1745. The interest of the public in the trial was intense and neither magazine could afford to ignore it. Both Thomas Astley, official publisher of the *London Magazine*, and Cave were ordered to appear before the Lords, both petitioned for forgiveness, both were reprimanded—Cave on his knees, Astley *in absentia* because of the gout—fined and discharged upon a promise to avoid future offenses. When asked how he presumed to publish the debates of Parliament, Cave answered that "he was extremely sorry for it, that it was a very great presumption; but he was led into it by Custom, and the Practice of other People; That there was a monthly Book, called 'The Political State' which contained Debates in Parliament, and that he never heard, till lately, that any Persons were punished for printing those Books." [18]

The Senate of Lilliput was immediately disbanded by Cave. The intrepid and impecunious young printer of the 1730's had become a mature, respectable, and prosperous publisher, and he was

[17] Johnson was solely responsible for the speeches appearing in the *Gentleman's Magazine* between July, 1741, and March, 1744. James Boswell's *Life of Johnson*, edited by George Birkbeck Hill (1887), I, 509.

[18] The cases of Cave and Astley are reported in Lords Journal, XXVII, 94, 98, 101, 103, 107, 108.

no longer willing to risk his valuable publishing properties.[19] The *London Magazine,* backed by the powerful syndicate which underwrote the journal, continued publication of a carefully edited account of the activities of its "political club." The magazine pointed out that it was no longer attempting to give particular speeches, but only to report the "substance of the debate by way of argument." [20]

In 1753 the House of Commons took note of the practice of including notes on Parliamentary proceedings in the form of letters to the editor such as began appearing in the *London Magazine* and issued a further restriction against publishing such reports "under any Pretense whatsoever." [21] This rule confounded the editors of the *London* and for a few years they made an attempt to disassociate the activities of the political club entirely from current proceedings in Parliament.[22] As the connection between the club and Parliament became less evident the reading public lost interest, and the debates were finally dropped in the August, 1757, issue.[23]

The Triweekly Press

By 1758 the monthly magazines had passed from the scene as purveyors of political and governmental information. Their place was taken by the host of new triweekly newspapers which arose to compete with both the monthlies and the older daily and triweekly journals such as the *Whitehall Evening Post,* the *General Evening Post* and the *London Evening Post.* The birth of these new competitors between 1757 and 1770 can be traced to the popular interest in the war with France, and, secondly, to an oversight in the drafting of the Stamp tax of 1757. Publishers discovered a loophole in the revenue act whereby a publication of six or more pages was liable to a tax of only three shillings *per edition,*[24] instead of

---

[19] In the June, 1752, edition Cave attempted with the greatest circumspection to revive the publication of speeches by publishing a letter to the editor in which a summary of some of the speeches was included. Cave died in 1754.

[20] Vol. 16, p. 353, August, 1747.

[21] Commons Journal, XXVI, 754 (10 April 1753).

[22] The phrase "in the character of ———" was dropped in the January, 1748, issue. Vol. 17, p. 105.

[23] Vol. 26, pp. 377-80.

[24] See above, Chapter 15, p. 321.

one or one-half penny per copy. *Lloyd's Evening Post and British Chronicle* began publication in 1757 followed by the *London Chronicle or Universal Evening Post* (1757), the *Universal Chronicle* (1758), the *Public Advertiser* (1758), the *Public Ledger* (1759), *St. James Chronicle or British Evening Post* (1761), the *Middlesex Journal or Chronicle of Liberty* (1769), and the *London Packet* (1770). As the appetite for news increased and production methods improved, new dailies made their appearance, the *Morning Chronicle* and *London Advertiser* in 1769 and the *Morning Post* and *Daily Advertiser* in 1772. By the time the leak in the Stamp tax was stopped in 1773 the new newspapers were well established and most of them were able to survive the tax of two pennies for six pages.

The competition between the new triweekly and daily journals for economic survival was keen, and sooner or later the publishers were impelled to attempt to outdo each other by reporting the proceedings of Parliament for an avid readership. Among the first to test the temper of Parliament were *The Public Advertiser, The London Chronicle, The Daily Adventurer,* and *The Gazetteer.* The very same day that their issues reached the streets of London (1 February 1760) with what they considered an innocuous item reporting the resolution of the House giving thanks to Edward Hawke for his victory over the French fleet, the Commons called the publishers to the bar, where they appeared and begged the pardon of the House. They were all released after a reprimand and payment of fees.[25] The order of 13 April 1738 was re-enacted as the current policy of the House.[26]

The House of Lords acted with equal dispatch against the *Public Advertiser,* published by Henry Sampson Woodfall, who later published the famous Junius letters. The House of Lords ordered the publisher to explain an item in the 20 May 1765 issue of his journal. Woodfall's testimony illustrates the contemporary pirating among the rival journals of the day. He testified that he copied the offending paragraph from the *St. James Chronicle.* He was fined £100. The publisher of the *Chronicle* explained to the Lords two days later that he had copied the item from the *Gazetteer and New Daily Advertiser.* He was also fined £100, but before he

[25] Commons Journal, XXVIII, 741, 745.
[26] *Ibid.*, XXIX, 206-7.

left the House it was pointed out that the same issue of his news-paper contained another item reflecting on "a Member of this House," and being before the bar he was fined an additional £100. The next day the printer of the *Gazetteer,* Charles Say, took his turn at the bar. In spite of his plea that he had a family of six children he was given the same fine as his predecessors.[27]

However active and even violent the competition between the triweekly journals, they were bound together by their common opposition to the restrictions of Parliament. Whichever way the publishers turned they found themselves facing citations for violating the rules against Parliamentary reporting or prosecutions for seditious libel by the courts. Incidents like the prosecution of Henry Baldwin, publisher of the *St. James Chronicle,* before the Lords in 1768 for publishing a letter written by John Wilkes, and the refusal of William Edmunds, printer of the *Middlesex Journal,* to reveal the author of the offending item on the ground that he had pledged secrecy only served to unite the newspaper publishers and to set the scene for a common front against Parliamentary authority.[28]

The Final Contest

By the spring of 1771 the time was ripe for a showdown. The House of Commons had lost touch with the country. The London publishers were united against its arbitrary authority. The city government in London was in the hands of the Parliamentary opposition, and such intrepid radicals as John Wilkes, alderman, and Brass Crosby, lord mayor, were ready for the fray. The printers backed by support from the city and its representatives in the House of Commons dropped all pretense of complying with restrictive resolutions of the House of Commons. Reports of Parliamentary news appeared in the triweekly newspapers more frequently and more fully than ever before, and more urgent and imperious became the knocking at the closed doors of Parliament by journalists who wanted admission as spectators and notetakers. On 5 February 1771 the House of Commons reaffirmed its ancient rule against reporting its proceedings and threatened prosecution against all

---

[27] Lords Journal, XXXI, 210, 212, 214, 215 (May, 1765).

[28] *Ibid.,* XXXII, 205, 208, 212, 425, 429, 570, 575. Edmunds persisted in refusing to divulge the author's name and was fined £100 and sentenced to a month's imprisonment at Newgate. *Ibid., p.* 575.

offenders.[29] The news of this action was duly reported in the tri-weekly press.

The incident which precipitated the bitter contest was engineered by John Wilkes. The following appeared in the *Middlesex Journal* (7 February 1771):

> It was reported that a scheme was at last hit upon by the Ministry to prevent the public being informed of their iniquity; accordingly on Tuesday last little Cocking George Onslow made a motion, "That the order against printing the Debates should be ready, and entered on the minutes of the day."
>
> Mr. Charles Turner opposed the motion with great spirit; he said, that not only the debates ought to be published but a list of the divisions likewise; and he affirmed that no man would object to it it unless he was ashamed of the vote he gave.
>
> Mr. Edmund Burke supported Mr. Turner's opinion; he said, that so far from its being proper to conceal their debates, he wished they would follow the ancient rule, which was to record them in the Journals.

This newspaper report and others like it in other journals of the same week point to the arrival of the political journalist. Boyer and his successors were both historians and tradesmen in information seeking to make money by the sale of information. The publishers of the triweekly newspapers of the 1770's were also tradesmen interested in profits, not only by purveying information but by serving it up "seasoned with opinions and prejudices in the interest of a political cause." No wonder Parliament was aroused. It was serious enough to have the secrecy of their proceedings violated and journalists printing what was said for the public to read, more frequently misrepresenting than representing, but here was a new threat—the proceedings presented from a point of view with the direct objective of influencing the votes of the members of the ancient assembly.

Although Parliament was under the domination of the court party, a sizable minority mostly from the city of London was eager for a contest with the government supporters. Backed by the people of the metropolis, these members had been fired by the recent Middlesex affair and were in a mood to defy openly the king's ministers in what they conceived to be the interests of their city constituents.

George Onslow, the member referred to in the *Middlesex*

[29] Commons Journal, XXXIII, 142 (5 February 1771).

Journal of February 7 as "little Cocking George," arose to defend
the privileges of the House of Commons as well as his own immunity from criticism.[30] He moved that the House immediately
proceed against the publishers of the offensive newspaper item.
John Wheble and R. Thompson, printers, were charged with publishing the debates contrary to order and were given notice to appear before the House. The printers sought advice from their London representatives and it would appear from subsequent events
that a defense strategy was devised with the connivance of the
Lord Mayor Brass Crosby and the two city magistrates and aldermen, John Wilkes and Richard Oliver. Ever since he had been refused his seat in Parliament, Wilkes was itching for a contest with
the government, and he seized on the order against the printers
as an opportunity to harass his old enemies. The printers were advised to ignore the summons which had been left at their homes
by the Serjeant at Arms. Upon their failure to appear the House
requested the king to issue a proclamation for their arrest, offering
a reward of fifty pounds. To add to the explosiveness of the situation, Onslow discovered that six other newspaper printers had been
guilty of the same offense, and it was moved after an extensive debate to proceed against them also.[31] The members from London
used all the tactics of Parliamentary procedure in an attempt to
defeat the motion. Its passage served to tighten the ranks of the
city printers and publishers in their opposition to the restrictions
on reporting the debates.

Following the tactics laid out by Wilkes, Wheble permitted
himself to be arrested by one of his workmen and appeared before
the city magistrate asking for his discharge. With judicial solemnity
the Alderman granted the request and ruled that the workman-
printer should be prosecuted for assault and false imprisonment,
at the same time issuing him a certificate that he had produced

---

[30] The principal accounts of this affair are to be found in *Parliamentary
History* (London, 1806-20), XVII, 58-119, 186-214; Commons Journal,
XXXIII, 142-289, *passim;* Annual Register, 1771, *passim;* Michael MacDonagh,
The Reporters' Gallery (London: Hodder and Stoughton, 1913), Chap. XX-
XXX.

[31] The offending newspaper publishers cited were William Woodfall,
Morning Chronicle and London Advertiser; Henry Baldwin, *St. James Chroni-
cle or British Evening Post;* T. Evans, *The London Packet or New Evening
Post;* T. Wright, *Whitehall Evening Post;* S. Bladon, *The General Evening
Post;* J. Miller, *The London Evening Post.*

the captive specified in the proclamation and was entitled to the reward of fifty pounds. And to make certain that the government did not overlook any of these incidents, Wilkes wrote a letter to the Secretary of State detailing the steps taken and protesting the legality of the proclamation. Thompson, the other printer, following the same procedure before Alderman Oliver, was released, and his captor was given a certificate entitling him to the reward. The rewards, incidentally, were never paid.

In the meantime a messenger of the House had apprehended the printer of the *London Evening Post,* one of the six added to the list by Onslow, but by prearrangement a city constable who was nearby ordered the messenger to take his prisoner before the Lord Mayor. Wilkes and Oliver were hastily summoned to the Mansion House and with dignified demeanor they demanded to know by what authority a citizen of London was arrested within the jurisdiction of the magistrates. The deputy serjeant at arms of the House of Commons arrived to defend his messenger and pointed out that he acted with the authority of a warrant issued by the Speaker of the House. Is this warrant backed by an order of a city magistrate? asked the mayor. No, was the reply. Then, said the mayor, the warrant is illegal and the prisoner is discharged. The printer immediately turned about and charged the messenger with false arrest.

When the news of the affair reached Parliament, there were cries of indignation. The privileges of the House were being undermined. Two of the three magistrates, the Lord Mayor and Alderman Oliver, were pre-emptorily ordered to attend in their places. The mayor and the alderman appeared in the House on March 19 and defended their conduct by insisting that they, as officials of the city, were obligated under their oaths of office, to uphold the franchises of the city which exempted its citizens from any legal process except that served by its own officers. These franchises, it was pointed out, had been recognized by Act of Parliament. In spite of repeated orders from the House, Wilkes refused to appear except in the character of a duly elected member.

In answer the government supporters argued that the honor and dignity of the House was at stake, that it was disgraceful to the House to allow its messenger to be imprisoned while following out the orders of the House, that as a consequence the entire structure of the privileges of Parliament was at stake. After an acrid debate on whether the Lord Mayor should be allowed to be heard by counsel (which was decided in the negative), the city's clerk was ordered to attend with the minutes of the proceedings before the three magistrates. The House gave way to its irritation by ordering him to erase the record and as a final fillip resolved that there should be no further proceedings at law in the case. Most of the supporters of the printers and the three London magistrates rose from their seats during these proceedings and left the floor of the House in disgust.

With passions still inflamed the court group proceeded to resolve that both the Lord Mayor and Alderman Oliver were guilty of a breach of privilege of the House for releasing the printer and for detaining the messenger of the House. It must be recorded that some of the more moderate members attempted to ease the situation by urging the two men to submit, but both remained adamant in their contention that they were only upholding the liberties of the citizens of London. The order to commit them both to the Tower of London was passed opposed only by the small minority that remained in the chamber.

A mob of London citizens greeted the two magistrates whenever they passed to or from Westminster during these proceedings. The crowd which appeared on the day the two men were sentenced, as reported in the *Annual Register,* was "prodigious, and great irregularities were committed; several gentlemen were insulted in the grossest manner, and some in very high office narrowly escaped with their lives." After a formal commitment by a vote of 202 to 39 and as the two convicted members were about to be conveyed to the Tower, a crowd took the horses from the coach and drew the vehicle in triumph through the city and would have manhandled the jailors were it not for the intervention of the Lord Mayor. While imprisoned in the Tower, the two officials were lavishly entertained at the expense of the city government.

The third magistrate, Wilkes, whom the government was reluctant to touch, did not share in these festivities. He remained discreetly at home, but in the Commons the question was raised, was he above or beneath the law. Forced to act, the government advisers solved the difficulty by ordering him to appear before the

House on April 8 and then promptly adjourned for its Easter recess to convene again on April 9. Face was saved.

The government managers, with their orders flouted, their commands disobeyed, and their contemners made into heroes by the London populace, took advantage of the Easter recess to formulate plans to extricate themselves from their uncomfortable position. It was decided that there was no going back, and a Special Commission was solemnly appointed by ballot to produce a solution. The committee sat regularly for a month and finally on April 30 presented its report to an expectant House and to still a more expectant public. After a lengthy historical review of Parliamentary privileges, the report recommended that J. Miller, printer of the *London Evening Post,* should be taken into custody. As Edmund Burke pointed out to the House, the Select Committee's report reminded him of the story of the mice who held a consultation on what to do with the cat that tormented them. They voted that the cat should be tied up, but unfortunately neglected to state how this should be accomplished. The report was adopted, Miller was not arrested, the messenger of the House was not prosecuted, and the city officials were released from the Tower at the end of the session when Parliament's authority normally terminated. Complete reports of these proceedings were carried in the London dailies and triweeklies. No move was made to prosecute the publishers, nor was the rule against reporting debates officially rescinded.

The joint victory of the newspaper publishers and the London magistrates was far from complete. The sanctity of the privileges of the House of Commons was preserved, but the House was never again to act in the same arbitrary way to defeat the right of the people to know what was taking place in the highest legislative body of the land. Not that this right was either openly or by indirection recognized. The Commons in 1771 yielded only because it felt it was more important to maintain its hereditary rights in theory than to put them to the test by force against a popularly supported and unified group of newspaper publishers. Secrecy of debate was still enjoined; the power to enforce such secrecy still existed but ceased to be exercised. For many years to come, offenses by newspapers were cited before the House but from now on the charge was not for *reporting* speeches but for *misrepresenting* them or for libelous attacks on the reputations of individual members.

William (Memory) Woodfall, editor of the *Morning Chronicle*, became famous for his remarkable ability to reproduce the speeches delivered in the House from memory. He "covered" most of the sessions of the Parliament which opened 22 January 1772. J. Miller, in his triweekly *London Evening Post,* gave a running report of the votes. Matters in which the community at large are so much interested, he said, should in their circulation be free as the air we breathe.

Even the House of Lords yielded its time-honored exclusiveness and secrecy. In 1775 the upper house almost precipitated a contest with the publisher of the *Public Ledger,* who like his fellow printers of 1771 was coached in his strategy by John Wilkes. The Lords wisely decided to let the matter drop rather than engage in a contest with the combined forces of Wilkes and the city newspapers. Like the Commons, the Lords confined themselves in the future to instances where the report was a misrepresentation or an imputation on the character of a member.[32]

Both Houses of Parliament retained an ancient and effective weapon against the newspaper reporters. The journalists could be cleared from either House as "strangers" on the motion of a member. No reporters were permitted to sit in the gallery in the early days of Parliament of 1772. In 1775 most of the famous debates on the relations with the American colonies were closed to reporters [33] under the Standing Orders. Fox, who sided with the majority in the affair of 1771, now argued vehemently in favor of admission of the press to the galleries on the ground that the British public had a constitutional right to know what was taking place in Parliament.[34] Gradually it became apparent even to the government supporters that the most effective way to prevent misrepresentation was to throw open the doors to all reporters, and in subsequent sessions orders to clear the gallery of strangers were rare. The new proprietor of *The Morning Chronicle,* James Perry, introduced a relay of reporters and in 1789 was able to give his readers a running account of the previous evening's session in his morning issue.

---

[32] Lords Journal, XXXIII, 198, 200; XXXIV, 324, 330, 331; XXXV, 575, 685, 692, 696.

[33] *Parliamentary History,* XVIII, 540.

[34] *Ibid.,* p. 1325.

The old orders prohibiting the report of debates were never officially wiped from the books. During the nineteenth century, however, the right of reporters to attend and report the sessions received increasing acceptance, beginning with the recognition of their occupancy of the back row in the strangers' gallery in 1803, the erection of a press gallery in 1831, and culminating in 1868 in the judicial recognition of the immunity of the newspaper publishers from libel appearing in the account of the proceedings.[35]

The Parliament that sat in 1771 never fully recognized the constitutional changes which it was accepting when it dropped its charges against J. Miller, publisher of the *London Post*. Not only was the ancient system shattered, but a new democratic movement was tacitly recognized in which the public as well as the members had an interest. Parliament was gradually opened to public view which in turn resulted in still more fundamental changes in the representative system. The bright light of publicity, the open and often irrational criticism of newspaper editors, the immediate and recurrent pressure of public groups—all served to accelerate the change from an independent to a responsible representative assembly. The freedom of the press to report to the public the actions and opinions of its representatives was a significant step toward a wider and more direct democracy.

[35] Wason *vs.* Walter, 4 L. R. Q. B. 73.

CHAPTER 18

Responsibility Under Law

In the seventeenth century the government's system for the control of the press was based upon "licensing," first under the royal prerogative and later under acts of Parliament, but by the opening of the eighteenth century this keystone of the earlier system had been found to be too cumbersome, too unwieldy, and too inefficient, and was eventually supplanted as the century progressed by criminal prosecutions under law, particularly under the law of seditious libel. Supplemented by control through taxation, by ministerial subsidization, and by strict regulation of Parliamentary reporting, criminal and Parliamentary prosecutions constituted the principal weapon of the government throughout the century.

The eighteenth century, the age of Enlightenment, the age of the "Philosophes," the age of "natural rights" and of "reason," witnessed the gradual but steady destruction of the traditional forms of control inherited from Tudor and Stuart times. In England in the second quarter of the century, the political theories of John Locke growing out of the Revolution of 1688 eventually penetrated the deeply ingrained attitude of the government toward the press, and for the first time in English history the phrase "freedom of the press" acquired a respectable as well as a concrete meaning. Freedom of the press in the first half of the eighteenth century meant freedom from licensing and nothing more. On the positive side, it meant that the press was responsible for the abuse of its freedom under the law, albeit a law derived in many cases from questionable sources. By the end of the century, however, most of the more obnoxious elements of this law were removed either by legislative enactment or by judicial construction. An account of the recognition and removal of these obstructions to free discussion is the subject of this chapter.[1]

The criminal law of the eighteenth century to which the press was subject can conveniently be discussed under four headings: (1) prosecutions for treason, (2) Parliamentary prosecutions, (3) general warrants, and (4) seditious libel. At the opening of the eighteenth century all four presented serious obstacles to free discussion through the press, but by the end of the century all were drastically curtailed as instruments of suppression.

Treason

As has been pointed out,[2] prosecutions of printers and publishers under the law of treason have been rare in English history. Only two printers were executed for treason in the entire seventeenth century, and only one in the eighteenth. On the other hand, convictions for seditious libel ran into the hundreds in both centuries. The various reasons for the failure of the government to make use of the rigorous death penalty under the law of treason in its continuing battle against subversive publications are not too clear, but it would appear that among such reasons were the relatively inflexible provisions of the original statute of treasons, the heavy penalty as contrasted in many cases with the ineffectiveness of the publication, and the ability of the government to maintain control through other more flexible means. The problem in the case of treason is to weigh the probable effects of the publication charged

---

[1] Bibliographic note: Excellent discussions of the problems and events covered in this chapter are to be found in W. S. Holdsworth's *History of English Law* (Boston: Little, Brown, 1924), X, 658-96; J. F. Stephen, *History of the Criminal Law of England* (London, 1883), II, 241-396; T. E. May, *Constitutional History of England* (1912 ed.), II, 1-59, 238-419; Edward Porritt, *The Unreformed House of Commons* (Cambridge: University press, 1903), I, 584-96. Especially valuable for this period is the study by Laurence Hanson, *Government and the Press, 1695-1763* (London: Oxford University press, 1936).

[2] See Chapter 13 for an account of treason in the seventeenth century.

against the accused in advance of the realization of those effects. Where the publication has not been successful in achieving its objective, the penalty of treason seems harsh and unwarranted; where the effects have been achieved, it is either too late to prosecute, or more direct participants in the treason than the publisher usually are available. A further handicap in the use of this remedy during the eighteenth century was the Act of William III [3] which required definite and precise standards of proof of overt acts before conviction.

Very little change in the substantive rules of treason as applied to publications was made during the eighteenth century. At the close of the seventeenth century it had been decided that neither spoken words nor unpublished written or printed words constituted treason in themselves. However, both written or printed words when published did constitute an overt act which could support a conviction for treason under the theory of constructive treason as laid down by Chief Justice Holt.[4] This construction made it unnecessary to enact special statutes on treason to cover the publication of subversive material. Nevertheless, early in the century an Act of Parliament, 6 Anne, cap. 7 (1707), made it treason to maintain by printing or writing that the Pretender or his offspring had a legitimate title to the crown of England. In spite of the uneasiness existing during the reign of the first Hanoverian king, this statute appears to have had little use. Although there was considerable literature produced supporting the title of the descendants of James II to the crown, most of it was printed on the continent and smuggled into England. In any event the main culprits were not the writers and printers but the organizers and the would-be assassins.

The only prosecution recorded under the statute was that of the impecunious eighteen-year-old printer's apprentice, John Mathews, who in 1719 was indicted for printing a pamphlet, *Ex ore tuo te judico, Vox Populi Vox Dei,* supporting the claims of the Pretender (James III) to the crown.[5] It appears from the scanty data on this young man that he had been in trouble with the

---

[3] 7 and 8 William III, c. 3.

[4] Charnock's Case, 2 Salk. 631 (1696).

[5] 15 State Trials, p. 1323.

authorities on previous occasions for printing seditious material on his mother's press. To the shame of the printing trade, no adequate defense was provided for the boy such as was advanced for the printer, William Anderton, in 1693. John Mathews was hanged at Tyburn 6 November 1720, aged nineteen, the only conviction for treason for publishing seditious material in the eighteenth century.[6]

Not until the end of the century did the government again turn to the law of treason in its attempt to regulate subversive publications. Alarmed by the revolutionary developments across the channel in France and fearful that the same or similar excesses might occur in the British Isles, the government took steps to punish the leaders of the republican movement. The common-law rules of seditious libel which had proved so effective earlier in the century were by this time rendered useless for government purposes by the Fox Libel Act (1792).[7] Arrangements were made to prosecute the principal officers of the Constitutional and London Corresponding Societies for high treason. These organizations had been advocating universal suffrage and annual Parliaments and were carrying on a campaign through their branch groups and through a proposed convention for achieving these objectives. The indictment charged the leaders under the doctrine of constructive treason with preparing for the overthrow of the king and the establishment of a republic. Although twelve men were indicted, the government dropped all prosecutions after juries acquitted both Thomas Hardy [8] and John Horne Tooke.[9] These trials did not overrule the doctrine of constructive treason,[10] but they indicated the difficulty of getting convictions from juries under such nebulous constructions. The next

---

[6] Two convictions for treason, that of Christopher Layer in 1722 and that of Thomas Deacon in 1746, appear to be based at least partially on published words. In the first case, the indictment charged that Layer published a seditious advertisement urging the people to take up arms and to levy war, but it should be pointed out that this publication was only a part of the indictment and was one of several overt acts charged against the accused. (16 State Trials, p. 94; 8 Mod. 82) In the second case, the accused, Thomas Deacon, was charged with compelling a printer to produce a paper urging the people to enlist in the rebellion. Again, as in that of Layer, this was one of several connected overt acts which formed the basis of the conviction. (18 State Trials, p. 366).

[7] 32 Geo. III, c. 60.

[8] 24 State Trials, p. 199.

[9] 25 State Trials, p. 1.

[10] Holdsworth, op. cit., VIII, 318.

year (1795) Parliament stepped in to make more concrete and authoritative the judicial constructions of the late seventeenth- and early eighteenth-century judges.[11] It is worthy of note that in spite of the judicial acceptance of the doctrine of constructive treason, this branch of the criminal law was seldom made the basis for the regulation of the press in the eighteenth century.

Prosecutions in Parliament

A continuing restraint on the press throughout the century was the fear of a citation before either the House of Lords or the House of Commons for an offensive publication. From the 1730's on when juries began to rebel in seditious libel cases, the two Houses of Parliament were the principal deterrents to free and open discussion of political questions through their power to punish a printer for what today would be considered harmless discussions of public issues. Perhaps the lack of attention by historians to the part played by Parliament in controlling the press is due to the fact that the prosecutions were handled with dispatch and without undue publicity and that the authority to punish was relinquished, or rather relaxed, without the dramatic and highly publicized contests which characterized the court trials for seditious libel. All in all, Parliament seems to have exerted almost as great a pressure on printers and publishers in the eighteenth century as did the common-law courts.

Both Houses of Parliament claimed the authority to summon, interrogate, and punish individuals who were charged with the dissemination of writings, which by various devices of logic were considered to be breaches of the privilege of Parliament. The exercise of such powers was not, as we have seen,[12] uncommon in the seventeenth century and was carried on throughout most of the eighteenth century by both Houses. The restrictions by Parliament extended to almost as wide a range of published materials as was covered by seditious libel and were, it would appear, more expeditiously enforced than the common-law rules.

The legal basis of the procedure in Parliament was the inherent right of the House to punish for infringement of its privileges. Even the common-law courts, which were gradually pre-

---

[11] 36 Geo. III c. 7.

[12] See above, pp. 112-16, 179-91, 275-79.

empting the judicial field, recognized the right of Parliament to determine cases concerned with breach of privilege and to assess punishment. The common law contended that, although violations of privilege were properly tried before Parliament, the question of whether a privilege existed was a question of law for the courts,[13] but this claim was never fully accepted by the House of Commons or by the legal profession until the nineteenth century.[14]

What types of publications were considered to be breaches of privilege and therefore punishable by Parliament? We have seen that both Houses scrupulously restricted the reporting of their sessions during the early part of the century.[15] In addition to these unauthorized reports, the following classes of writings were considered to be punishable by action of the House: (1) publications in the nature of a personal libel on a member; (2) reflections on the House or on Parliament in general; (3) reflections on the government including aspersions on the king and his ministers; (4) certain types of obscenity and blasphemy. Both Houses imposed their punishments on writers as well as on printers, publishers, and procurers, or on any combination of persons concerned in producing the offensive publication, both Houses being careful, however, not to punish a member of the other House. When no author's name appeared on the printed matter, the printer was summoned to appear, and if he revealed the author he was frequently released, although occasionally he was sentenced along with the author and publisher.

The House of Lords was particularly zealous in protecting the personal reputation of its members. The largest single class of punishable writings in this House in the eighteenth century, as revealed by the *Journals,* was libels on members. These cases were ordinarily raised by the member defamed who called the attention of the House to the breach of privilege. An example is the prosecution for a libel on the Earl of Hertford in the *London Evening Post* and in the *London Gazetteer* (1764). Meres, the printer of the *Post,* and Say, of the *Gazetteer* (who admitted he copied it from the

[13] Rex *vs.* Knollys, 1 Ld. Raym 10 (1695); Ashby *vs.* White, 14 State Trials (1704).

[14] Holdsworth, *op. cit.,* X, 539.

[15] See above, pp. 286-87.

Post), were both fined £100.[16] Although the proceeding in such a case was not conducted with all the forms of a judicial hearing, the presence of the chancellor and justices in the Lords kept that body from disregarding all forms of a regular trial. In at least one instance a complaint of a libel on a Lord resulted in a verdict in favor of the author.[17]

The House of Commons, whose judicial functions began to decline in the middle ages and had almost disappeared by the eighteenth century, insisted, like the Lords, on its right to punish breaches of its privileges and to proceed against a writer or printer for reflections on one or more of its members.[18] Punishment for such libels, however, was practically abandoned by the Commons in the eighteenth century.

Disparaging comments on the proceedings of Parliament (as distinct from news accounts of such proceedings which are discussed in Chapter 17) were considered to be a breach of privilege in both Houses and therefore punishable by summary action. However, during the reigns of the first two Georges there were few such prosecutions in this category. An instance is the complaint in 1724 by the Lords, who considered themselves libeled in a book, *A New Description of England and Wales with the Adjacent Islands,* published by a syndicate of booksellers. All were called before the bar and exculpated themselves by revealing the author as David Jones and the printer as James Bettenham. A committee searched the precedents of the House and produced a report of seventeenth-century instances of actions "to vindicate the honour of the House," citing punishments of from £500 to £1,000. The publishers and the printer were kept in custody while a search went on for the missing author. A week later Mrs. Jones appeared to testify that her husband was beyond the call of the House, having died six weeks previously. Publishers and printers were reprimanded and released after paying fees.[19]

In the Commons, both members as well as nonmembers were brought to the bar for publications which were considered to be an affront to the dignity, or a reflection on the proceedings, of the

---

[16] Lords Journal, XXX, 508, 511 (15 March 1764).

[17] *Ibid.,* XXIII, 399, 406, 407 (21 April 1729).

[18] See Commons Journal, XIII, 230 (27 February 1699-1700).

[19] Lords Journal, XXII, 349, 350-51, 355, 359, 360, 362, 387, 390.

House. The largest number of offenders were by far the news-paper printers and publishers. Both John Tutchin of the *Observator*,[20] and Samuel Buckley of the *Courant*,[21] the first daily news-paper, were cited before the Commons for uncomplimentary references to its activities. The Commons, however, unlike the Lords felt it necessary to confirm its right to commit for publications by adopting (1701) a set of rules:

> Resolved: (1) That it is the opinion of this Committee, that to assert, that the House of Commons is not the only Representative of the Commons of England, tends to the subversion of the Rights and Privileges of the House of Commons, and the fundamental Constitution of the Government of this Kingdom.

> (2) That it is the opinion of this Committee, that to assert the House of Commons have not the power of commitment, but of their own members, tends to the subversion of the Constitution of the House of Commons.

> (3) That it is the opinion of this Committee, that to print, or publish any Books or Libels, reflecting upon the Proceedings of the House of Commons, or any member thereof, for, or relating to, his service therein, is a high violation of the Rights and Privileges of this House of Commons.[22]

Citations before the Commons for violation of the above rules were infrequent during the early eighteenth century except for a spurt of activity following the abortive uprising of 1745, but by 1770 when a complacent and corrupted House became one of the instruments employed by George III to re-establish the powers of the crown, the prosecutions for libels of the House became more frequent. In 1774 the House proceeded against Henry S. Woodfall, publisher of the *Public Advertiser*, in which the offensive and seditious letters of Junius appeared. The proceedings in this case indicate the confusion which prevailed both in and out of Parliament during these exciting days.[23] Woodfall named the Reverend John Horne (later Tooke) as the author. At the bar the clergyman, turned lawyer, demanded evidence of his authorship. It was pointed out that the evidence presented by Woodfall could not be accepted

---

[20] Commons Journal, XIV, 336-37, 340 (14 February 1704).

[21] *Ibid.*, XVII, 175, 182 (8 April 1712).

[22] *Ibid.*, XIII, 767 (26 February, 1701).

[23] *Ibid.*, XXXIV, 452-53, 456, 464-65, 472, 492 (February 7-24, 1774).
See also *Parliamentary History of England* (London, 1806-20), XVII, 1003-50.

since he was already branded as the guilty publisher and therefore incapable of testifying. Unable to produce other witnesses, the Commons, to the satisfaction of the opposition, was forced to release Horne, but turning to the unsuspecting printer, kept him in prison from 14 February 1774 to March 2 and assessed fees amounting to £72.[24]

Parliament's authority to control public discussions reached its apex in its contention that it was a breach of privilege to publish unfavorable comments on the central government and its administration. A reflection on the king was, of course, considered to be a reflection on the government. There appears to be little difference in the eighteenth century between Parliament's concept of a "reflection on the government" and the common-law definition of seditious libel. In both Houses, this type of publication brought more persons, both members and nonmembers, to the bar than any of the other categories heretofore mentioned.

The peers being, perhaps, more circumspect in their language, there is no record of a prosecution in the House of Lords of a member for writing or circulating seditious comments on the government. In the House of Commons, on the other hand, both Richard Steele (1713-14) and John Wilkes (1769) were expelled for subversive political writings. Wilkes, who had already been convicted for seditious libel in the courts (*North Briton,* No. 45)[25] and who was currently serving his sentence for that crime, was cited in the Commons as being responsible for the publication of an offensive item in the *St. James Chronicle* (December 8-10, 1768). The item consisted of a letter supposedly written by Lord Weymouth, secretary of state, in which the peer urged the use of the militia in the recent St. George's Field riots with a pointed introduction by Wilkes holding Lord Weymouth responsible for the resulting bloodshed. The House of Lords took up the matter of a libel on one of its members on 13 December 1768, but upon discovering that Wilkes, still a member of the House of Commons, was the author, decided to proceed cautiously and to confer with the lower house.[26] The Commons impetuously took the lead and proceeded against its

---

[24] An itemized account of these fees is published in the Appendix to Vol. 1 of John Wade's edition of *The Letters of Junius* (London, 1868).

[25] See below, pp. 384-85.

[26] Lords Journal, XXXII, 205, 208, 212.

member for a breach of privilege. That the offensive publication
was also a libel on a member of the Lords did not deter the lower
house from voting the publication a libel on the government and
expelling the author.[27]

By far the largest number of prosecutions by the House of
Commons for published criticisms of the goverenment were directed
against nonmembers, principally newspaper publishers. Early in the
century the House adopted the time-honored as well as time-con-
suming procedure of appointing a committee to investigate libels
on the government. The publishers of the *Evening Post* (E. Barrington) [28] and of the *Weekly Journal* (Mist) [29] were turned up by one
of these committees and after several delays were imprisoned and
finally discharged after paying fees. In 1740 the publisher of the
Daily Post, John Meres (Meere), suffered the same penalty.[30]
Where neither the author nor the publisher of a libelous pamphlet
could be ferreted out, the paper was burned by the common hangman in public display,[31] a practice inherited from the previous
century and continued until the time of the American Revolution.
Punishment by the Commons was limited to imprisonment during
the session of Parliament and payment of customary fees, whereas
the Lords could theoretically imprison an offender indefinitely as
well as fine him a substantial sum. By 1770 either because of the
limitations on the punishment or because of a growing deference
to the jurisdiction of the criminal courts, the House of Commons
adopted the practice of petitioning the king to order a prosecution
of the offending publishers before the common law courts.[32] Among
the last of such libels considered by the Commons during this
period were the pamphlets, *The Present Crisis with Respect to*

[27] Commons Journal, XXXII, 108-9, 113, 175-76, 178-79. This, according
to the Commons Journal, was the second occasion on which Wilkes was
formally expelled. He was expelled for publishing the *North Briton* in 1764.
In the case of the Middlesex elections he was four times denied a seat but was
not expelled.

[28] *Ibid.*, XVIII, 194-95, 200, 300, 458, 466, 468. These proceedings extended over more than a year, June, 1715, to July, 1716.

[29] *Ibid.*, XIX, 562-63, 564, 565, 567 (27 May–3 June 1721).

[30] *Ibid.*, XXIII, 545, 546-47, 560-61, 563, 643, 702.

[31] *Ibid.*, XXIX, 874-75 (24 February 1764).

[32] See order of the attorney general to proceed against Woodfall, 16 February 1774. *Ibid.*, XXXIV, 464. Also 14 December 1795, *Ibid.*, LI, 231-32.

America and *Crisis No. 3*, which were voted as scandalous libels on the king and which, with the concurrence of the House of Lords, were publicly burned on 7 March 1775.[33] Toward the end of the century Parliament became engrossed in its legislative functions and, without resistance or publicity, quietly abdicated its functions as a prosecutor and judge of seditious libels in favor of the attorney general and common-law courts.[34] So quietly was the transition made that little notice has been given to the active control which Parliament exercised over the press through its authority to punish for breach of privilege.[35]

Secretaries' Warrants

A criminal prosecution for seditious libel, as has been pointed out, was the principal instrument of the government in its program for control of the press throughout most of the eighteenth century. The apprehension of offenders and the collection of evidence on which to base a prosecution were problems which were simplified by the use of what has been described as "general warrants." These warrants were issued by the secretary of state to the king's messengers directing them to arrest the "authors, printers, and publishers" of certain specified publications and at the same time to search and seize any papers which might be useful in the prosecution for seditious libel.

The following is an example of an eighteenth-century general warrant (preamble omitted):

These are, in His Majesty's Name, to authorize and require you, taking a Constable to your Assistance, to make strict and diligent Search for the Authors, Printers, and Publishers of a seditious and scandalous Weekly Paper, entituled The North Britain, beginning with No. 1 and ending with No. 25, printed by G. Kearsley in Ludgate Street; and Then, or any of Them, having found, to seize and apprehend, and to bring, together with Their Books and Papers, in Safe Custody, before me, to be examined concerning the Premises, and further dealt with according to Law; In the due Execution whereof all Mayors, Sheriffs, Justices of the Peace, Constables, and all other His Majesties Officers, Civil and

---

[33] *Ibid.*, XXXV, 158-59.

[34] The House refused to take any action on a pamphlet presented to it in 1792. *Ibid.*, XLVIII, 15.

[35] This power seems not to have been exercised in the early U.S. legislative assemblies.

Military, and Loving Subjects whom It may concern, are to be aiding
and assisting to you as there may be occasion. And for so doing This shall
by your Warrant, Given at St. James's the Eighteenth Day of November,
1762, in the Third Year of His Majesty's Reign.[36]

Under the authority of warrants similar to that set out above,
the king's messengers were able to arrest any person who was
suspected of having a hand in the publication of a seditious libel
and at the same time to search the homes and offices of suspected
persons and take possession of any incriminating papers which
might be found.

It was inevitable that those persons who possessed the temerity
to express criticism of the government should seek to avoid penalties
by concealing their authorship of offensive publications. The anonymous pamphlet, as well as newspaper, became common practice.
At the same time, there evolved the ethic that the printer or publisher would protect, as far as possible, the anonymity of the author
or sponsor. In several instances the printer would accept the sentence under seditious libel rather than reveal the name of the
author.

By the opening of the eighteenth century the power of arresting officers in ordinary cases of felony had been strictly circumscribed in the interest of the liberty of the subject. Warrants must
describe with certainty the person who was to be arrested.[37] Why,
then, were "general warrants" for the search and seizure of unnamed
persons permitted in cases of seditious libel? How many such warrants were issued in the eighteenth century it is impossible to say,
but it is apparent from the available records that they were employed whenever the authorities were unaware of the identities of
the culprits.

The origin of this practice can be traced back to the original
charter to the Stationers Company in 1557 by which wide powers
of search and seizure of illegal printing were granted to the officers
of the trade organization.[38] These wide powers were confirmed by
the Star Chamber decrees of 1586 and 1637 and were exercised
by the officers of the Company up to the time of the Restoration.

---

[36] Add. Mss. 22131, f. 31a, b. The warrant is signed by Lord Halifax,
secretary of state.

[37] Holdsworth, *op. cit.*, III, 599-604; *Ibid.*, X, 659.

[38] See below, pp. 82ff.

Under the terms of the Regulation of Printing Act of 1662, many of the powers formerly exercised by the Company were transferred to the office of secretary of state, among them the authority to make arrests and seize papers. The legal authority of the Surveyor of the Press, Roger L'Estrange, to make searches and arrests was based on this and succeeding acts of Parliament. When the office of Surveyor of the Press was abolished, the secretaries of state continued to issue warrants to their messengers to apprehend persons suspected of engaging in illegal printing. These warrants assumed various forms, frequently mentioning the name of the persons to be arrested and occasionally issued in the general form without names. It is obvious that the authority to issue a general warrant for the arrest of unnamed persons suspected of participating in the publication of libelous matter was extremely useful to the secretaries of state in carrying out the program of control of the press.

Since general warrants were illegal and unconstitutional in the apprehension of suspected persons in other types of felonies, it is surprising that no attempt was made earlier in the century to contest the legality of such warrants when applied to persons suspected of seditious libel. The question was finally raised in a series of court proceedings growing out of the publication of newspapers opposed to the policies of the early favorite of George III, Lord Bute. Operating behind the scenes was Lord Temple, leader of the principal opposition faction among the Whigs, and in the forefront was John Wilkes, whose services in behalf of Parliamentary reporting have already been described.[39]

The first publication to take the field against George III's Tory ministry was the weekly newspaper, *The Monitor*, edited by Arthur Beardmore, which had begun publication in 1755. To combat the attack, the government proceeded along two lines, the sponsorship of a newspaper to counteract the *Monitor*, and if that did not work, a prosecution for seditious libel. On 26 May 1762 the *Briton* entered the field on the side of the government with T. G. Smollett as editor and chief writer. Within a week the political tacticians of the Temple group launched a second opposition newspaper, the

---

[39] See above. Detailed account of the contest between the ministerial press and the opposition press is to be found in George Nobbe, *The North Briton* (New York, 1939) and L. B. Namier, *The Structure of Politics at the Accession of George III* (London: Macmillan, 1929).

North Briton. The identity of the editor and author, John Wilkes, was not revealed on the publication in order to avoid a prosecution for seditious libel. The following week saw the appearance of the second government paper, *The Auditor,* edited by Arthur Murphy, to assist the *Briton.* The newspaper battle was on and continued throughout the summer of 1762; the *Briton* and the *Auditor* versus the *North Briton* and the *Monitor.*

Apparently realizing that the government newspapers were unsuccessful in counteracting the opposition writers, the ministry prepared to unleash its second weapon, a prosecution for seditious libel. A warrant for the arrest of the editor of the *Monitor,* Arthur Beardmore, and for the seizure of his papers was issued by the secretary of state, Lord Halifax. A similar warrant was issued for the arrest of John Entick (Entinck), one of the writers for the *Monitor,* and for the seizure of his papers. Since both Beardmore and Entick were well known as the writers for the *Monitor* and had made no attempt to.keep their association with that newspaper secret, the warrants were made out in their names. The warrants were served, and both Beardmore and Entick were arrested on 11 November 1762. Entick's house was searched and his papers carried off. In the meantime, the attorney general had examined the contents of the *North Briton* and gave his opinion that nine of the issues were seditious. Both Beardmore and Entick were released from custody a week after their arrest, either because the government felt it did not have a sufficient basis for prosecution or because it decided to go after bigger and more important game, the authors of the *North Briton.* On the basis of the attorney general's opinion, Lord Halifax, secretary of state, issued on November 18 a general warrant for the arrest of the authors and publishers of the *North Briton.* This warrant, however, was never served.

Parliament reassembled on November 25 and both the *Monitor* and the *North Briton* continued to irritate the king's favorite, Lord Bute. With the end of the year 1762, the *Monitor* suspended and the anonymous *North Briton* continued to fight alone. No attempt was made to serve the November warrant against its authors.

The new session of Parliament opened on 19 April 1763. Lord Bute had already resigned as first lord of the treasury. With Bute gone, the sponsors of the *North Briton* took counsel to consider whether they should continue the contest with the crown and its ministers. It was decided that George Grenville, brother of Temple, who replaced Bute, was still a tool of the king and had deserted the Whig principles, and April 23, No. 45 of the *North Briton* appeared on the streets of London with a pointed criticism of the king's speech at the opening of Parliament earlier in the week.

The irate king conferred with his Council, and on April 26 a new general warrant was issued by Halifax calling for the arrest of the "authors and printers" of the *North Briton*. Within three days some forty-eight arrests were made under the authority of the warrant. The first to be taken into custody was Dryden Leach, who had printed one of the earlier numbers of the newspaper. Next, George Kearsley, publisher of the paper, and several of his servants were arrested. When questioned by the messengers, he named Richard Balfe as the printer of No. 45 and John Wilkes as author. Balfe and his workmen were arrested the same day. On the basis of information obtained from Kearsley and Balfe, the government proceeded to arrest Wilkes and to seize his papers in spite of the fact that he was at the time a duly elected member of Parliament. Wilkes and his friends were prepared for the contest and immediately sued out a writ of habeas corpus, and at a hearing held before Chief Justice Pratt (later Lord Camden) on May 6, the author was ordered released on the ground that he was protected by his Parliamentary privilege.

Within a month suits were brought by various of the forty-eight persons taken up under the general warrant to collect damages for unlawful arrest and search and seizure of papers. The first case was brought by Huckwell, one of Leach's printers, and he was awarded £300 for false arrest. The next day (7 July 1763) Balfe and twelve of his compositors recovered £200 each. However, the principal case was brought by Wilkes himself in December, and he was given £1,000 damages.[40] Next Leach, the early printer of the *North Briton*, collected £300.[41] Beardmore, editor, and Entick, writer, for the *Monitor*, were also given £1,000.[42] The final suit was brought by Wilkes against Lord Halifax five years later (1769) in

---

[40] Wilkes *vs.* Wood, 19 State Trials, p. 1153. The House of Commons passed a resolution condemning the general warrants on 17 February 1764 by a vote of 232 to 218. Commons Journal, XXIX, 846.

[41] Leach *vs.* Money *et al.*, 19 State Trials, p. 1001.

[42] Entick *vs.* Carrington, *Ibid.*, p. 1029.

which the intrepid author of No. 45 recovered £ 4,000.[43] It has
been estimated that the total cost of these suits to the government
amounted to more than £ 100,000.[44]

Three questions were raised in these cases, (1) did the secretary of state have power to issue a general warrant, (2) did he have
authority to issue any kind of warrant, and (3) did he have authority to order search and seizure of papers. The answers to these
questions were finally given in two principal cases, Leach vs. Money
and Entick vs. Carrington. The first question, the validity of the general warrant, was decided by Lord Mansfield in the case of Leach vs.
Money. The case was argued twice. After the first argument, Lord
Mansfield and the entire court made a clear ruling that such warrants, even in the case of seditious libel, were illegal. However, on
the second argument, the judges avoided the main issue by ruling
that since Leach was not the author, printer, or publisher of the
North Briton, No. 45, he was outside the scope of the warrant, and
therefore entitled to damages for false arrest.

The case which finally determined the second and third issues
was Entick vs. Carrington [45] decided by Lord Camden (8 November 1765). Counsel for the crown justified the powers of the secretary to issue a warrant in the case of seditious libel on four
grounds: (1) that the secretary as a privy councillor had authority
to issue warrants, (2) that as a justice of the peace, he also had
such powers, (3) that he had in long-continued practice exercised
this power which was recognized by the courts, and, (4) that such
a power was necessary for the safety of the state. Lord Camden
effectively disposed of all these arguments in a brilliant opinion.
He pointed out that individual members of the privy council had
authority to order arrests only in the case of high treason, and he
effectively demolished the argument that the secretary held the
powers of the justice of the peace. With historical accuracy, the
Chief Justice traced the development of the secretary's powers in
case of libel to the Licensing Acts and concluded that powers so
derived were contrary to the common law even though they had
been employed for more than one hundred years. In answer to

[43] Wilkes vs. Lord Halifax, Ibid., p. 1406.
[44] H. R. Fox Bourne, English Newspapers (London: Chatto & Windus,
1887), I, 172.
[45] 19 State Trials, p. 1029.

the final argument that the security of the state demanded that the secretary exercise such powers, Lord Camden pointed out that if such authority was necessary for the public welfare it must be set up by legislative enactment rather than by common law. Thus, a practice more than one hundred years old, a practice which brought terror into the lives of hundreds of printers and writers, was abolished. Sir William Holdsworth, historian of the English law, calls the decision by Lord Camden in Entick *vs.* Carrington, "a masterly performance—remarkable for the breadth and insight of its historical learning, and for its mastery of the principles of the common law." [46] It is also a masterly performance in delineating the principles of freedom of expression and of the press.

Wilkes was later prosecuted for the authorship of No. 45 on an information by the attorney general and was sentenced to fine and imprisonment. The House of Commons also expelled him for the same crime. However, as a result of the court decisions growing out of the arrests, particularly the decision of Lord Camden in Entick *vs.* Carrington, the last of the arbitrary powers of the executive derived from the Regulation of Printing Acts was destroyed.

Seditious Libel

The major contest between the government and the press in the eighteenth century arose over the procedural practices in the law of seditious libel. A prosecution for this common-law crime, the principles of which had been developed in the second half of the seventeenth century,[47] was the most useful single weapon available to the government in its conflict with recalcitrant printers and publishers. Although no attempt has been made to canvass the total number of such prosecutions during the eighteenth century,[48] they were sufficiently frequent to remind the temeritous printer of the risks he was taking in publishing unfavorable comments on the government or on its principal officers.

The law of criminal libel as inherited by the eighteenth cen-

---

[46] Holdsworth, *op. cit.*, X, 672.

[47] See above, pp. 269-75.

[48] Arthur Aspinall reports the claim that there were about seventy prosecutions during the first thirty-one years of the reign of George III. These include all types of libel, defamatory and obscene as well as seditious. *Politics and the Press* (London: Home and Van Thal, 1949), p. 41.

tury was basically the same as that developed during the reigns of Charles II and James II out of the remnants of Star Chamber precedents. Nowhere did the Revolution Settlement of 1688/9 or the famous Bill of Rights mention specifically freedom of speech or of the press, although several aspects of these freedoms were undoubtedly implicit in the Revolution principles. Fundamental human freedoms as recognized at the end of the seventeenth century included safeguards for life and property but did not extend to protection for the basic freedom of expression. However, toward the end of the eighteenth century, political theories had drastically revised the relationship between the governors and the governed, and the first fruit of this change was a demand for a wider liberty to discuss and criticize government men and measures. In no other field is this conflict between old and new theories so dramatic as in the field of seditious libel, and in no other arena were the contestants so evenly divided or the principles so ably defended.

The following discussion of the developments in seditious libel in the eighteenth century is divided roughly into four chronological parts; the first from 1704 to 1730 during which the legal principles of the previous century were carried forward; the second from 1730 to 1760 which witnessed the beginning of the revolt of juries and the failure of prosecutions; the third from 1760 to 1780 including the conflict between Lord Mansfield and both Wilkes and the "Junius" publishers; and the last from 1780 to 1792, the climax of the conflict with both Lord Mansfield and Lord Erskine on the stage and with Fox's Libel Act as the final curtain.

The technical rules for a criminal prosecution for seditious libel were laid down shortly after the opening of the century by Chief Justice Holt in Tutchin's case.[49] Although the charge to the jury was somewhat ambiguous in this case, there is no doubt as to what Lord Holt considered to be seditious. Whatever lessened the affection of the people for the government was criminal. The jury was to determine whether the person prosecuted was the publisher and whether the words as published conveyed the meaning contended for by the prosecution. The judge on the basis of the jury's verdict would, as a matter of law, determine both the

[49] 14 State Trials, p. 1095 (1704).

criminal intent (to be inferred from the words) and the illegality of the published language.[50]

Only occasionally was it necessary for the government to crack the whip of seditious libel to remind the printers and publishers of their proper function. An example is the prosecution of the persons responsible for the publication of Mist's *Weekly Journal*, No. 175, 24 August 1728. Mist had been punished previously by the House of Commons for reflections on the government,[51] but his newspaper was carried on somewhat surreptitiously by a group of associates. Informations were filed by the attorney general against John Clark, pressman, Robert Knell, compositor, and Joseph Carter and Richard Nutt, apprentices, for printing and published the offensive newspaper. Although the jury found them guilty of printing only, each was sentenced to the pillory and to prison, the printers for six months and the apprentices for one month.[52]

The leading case of this early period of the eighteenth century was the trial of Richard Franklin (Francklin) for publishing the *Craftsman*, a political paper edited by Nicholas Amhurst. The particular issue which brought on the prosecution was one in which the recent treaty of peace between France, Spain, and England was severely criticized. The contumacious Franklin had been frequently prosecuted and imprisoned for libel both by the courts and by Parliament. At this trial,[53] which attracted wide attention among the London printers and publishers, Franklin was ably defended by counsel, but Lord Chief Justice Raymond gave a clear and unequivocal instruction to the jury to find the printer guilty if in their opinion the evidence showed that he was the publisher and that the article complained of referred to the king and his ministers as charged in the information. The jury found the printer guilty of publishing the libel and he was fined £100, imprisoned one year, and ordered to provide security for his good behavior for seven years in the amount of £2,000.

Sometime during the second quarter of the century there arose

---

[50] Although Justice Holt's charge to the jury is inconsistent in parts, and not too clear in others, it would appear that he was attemping to apply the law as established by the courts in pre-Revolution days.

[51] See above, p. 373.

[52] The cases are reported in 1 Barn. K. B. 305, 306, and in a note in 17 State Trials, p. 667.

[53] *Ibid.*, p. 672 (1731/32).

a steady but as yet unimpressive demand for a wider freedom of expression, particularly in the public newspapers. The phrase, freedom of the press, became increasingly current and it is to be found mentioned in the courts as early as 1732 [54] and in the House of Commons in 1738.[55] The case which fired the country arose not in the hallowed shrine of English justice at Westminster but in a colonial court room in the remote province of New York. John Peter Zenger was charged with a libel on the royal governor, but an inspired appeal by the aged but able Philadelphia attorney, Andrew Hamilton, impelled the jury to bring in a verdict of not guilty in spite of the evidence that Zenger had published the offensive newspaper.[56] Although the Zenger case was never cited seriously in an English court of law, the publication of the trial in four editions in London within one year (1728) undoubtedly set an example for English juries to follow. A new edition of Milton's *Areopagitica,* the first since the original publication in 1644, accomplished what the original failed to achieve—it aroused public support for the philosophical principles of freedom of the mind.

A widely publicized revolt of a London jury against the judge's instructions occurred in 1752 in the prosecution of William Owen, a bookseller, for publishing a pamphlet accusing the House of Commons of acting unjustly in committing one Alexander Murray to prison for riotous conduct during an election. One of the counsel for the bookseller was Charles Pratt, the future Lord Camden, who in this case as later in Parliament contended that the jury should be permitted to pass on the guilty intent of the publisher. Chief Justice Lee followed the practice of his predecessors in his instructions to the jury, but in spite of the evidence that Owen had published the pamphlet, the London jury, following the example of the New York jury, brought in a verdict of not guilty.[57]

A conviction two years later (1754) was, as reported by Lord Mansfield, the first to be obtained from a London jury in twenty-seven years.[58] By mid-century it had become obvious that the tech-

---

[54] *Ibid.*

[55] April 13, *Parliamentary History,* X, 800.

[56] 17 State Trials, p. 675. See also bibliography in Livingston Rutherford, *John Peter Zenger, His Press, His Trial* (New York: Smith, 1941).

[57] 18 State Trials, p. 1203.

[58] Rex *vs.* Nutt, cited by Lord Mansfield in his opinion in the *Dean of St. Asaph's Case,* 21 State Trials, at p. 1038.

nical rules of seditious libel were out of tune with the developing concept of the constitutional relation between the government (and its officers) and its subjects. The trade printers, turned newspaper publishers, found a ready market for their wares and were encouraged in their criticisms of the government both by the maturing London middle class and by those factions in the governing class which found themselves out of office. In 1760 George III embarked on his purpose to restore the constitutional position of the crown, at least partially lost to the great Whig families after the Hanoverian accession. One by one the king dismissed those ministers whose independence of the crown made them obstacles in his path to personal rule. If the Whig families could maintain their powers by corruption, so could the king take over by the same methods. Thus was the stage set for the bitter and prolonged conflict between the king and such ready and versatile opponents as John Wilkes and the anonymous "Junius." With Parliament corrupted and under the finger of the king and his subservient ministers, the contest was removed from the halls of Westminster to the London newspapers. The printers and publishers became the willing instruments by which the opposition sought to curtail the powers of the crown, to reinstate the Whig families, and of even more importance to them, to establish the rights and liberties of London tradesmen. Into this melee were brought two weapons of questionable efficacy, the secretary's warrants, which we have seen were declared illegal by Lord Camden,[59] and the prosecution for seditious libel with its technical rules of procedure.

After consulting with the leading legal authorities of the times, including the retired chancellor Lord Hardwicke, the king's ministers proceeded with the prosecution of Wilkes for seditious libel based on the now famous No. 45 of his newspaper, the *North Briton*. The news of the prosecution and of the unsuccessful attempts to arrest the editor under the authority of a general warrant was given wide publicity in the London newspapers and served to direct the attention of the public to the basic issue of freedom of the press. However, the Wilkes prosecution,[60] like that of Zenger, made little or no change in the fundamental law of seditious libel. One innovation in this prosecution was the omission in the informa-

---

[59] See above, pp. 379-80.
[60] 19 State Trials, p. 1075.

tion of the epithet "false," which heretofore had been invariably included in describing the nature of the offensive words.[61] The omission was probably deliberate in order to avoid argument at the trial of the nature of the proof required. Wilkes was convicted in his absence from the country, and the conviction, both for sedition and for blasphemy ("Essay on Woman"), was affirmed by the House of Lords.[62] However, the sentence of outlawry was reversed by the Court of King's Bench.[63]

The event which focused public attention on the rules of procedure in trials for seditious libel was the prosecution of the publishers of the letter of Junius (No. 35) [64] which directly attacked the king as the source of alleged evils in the central administration. Even Wilkes, in spite of his intense hatred for George III, had observed the formalities by pretending a deference for the king while castigating his ministers. Junius, however, shielded by his anonymity, called upon the king to admit his mistakes, reverse his policies, dismiss his advisers, and to withdraw from his interference in Parliament. The letter ended with a warning which was almost a threat: "The Prince who imitates their [the Stuarts'] conduct, should be warned by their example; and while he plumes himself upon the security of his title to the crown, should remember that, as it was acquired by one revolution, it may be lost by another." [65]

The letter appeared on the morning of 19 December 1769 in Henry Woodfall's *Public Advertiser*. The regular edition, plus a special issue of 1,750 copies, was sold out by noon. The letter was reprinted in John Miller's *London Evening Post* of the same evening and was carried in full the following day by most of the London press, including the *Gazetteer*, printed by Charles Say, and the *Independent Chronicle* by George Robinson. The *St. James Chronicle* (Henry Baldwin) carried it on December 21, and Miller republished the text in his monthly publication, *The London Museum*, on 1 January 1770. Its sale was tremendous, and the speculation as to the outcome of the issue now joined with the crown was no less absorbing than the charges themselves.

[61] See copy of the information as reported in 19 State Trials at p. 1382.
[62] Lords Journal, XXXII, 222.
[63] 19 State Trials, at p. 1115.
[64] See *The Letters of Junius,* edited by C. W. Everett (London, 1927).
[65] *Ibid.,* p. 148.

Junius remained discreetly silent all during January. If the original publisher, Woodfall, with whom Junius had been in correspondence, knew or guessed at the identity of the author, he was also silent. The government advisers must have concluded that it was futile to try to flush out the letter writer, as no attempt was made at the subsequent trial of Woodfall to trace the author, although undoubtedly attempts were previously made to get the printer to reveal his identity.

On 23 January 1770 informations [66] were filed by the attorney general charging the five printers mentioned above, together with John Almon, from whose Piccadilly bookshop a copy of the *London Museum* had been purchased by a government agent, charging them with the publication of a seditious libel on the king and his government.[67] Almon, the bookseller, was first brought to trial on 2 June 1770. Why Almon first, since of all six he had the least to do with the publication of the Junius letter? It must be remembered that aside from the Wilkes prosecution in his absence in 1764, the attorney general had been unable to control the verdicts of London juries in libel cases. Almon, who had offended the authorities on several previous occasions in his *Public Register*,[68] was a resident not of London but of the city of Westminster and would be tried by a Westminster jury. Besides, if a mere seller of libels could be convicted, it would tend to frighten all booksellers as well as publishers.

At the trial [69] Almon was ably defended by Mr. Serjeant John Glynn, the distinguished counsel for Wilkes and other opponents of the king. In his speech to the jury Glynn pointed out that the letter complained of was sold by one of Almon's servants during his absence and that on his return the rest of the edition was sent back to the printer. How, under these circumstances, asked the defendant's counsel, could Almon be accused of a criminal intent to libel the king? Lord Mansfield in his charge to the jury presented only two grounds for consideration: (1) whether Almon published the paper, and (2) whether the paper carried the sense attributed to

---

[66] The use of informations *ex officio* was limited in 1819, 59 Geo. III, c. 12.

[67] 20 State Trials, p. 821 (note).

[68] Almon had also offended the government by his publication of the notorious "A Letter Concerning Libels" (1765).

[69] 20 State Trials, p. 803.

it by the information. He pointed out that a sale in a shop was a publication and that the master was responsible for the acts of his servant. The jury found the bookseller guilty.

Encouraged by this conviction, the prosecutors proceeded against Henry Woodfall on June 13 before a London jury.[70] Here again Mr. Serjeant Glynn, as counsel for the defense, contended that if the jury were convinced that the Junius letter was not published with intent to defame the king but "freely to canvass the acts of government," the publisher should be acquitted. Lord Mansfield gave his charge to the jury along the same lines as that given in the Almon case, pointing out that if the contents of the letter were not criminal (a decision reserved for the judge) their verdict of guilty would do no harm. After deliberating more than nine hours, the jury returned a verdict of "guilty of printing and publishing only." Both prosecution and defense presented motions, the first to enter the verdict as guilty and the second to discharge the printer under the verdict. The motions were argued on July 3 and decision was reserved until the next term of court.

The next two trials, those of John Miller and Henry Baldwin, were held on July 18. The same charges were made by the attorney general, the same defense was made by the same counsel. Lord Mansfield's charge to the jury followed the same tenor as in the previous cases with this curious addition: ". . . to be sure the jury, in every cause, may make an end of the question, whether they have not a right to find that verdict. If you take upon you to determine the law, you must, for the sake of your consciences, be sure to determine according to law, and you must be sure that the law is, that such a paper may be printed and published, of the tenor you find it." [71] Was the eminent chief justice slipping over to the position of Mr. Glynn? The sharp eyes of Junius noted this deviation from the previous charges, and in a public letter to Lord Mansfield he points out the discrepancy.[72] The trial was over by noon, and upon the retirement of the jury the court proceeded immediately to the trial of Henry Baldwin, publisher of the *St. James Chronicle*. Although no reliable account of this trial has apparently been preserved, Junius points out that the charge to the jury in this case was

[70] *Ibid.*, p. 895.
[71] *Ibid.*, p. 894.
[72] *Letters of Junius,* Everett ed., p. 180.

even more lenient than in the Miller case.[73] In any event the Baldwin jury retired at 4 P.M. and returned before six with a verdict of Not Guilty. The Miller jury had more difficulty coming to a decision and did not come in with its verdict of Not Guilty until half past seven. I can find no record that after these verdicts either Charles Say or George Robinson was ever brought to trial.

At the next term of court, the judges of the King's Bench ruled that Woodfall was entitled to a new trial.[74] No new trial was ever prosecuted by the government attorneys on the ground, it was claimed, that one of the original jurors walked off with the prosecutor's only copy of Woodfall's newspaper. Almon was brought up for judgment on November 28, the sole convicted seditionist, and was fined 10 marks and bonded for his good behavior for two years in the sum of £800.

Reports of the series of Junius trials were carried in the London newspapers and resulted in widespread public discussion in London and in the halls of Westminster. Undoubtedly Lord Chief Justice Mansfield was under considerable pressure during these trials, both from the king and his friends on the one side and from the London populace and the Whig opposition on the other. In the House of Commons (6 December 1770) Mr. Serjeant Glynn moved for an enquiry into the administration of criminal justice, an enquiry which was stifled by the ministry.[75] A few days later the Chief Justice, in an apparently agitated state of mind, called a special session of the House of Lords and without ado presented that body with his opinion in the Woodfall case without recommendation.[76] This unusual procedure surprised the Lords, but they were still more surprised when Lord Camden seized the opening to propose a series of six questions to the Chief Justice:

1. Does the opinion mean to declare, that upon the general issue of Not Guilty, in the case of a seditious libel, the jury have no right by law to examine the innocence or criminality of the paper, if they think fit, and to form their verdict upon such examination?

---

[73] *Ibid.*, John Walter, later founder of the London *Times*, was a member of the Baldwin jury. *History of the Times* (1935), I, 56-57.

[74] 20 State Trials, p. 917.

[75] See *Parliamentary History*, XVI, 1211-1301; a previous attempt to limit the attorney general's authority to issue informations *ex officio* was also defeated. *Ibid.*, p. 1211.

[76] *Ibid.*, p. 1312.

2. Does the opinion mean to declare, that in the case above mentioned, where the jury have delivered in their verdict Guilty, that this verdict has found the act only, and not the law?

3. Is it to be understood by this opinion, that if the jury come to the bar, and say that they find the printing and publishing, but that the paper is no libel, and in that case the jury have found the defendant Guilty generally, and the verdict must be so entered up?

4. Whether the opinion means to say, that if the judge, after giving his opinion of the innocence or criminality of the paper, should leave the consideration of that matter, together with the printing and publishing, to the jury, such a direction would be contrary to law?

5. I beg leave to ask, whether dead or living judges, then absent, did declare their opinions in open court, and whether the noble lord has any note of such opinions?

6. Whether they declared such opinions, after solemn arguments, or upon any point judicially before them.[77]

Lord Mansfield replied that this method of raising judicial questions was unusual, but instead of insisting on a regular procedure, he indicated he would take up the questions at an early date. The date turned out to be 1783, thirteen years later.

The public uproar which accompanied the Junius prosecutions convinced both the government attorneys and the justices of the difficulty, if not impossibility, of obtaining convictions for seditious libel in the present state of public opinion. It was also apparent that among certain Parliamentary leaders and judicial lights, there were serious doubts of the validity of Lord Mansfield's exposition of the function of the jury in these prosecutions. Unfortunately, no appeal was taken from the Almon case to the House of Lords. If the law had been settled at this time along the lines contended for by Lord Camden and Serjeant Glynn, there would have been no need for Fox's Libel Act nor would there have been a need for the hundreds of provisions still to be found in American constitutions giving the jury the right to try both the law and the facts in libel prosecutions. Tactically the battle was won by the London newspapers and their supporters since juries refused to convict; theoretically the law remained as Lord Mansfield and the government prosecutors contended.

Lord Mansfield's composure returned as pressures from both the crown and the London journals relaxed, and by 1783 [78] he was

---

[77] *Ibid.*, p. 1321.

[78] Lord Mansfield gave a somewhat inconsistent charge to the jury in the

again ready for the battle, secure in his conviction that a jury had no right to pass on the libelous or seditious nature of the publication. The climax of the century-long conflict, with the Chief Justice and John Erskine as the opponents, took place in the Court of King's Bench on a motion for a new trial in the conviction of the Dean of St. Asaph.[79] The clergyman had published a "Dialogue" which urged constitutional reform in Parliamentary representation and which, it was alleged, incited to rebellion.

Erskine presented four main arguments why the entire case should have been left to the jury: (1) the criminal intent, as in all crimes, is an essential ingredient of the crime of seditious libel and should be found by the jury as a matter of fact. Mansfield answered that the criminal intent was not a necessary ingredient but was a conclusion of law to be inferred from the facts.

(2) Erskine contended that since the verdict of Guilty or Not Guilty was a general verdict, the jury had the right as in other crimes to decide the whole matter. Mansfield's retort was that the procedure in seditious libel was "peculiar" and different from that of other crimes.

(3) Erskine's third argument was that a general verdict with the limited meaning of a special verdict was likely to cause injustice to the defendants. Elaborating, he pointed out that the whole case was not necessarily on the record so that it could adequately be reviewed by the judges. Mansfield replied that what was not on the record could be submitted in evidence to the jury and that later the judges could be asked their opinion on the nature of the words as published and as amended by any evidence available. Erskine failed to make the point clear that a person accused of libel would be put to the expense of a trial in advance of a determination by the judges of the nature of the words.

(4) Lastly, Erskine appealed to former cases and dicta to support his position as to the procedure in libel cases. Mansfield admitted that many of the earlier cases were inconclusive and sometimes ambiguous and gave a detailed review of cases since the Revolution. He might have gone back further to the decisions of Restoration judges whose opinions would have supported his case,

---

trial of John Horne (Tooke) in 1777. The charge is at least different from that delivered in the Baldwin case. 20 State Trials, pp. 759-63.

[79] State Trials, p. 876 (1783/4).

but he omitted these as well as the still more remote Star Chamber precedents.

As the result of the court's insistence on the nature of a trial for criminal libel at common law and the concurrence of the judges in Parliament, numerous requests were made for statutory changes.[80] Finally in 1792, with the support of Pitt, Burke, and Lord Camden, Fox's Libel Act was passed.[81] The act, in a declaratory form, reversed the views of Lord Mansfield and the judges and adopted those of Lord Erskine and Lord Camden. It established four propositions: (1) the jury may give a general verdict on the whole issue in a libel case, not on the publication and innuendoes only, (2) the judge may at his discretion direct the jury as in other cases, (3) the jury may give a special verdict if it wishes, and (4) the defendant may move in arrest of judgment after conviction by a jury.

Lord Mansfield's main contention in support of the limited function of juries was that otherwise the law as to what is is seditious or libelous would be uncertain. Unfortunately, the law was uncertain where juries refused to convict. Under Mansfield's position the law would have been certain only if the seventeenth- and early eighteenth-century rule that any reflection on the government was seditious prevailed. Such a rule was inconsistent with the changing position of the government as responsible to, as well as representative of, its constituents.

Fox's Libel Act, unfortunately, came too late to be included in the fundamental law of the now independent American colonies. In the United States the common law of seditious libel was changed to conform with that of England by numerous provisions in state constitutions. These provisions, although not as clear or as detailed as the English Act, were nonetheless effective in abolishing the archaic procedures of Mansfield's common law. The common wording was ". . . and in all prosecutions for libel the jury shall be the judges of the law and the fact as in other cases." [82]

Lord Mansfield's statement, looking backward, summarized

[80] *Parliamentary History,* XVII, 53, 73; *Ibid.,* XXIX, 551.

[81] 32 George III, c. 60.

[82] See Appendix to W. R. Arthur and R. L. Crosman, *Law of Newspapers* (2d ed.; New York: McGraw-Hill, 1940), for the text of these constitutional provisions.

the freedom of the press in the eighteenth century. The Chief Justice, the conservative exponent of a developing common law, said: "To be free is to live under a government by law. The liberty of the press consists in printing without any previous license, subject to the consequences of law." [83] We have come a long way since Henry VIII issued his first list of prohibited writings.

Lord Erskine's statement, as set out in his defense of Thomas Paine for publishing *The Rights of Man,* looks forward and sets the stage for the future development of liberty of discussion on both sides of the Atlantic.

Erskine, the product of the age of "enlightenment" and "rationalism," said: "The proposition which I mean to maintain as the basis of the liberty of the press, and without which it is an empty sound, is this: that every man, not intending to mislead, but seeking to enlighten others with what his own reason and conscience, however erroneously, have dictated to him as truth, may address himself to the universal reason of a whole nation, either upon the subjects of government in general, or upon that of our own particular country." [84] The eloquent English statesman phrased a theory of freedom of the press, but the application and maintenance of this liberty fell to the thousands of relatively unknown writers, printers, and newspaper publishers who in the nineteenth century translated this statement into a working principle.

---

[83] 21 State Trials, p. 1040.
[84] 22 State Trials, p. 414.

INDEX

Auernor, Master, 145
Austen, Robert, 209n, 229
Authors, 248n; complaints against piracy, 171; name required, 308, 310; subsidized, 328-35

Badcock, William, 269n
Badger, Thomas, 206
Bainham, James, 45
Baldwin, Henry, 356, 358n, 385, 387-88, 390n
Bale, John, 55
Balfe, Richard, 378
Ball, William, 228
Ballads, 73, 135, 143n, 144, 157, 212n, 223
Bamford, Henry, 93
Bankes, Richard, 29, 38
Banks, Thomas, 204
Barker, Christopher, 33, 39, 65n, 69, 74, 92, 128, 171
Barker, Christopher II, 128, 172n, 245, 280n
Barker, Mathew, 228, 229
Barker, Robert, 33, 75, 76n, 128, 129
Barker, Robert II, 128
Barkstead, John, 230
Barrington, E., 373
Barwick, G. F., 49n
Bastwick, John, 111n, 121, 122-23, 124, 125, 199
Bates, Thomas, 208
Bayfield, Richard, 45
"Beacon Firers," 226-27
Beardmore, Arthur, 376, 377, 378
Beddle, John; see Bedill, John
Bedford, Duke of, 334, 344
Bedill, John, 49n, 65
Bellamy, John, 175
Berkenhead, Sir John, 207, 241, 291
Berthelet, Thomas, 32-33, 38, 43
Betthenham, James, 370
Bible, 42, 46, 48; printing, 37, 38, 47, 75, 130, 169, 172, 222, 228, 229, 248; see also Tyndale; Coverdale
Bill, Charles, 245
Bill, John, 128, 172n, 245, 280n
Bill of Rights, 275, 300, 381
Binders, 59
Bishop of London, 83, 86, 90, 93, 94, 138, 239, 240; as licenser, 44, 58, 59, 61, 62, 63, 72, 143, 145, 146, 242, 243
Bishop, George, 33, 208, 209n
Bishop, Zachary, 222
Blackstone, William, 7, 9
Blades, William, 23n, 24
Bladon, S., 358n
Blaiklock, Lawrence, 208, 211
Blakes, Andrew, 86
Bland, Dr. John (?), 341
Blasphemy, 369, 385
Blocking entry, 79, 135, 152
Blount, Charles, 243n, 244n, 261n
Blunden, Humphrey, 208n, 209
Boccaccio, 145
Bohun, Edmund, 243n, 244, 260n
Bolingbroke, Lord (Henry St. John), 308, 329, 337, 340
Bond; see Recognizance
Bond, ———, 287
Bonner, Edmund, 55
Booker, John, 187
Books, imported, 229, 240, 262; library copies, 241; prohibited, 2, 45, 46; seditious, 222, 240-41
Booksellers, 240, 258; foreign, 25
Border, Daniel, 224, 225
Bosanquet, E. F., 247n
Bostock, Robert, 189
Boswell, James, 353n
Bourne, H. R. Fox, 379n
Bourne, Nicholas, 136, 149n, 151, 152, 153, 155, 156, 157, 159, 160, 174, 233
Bourne, Robert, 75, 77
Bowler, James, 155
Boyer, Abel, 301, 337, 347, 350, 351, 357

Brabourn, D. Theophilus, 243
Bradford, Gladys, 120n
Bradshaw, John, 221
Bragg, Benjamin, 278
Brandeis, Louis D., 11
Brandon, Lord of (Gerard), 276
Bray, Dr. William, 184
Breach of privilege; see Parliament
Brent, Sir Nathaniel, 143, 187, 212
Brewster, Thomas, 171n, 269n
Bribery; see Subsidy
Bridge, Major, 227
Bridges, Dr. John, 98
Briefe Relation, 224
Bristol Postboy, 314n
British Journal, 342
Briton, 376, 377
Bromhell, Thomas, 295
Brooke, Nathan, 269n
Browne, Jo, 204
Browne, Joanne, 269n
Bruce, John, 96n
Brudenell, John, 255n
Buck, George, 67
Buckley, Samuel, 279, 309, 327, 328, 335, 338, 341, 343, 371
Buckley, Stephen, 185
Buckner, William, 145n
Burbie (Burby), Cuthbert, 81
Burke, Edmund, 357, 361, 391
Burton, Henry, 111n, 121, 122, 123, 125, 140n, 144n, 155, 199
Bute, Lord, 376, 377-78
Butler, Edward, 268n
Butter, Nathaniel, 140, 145, 148, 149, 151, 152, 153, 154, 155, 156, 157, 159, 160, 203, 233
Butter, Thomas, 93
Byddell, John, 49n, 65
Bynneman, Henry, 39, 97, 98, 103n
Byrde, William, 39
Byrom, H. J., 83n, 90n

Caley, Robert, 71
Calvert, Elizabeth, 253
Calvert, Giles, 171n

Calvert, Sir George, 151, 153, 154
Calvin, John, 79n
Cambridge printers, 69, 70, 78, 239
Camden, Lord, 7, 9, 11, 378, 379-80, 383, 386, 388, 389, 391
Camden, William, 92n
Campbell, William, 32n
Campion, Edmund, 60n
Cane, ——, 182
Care, Henry; see Carr, Henry
Carlson, C. Lennart, 349n
Carr, Frank, 117n
Carr, Henry, 269n, 271n, 272, 273, 297, 298n
Carr, William, 276
Carter, John, 89
Carter, Joseph, 382
Carter, William, 88, 89-90, 265
Cartwright, Thomas, 60, 95n, 96, 97
Case of the Seven Bishops, 274
"Cato," 339, 340, 342
Cave, Edward, 349, 350-51, 352, 353-54
Cawood, John, 33, 89
Caxton, William, 22-24, 32n, 65, 246n
Censorship; see Licensing
Certain Informations from Several Parts of the Kingdom, 207-8
Challoner, Thomas, 190
Chamberlain, John, 148, 149n, 150
Champion, 344
Chapman, Laurence, 208, 211
Charles I, 3, 107, 108, 111n, 114, 121, 128, 129, 156-57, 158n, 168n, 228, 237, 250, 260n, 290
Charles II, 3, 6, 10, 232, 233, 238, 239, 241, 250, 266n, 275, 281, 282, 289, 290, 296, 297, 298, 299, 302
Charlewood, John, 78n, 88, 93, 94
Church of England, 27, 58, 95, 109-10, 241, 243; control of printing, 137-40

Church of Rome, 27, 110; control of printing, 41-46, 47, 58; *see also* Roman Catholic
Churchill, John, 280
Cicill (Cecil), William, 53, 54
City Mercury, 295
Clarendon, Earl of, 296
Clark, John, 382
"Clear and present danger," 11-12
Clowes, John, 229
Clyde, W. M., v, 197n, 216n, 228, 232n
Coates, Richard, 175, 223n
Cobbett, William, 279, 309n
Coe, Andrew, 205, 209n
Coffeehouses, 287, 296
Coke, Edward, 113, 117, 119n, 137n
Coles (Cowles), Francis, 186, 204, 206, 208
Coles, Peter, 189
Collet, Collet 'Dobson, 310
Collings, Richard, 208n
Collins, Thomas, 172n
Colpeper, Sir John, 180
Combs, ——, 299
Commons, House of, 180-83, 306, 346; Boyer's reports, 347-48; committee for printing, 180ff., 214; committee on examinations, 169, 175-76, 189, 191, 199, 207, 214; committee reports, 349; contest with Wilkes, 358ff.; libels on, 370; 373; licensing, 261ff.; newspaper reports permitted, 361-62; official printing, 204ff.; order of 1648, 214n; orders to Stationers Company, 174, 204; propaganda by, 183, 189, 204; prosecution of newsbooks, 211-12; prosecution of newsletters, 285-86; prosecution of newspapers, 278; protestation, 115, 205; reflections on proceedings, 277-79; reports of king's trial, 216; reports of votes, 281, 282-84; rights of authors, 171; recess reports, 352; secrecy of debates, 102-8; special enforcement committees, 189; suppression of diurnals, 205; Woodfall case, 371ff.; *see also* Parliament
Commonwealth, 221-25
Communism, 10, 11-12, 13
Complete Intelligencer, 209
Concanen, Mathew, 341
Constructive treason, 266, 366
Continuation of the News, 206
Cook, Edward, 244
Cooke, Thomas, 344
Cooke, William, 203, 204
Cooper, Thomas, 96
Copyright Act of 1709/10, 249
Copyrights, 72, 74-82, 130, 135, 172-73, 223, 248-49, 262, 312; in editions, 79; in translations, 79; *see also* Patents
Corbett, Miles, 180, 212n
Corn-Cutter's Journal, 343
Corontos, 129, 147-56; failure of, 160-61; foreign, 148-50, 154; licensing of, 151, 153, 160; petitions to publish, 157-59; monopoly in, 151-52, 156-60; suppression of, 150, 155-56; warrant for, 159; *see also* News, foreign
Corresponding societies, 367
Corsells (Corsellis), Frederick, 22, 23
Cotes, Richard, 171n
Cottington, Lord, 151, 153, 155
Cotton, John, 299
Cottrell, James, 226
Council, 28-29, 31, 39, 46, 49, 50, 54, 60, 74, 75, 92, 135; as enforcement agency, 86, 250-52; licensing of news, 153; suppression of news, 151, 155-56
Council of State, 217, 219, 220, 221-23, 225-30, 289, 290
Council Order of 1566, 58-59, 69, 72, 83

East, Thomas, 79n, 93
Ecclesiastical court, 43, 98; *see also*
High Commission
Edinburgh Courant, 330
Edmunds, William, 356
Edward III, 266, 268n, 350
Edward VI, 33, 51-54
Eeles, Robert, 177-78, 190
Eeles, Mrs. Robert, 177
Eliot, Sir John, 116
Elizabeth, Princess, 113, 148, 152
Elizabeth I, 1, 2, 3, 6, 10, 28, 30,
71, 78, 87, 91, 95, 97, 101, 102,
103, 107, 108, 110, 115, 128,
131, 136, 152, 239
Englishman, 333
English Post, 325
Entick (Entinck), John, 377, 378,
379, 380
Entick *vs.* Carrington, 378, 379,
380
Erskine, Sir Thomas, 5, 7, 9, 11,
381, 390, 391, 392
Escott, T. H. S., 340, 341n
Evans, F. M. G., 253n
Evans, Thomas, 358n
Evelyn, Sir John, 180
Everett, C. W., 385n
Eversden, Henry, 254
Examiner, 313, 314, 332, 337, 338
Exeter Mercury, 348n
Eyre, G. E. B., 188n, 204n, 225n,
290n

Fairfax, Thomas, 213, 216, 221
Faithful Scout, 225, 226, 231, 289
Faques (Facques), William, 32
Farnaby, Thomas, 187
Farwell, John, 269n, 274n
Faucett, Bernard, 186
Fawcett, Thomas, 206
Fawne, Luke, 226
Featherstone, Henry, 169, 170n
Field, John, 95, 96, 171n, 172n,
211, 228, 281
Fielding, Henry, 330, 334, 344

Figgis, J. N., 109n, 112n
Firth, C. H., 173n, 187n, 213n,
222n
Fisher, John, 42, 43, 45
Flower, Francis, 39, 75n, 92
Floyd, Edward, 112, 113, 114n
Flying Post, 278, 301, 313, 314,
325, 341
Ford, Charles, 327
Foreign news, 147ff., 233, 324;
see also Corontos
Fox, Charles J., 345, 362
Fox's libel act, 367, 391
Foxcroft, George, 230
Foxe, John, 43n, 44n, 45n, 76n
Foxford, Richard, 43n
Franck, John, 171n, 181
Frank, Dr., 243
Franklin (Francklin), Richard, 382
Fraser, James, 244, 260n, 300
Frederick, (Elector), 148, 150
Free Briton, 341, 342, 343
Freedom of speech; in Parliament,
100-3, 115-16
Freedom of the press; abolition of
licensing, 262; during interreg-
num, 174, 191-201, 220ff., 232-
33; end of 17th century, 301-2;
during 18th century, 305ff.,
364ff., 381, 383, 391-92, Level-
lers on, 200ff., 226-27; theories,
5-13, 89; Toland on, 318; *see
also* Milton, John.
Freeholder, 332, 338
Freethinker, 338
French Intelligencer, 225
Frere, W. H., 95n
Frost, Gaulter, 224
Fry, Francis, 37n

Gage, William, 185
Gairdner, James, 44n, 45n
Gardiner, Stephen, 55
Gardiner, S. R., 109n
Gay, John, 340

Gellibrand, John, 253, 254n, 300
Gellibrand, Samuel, 226
General Evening Post, 354, 358n
General warrants, 253-54, 374-80
Gentleman's Magazine, 350, 352, 353-54
George, Prince, 325
George I, 10, 319, 327, 328, 335, 338
George II, 334, 344
George III, 6, 9, 312, 322, 345n, 371, 376, 380, 384, 385
Giddins, Robert, 349
Gloucester Journal, 349
Glynn (Glynne), John, 180
Glynn, John, 9, 386, 387, 388, 389
Goade, Thomas, 145n
Godden, G. M., 344n
Godolphin, Sidney, 330, 332, 336
Gooch, G. P., 41n, 110n
Goodman's Fields Press, 198
Goodwin, John, 227, 233
Gordon, Thomas, 335, 339, 340, 342, 351
Goslin, Elizabeth, 254
Gough, John, 37, 43
Gough, William, 227
Grafton, Richard, 29, 33, 37, 38, 47, 48, 50, 65
Graham, W. J., 314n
Grant, James, 308n
Graydon, John, 325
Greensmith, John, 208
Greg, W. W., 59n, 61n, 68n, 80
Grenville, George, 378
Grey, Isaac, 227
Griffin, Edward, 211, 225
Grimston, Harbottle, 180, 182
Grindal, Edmund, 62
Grub Street Journal, 341
Grumbler, 338
Guardian, 333
Guest, Robert, 287
Guthrie, William, 344, 352-53

Habeas Corpus Act, 255

Hale, W. H., 139n
Halifax, Earl of, 331, 352, 375, 377, 378, 379n
Hall, Arthur, 102-3
Haller, William, 192n, 196n, 198, 200n
Ham, John, 136
Hamilton, Andrew, 383
Hammond, Dr. John, 93
Hammond, John, 205n
Hancock, Jasper, 299
Hanmer (Hanmere), Sir Thomas, 348
Hanson, Laurence, v, 319n, 323n, 325, 336, 337, 343, 365n
Hardwicke, Earl of, 384
Hardy, Thomas, 265n, 367
Hare, Dr., 341
Harley, Robert, 308, 326, 327, 328, 330-31, 333, 336, 337, 338, 339, 348
Harris, Dr., 145
Harris, Benjamin, 269n, 271n, 272, 297, 301
Harris, William, 136
Harrison, G. B., 95n, 152n
Harsnett, Samuel, 94
Hart, W. H., 270n
Hartlib, Samuel, 192
Hartwell, Abraham, 62, 63
Harvey, Gabriel, 63
Hatton, Ragnhild, 327n
Hawke, Edward, 355
Hawkers, 322; suppression of, 190-91, 209n, 213, 223, 231, 252, 320
Hawkins, Sir John, 351n
Hayhurst (Hurst), Robert, 242n
Hayward, John, 94, 95n
Heads of All Proceedings in both Houses of Parliament, The, 205
Heads of Several Proceedings in Both Houses of Parliament, 203
Henry, Prince, 152
Henry VI, 22
Henry VII, 30, 32, 127

Henry VIII, 2, 9, 10, 21, 26, 27, 30, 31, 36, 37, 42, 44, 45, 46, 47-51, 53, 66, 74, 108, 109, 392
Heraclitus Ridens, 298
Heresy, 42, 45, 48-49, 55, 240
Hermit, 314n
Herne, Richard, 174, 186, 206
Heron, Mr., 244
Heylin, Peter, 207
Hickes, James, 291n, 294-95
Hickes, Margery, 254
Hicks, William, 177
High Commission for Causes Ecclesiastical, 69, 70, 86, 90, 97, 100, 134, 136, 138-41, 143, 232; abolition of, 166; prosecution of Bourne and Butter, 155
"High Fliers," 319
Hill, George Birkbeck, 353n
Hills, Henry, 171n, 172n, 245, 281
Historian, 314n
Hitton, Thomas, 45
Hoadley, Benjamin, 340
Hodgkins, John, 88, 99, 100
Hodgkinson, Richard, 293
Holdsworth, W. S., 28n, 108n, 267n, 270, 273, 274, 275, 365n, 380
Holland; proclamation against corontos, 150
Holland, Sir John, 180
Holles, John, 116
Holmes, Oliver W., 11
Holmes, William, 88, 93
Holt, Sir John, 271, 276, 366, 381, 382n
Hoppe, H. R., 75n, 92n
Horman, William, 35
Horne, John; *see* Tooke, John Horne
Horton, ——, 287
How, John, 278
Huckwell, ——, 378
Hudson, William, 119n
Hulme, E. W., 34n, 39n

Hume, Alexander, 86
Humphreyville, William, 182, 205
Hunscott, Joseph, 138, 171n, 175, 176-77, 186, 199n, 206, 223n
Hunt, F. K., 316n
Husband, Edward, 171n, 172n
Hutchins Commission, 12
Hyp Doctor, 341

Ibbitson, Robert, 215n, 225, 230
Impartial Scout, 224
Independent Chronicle, 385
Independents, 212, 220, 226-27
Index of prohibited books, 2, 45, 46
Information; *see* News
Ingler, William, 208
Injunctions of 1559, 56-59, 69, 72
Innes, Robert, 290, 291
Instrument of Government, 219
Intelligencer, 293
Islip, Abbott, 23, 24

Jackson, Ralph, 81
Jacobite's Journal, 344
James I, 3, 6, 107-10, 112, 113, 114, 115, 128, 129n, 131, 139, 142, 148, 150, 154, 161, 228, 246, 247n
James II, 250, 264, 268, 274, 275, 282, 297, 299, 366, 381
James III, 366
Janeway, Richard, 269n, 281
Jefferson, Henry, 77
Jefferson, Thomas, 7, 11, 13
Jeffes, Abel, 85, 94
Jeffries, George, 264
Jenkins, Sir Leoline, 252
Jennings, Theodore, 215
Johnson, Samuel, 6, 330, 334-35, 350, 352-53
Jones, David, 370
Jones, Richard, 72
Jones, William, 140
Journalism, 220; history of, v-vi, vii
Journals; *see* Newspapers; Magazines

Stationers Company
Mathew, Thomas (pseud.), 47
Mathews, John, 366-67
Matthews, Augustine, 140
May, T. E., 365n
Maylour (Mayler), John, 49n
Maynard, John, 174, 180
McIlwain, C. H., 108n, 111n, 112n
McKerrow, R. B., 57n, 89n, 133
Mead, Joseph, 148, 149, 151n, 154n
Mead, Robert, 169
Mearne, Sam, 253, 258
Medley, 313, 314, 337, 338
Melancthon, 29
Mercator, 315, 338
Mercuries; see Newsbooks
Mercurius Aulicus, 207, 222, 241, 290, 291
Mercurius Bellonius, 225
Mercurius Britannicus, 196, 208, 209, 210, 213, 226, 230, 231
Mercurius Civicus, 208, 213
Mercurius Democritus, 225
Mercurius Elenchichus, 214
Mercurius Elencticus, 222
Mercurius Fumigosus, 231, 290
Mercurius Honestus, 290
Mercurius Melancholicus, 214, 222
Mercurius Militaris, 222
Mercurius Phanaticus, 290
Mercurius Phreneticus, 225
Mercurius Politicus, 224, 225, 230, 289, 291, 331, 339
Mercurius Pragmaticus, 214, 222, 225
Mercurius Publicus, 289, 290, 291
Mercurius Rusticus, 207, 211
Mercurius Scoticus, 225
Mercury, 295
Mercury women, 211; see also Hawkers
Meredith, Christopher, 175, 223n
Meres (Meere), John, 369, 373
Merest, ———, 227
Messengers of the press, 252, 254n

Middlesex Journal, 355, 356, 357
Middleton, Conyers, 23
Middleton, William, 49n
Midgley, Robert, 243
Military warrants, 221-22
Mill, John Stuart, 9, 13
Miller case, 388
Miller, Mr., 168n
Miller, Abraham, 223n
Miller, George, 169, 175
Miller, John, 358n, 361, 362, 363, 385, 387-88
Milton, John, 3, 9, 101, 140, 189, 192, 195-97, 224, 225, 227, 233, 238, 261, 383
Mist, Nathaniel, 339, 373, 381
Moderate, 214, 216, 223n
Moderate Intelligencer, 213, 215-16, 224n
Modern Intelligencer, 225
Mohun, Charles, 286
Monck, George, 289, 290
Monitor, 376, 377
Monopoly; attack by Lilburne, 200; before Council of State, 227-29; in news, 151, 152, 156-60; petitions for, 157-59, 307; see also Patents
Montague, Richard, 112, 114
Moon, Richard, 255n
Moore, George, 158, 246n
Moore, Richard, 180
More (Moore), John; 129, 171
More, Sir Thomas, 42n, 45
Morice, Sir William, 295
Morison, Stanley, 203n, 316n, 320n
Morley, Caleb, 130
Morning Chronicle, 345, 355, 358n, 362
Morning Post, 355
Moxon, James, 225
Muddiman, Henry, 285, 289-90, 291, 292, 293, 294-95, 296, 298
Muddiman, J. G., vi, 149n, 196n, 208n, 222n, 232n, 291n, 295n, 296n, 297n

403

Munk, ———, 222
Murphy, Arthur, 377
Murray, Alexander, 383
Muttershead, Edward, 223n
Myddleton, Mistress, 70

Nalson, John, 184
Namier, L. B., 376n
Nationalism, 26
Natural law, 7
Neak, Robert, 93
Needham, Marchmont, 190, 196, 210-11, 214, 224, 231, 289, 290n, 291
Negus, Samuel, 318, 319n
Nevill, Alexander, 79n
Newberry, Nathaniel, 152, 154
Newberry, Ralph, 33
Newbolt, William, 268n
Newcomb (Newcombe), Thomas, 171n, 172n, 223, 225, 230, 231, 245, 294
New learning, 26-27
Newman, Humphrey, 99
News, 293; demand for, 147-48, 202ff., 220; domestic, 202ff., 204n; foreign, 147ff., 233, 324; monopolies in, 289-95; of Parliament, 230, 346-63; political, 324ff.; provincial, 324; suppression of, 50, 53, 230, 231, 299-300, 307; *see also* Corontos; Diurnals; Newspapers
Newsbooks, 144, 149ff., 191, 203ff., 220, 230-31; censorship of, 207ff., 213, 223; legality of, 298, licensed, 207-8, 224-25, 300; restoration, 289-95; royalist, 207; suppression of, 298
Newsdealers, 322
Newsletters, 148, 285-88, 294, 295, 296, 299, 339, 348
Newspapers, 252; census of, 318; circulation of, 325; dailies, 355; patent for, 292ff.; production of, 203; prosecutions, 298; tax on,

311ff., 317-20; triweeklies, 354ff.
Nicholas, Sir Edward, 231, 255, 290, 291, 292
Nichols, J. G., 65n
Nicholls, John, 180
Nicolas, Sir Harris, 28n
Night Post, 314n
Nobbe, George, 376n
North Briton, 372, 376n, 377, 378, 379, 384-85
North, Francis, 247, 299
North, Frederick, 321
Northumberland, Earl of, 52
Norton, Bonham, 75, 129
Norton, John, 38, 75, 93, 129, 206
Norton, Roger, 171, 248, 258
Notary, Julyn, 25
Nutt, Richard, 382
Nycolson, James, 47

Oates plot, 250, 297
Oates, Titus, 250, 273, 297
Obscenity, 369
Observator, 298, 299
Observator, 275, 278, 313, 314, 371
Observer, 278
Occurrences from Foreign Parts, 289, 291
Official newsbooks, 224, 225, 233, 290ff., 296
Official newspapers, 323-28
Oldenburg, Henry, 243-44
Oldisworth, William, 338
Oliver, Richard, 358-59, 360
Onsloe, Sir Richard, 209
Onslow, George, 357-58, 359
Orange Gazette, 300
Order in Council, 251
Orwin, Thomas, 70
Osborne, Thomas, 343
Ostwood, James, 270n
Overton, Richard, 190, 196n, 197-98, 199, 200
Owen, William, 383
Oxford (printing), 25, 69, 70, 171n, 239, 243n, 248

Pocklington, John, 184
Political clubs, reports of, 353-54
Political journals, 316, 335-45; census of (1723), 318, 319, 324
Political State of Great Britain, 347-48, 350, 351, 353
Political writers, 328-35, 343
Pollard, A. F., 26, 52n
Pollard, A. W., 35, 37n, 66n
Poplar, Dr., 243
Porritt, Edward, 365n
Pory, John, 148, 156n, 157n
Post Boy, 325, 337
Post Man, 325, 326
Pratt, Charles; *see* Camden, Lord
Prerogative power, 27, 30, 59, 93, 109, 237-38, 242, 300; to suppress news, 156, 298
Presbyterians, 193, 198, 199, 220, 226-27
Present State of Europe, 314
Present State of Great Britain, 314
Press; at Finsbury, 222; at York, 222, 239; Royal Commission, 12; *see also* Freedom of the press
Press warrants, 253-54
Price, W. H., 34n, 129n
Pride, Thomas, 227
Primer, 51
Printers, 8, 25; foreign, 31-32; number of, 56, 69, 134, 137, 239; official, 32-33; Parliamentary, 171n, 281; royal, 245
Printing; introduction of, 22-25; history of, vi, vii
Printing privileges, 33-37; *see also* Copyright
Printing "stocks," 130, 135, 167, 245
Prior, Matthew, 337
Privileges of Parliament; *see* Parliament
Privy Council; *see* Council
Proclamations, 29-30, 52, 53, 54, 55, 60, 115, 142, 238, 242, 250-51, 296, 299, 307; of 1529, 44-45; of 1530, 45-46; of 1538, 36-37, 48-50; of 1544, 50; of 1546, 51; of 1551, 54; of 1621, 150; of 1623, 154
Protestant Domestic Intelligence, 297
Protestant Mercury (Exeter), 348n
Protestant Postboy, 314
Protestation, 115, 204
Protester, 344
Prothero, G. W., 100n, 110n
Provincial press, 317-18
Provost marshalls, 222
Prynne, William, 111n, 121, 122, 123-25, 137n, 140n, 141, 145, 155, 199
Public Advertiser, 355, 371, 385
Public Intelligencer, 231, 289, 291, 294
Public Ledger, 355, 362
Public opinion, 179, 192, 221, 328ff., 346
Public Register, 386
Pulteney, Sir William, 340, 352
Purfoot, Thomas, 83
Puritan, 2, 3, 61; literature, 139; printers, 95-100; theories on press, 191-201, 232-33; writers, 60, 89; *see also* Martin Marprelate tracts
Putnam, G. H., 43n
Pym, John, 114
Pynson, Richard, 32, 35, 65

Quo warranto proceedings, 252, 258

Raikes, Robert, 349
Rait, R. S., 173n, 187n, 213n, 222n
Ralph, James, 344
Rambler, 314n
Rand, B., 261n
Rastell, John, 35
Raworth, John, 175
Raymond, Sir Robert, 382
Read, James, 348

Recognizance, 49, 53, 55, 59, 69, 142, 206, 222, 223, 231, 239, 255, 258
Redmon, Robert, 29
Reed, A. W., 35n, 36, 37n, 43n
Reformation, 27, 90, 124, 191, 197; literature, 45, 51
Remembrancer, 344
Rente, Thomas, 85
Reports of Parliament, 4, 215, 279-88, 346-63
Review, 314, 315, 330, 336, 337
Revolution of 1688, 7-8, 265, 300, 328, 364, 381
Rhapsody, 314n
Ridpath, George, 301
Rivers, Earl, 24
Rivington, Charles Robert, 68n, 168n, 188n, 204n, 225n, 290n
Rix, S. W., 244n
Roberts, James, 38
Robinson, George, 385, 388
Robinson, Henry, 3, 192, 194, 196n
Rogers, Abigail, 211
Rogers, Owen, 77
Roman Catholic; literature, 83, 90, 139; presses, 319; *see also* Church of Rome
Roper, Abel, 172n, 301, 337
Rothwell, John, 226
Roundhead, 220
Rouse (Rous), Francis, 180
Rowland, William, 287
Royal Commission on the Press, 12
Royal Society, 243
Royalist, 220; press, 207, 221-22, 223-24
Roycroft, Thomas, 258
Royston, Richard, 190, 269n
Rump Parliament, 219-20
Rushworth, John, 115n, 124, 146n, 208, 209, 212, 213, 224, 225, 230
Russia, 12-13
Rutherford, Livingston, 383n
Rutter, Ralph, 253
Ryehouse plot, 250

Rymer, Thomas, 38n
Ryves, Bruno, 207

Sacheverell, Henry, 278
St. Albans, 25
St. Asaph, Dean of, 383n, 390
St. James Chronicle, 355, 356, 358n, 372, 385, 387
St. John, Henry (Bolingbroke), 308, 329, 337, 340
Salisbury, John, 277, 278
Sandes, George, 130
Say, Charles, 356, 369, 385, 388
Sayer, Edward, 246
Scandalum magnatum, 118-19
Scobell, Henry, 171n, 224, 225
Scofield, Cora, 61n
Scolar, John, 36n
Scots Postman, 330
Scottish Dove, 208, 211, 213
Scroggs, Sir William, 264, 271, 272, 273, 298n
Secord, A. W., 315n
Secretary of State, 247, 250, 359; as licenser, 242, 243; as publisher of *Gazette*, 323ff.; contest with *North Briton*, 378ff.; control of press, 252-55; examinations before, 255; press warrants, 253-54, 374-80, 384
"Security System," 312
Sedition, 48, 52, 60, 91, 179, 240-41, 271, 299, 300; prosecutions in Parliament, 275ff.; *see also* Seditious libel
Seditious libel, 2, 4, 5, 117-20, 253n, 269-75, 367, 372, 374, 375, 380-92; intent in, 273; in United States, 391; Junius, 385-89; jury, 273-74, 383, 387ff., 391; truth as defense, 274; see also *Libellis Famosis, de*
Selden, John, 180
Sellers, John, 245n
Separatists, 193, 197
Seres, William, 38, 54, 76
Seven Years War, 321

Several Proceedings in Parliament, 224, 225, 230, 231

Seymour, John, 247, 259

Seymour's case, 247

Shaaber, M. A., 149n

Shaftesbury, Earl of, 297

Shelbourne, Earl of, 345

Sheppard, Samuel, 221, 225

Sibthorp, Robert, 146

Simms, Valentyne, 99

Singleton, Hugh, 82n, 83, 88, 89, 90-92

Smallridge, ———, 299

Smith, David Nichol, 327n

Smith, Francis, 269n, 298

Smith, George, 190, 208, 211

Smith, J., 205

Smith, John, 54

Smollett, Tobias G., 330, 334, 376

Snowden, Thomas, 269n

Somers, John, 331, 332

Somerset (protector), 51, 52

Sovereignty, 6-7

Soviet system, 12-13

Sparke, Michael, 140-41, 155, 169, 170n, 227

Spectator, 313, 314-15, 316

Speed, John, 229

Speed, Samuel, 246

Spencer, Thomas, 140n

Stafford, Simon, 71

Stallard, Dr., 62, 63

Stamp Tax, 4, 306-22, 345; American, 321; avoidance of, 315-17, 321; first act, 307-11, 312-18; income, 315, 320, 321; provisions of 11 Geo. I, c. 8, 319; Pitt's tax, 320-21, 354; North's tax, 321-22; repeal of, 322

Stanford, Lord, 210

Stanley, John, 349

Stansby, William, 154

Star Chamber, 29, 39, 58n, 75, 76, 94, 120-26, 166, 228, 232, 237, 270; *see also* Star Chamber decree.

Star Chamber decree; of 1586, 2, 5, 61-62, 69-70, 72, 84-85, 141, 142, 375; of 1637, 2, 5, 134, 142, 144, 375

Starkey, John, 276

Stationer, 65, 71

Stationers and newspaper makers company, 68n

Stationers Company, 2, 4, 5, 7, 59, 60, 62, 63, 64-67, 90, 92, 96, 97, 134-36, 187, 220, 229-30, 232-33, 375; conflict within, 167ff.; licensing, 71-74, 143ff.; membership, 66-67; officers, 67-68; search and seizure, 82-88, 90, 135-36, 174-78, 206, 210, 222, 223, 257-60, 300; "stocks," 130, 135, 245, 258; quo warranto, 252, 258; *see also* Acts for Regulation of Printing; Court of assistants; Patents

Stationers guild, 64-65

Stationers hall, 85

Stationers Register, 58, 62, 187, 188, 241, 248; blocking entries, 79, 135, 152; registration of Corontos, 152, 172; of diurnals, 209; of newsbooks, 223, 290

Statute of monopolies, 131

Steele, Richard, 314, 315, 326, 330, 333-34, 372

Steele, Robert, 30n, 44n, 91n, 113n, 129n, 154n, 171n, 183n, 205n, 238n, 296n, 307n

Stephen, J. F., 267n, 270, 274, 365n

Stephen, Leslie, 261n

Stephens, Robert, 253, 267, 300

Stevens, D. H., 333

Stirrop, Thomas, 85

Stockum, P. Jon, Jr., 149n

Stow, John, 22, 23n, 24, 58n, 83, 89n

Stradling, Dr. George, 243

Streator, John, 172n, 262

Strickland's case, 101n

Walkadyn, ———, 175
Walker, Rev., 244
Walker, Henry, 185, 190, 206, 212, 216n, 224
Walker, Thomas, 185
Walley, Edward, 215
Walley, Henry, 207, 208, 209
Wallye (Walley), John, 71
Walpole, Horace, 341
Walpole, Sir Robert, 9, 10, 318, 319, 334, 338, 340, 341, 342, 343, 344, 350, 352, 353
Walsingham, Francis (pseud.), 342, 343
Walter, John, 388n
Walthoe, John, 343
Walwyn, William, 3, 192-94, 196n, 197, 200
Ward, Robert, 182, 205
Ward, Roger, 75, 85, 88, 93, 94
Wardner, Walter, 158
Wareham, William, 42
Watkins, Richard, 38, 39, 73
Webb, Nathaniel, 226, 238n
Weekly Advertisements, 295
Weekly Discovery, 298
Weekly Information, 290
Weekly Intelligencer of the Commonwealth, 224, 225, 231
Weekly Journal (Mist's), 331, 339, 341, 373, 382
Weekly Journal (Read's), 348
Weekly Packet, 311, 314
Weekly Pacquet of Advice from Rome, The, 272, 297
Weekly Register, 341
Weekly Worcester Journal, 314n
Wells, John, 184-85
Welsh, Richard, 38
Wentworth, Peter, 89, 101-2, 104
West, Richard, 186, 206
Weymouth, Lord, 372n
Wharton, George, 238n, 242
Wheble, John, 358
Whig Examiner, 332, 337

Whig party, 308, 328, 331, 332, 333, 337, 338, 384
Whistler, Mr., 182
White, Mr., 181, 182
White, Edward, 73
White, Robert, 190, 208, 210-11, 216
White, Thomas, 190
Whitechurch, Edward, 38, 47, 48, 50, 65
Whitehall Evening Post, 331, 339, 354, 358n
Whitgift, John, 61, 62, 63, 97, 98, 239
Wickham, John, 253, 267
Wickwar, W. H., v
Wight, John, 83
Wigston, Roger, 99
Wilcocks, Thomas, 96
Wilford, John, 351
Wilkes, John, 5, 8, 101, 356, 357, 358-59, 360, 362, 372, 373n, 376, 377, 378, 379n, 380, 381, 384-85, 386
Wilkes, Sir Thomas, 33
Wilkins, David, 42n, 66n
Wilkins, William, 343
William III, 4, 244, 250, 260n, 300, 301, 312, 330
William and Mary, 1, 250n, 283, 300
Williams, ———, 282n
Williams, Dr. Daniel, 61n
Williams, J. B.; *see* Muddiman, J. G.
Williams, Oliver, 290-91
Williams, R. F., 148n, 156n
Williams, Robert, 205
Williamson, Joseph, 244, 252, 257, 259, 285, 292, 294-95, 296, 323
Willie, John, 129
Wilson, J. D., 98n
Wilson, John, 223n, 253
Wilson, Robert, 185
Wilson, Sir Thomas, 158n
Wilson, William, 185
Wimbledon, Lord, 156

Windebank, Sir Francis, 156
Winnington, Sir Francis, 273, 282
Winter, Thomas, 175
Wither, George, 129, 132, 133, 168n, 254
Wolfe, John, 69, 75, 77, 78, 88, 89, 92-95, 103, 132
Wolfe, Reyner, 57
Wolsey, Cardinal, 42
Wood, Michael, 55
Wood, Robert, 182, 205, 225
Woodfall, Henry Sampson, 355, 371, 373n, 385, 386, 387, 388
Woodfall, William, 358n, 362
Worall, Dr., 153
Worman, E. J., 25n

Wren, Matthew, 124
Wright, H. G., 103n
Wright, John, 171n, 181, 188, 205, 208, 223n
Wright, T., 358n
Wright, William, 93, 129
Writers; see Authors
Wydville, Anthony, 24
Wyer, Robert, 44
Wyse, Andrew, 73

Yard, Robert, 301, 325
Yeale (Yale), Thomas, 58
Yelverton, Christopher, 212n

Zenger, John Peter, 383, 384